THE BATTLE OF

C000152017

Five Hundred Copies of this Work have been printed,

of which this is No 240

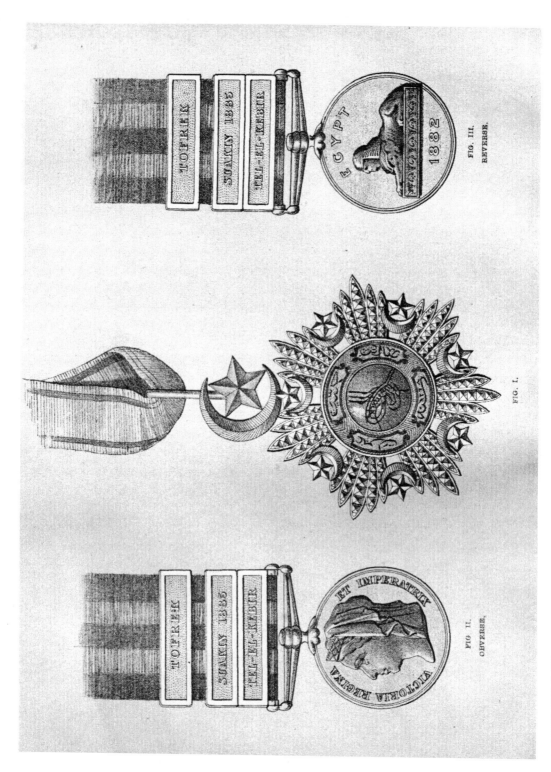

FIG. III.
REVERSE.

TOFREK

SUAKIN 1885

TEL-EL-KEBIR

EGYPT

1882

FIG. I.

FIG. II.
OBVERSE.

TOFREK

SUAKIN 1885

TEL-EL-KEBIR

ET IMPERATRIX

VICTORIA REGINA

McLAGAN & CUMMING. LITH. EDIN.ᴿ

ORDER OF THE MEDJIDIE, AND MEDAL FOR EGYPT.

THE

BATTLE OF TOFREK

FOUGHT NEAR SUÂKIN, MARCH 22ND, 1885

UNDER

MAJOR-GENERAL SIR JOHN CARSTAIRS M'NEILL,

V.C., K.C.B., K.C.M.G.

IN ITS RELATION TO THE MAHDIST INSURRECTION IN THE EASTERN SUDAN
AND TO THE CAMPAIGNS OF 1884 AND 1885

The Naval & Military Press Ltd

published in association with

FIREPOWER
The Royal Artillery Museum
Woolwich

Published by
The Naval & Military Press Ltd
Unit 10 Ridgewood Industrial Park,
Uckfield, East Sussex,
TN22 5QE England
Tel: +44 (0) 1825 749494
Fax: +44 (0) 1825 765701
www.naval-military-press.com

in association with

FIREPOWER
The Royal Artillery Museum, Woolwich
www.firepower.org.uk

The Naval & Military
Press

MILITARY HISTORY AT YOUR
FINGERTIPS

… a unique and expanding series of reference works

Working in collaboration with the foremost
regiments and institutions, as well as acknowledged
experts in their field, N&MP have assembled a
formidable array of titles including technologically
advanced CD-ROMs and facsimile reprints of
impossible-to-find rarities.

*In reprinting in facsimile from the original, any imperfections are inevitably reproduced
and the quality may fall short of modern type and cartographic standards.*

Printed and bound by Antony Rowe Ltd, Eastbourne

OFFICERS LIBRARY · R.M.L.I. · FORTON

PREFACE.

N prefacing the following work with a few remarks, according to time-honoured custom, it would be mere affectation to offer either apology or excuse for bringing it before the Public.

Even on the hot sand of the desert, the blood so lavishly expended on March 22nd, 1885, was not dry, and, if we except those dragged from the interior of the zeribas, not the body of an Arab on the battlefield had been touched, ere already, four thousand miles off, intelligence of the fight was being spread throughout London like wildfire. By the next morning, through every agency the Press could command, in forms so distorted as to be almost grotesque in their absurdity, over Britain and the civilised world, a similar result took place.

Raised to lips panic-stricken, and in the first hot haste of the "unexpected," ignorant of all that was essential even to a moderately-accurate statement of the facts, Rumour's brazen clarion could but ring out notes of discredit and dismay. On every doubtful point, one rule of judgment only was recognised—that they must be sinners above all men on whom had fallen the Siloam-tower of a strategy shattered at its first contact with stern reality.

Of this strategy the action at Tofrek formed no part; and whether the statement that "no fighting was anticipated" be true or not, certainly none was intended. It formed the unexpected result of a Movement only preparatory to more warlike operations, and in which fatigue-duty, not fighting, was the order of the day. To dissociate the action referred to from the general line of strategy being pursued at the time when it was fought, would be indeed impossible, even were it desired, whatever there was in the day's events of exceptional weakness, mischief, or loss, being demonstrably deducible from it, as cause and effect.

The distinctive position the action at Tofrek thus naturally assumes is due, as stated, not to any choice or intention on the part of Head-Quarters at Suâkin, but to the fact that the Arab, in the exercise of his belligerent rights, chose to precipitate a battle which the Authorities hoped would take place, not in the bush, but amid the rocky defiles at Tamai or Tamanieb; not with a semi-combatant Force, burdened with fatigue and convoy-duties, but with the entire strength of the Expedition, prepared at every point to crush the enemy, if, biding Head-Quarters' time, he would be so chivalrous as to assemble *en masse*, "attack the Squares in large numbers, be repulsed," and then, demoralised and decimated by machine gun and rifle fire, "be cut up by the Cavalry."

The Arab, however, chose to follow methods of his own; and so, under the most disadvantageous circumstances, without special warning, or precedent preparation, the Force sent off on the 22nd to carry out the preliminary work of constructing and storing an Advanced Depôt or Secondary Base, was compelled, single-handed, to achieve the ultimate object of the Campaign, and to do this *with all the wreckage of a surprised and discomfited strategy tumbling about its ears.*

True, according to the ingenious logic of the Press, the chief sinners were necessarily those upon whom the strategic tower fell; and so, with scant acknowledgment for what was achieved, and much discredit and obloquy for what it cost, this gallant deed of arms was pronounced " absolutely nothing but a negative victory "![1] and in the very act of superseding the cumbrous and abortive strategy being pursued at Suâkin, was stigmatised as " absolutely barren of strategical results " !

" Negative victory " was indeed a complimentary term compared with others used by the hasty critics of the Press, who, without scruple, freely credited the General in Command with every mischief that befell. As the most galling imputation that could be levelled against a high-minded and honourable man—the most fatal stab that could be inflicted on a reputation won by hard and successful service in various quarters of the globe—he was charged with permitting himself to be " surprised " ! with having his troops in an " unprepared state " ! and neglecting the most ordinary precautions a wise and wary General would naturally adopt !

Reserving the detailed examination of assertions such as these, we will only say that most assuredly neither was Sir John M'Neill surprised, nor the Force under his Command. Charges of " surprise " and " want of preparation " lie entirely at the door of the strategists who affirmed and believed that by the operations of the 19th and 20th the right flank of the British advance on Tamai had been adequately protected, and the Arab tribes effectually overawed, and, on the strength of this belief, as was clearly recognised at the time, made every preparation possible for a " first-class disaster."

[1] *Vide* p. 241.

b

On their own showing, it is indeed evident that not one special who reported, not one editor who commented, on the events of the 22nd, was in the slightest degree aware what the defensive dispositions of the troops really were, or whether any preparations were made for the eventuality of an attack at all; the natural inference being that none existed. Of the fact, especially, that two-thirds of the whole Force—practically the entire Indian Contingent—were under arms throughout the day, nothing was known. The Rallying Square, composed, until about two o'clock, of *all* the British troops not engaged in fatigue duty, fared little better; in the *Daily News*[1] it masquerades as forty Royal Marines engaged in wood-cutting, who form a small square and kill a hundred rebels; in other cases it is two companies of the Berks, caught dining, lunching, or engaged in other avocations, who also improvise a square, and perform wonders. In every instance it receives prominence merely as a chance incident standing out in relief against a background of disorder and confusion. That the story is a mere burlesque of one of the stated military dispositions of the day is never once recognised.

That within a very few moments effective order of battle could have emerged out of the state of matters so depicted is incredible. This order already existed in full force, and by it the real stress of the attack was undoubtedly borne. Within it were embraced the entire Indian Contingent; and that six Companies of the 17th Native Infantry broke their formation was no fault of the General. Although, as the intended garrison of the redoubts, being naturally occupied in strengthening the defences, this order equally included the Berks and the Royal Marines, and more especially that half battalion of the Berks forming one fourth of

[1] March 24th, 1885.

the original Rallying Square, whose doings were travestied in a manner so ridiculous.

It was not known in London, it was not known at Suâkin, it may not have been surmised even at Tofrek, but it is a fact, nevertheless, known to us now, and which it is useless to deny, that, so far as the Arabs were concerned, on the 22nd of March was fought the pitched battle of the Campaign—a battle which they strained every nerve to convert into a victory, and only failed because they found the combined Imperial Forces to be absolutely invincible. Invincible, under dispositions the best possible to be made in a day intended for fatigue duty and not for fighting. Invincible, even when caught in tactical toils, discomfited as soon as tested, and, at the first contact with stern realities, collapsing in irremediable ruin. The Arab attack, to the Head-Quarters' strategy, proved as the iron to the earthen pot ; but happily confronted with still sterner metal, even the iron pot was dashed in pieces.

In making these statements I trust the reader will not think undue advantage is being taken of the Preface, or the argument in too great a degree anticipated. In a case like the present where a particular event has been dragged into a most unenviable notoriety, and the Public mind so systematically abused, it is essential that the most vital point, upon which the whole question as to the incidence of responsibility turns, should be placed distinctly in the foreground. In so doing, one duty only is ours, and that is, without fear or favour, clearly to see, and uncompromisingly to state, all the essential facts as they really were. We propose to do this still further, not as a discussion argued on merely military grounds, but in such a way as shall carry conviction to the mind of every intelligent reader, and form a genuine narrative of what experience has proven to be by far the most important and decisive conflict of the two Campaigns on the Red Sea Littoral.

As a guarantee for the substantial accuracy of the various statements made, it may be mentioned that, in addition to communicating much valuable information, the proof sheets of this work have had the advantage of being carefully revised by Officers of Rank who were present at the action. In returning the proofs with a few emendations, General Hudson states, "It has been quite surprising to find what an amount of ignorance still prevails on the subject of the occurrences in the Soudan, and especially regarding the events of which you propose to treat." An Officer on the Indian Staff, who occupied an important position on the 22nd, also writes, "I have read the proofs you so kindly sent me with the greatest interest; and, indeed, I can find in my experience of the day's proceedings nothing to add to the ample information which has been collected by you. I can find no one point in your description of the operations with which I disagree; and curiously enough, although I have talked the business over with lots of men who were there, you have thrown up a lot of resh light which I had no idea of."

While sparing no effort to ensure accuracy, in dealing with operations involving so much varied and complex detail, and where, especially at the most critical juncture, the attention of every one engaged was thoroughly pre-occupied with, and concentrated upon, particular duties, it is scarcely possible on special points to secure unanimity of opinion, or wholly to avoid error. Happily this remark is least applicable to those broader aspects of the question with which we have chiefly to do. All the leading facts are now beyond dispute; and in their bearing on the incidence of responsibility may be said to compel admission on the part of every one able to appreciate their significance. Authoritative statement has taken the place of sensational inaccuracy, and laid a wholesome restraint upon the virulence of personal attack, for a considerable time after the action only too freely indulged in.

Whether the reader agrees with the line of argument pursued or not, and whatever difference of opinion there may be on matters of detail, of one thing he may rest assured, that, between the day's experiences as undergone by the military man, Officer or private, and the manner in which its more sensational events were dealt with by the Press, there exists the greatest possible contrast. The brief period embraced in the Arab assault excepted, the duties of the day were of the most toilsome and harassing character, involving the most concentrated attention, the most studious care for innumerable details, all necessary to the successful discharge of the work prescribed. As to the "special" alone was given a free hand and no other duty save to inquire into all that was being done, and to learn by personal observation, *if he chose*, the various precautions adopted, and dispositions made, so only to him was it given to play "high jinks," and disport himself so confidently before the "eye of the world."

In the name of an honourable, a gallant, and a laborious profession, I must be allowed to protest not merely against the special misrepresentations indulged in, but still more against the entire spirit and tone in which the various Press criticisms were conceived. Not only was it false to all the main facts, and utterly unworthy of the subject, but it presupposed an inversion of all those relations which ought to exist between the Press and an Army engaged in active operations in the field. In granting, in the Public interest, exceptional opportunities for acquiring information, the War Office had no intention to delegate its own functions to an irresponsible tribunal, or to afford facilities by which, with the world-wide speed and certainty of telegraphic communication, those nobly doing their duty under most adverse circumstances were to be robbed behind their backs of honour and fair fame. This gross abuse of War Office privileges has been very well dealt with by the trenchant pen of Major Elliott, in an article on "British Generals and War Correspondents as Umpires-in-Chief," appearing in the *Illustrated Naval and Military Magazine* for July 1885, the bulk of which is given in the Appendix.[1] The lapse of time has only added weight to its pungent and incisive sentences, and it is to be hoped that this and other protestations may tell advantageously on future relations between the Sword and the Pen in its too often most ill-informed and fugitive, most irresponsible, yet most dangerous, sphere of influence. In the first flush of high-wrought interest, combined with inadequate information, feeding the insatiable curiosity of the Public with crude and misleading statements, what in error is said, and still more, what through sheer ignorance is left unsaid, becomes at once a fruitful source of irreparable mischief. Seldom or never does there follow retractation or apology; the false start, sedulously pursued, but serving anew to illustrate the old adage, "Humanum est errare, diabolicum perseverare." To the fireman it has been said, the first five minutes are worth the succeeding five hours, at a conflagration. At Suâkin, in March 1885, sadly was there missed the quick eye and ready hand of Admiral Hewett, prompt as in 1884

[1] *Vide* Appendix V.

to "shoot folly" when, out of a too fertile *nidus* of ignorance and panic, it first rose upon the wing.

Among the principal reasons contributing to defer the publication of this work may be mentioned the unexpected delay in the issue of the Official Report regarding the Campaigns in the Eastern Sûdan. It is evident that on many controverted topics private inquiry cannot be expected in any degree to equal that instituted by Authority. Even under the most favourable circumstances, and with every source of information at command, it is difficult, often impossible, to harmonise conflicting statements, and it can only be hoped that the points of divergence or of discrepancy may not be found too great.

The introduction of a special chapter on the Indian Contingent, although necessarily retarding the work a little, is matter for congratulation rather than regret. Preceded as it was by the resignation of a Cabinet Minister, the extraordinary outburst of political rancour which greeted the advent of a small Indian Force into the Mediterranean in 1878 must always surround any succeeding Expedition with a special interest. In the heated atmosphere of partisan strife, it seemed indeed as if by this simple event the very bases of the British Constitution were being menaced. For the notice of the Expedition of 1885, a most interesting Memorandum, very kindly contributed by Major-General Sir John Hudson, K.C.B., forms the leading groundwork. A connected account of the Expeditions prior to that of 1882, undertaken from India beyond the *kalapani*, being still a desideratum, may excuse, I trust, the very brief notes prefixed. To Sir John Hudson I am also indebted for the very curious record of the Digna family, drawn up by Brewster Bey, embodied in the

Appendix, where will also be found a large amount of documentary and other illustrative matter, not otherwise easily accessible to the general Public.

In conclusion, I trust the reader will not consider that, in certain cases, the language employed is too strong, or the opinions expressed too emphatic. It must be remembered that, but for the mischievous and most reprehensible intervention of the Press, in matters upon which it was necessarily for the time being entirely uninformed, this book would not have been written.

From a military point of view, coolly and dispassionately considered, the whole question at issue lies in a nutshell. The elaborate precautions adopted at Hashin, and not less so in the advance on Tamai, show that, when it was intended to beat up the enemy and, if possible, force him to fight, Head-Quarters was fully alive as to the measures requisite in combating such a foe. *Per contra,* on the 22nd, the reversal of all these conditions, is an exact index, not only of the pacific intentions, but still more, the confident belief, entertained at Head-Quarters, that further operations were completely safeguarded by the fortified post established at Hashin. Hence, the reduction of the Cavalry strength down to a mere fringe of stationary outposts, while the enormous Convoy, instead of being kept well in the rear, as on the occasions noted, and laid down in the first or written Instructions, was sent, as the event proved, right out into the very forefront of danger. Over arrangements like these, no one at Tofrek on the 22nd had the very slightest control, the only option left to the Generals, as to the rest of the Force, being to do their duty "UNDER THE CIRCUMSTANCES." This term, however, must include not merely matters of accidental, local, and momentary importance, but, *all the circum-*

stances materially affecting the fortunes of the day, including the character of the enemy, his mode of attack, the special tasks the Force was sent out to perform, and, above all, the general nature of the strategy being pursued at Suâkin. The more attentively these are considered, and the more vital the consequences of arduous and unexpected duty most effectively discharged, I do not hesitate to say the more ungenerous will the animadversions of the Press appear to have been.

More especially is this the case with regard to any implied remissness or dereliction of duty on the part of the General in Command. To any one personally acquainted with Sir John M'Neill, either in civil or military life, and who knows that ever watchful promptitude and presence of mind, under circumstances of danger and difficulty only roused into higher, keener, more concentrated activity, the charge carries its own refutation along with it. To those not so favoured, the facts themselves clearly realised must compel conviction against all detractors. Let there be considered the brief period given—measureable not by minutes but by seconds —to spring from working into fighting form, and to surround these zeribas with a storm of leaden hail under which nothing lived; the space of time, also marvellously brief, within which the whole work had to be done, and by the terrible and decisive vigour of a repulse, in twenty minutes score not a "negative," not a transient, but a final and effective Victory.

Above all, let there be considered the character of the attack, and of the enemy at whose hands it was sustained. To military men the precise nature of the assault delivered is known as "shock tactics," but in the present case it was "shock tactics" in their most determined and dangerous form. This mode of

c

attack is precisely similar to that recently advocated by General
Boulanger as best adapted to the peculiar genius and characteristics of the French Army, and as the most appropriate to be
employed in a war, such as Europe has not seen for many a day,
between two great and civilised nations. Yet I doubt very
much whether, with all his *elan* and courage, the Frenchman could
at all equal the Mahdi's Dervishes—picked men as they were—
in the determined fury of their onset, or the reckless indifference
with which they rushed onward, and charged right home to certain death. If mortal power, inspired with the deadliest hatred,
hurling itself forward in serried masses, and, at a few seconds'
warning, closing with its enemy in a death-grapple, could have
broken his ranks, this would have been effected on the 22nd, with
all the speed and the certainty of lightning. Happily such was
not the case, the disciplined and well organised antagonist being
but welded to a higher temper, and stimulated to a more obstinate
resistance. Yet we are asked to believe this would have happened
equally with the "specials'" Donnybrook fair! It is incredible.
Much less than twenty minutes of Arab sword and spear would
have sufficed to sweep it from the face of the earth.

With considerations like these in view, I have little doubt the
reader will endorse the words of Sir John Hudson, when, in a
letter with which he has favoured me, referring to the effect of the
action at Tofrek on the Arabs themselves, as ascertained through
subsequent inquiry by Brewster Bey, he states, "That they were
immensely impressed with the losses they sustained on that
occasion, and were thoroughly astonished at finding themselves so
completely beaten when they MADE SURE OF VICTORY."

With regard to the more permanent and enduring results of this action, I will only quote the words of a well-known military writer; words which, as applicable alike to all battles in any degree claiming to be decisive, have a scope much beyond their immediate reference, viz., an action where the casualties are comparatively few :—

"There are some critics who judge of the importance of a battle solely by the amount of the slaughter produced on both sides. There is no need for me, I am certain, to point out to the intelligent reader that the criterion thus set forth is altogether a false one. *The status of a battle can be decided only by the results. If these results prove decisive—decisive, that is, of the campaign; decisive as to the consequences; decisive as to the future permanent position of the combatants*—then, though the casualties be ever so few, that battle is a decisive battle."[1]

Of the three *criteria* mentioned—the campaign in progress—the immediate consequences—the permanent relations of the combatants,—each must, in its measure, stamp the action at Tofrek as being emphatically decisive, and in this respect it may be usefully compared with that fought at Tamai in 1884. The British strength was in both cases approximately the same, but in all other respects, the character of the *locale*, the duties and avocations of the day, the object of the movements, in short, everything that may be classed as "circumstances," the contrast was very great. Both actions practically closed the respective campaigns, further operations being due rather to the want of adequate information than real necessity; they were summarily stopped in fact by the enemy, who, refusing further to fight, withdrew into waterless and inaccessible localities where the British Force could not follow. So far then the actions were equally effective, but at this point the

---

[1] *The Decisive Battles of India,* by Colonel G. B. Malleson, C.S.I. Preface, p. xi.

analogy terminates. In a battle of any importance the immediate "consequences," the "fruits of victory," are very various, and entirely dependent on circumstances. The result may be a large acquisition of territory, the command of important strategic positions, the capture of strongholds, magazines, munitions and prisoners of war. To gain such advantages is the great reason why battles are fought, but whether these results be temporary or enduring must depend on the subsequent "fortune of war." The bare possibility of results like these was entirely awanting in the Eastern Sûdan, and seldom have the British Arms been carried into a more restricted and barren field. A secure Base, immunity from attack, the Suâkin-Berber route kept open, were the only attainable "consequences" of any action, or even of a campaign. It was no fault of General Graham, or those under his Command, that towards objects like these the battle of Tamai produced not the slightest effect. On the departure of the Expedition in 1884, as previous to its arrival, Suâkin was only safe through the constant presence of a British Naval and Military Force. Even so defended, it was the object of perpetual night attacks, the Royal Marines in the course of the succeeding year having been over 300 times under fire, and if not technically besieged, were at least effectually shut up within their camping lines, the enemy being masters of the entire surrounding district.[1]

[1] The principal informant on this point was Commodore Molyneux, of H.M.S. "Sphinx," stationed at Suâkin. Writing to Vice-Admiral Lord J. Hay, under date July 14th, 1884, with reference to the persistent night attacks and proposed occupation of the "Salt Wells" made use of by the Arabs, much to the annoyance of the garrison, he states: "We shall then, I think, have done all that we can do, while maintaining a defensive attitude, to keep the enemy at a distance, though firing as they do in the air at extraordinarily long distances, there must always remain a certain amount of risk to life." (*Parl. Papers*, Egypt, No. 35 (1884), p. 8.) In another communication of the same date, he states that Osman Digna was doing all in his power to induce the friendly and neutral tribes to join him, and having the power to carry off their women and flocks, and seize their wells, "the Chiefs of the tribes have accordingly,

With the second, also disappears the third of the *criteria* laid down by Colonel Malleson. On the influence of Osman Digna over the tribes, and the numerical strength of his following, the battle of Tamai had practically no effect. The truth is, that after the departure of the Expedition, or perhaps stimulated by it, matters became worse rather than better, and in a communication to the Vice-Admiral of date August 6th, Commodore Molyneux mentions "The enormous concentration Osman's efforts had succeeded in forming about the end of Ramadan, when, by all accounts, his force was at least double what it was before the English arrived, and was estimated at 17,000 men."[1] In 1884 Ramadan commenced 25th June, and terminated 24th July, at which date this large force must have been assembled, agreeing pretty closely with Consul Cameron's estimate, that in 1884-85 the Northern Hadendowas under Osman Digna's influence "must have numbered at least 15,000 desperate fighting men."[2] As the autumn advanced, these numbers fell off, owing to failure in the supplies of food, but towards the close of November Commodore Molyneux states that

"The rebel forces are gradually regaining their strength at Tamai and Handoub, and Suakin is now as closely invested as regards communication with the interior as ever.

in self-defence, given in their submission to him." His following was then estimated at from 8000 to 10,000 men. (*Ibid.* p. 9.)

On the 18th he writes—"Osman says he will attack the Beni Amers south, and Amarars to the north ; *he has never had so large a following*, and talks of attacking this during Bairam" (*Ibid.* p. 49). And on the 26th the Mahdi's advice to Osman is given —"Not to risk attacking entrenchments but to fight if troops come out." (*Ibid.* p. 50.)

At the same time some interesting infor-mation is given as to the tactics pursued by an Arab camel corps.

"This rebel camel corps seems to be well trained ; they lie quietly concealed behind the bushes, and when they see their oppor-tunity, mount, and endeavour by a rapid turning movement to cut off the retreat, and when close, within 300 or 400 yards, the camels all drop together, and the riders dismounting, come on with their spears at a brisk pace." (*Ibid.* p. 50.)

[1] *Parliamentary Papers*, Egypt, No. 35 (1884), p. 61.   [2] *Vide* Appendix II.

"Osman Digna is practising his old tactics of oppression and coercion, combined with judicious lying, and as we show no signs of moving, self-preservation obliges the tribes who have lately been ready to co-operate with us to rejoin him." [1]

As time advanced matters only grew worse, both in the investment of Suâkin, and the oppressions and punishments by death, inflicted by Osman Digna, on those whom Commodore Molyneux terms "the friendly and neutral tribes."

The town itself held only by physical force against an ever-watchful and pertinacious enemy, such then was the actual state of matters at Suâkin in 1884-1885. The spring tournament, too late in its inception, and beating a hasty retreat, not before the Arab but the climate, seemed only to aggravate a situation which, at the cost of six weeks' operations and two well-fought battles, most assuredly it did not, and could not settle. On the contrary, the influence of Osman Digna continued steadily in the ascendant, until the fall of Khartûm, and the course of events on the Nile, rendered his position so important, that a second Expedition was deemed an imperative necessity. From a military point of view, of the two insurrectionary leaders, the Mahdi's Lieutenant was really the most dangerous. From a critical and difficult position, the Nile Expedition withdrew without serious interference from an enemy who seemed chary of descending below the Nile junction, but on the Red Sea Littoral, the rebel chief was able to threaten both the British position at Suâkin and the Suâkin-Berber route.

The most undeniable and significant proof of Osman Digna's importance, of the confidence reposed in him, and of the intimate relations between the two rebel centres, was the appearance of a Mahdist contingent at Tofrek. Such an event had not previously

---

[1] *Parliamentary Papers*, Egypt, No. 1 (1885), p. 109.

occurred in the Eastern Sûdan, and it is evident that in being thus specially recognised and reinforced from Khartûm, the rebellion in that province had attained its culminating point. It matters not under what form further advance had taken place, or under what General, a decisive conflict was certain to occur between this determined and powerful reinforcement and the British troops. The earliest opportunity did occur on the 22nd, and that under exceptionally favourable circumstances for the enemy, and we know the result.

Struck through all its ramifications, as with a fatal blow, the backbone of the rebellion on the Red Sea Littoral was finally broken, the power of Osman Digna crushed, and his influence over the tribes effectually annihilated. Of these facts, over two years' experience must have convinced the most gainsaying; while, at Suâkin, the unwonted phenomenon of an unmolested Indian garrison, succeeded by an equally unmolested Egyptian garrison, promise the permanent restoration of peace in that disturbed locality.

Of the three *criteria* laid down by Colonel Malleson, the third, and by far the most important, is thus specially applicable to the action at Tofrek, and in the manner in which it affected the "future permanent position of the combatants," has left nothing more to be desired.

As still further elucidating the remarks just made, I need only refer to the place held by the Battle of Tofrek in the list of honours awarded by the Government in the course of the recent Egyptian Expeditions. To the medal granted for service in Egypt and the Sûdan, during any of these Expeditions, eight[1] clasps have been superadded. Two of these, "The Nile 1884-85," and "Suakin, 1885," cover service in the localities noted within certain dates,

---

[1] Exclusive of the composite clasp "El Teb-Tamaai."

irrespective of presence at any particular engagement. The other six were issued only to those actually present at the critical battles of the four Campaigns, viz., "Tel-el-Kebir," "El Teb," "Tamaai" (1884), "Abu Klea," "Kirbekan," and "Tofrek."

In the decisive character of their immediate results, and the profound impression produced upon the enemy, between the two latter actions, a striking analogy is traceable. As an appropriate accompaniment then to Lord Wolseley's terse and admirable characterisation of the work effected at Tofrek in "destroying Osman Digna's power in the hard fought action of the 22nd March, under Major-General Sir J. M'Neill,"[1] with the extract from the Official Report[2] of General Brackenbury, in which the results of the action at Kirbekan are summed up, this Preface may be very fitly closed :—

"The crushing effect of the action of the 10th February at Kirbekan is best shown by the fact that after that fight the enemy allowed us to march unmolested to the farthest limits of the Monassir country, to take successively all the positions they prepared for defence, and subsequently to retire through the same positions without firing a shot or offering us any opposition."

WILLIAM GALLOWAY.

June 21, 1887.

---

[1] Despatch, *London Gazette*, Aug. 25th, 1885.

[2] *Parliamentary Papers*, Egypt, No. 13 (1885).

CONTENTS.

CHAPTER I.

PRELIMINARY.

CHAPTER II.

THE INSTRUCTIONS.

d

CHAPTER III.

THE PARADE AND MARCH OUT.

CHAPTER IV.

THE ZERIBA.

CHAPTER V.

THE BATTLE.

CHAPTER VI.

THE INDIAN CONTINGENT.

CHAPTER VII.

RETROSPECTIVE.

CHAPTER VIII.

THE PRESS AND THE BATTLE.

APPENDICES.

I.

II.

III.

IV.

e

V.

VI.

VII.

VIII.

IX.

X.

XI.

XII.

ILLUSTRATIONS.

MINOR ILLUSTRATIONS.

DESCRIPTION OF PLATES.

FRONTISPIECE.

Figure I. of this plate shows the Order of the Medjidie, 2nd Class, as granted in 1882 by His Highness the Khedive of Egypt, under authorisation of His Imperial Majesty the Sultan, to H.R.H. the Duke of Connaught and various Officers of the British Army for service in Egypt.

This Order was first instituted by the Sultan Abdid Medjid in 1852, and formed one of the prized decorations for the Crimean War. Its distinctive features are a star of seven points, with an equal number of crescents inclosing stars of five points, in the intermediate spaces, with the Imperial Cipher in the centre; the decoration being suspended from a crescent and star, and the ribbon red with a green stripe on either side. There are five classes, distinguished chiefly by the varying size of the star.

Figures II. and III. show the obverse and reverse of the Medal granted by the British Government for service during the Egyptian Campaigns, the obverse carrying Her Majesty's head with the diadem and veil, and surrounded with the legend "Victoria Regina et Imperatrix ;" the reverse a sphinx, with the word "Egypt." Only Medals granted for the first Campaign carry the date 1882. A notice of all the clasps accompanying this Medal have been already given in the Preface, pp. 21-22. The ribbon is blue, with two white stripes.

PLATE I.

This is merely a section, *facsimiled to exactly the same scale*, of the large Map of the country adjacent to Suâkin, issued by the War Office for the use of the Field Force serving in the Eastern Sûdan. The original includes an area of about thirty square miles, with an extension of sixteen or seventeen miles westward on the Suâkin-Berber route. These limits extend considerably beyond any operations undertaken in 1885, and if the line of Railway be excepted, every point of interest in the Campaign of that year is embraced within the more restricted area shown on Plate I. The only variation permitted has been a more distinct demarcation of the Lines of the British Advance on Tamai in 1884 and in 1885, the former being tinted a *blue* colour, and the latter *red*. The *yellow* line marks the comparatively clear and unimpeded track of a khor distinctly defined on the Intelligence Department Map, along which, according to a belief very generally entertained amongst those who were best informed in the Force at Suâkin, the advance on the 22nd *ought to have taken place,* but how this error arose or to whom the mistake is to be attributed is by no means apparent. One thing is certain, that, to use the words of an officer present at the action, "The general statement, over and over repeated at the time, and never to my knowledge contradicted, was, 'They missed their way.' I am unable to say how, or to whom, the blame attaches."

PLATE II.

PLANS OF GENERAL M‘NEILL'S ZERIBA AT TOFREK.

At pages 62 and 63, the mode of constructing a zeriba has been described, and also the successive changes that formed at Tofrek underwent. In its first stage it embraced over a thousand yards of thorn fencing, in the redoubts there being from five to six hundred yards of trench in addition. In the latter part of the operations, the entrenching tools invented by Major Wallace were largely employed, a detailed notice of which will be found in Appendix X. During the process of construction, and with the Transport Train being continuously disloaded and withdrawn, a variety of service-openings were necessarily left while these operations were in progress; but they were afterwards closed up, and the fencing made good.

We have seen, at page 63, that on March 30th, in order to liberate one of the Battalions for the proposed operations at Tamai the zeriba underwent a complete alteration. By utilising the Commissariat stores this was done very rapidly and well under the superintendence of Lieutenant-Colonel Edward Pemberton Leach, V.C., C.B. The zeriba was thus in existence for exactly a fortnight—one week as a thorn-fenced enclosure, one week as a reduced and fortified work. If the reader will turn to Appendix XI. he will find that the first form was precisely similar in arrangement to the improvised squares formed by the Grenadier Camel Corps with the Nile Expedition. There, when an alarm arose, the camels were all knee-lashed or hobbled, in one great square, the riders forming up in smaller squares at the opposite angles, and were thus able to protect by a flanking fire every side of the central camel square.

It is stated, at p. 84, that in order to avoid drawing the enemy's fire, for the first night no tents or lights were permitted. With the camels carrying the Staff baggage, two Indian tents, weighing about fifty pounds, pertaining to Sir John M'Neill had been brought out, one of these was handed over for the use of Colonel Huyshe of the Berkshires, and Sir John got into the other on the Tuesday. From first to last, it was not only to the majority an outdoor bivouac, but for these eventful ten days, from the Generals downwards, no one undressed, and toilette or ablutions there were none. In compliance with the requirements of Sir Charles Napier's celebrated "kit," one of the Staff happened to have a piece of carbolic soap; but where there was no water, to use it as a detergent being impossible, it was scraped and devoted *pro bono publico* to plug the nostrils during sleep, and thus secure some degree of protection against the polluting influences of defunct Arabs and camels. Towards the close of the operations the same Officer, for half a sovereign, having become possessor of a large Indian bottle of soda water, instead of quenching his thirst preferred to indulge in the unwonted luxury of a wash.

The action on the 22nd brought consequences with it which were not at first anticipated. Under similar circumstances, for sanitary reasons, it is usual for a Force to leave the vicinity of the battlefield as quickly as circumstances permit. It was so in all the other actions in the Eastern Sûdan; but in the present case to do so was impossible. For the first time in the history of these Campaigns, the Arabs made an exception to their invariable, their traditional practice, and attacked a defensive position. Under a tropical sun, the result to the defenders was a field encumbered with a mass of dead Arabs and animals, which even burial could not effectually dispose of. It was suggested from Head-Quarters that to get rid of this most disagreeable and insanitary *entourage*, the zeriba should be removed a mile and a half to the right, which would place it directly on the Tamanieb road; but the Force was tied, by the necessity of keeping by their water supply, which, stored as it was in the large iron tanks, requiring, even when quite empty, ten men to lift them on to a mule cart, it was impossible to remove. It was thus compelled to reverse Napoleon's dictum, that "an army *moves* by its stomach," and remain fast anchored by the reservoirs it had cost so much labour slowly to fill. Even when the Convoy got out on the forenoon of the 23rd it was remarked that a sickening odour was already tainting the air, but as time wore on, and of each recurring day it could only be said—

> "Now, by my life, this day grows wondrous hot;
> Some airy devil hovers in the sky,
> And pours down mischief:" (*King John*, Act III. Scene 2)—

to those compelled to bivouac and carry on all necessary duties and avocations in so pestilential an atmosphere, was indeed by no means an agreeable task. A report appeared at the time, stating that the health of the troops was being seriously affected by the nauseous effluvium, and of the various cases of sickness reported in the zeriba, Sir John M'Neill requested the doctor particularly to note any that might be due to the prevalent odours, but he was not able to trace even one instance, attributing the safety of the men very much to their living entirely in the open air. The greatest danger would have been to the wounded, as it would have been almost impossible under such circumstances to keep their wounds healthy or free from gangrene; but these cases were removed to the Base at the earliest opportunity.

With reference to this disagreeable aspect of military operations, the following remarks, which appeared during the currency of the Campaign, may be quoted :—

"It is not astonishing that the accounts of recent operations in the Soudan should have excited, to use a very mild expression, uneasy feelings here, and that the details furnished by the special correspondents should cause disgust and something like indignation in the country. It would not be surprising, therefore, if the Generals who are compelled by the orders of Government to engage in operations which as soldiers they must loathe, were to order the correspondents to remain in camp whenever 'razzie' like the successful expedition discussed in the House on Thursday are undertaken, or to direct the censors to water their despatches very copiously. But what is to be done in the case of private correspondence and letters from officers and soldiers? The most highly coloured—'graphic' is the word—of the after-the-battle scenes we have read was sketched with exceedingly great power by an officer, who described the sights which met the eye (and who gave a strong idea of the odours which filled the nostrils) of those who were obliged to traverse the field where the Arabs slain in Graham's and M'Neill's combats were rotting between Suakim and the zerebas; and the public shuddered, the friends of humanity were shocked, and the newspapers uttered exclamations of horror in type, as though they expected all the graves to bloom with flowers, and the air to be perfumed with sweets. It is sanctimonious affectation of tenderness, and humane sympathy is morally very offensive. War is dreadfully serious business. A General cannot treat an enemy as an angler for pike treats a frog, 'as though he loved him.' Much as he may be tortured by the cruelty of the measures by which he is obliged to effect the end he is under orders to execute, he must carry them out. But there is a limit.

There is no law, human or military, to justify barbarous acts even against barbarians. Our officers in Africa are under the eye of very severe criticism in Europe . . . As to bad smells and ugly sights, the public may be quite sure that battle-fields under the best conditions are disagreeable. They must not affect the airs of Hotspur's fop—and 'as the soldiers bore dead bodies by, he called them untaught knaves, unmannerly, to come betwixt the wind and his nobility;'—but accept the results, with the 'trimmings' of gorged vultures and prowling hyænas, pariah dogs, and the like, which may be served up as a dish of horrors as long as the war and the liberty of pen, ink, paper, and press endures."—*Army and Navy Gazette,* May 9th, 1885.

The fact of this large amount of carrion, human and bestial, lying uncon-. sumed for so long a period in a tropical country, is a striking evidence of the very scanty fauna inhabiting these arid and desert wastes. Had the scene of the fight lain in India, what with *Raptores* and *Carnivores* innumerable, vultures, hawks, adjutants, hyænas, *et hoc genus omne,* all constantly at work in large numbers, the whole ghastly *entourage* would have been cleared off in a very short time. It was afterwards discovered, when too late to be of any service, that in the vicinity, near the junction of the Tamai and Tamanieb routes, there were some dry wells, which might have been used as burial pits, and then covered up. With reference to the dead camels also, a useful idea afterwards occurred, viz., to deal with them as the Highland sportsman does with the stag he has shot—gralloche it, *i.e.,* rip the animal open, disembowel it, and bury the entrails, in which case under the burning sun of the tropics the carcase would soon become a desiccated mummy.

"All the dangers and glories of the grand advance"[1] brought to a final close, with the return from Tamai, and the reported desertion of Tamanieb by the enemy, the purpose of the zeriba had been served, and it only became necessary to remove the large accumulation of stores brought together with a view to much more protracted operations. The defences of the zeriba and its redoubts, as modified on March 30th, were largely constructed of biscuit boxes and other packing cases, which had been piled into ramparts and various defensive constructions not originally contemplated by the Commissariat Department. Without adequate preparation the removal of these stores would have been a tedious and troublesome business. When the Force returned from Tamai on April 3rd it bivouacked overnight at the Tofrek zeriba, marching into Suâkin the following morning; the 28th Bombay Native Infantry and a detachment of the Royal Navy with two Gardner

[1] *Daily Telegraph,* March 27th, 1885.

f

guns being left as a guard.   On going into Suâkin with his Brigade on the
4th, Sir John M'Neill left the zeriba in charge of a very active and intelligent Special Service Officer, Major, now Lieutenant-Colonel, Robert C.
D'Esterre Spottiswoode of the 10th Hussars.   Being informed the previous
day that a Convoy would come out on the 6th to remove the stores and dis-
mantle the zeriba, he set to work and got everything in readiness.   It would
have been very inconvenient and occupied much time to have had the
camels led up into the zeriba, and especially into the redoubts and small
works, and there loaded.   All small things, such as cases, water-tins, etc., were
accordingly brought outside, and arranged in long double lines, so that the
camels, led in between them, had only to kneel down, get loaded, and move
off.   The Convoy on going out on the 6th found matters accordingly in a
very forward state.   It was composed of the 2nd Brigade,—Berkshires, East
Surrey, and Shropshires, under Sir John M'Neill, to these being added the
15th Sikhs, a force of over 2600 all ranks.   They left Suâkin at 5.30 A.M.,
arriving at the zeriba at 8.30.   The Diary itself admits that "owing to systematic arrangements the work was promptly and thoroughly effected.   Nothing
was left on the ground."[1]   So thoroughly effective had all the preparations
been that the return journey was commenced at one o'clock, and Suâkin
reached by 4.30 P.M.

     In these operations the 28th Bombay Native Infantry did excellent
service, the whole Regiment having turned out as a fatigue party.   The stores
which had been taken out with so much labour were thus brought off, to the
last truss of mouldy-hay, nothing remaining save the brushwood fence, this
being afterwards burnt on May 1st by a party of Mounted Infantry and 9th
Bengal Cavalry.   It will be noticed on Plate II. that, in its second stage, the
zeriba is crossed diagonally by a traverse of hay nine feet high.   The hay
being compressed and in bales, the object of this arrangement was in the
event of an attack to stop bullets and other missiles from crossing the zeriba.
This hay brought from India was found to be very mouldy and indifferent
in quality, but was all scrupulously removed even to the last truss.   So much
water had also been brought out that even the enormous force of men,
followers, and animals bivouacking at the zeriba on the night of April 3rd,
were unable to produce much impression on the 30,000 gallons of water
stored at the cost of so much time and labour.   On the 6th, accordingly, for
once men and animals were allowed to drink their fill and sate themselves
from the abundant supplies.   What still remained unconsumed was poured

---

[1] *Vide* Appendix III. p. 343.

out on the parched and burning ground, and the tanks, both iron and canvas, carried off. So great was the superfluity that General M'Neill, seeing a large pool formed by the discharged fluid, rode his horse into it fetlock deep, for the mere pleasure, in this truly "dry and thirsty land," of letting him stand for a short time with his feet in the refreshing water.

At the close of Chapter V. it is mentioned that the British dead were interred in large trenches dug on the northern and western sides of the zeriba, and in default of any better method were decorated in Arab fashion with stones. This practice seems widely prevalent in this portion of Africa, as Mr. Hamilton tells us :—

"The graves are covered with oblong heaps of stones about a foot high : along the ridge of many of them a quantity of white salt, sometimes of white pebbles, is heaped up."—*Sinai, the Hedjaz and Soudan,* p. 222.

In Abyssinia the practice occurs in a still more artificial form :—

"About three miles from Koomaylo we came upon a very curious burial-place. It was in a low flat close to a gully, and covered a space of perhaps fifty yards square. The graves were placed very close together, and consisted of square piles of stones, not thrown together, but built up, about three feet square, and as much high. They were crowned by a rough pyramid of stones, the top one being generally white. Underneath these stone piles was a sort of vault."—*The March to Magdala,* by G. A. Henty, p. 54.

"Near the wells [at Koomaylo] is another large graveyard : the tombs here are rather more ornate than those I have already described, some of them being round, and almost all having courses of white quartz stones. Upon the top of many of these tombs are two or three flat stones placed on end, and somewhat resembling small head-and-foot stones. As there is no inscription upon them, it would be curious to find out the object with which the natives erect them."—*Ibid.* p. 58.

The curtain falls upon Tofrek with an event directly due to the unprincipled attacks so persistently made regarding the conflict of which it had been the scene. On the morning of the 10th of May, General Lord Wolseley, who had arrived at Suâkin from the Nile on a visit of inspection, rode out to the zeriba. He was accompanied by General Graham ; Sir George Greaves, Chief of the Staff at Suâkin ; Brigadier-General Hudson ; and the whole Staff, a body of Cavalry under General Ewart acting as escort. General Hudson fully explained to Lord Wolseley the various defensive dispositions of the troops, the circumstances under which the Arab attack took place, and the decisive manner in which it was repelled. The effect of this personal inspection on his Lordship's mind may be judged of from the subsequent despatch, already quoted in the Preface, and in the reference to the subject in a speech delivered at the Mansion House, on Wednesday, the 29th July 1885, also quoted at page 223.

PLATE III.

GROUP OF MAHDIST DERVISHES.

The unwonted, and, so far as we are aware, the solitary instance in which a Contingent of Mahdist Warriors or Dervishes made their appearance in the Eastern Sûdan having been at the Battle of Tofrek, it may be of interest to notice a few of their more distinctive peculiarities. These lie chiefly in the costume worn, and especially in the head-gear. In weapons, and in habitudes also, they in no way differ from their compatriots; but one remarkable custom they do abjure, and that is the peculiar mode of dressing the hair, almost universally prevalent amongst the Sûdanese Arabs. Their characteristics have been very vividly sketched by a traveller to whose writings we will have occasion frequently to refer.

"It was something new to find ourselves in the midst of the naked savages who here surrounded us. They answer the description given of the Troglodytes, whose descendants they probably are, though they of course claim an Arab lineage. Tall, slim, active-limbed, with regular and delicate features, they look like animated statues of bronze. Their skin is a deep chocolate-brown, and their heads, which are uncovered, bear a close and thick natural protection of curly hair, in which feature, and in which alone, they approach the negro type. Their only garment is a cotton cloth, about four yards long, worn round the waist, its two ends, which are frequently adorned with broad stripes of crimson silk, being thrown crossways over either shoulder, or wound round the body like a belt. Their sandals of camel hide are generally made with a long tongue of leather, which falls from the instep over the greater part of the foot. As ornaments, rather than as instruments of devotion, they wear a rosary of wooden beads round the neck, and a bunch of amulets, secured in little leather drums, tied round the left arm, with sometimes the addition of a short knife, whose sheath is fastened to the same string. A wooden skewer, serving as a comb, is stuck in their thick hair which some wear in a round mop-like crop; but most of them dress it in long ringlets, falling square from the temples round the head, and reaching over the shoulders, while a toupet of shorter hair on the forepart of the head stands straight up over the brow. The ringlets are smeared over with grease, which, when newly put on, gives them the appearance of being powdered. Others use a composition of pounded sandalwood and cloves kneaded with camel's grease, which gives a yellow colour to the hair. I saw one dandy whose toupet was thus coloured yellow, while the falling ringlets behind were white."—*Sinai, the Hedjaz, and Soudan,* by James Hamilton (London, 1857), p. 196.

This extraordinary coiffure, with all the inevitable filthiness attending it, is entirely discarded by the Mahdist Dervish, who crops his hair, and wears a round low-crowned cap of plaited straw or parti-coloured cloth. The most peculiar feature is, however, the tunic, with its patchwork decoration, which may be said to have constituted the uniform of the Mahdi. These tunics are merely loose gowns of unbleached cotton drawn over the head, with open sleeves coming well down the arm. The formation of the dress itself is extremely simple, all the skill and labour being bestowed upon its decoration. Although the taste displayed may not be of a very high kind, and savour more of a pantomime than of a military uniform, considerable ingenuity is displayed in studding the simple garment with parti-coloured patchwork, no two specimens being decorated exactly alike.

To describe one or two typical examples will be the best way to give the reader a clear idea as to the general characteristics of this novel costume. In Plate III. the warrior on the right wears a tunic, of which a leading feature is two dark blue stripes, and a central red one crossing the chest diagonally from the shoulders and meeting in the centre. From this point a line of diamond-shaped patches, with a central oblong patch, runs down the middle of the skirt. The colours are again dark blue and red alternately, some of the diamonds being halved between the colours. This arrangement is repeated at the two sides. Between these central and side lines there runs another, formed of much smaller diamonds, with oblongs composed of both colours. The neck, sleeves, and skirt are bound in red and vandyked in dark blue. In the centre of the chest is a dark blue spot with a red circle round it. On the sleeves, enclosed within a red border, there is a long stripe of the small diamond patches introduced on the sides of the tunic, and between this stripe and the armpit is a cruciform patch of dark blue cloth bordered with a red edging. Another tunic which I have seen, dreadfully besmeared with blood, and pierced with bayonet or bullet holes, was bordered and vandyked in a similar style to the last round the neck, sleeves, and skirts, but decorated with circular patches of cloth, also clipped vandyke-fashion. Of a third tunic the most distinctive peculiarity is a large tippet, or camaille, as in the days of chain-armour it would have been called, covering all the upper part of the chest, and formed of a genuine Scotch tartan, showing a good-sized check of red and green squares with a yellow stripe running through it. The front of this tunic has three oblong patches of brown and black woollen cloth disposed down the middle with small pieces about an inch square, set on diamond-fashion on the four sides. Similar patches run down the sides, and the bottom of the skirt has a triple border, first of red, then a band of dark cloth, surmounted by a van-dyked edging of yellow. These tunics are all decorated in the same style on back and front, so that the garment can be put on indifferently either way.

The standard borne by the warrior on the left carries an inscription to the same purport as that shown on Plate IV., only not so complete, the lines also running the reverse way. It will be noticed that the spears are all shod with iron. This is done in order to give weight and impetus to the spear when thrown at an enemy, the weapon being aimed and propelled through a circular orifice cut on the edge of the shield. It will be noticed that the Arab in a sitting posture has in his hand a knobkerry or throwing-stick, which is flung with great force at the face of an opponent from a few yards distance, the thrower then rushing on with sword and spear to take advantage of his adversary's confusion.

Sir Samuel Baker gives a very minute account of the shields used by the Arabs. Of these there are two kinds, the second being the form most usually met with in the Eastern Sûdan, of which our author states that it "is circular, about two feet in diameter, with a projection in the centre as a protection for the hand. When laid flat upon the ground the shield somewhat resembles an immensely broad-brimmed hat, with a low crown terminating in a point. In the inside of the crown is a strong bar of leather as a grip for the hand, while the outside is generally guarded by a strip of the scaly hide of a crocodile.

"The skins most prized for shields are those of the giraffe and the rhinoceros; those of the buffalo and elephant are likewise in general use, but they are considered inferior to the former, while the hide of the hippopotamus is too thick and heavy.

"The hide of the giraffe is wonderfully tough, and combines the great advantage of extreme lightness with strength. The Arabs never ornament their shields; they are made for rough and actual service, and the gashes

upon many are proofs of the necessity of such a protection for the owner."—
Nile Tributaries of Abyssinia, p. 168.

PLATE IV.

FIG. 1.—MAHDIST STANDARD, CAPTURED BY MAJOR THOMAS F. DUNSCOMB BRIDGE, ROYAL MARINE LIGHT INFANTRY.

The circumstances under which this flag was captured having been narrated at page 76, it only remains to describe the trophy itself, which is now in the possession of the Major's family.

The flag measures four feet nine inches in length, by three feet nine inches in breadth; the material is rather thin unbleached cotton cloth, with a red worsted border carried round the three sides, from two and a half to three inches in width, hemmed and firmly sewn together in short lengths, the sewing being all done with strong white cotton thread. On the fourth side both the cotton and worsted border are folded over two and a half inches, firmly sewn down, and closed at the top, thus forming a long pocket for the insertion of the staff, which does not appear to have had any other means of attachment.

The Arabic inscription runs in three irregularly spaced lines, on the upper half of the standard, the letters averaging four to five inches in depth, being formed by narrow strips of red cotton cloth, turned in at the edges, and sewn down with white thread, so forming a narrow line under a quarter of an inch in breadth. The inscription thus appears only on one side, and some of the characters are so ill formed that Sir William Muir, K.C.S.I., Principal of Edinburgh University, who has kindly favoured me with a translation, found them undecipherable. According to this eminent Orientalist, the inscription presents the ordinary Mohammedan formula, the transliteration and translation being as follows :—

Transliteration.

LA ILÂHA ILLA ILÂHU ; MOHAMMED
RASULU HÛ ; MOHAMMED AL MEHDI (SALA ?)
ALLÂHU (illegible) ALLÂHU ALEIHI WA SALLAM.

Translation.

There is no God but the Lord ; and Mohammed
is his Prophet ; Muhammed al Mehdy (the Guide)
The Lord (bless ?) him (illegible) and give him peace.

It will be noticed that above the second line there is a small hole, where the flag has been pierced by a bullet, and a red selvage line runs down near the end of the inscribed lines.

Fig. 2.—Sûdanese Charm Box from Suâkin.

This object, usually worn on the left arm, is chiefly formed of leather, and consists of two parts :

1st, A circular box or drum, one inch and a half deep by one and a quarter in diameter, covered with leather, and containing some verses of the Koran written on paper, supposed to render the wearer as one of the *Mu'mim*, or faithful, proof against the bullets and lethal weapons of the *Kaffir*.[1] The box is of course understood to be hermetically closed, and to undo it would destroy the efficacy of the charm.

2nd, An armlet, formed of a double circle of twisted thong, with the extremities drawn into a knot, the loose ends being left free, as shown in the drawing. Beneath this the attachment with the box is formed by a fold of the leather casing being carried round the two twisted thongs forming the armlet, and there very neatly and tightly sewn in. The entire object displays a good deal of skill and ingenuity in the use of very simple materials.

Fig. 3.—Sûdanese Snuff Box from Suâkin.

This is merely a little gourd, fruit of one of the widely-distributed family of the *Cucubercitæ*, in its natural state. It is two inches in diameter, and has a small orifice one-third of an inch wide neatly cut in the top, with a leathern

[1] *Kafir* (plural *Kafirun*), lit. "the coverer," one who covers up or conceals, hides or denies the truth, and in this sense extensively used throughout the East as a term of religious reprobation ; while in its primitive meaning of hiding, covering, it is also expressive of such sacred ideas as expiation and atonement, by sacrifice, prayer, or alms.

By a curious anomaly, the cognate form in the Hebrew is connected with the holiest and most sacred associations known to the Jew, giving its name to the Mercy Seat and leading ceremonial observances.

Various other terms are also used to designate those outside the orthodox Mohammedan pale, *e. g.*—

Mushrik, one who gives companions to God ; applied equally to Christians who believe in the Trinity and to idolaters.

Mulhid, one who swerves from the truth.

Zandíg, an infidel, or a Zend worshipper.

Munafíg, one who secretly disbelieves in the divine mission of Mahomet.

Murtadd, an apostate from Islam.

Dahri, an atheist,—all who deny the Divine existence.

Waṣaníy, a pagan or idolater.

    Vide Hughes's *Dict. of Islam.*

plug three-quarters of an inch long acting as a stopper. This little contrivance is very ingeniously made out of tiny strips of leather, the strip forming the core being folded up longitudinally, so as to present a solid extremity either way, while the head is formed by another strip wound round the top, and neatly tucked in at the ends. The contents of the box are not used in the ordinary European fashion,—instead of being taken up through the nostrils, being swallowed, or rather bolted. The *modus operandi* is very well described by Mr. Hamilton; when relating how Arabs snuff, he states :—

"This they carry in a small hollowed nut, and take it in a fashion which I recommend to European amateurs as less dirty than the usual one. A large pinch is shaken out on the back part of the hand, between the thumb and forefinger, in the same way as the Highlander administers to himself this luxury, and it is then chucked, not up the olfactory canals, but into the mouth, and swallowed without chewing. As nitre is added to the leaf which the Western Arab chews, so here they mix the ashes of the wood fires with their snuff, and one seldom passes the place where an encampment has been, without seeing the camel men turn aside to gather the ashes of the dead fires."—*Sinai, the Hedjaz, and Soudan,* p. 224.

If, in being taken up from the back of the hand, an analogy is presented to a custom occasionally found in Scotland, in a mode of snuffing which must altogether fail in tickling the olfactory nerves, the term "sneeshin" would be quite inapplicable.

PLATE V.

SÛDANESE WEAPONS.

As the scene, from the remotest ages, of incessant tribal and internecine war, Africa has long been distinguished for the variety, the peculiar character, and in many respects the excellence, of its weapons of war. The art of destroying human life, and of inflicting torture of the most cruel and relentless kind, has found ample scope amongst its teeming populations. In arts like these the Sûdan and Central Africa are second to none. The weapons represented on Plate V. are only a few, out of an endless variety of types sufficient in themselves to form an ethnographical collection of no mean interest.

Figures 1 and 2 represent weapons preserved in the Museum of Science and Art, Edinburgh, and are of special interest from being incidentally associated with the late General Gordon when Governor of the Sûdan. The barbed spear-head (Fig. 1), which is drawn full size, was thrown at him in the usual way, and passing through his coat struck a tree behind. The plain elongated spear-head (Fig. 2), which, like all the remaining examples, is drawn under half-size, was used by General Gordon's servant in killing the man who threw the small spear.

Figures 3 and 4 are illustrations of a very formidable type of weapon extensively used in the Central Sûdan. Sir Samuel Baker describes a weapon of this kind as used by the Tokrooris, a tribe of Mohammedan negroes living on the confines of Egyptian and Abyssinian territory :—

"They are armed with lances of various patterns. Their favourite weapon is a horrible instrument barbed with a diabolical intention, as it can neither be withdrawn nor pushed completely through the body, but, if once in the flesh, there it must remain. This is called the chimbāné ; it is usually carried with two other lances with plain heads."—*Nile Tributaries of Abyssinia*, p. 511.

Figure 5 illustrates the plain-headed style of lance referred to by Sir S. Baker, and which is of course the most usual form of weapon, differing chiefly in point of size, from a blade four inches in breadth, and including the socket, about eighteen inches in length, down to half these dimensions. The savage-looking implement (Fig. 6) is, with the handle, also about eighteen inches long, and is used chiefly for hamstringing camels and other large animals ; but, as may easily be judged, would be a terrible instrument howsoever used. Weapons precisely similar were found by our troops in use in Abyssinia.

"The natives completely swarm about our camp [Senafe]. The men do not do much, but loiter about with their swords and spears and shields made of elephant hide. These spears are really formidable weapons. They are from six to ten feet long, and weighted at both ends, and the natives are able to throw them with great force and considerable accuracy for a distance of over thirty yards. These would be ugly weapons in a hand-to-hand fight in a bush ; but as it is, against a disciplined force armed with firearms, they are simply absurd ; and I have seen no offensive weapons, such as bows or arrows—which could be used with effect against us during the passage of a defile—in their possession since my arrival in the country."—*The March to Magdala*, by G. A. Henty, p. 91.

With regard to the diagram, page 149, it may be remarked that, owing to the restricted breadth of type, the Cavalry cordon formed by Major, now Lieutenant-Colonel, Francis J. Graves, round the recovered camels and baggage animals, is unavoidably shown in too compressed, and therefore too crowded, a formation. What with detachments of the 20th Hussars, 5th Lancers, and 9th Bengal Cavalry, as mentioned at pages 79, 80, there was present a combined Cavalry Force, in all, over three hundred strong. This was largely due to the precautions adopted by Major Graves, who, from information received in the bazaar in the course of the morning, fully expecting there would be a fight, requested that the normal strength of his Squadron might be increased. This gave him the whole of the Regimental signallers, two extra Officers, Surgeon N. Leader, and two Hospital orderlies, raising the Squadron from about ninety, to a hundred and ten. Forage and rations were also taken, and every preparation made for eventualities. In addition to what has been stated at pages 79-81, after-inquiries seem to show that about two hundred of the Bengal Native Infantry, and followers, as well as several British Officers and men, got back to the zeriba under shelter of the Cavalry. Arrived there, his little Force was drawn up by Major Graves, as a central and two flanking supports to the cordon, facing outwards of course, and describing a much larger and more open arc than it has been possible to show on page 149.

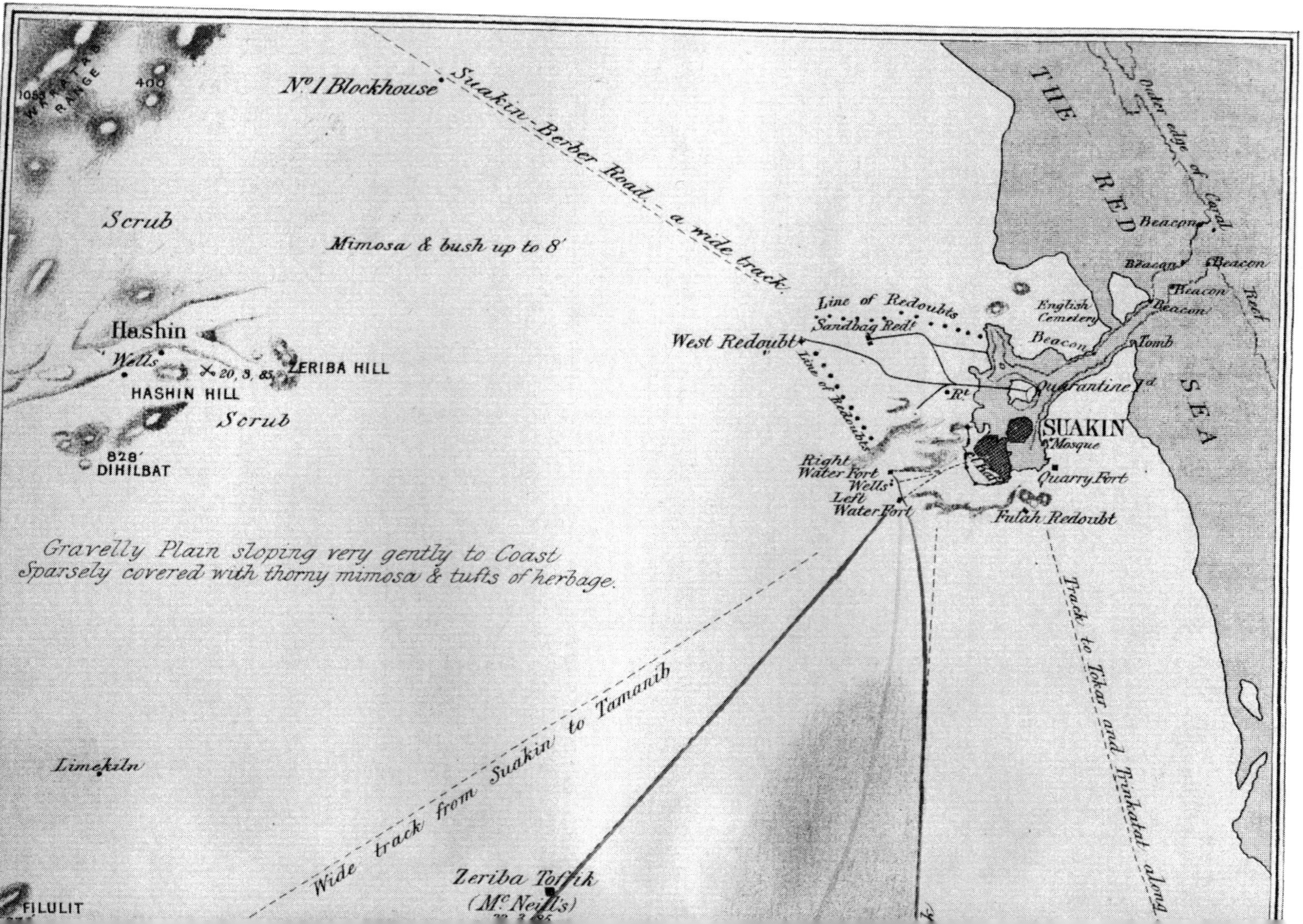

THE RED SEA

Outer edge of Coral Reef

Beacon
Beacon
Beacon
Beacon

SUAKIN

Track to Tokar and Trinkatat along

Quarantine I.

English Cemetery

Mosque

Quarry Fort

R.C.

Beacon Tomb

Fulah Redoubt

Line of Redoubts

Sandbag Redt

Line of Redoubts

West Redoubt

Right Water Fort Water Wells

Left Water Fort

Suakin-Berber Road. — a ride track.

Nº 1 Blockhouse

Mimosa & bush up to 8'

Wide track from Suakin to Tamanib

Zeriba Toffik
(Mc.Neills)

Scrub

ZERIBA HILL

Scrub

Hashin

Wells

× 20, 3 &c.

HASHIN HILL

828'
DIHILBAT

MC. NEILLS 100
9 MILES
400

Gravelly Plain sloping very gently to Coast
sparsely covered with thorny mimosa & tufts of herbage.

Lime Kiln

FILULIT

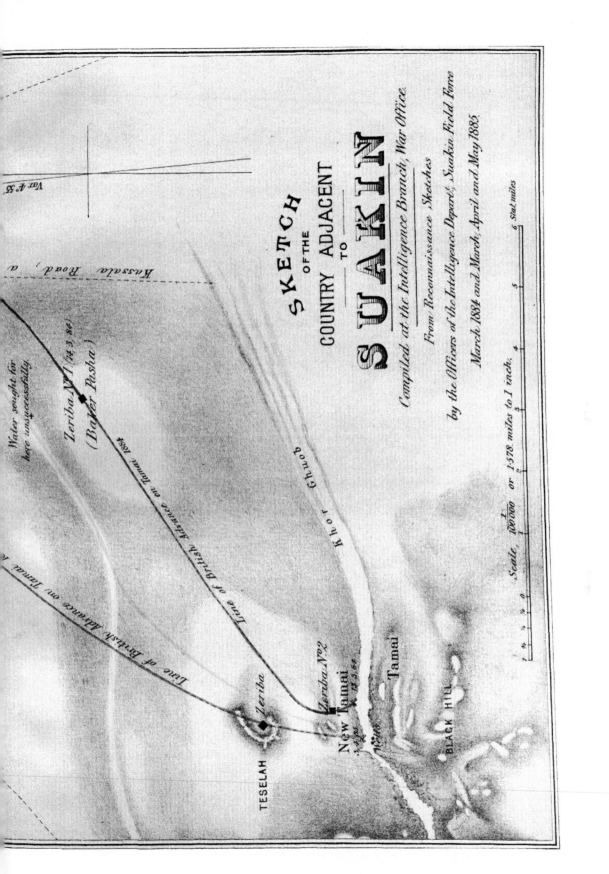

SKETCH
OF THE
COUNTRY ADJACENT
TO
SUAKIN

Compiled at the Intelligence Branch, War Office,

From Reconnaissance Sketches

by the Officers of the Intelligence Depart, Suakin Field Force

March 1884 and March, April and May 1885.

Scale, $\frac{1}{100,000}$ or 1·578 miles to 1 inch.

Stat.miles

Var. 4° 35'

Hassala Road

Water sought for here unsuccessfully.

Zeriba Nº 1 (24. 3. 85)
(Baker Pasha)

Line of British Advance on Tamai 1884

Line of British Advance on Tamai 1885

TESELAH

Zeriba

New Tamai

Zeriba Nº 2

Tamai

Khor Ghuob

BLACK HILL

CHAPTER I.

OFFICERS LIBRARY P.M.L.I. GORTON

PRELIMINARY.

"The wretched peasant, with that filthy cloth, which you see, is a determined warrior,
who can undergo thirst and privation, who no more cares for pain or death than if
he were of stone. The young fellows even have a game by which they test who
will bear the lash of the hippopotamus whip best.[1] They are in their own land;
the pains of war are their ordinary life; and they are supported by religion of a
fanatical kind, influenced by the memory of years of suffering at the hands of an
effete set of Bashi Basouks. No; if our Kentish or Yorkshire boys are to come up
to help me, it is not with my wish, UNLESS WITH THE GREATEST PRECAUTION."—
GENERAL GORDON'S JOURNALS: *sub 24th September* 1884.

IN the various campaigns entailed by the Egyptian policy
of the late Government no incident has been more
severely or unjustly animadverted upon than the action
fought near Suâkin on the 22nd of March 1885, under
Major-General Sir John Carstairs M'Neill.

For a day or two previous to this event it was known that
active operations had recommenced in the Eastern Sûdan.
Telegraphic accounts had already appeared of the advance upon
Hashin, while the lists of killed and wounded brought home to the

---

[1] "The Hamitic race are bigoted Mohammedans, and to them no sacrifice is
counted great in the cause of religion.
Among the tribes of the Red Sea there is
a custom of deferring the rite of admission
to the Moslem creed until puberty, when
it is performed in public by a process of
such utter agony, of a barbarity so shocking,
that it cannot be described here. The
torture is borne, as a point of honour,
without murmur or tremor, and as a
test unsurpassable of resolution, fortitude,
and control of emotion."—"The Native
Races of Egypt and the Soudan:"—
Army and Navy Gazette, 31st January
1885.

public mind the inevitable price of war. It was also known that the Arab tribes, assembled in considerable strength under the influence of Osman Digna, were in a dangerous and aggressive mood.

All available experience went to prove that the British Army was confronted with an enemy against whose artifices no precautions could be too great, and adequately to cope with whom would demand not only the highest qualities of courage and endurance, but constant and sleepless vigilance. Not only was the Expedition, while yet in course of formation, practically confined within its camping lines, but these lines themselves were systematically invaded with the most daring impunity.

If not formidable in resources or acquaintance with the arts of civilised warfare, in the Arab there was combined, with the reckless daring of the fanatic, the ruthless truculence of the assassin. Untrained in military discipline, the Sûdanese hordes were yet bound as in corporate unity by the ancient hatred of the Moslem to the Christian, of the Crescent to the Cross,—all the worst traditions of that bigoted and intolerant faith finding full scope in the new uprising under the banner of the Mahdi.

Nor could it be doubted that, versed in turning to effective account all the resources of a baleful superstition, their leader, the astute and crafty ex-slave merchant of Suâkin,[1] who owed the

---

[1] "Osman Digna's whole relation to the revolt and the amalgamation in him of religious, political, and mercantile aspirations, are hard to comprehend. A broker and trader, and principally a slave trader in Suakin and Jeddah, he received a severe financial blow when, some six years ago, a British cruiser captured two slave dhows full of victims, on the way to Jeddah. Osman Digna's trade then fell from bad to worse, his house property in Suakin was all mortgaged, and he became hopelessly involved. Being of no great distinction by birth, his selection by the Mahdi to lead a religious rebellion in these parts is not in accordance with the structure of Arab society and feeling, and is attributed to the accident that Osman Digna, in one of his incursions far south for slaves, met the Mahdi, who formed a high estimate of his ability and of his influence acquired through successful trading.

"If this history be trustworthy, passions, for other objects than holiness, are the keynote of Osman Digna's character and motives, and it is against all probability that he will cast his goods and his position into the broken balance of battle. He is no ignorant fanatic, and he cannot himself believe the myths which he multiplies in order to control his followers. Still, all say that he will fight."—*Times*, 10th March 1884. *Vide* also Appendix II.

meddlesome humanitarianism of the West so deep a grudge, would if fitting opportunity occurred, in the most malign and murderous meaning of the words, " Cry 'Havoc,' and let slip the dogs of war !" [1]

These dogs were already baying at every outpost of the Army, licking up every life that crossed their fiend-like path. Keen of eye and noiseless in step as hyænas, in the dense gloom of the tropical night they slipped past pickets and sentries, straight into the tents of the sleeping soldiery, driving keen-edged sword or spear into the unconscious forms around them. Enemies such as these were indeed but a sample of thousands more to whom murder and rapine were as familiar as the air they breathed. Wherever the eye could turn over these arid plains, dense bush, rocky ravines, and distant hills, the land might be said to swarm with wolves rather than with men. At a season of the year, too, when European troops ought to be withdrawn, not landed. Such was the enemy the various Corps composing the Expedition of 1885, were suddenly called upon to face.

Truly may it be said of every man who set his foot upon that fateful shore, that he carried his life in his hand; and if, at the close of the campaign, it was his good fortune safely to return, that return would be due not to any grace or favour of the foe, but to the wise precautions, to the skilful strategy, and good handling of the Generals; to his own courage, promptitude, and presence of mind; and to the superiority of the arms of precision, of offence and defence, placed at his disposal. Those who went did so at the call of duty— imperative and not to be gainsaid; the reason why they went was directly due to one of the direst exigencies of Governmental blundering which has ever disgraced the political annals of this country.

The Suâkin Expedition of 1885 sprang up as a direct sequel to the fall of Khartûm. In strength and resources the Force intended for the relief of that beleagured town and its brave defender had been calculated for one eventuality only, viz., that Khartûm should be found safe and General Gordon alive. It was despatched at the eleventh hour in the vain hope, too frequently entertained in human affairs, that the final, the predicted hour of Fate and Doom, would never arrive. All illusions to the contrary, in a form more ruthless and ghastly than the most pessimistic imagination had ventured to conceive, that hour unfortunately came at last.

Five months of incessant toil by desert and waterway; the gauntlet run in a rapidly-falling river of a thousand miles of cataracts, portages, swift currents, concealed rocks, and other obstructions; herculean labours under an African sun, carried out with the utmost enthusiasm, and animated by a Great Hope, ended by conferring on the Nile Expedition *one privilege.* Buried in the heart of the Sûdan, whether in the camps at El Gubat or Abu Klea, punishing the murderers of Colonel Stewart in the Dar Monassir or with Head-Quarters at Korti, foremost of all their countrymen, amid the deep silence of the desert, on their keenly attent and listening ears, fell the first notes of the fatal announcement of General Gordon's death, and the capture of the town he had so long and so gallantly defended.[1]

[1] The following quotation from the *Army and Navy Gazette* for February 7th 1885 will show the temper of the country immediately on the receipt of this disastrous intelligence. Lord Wolseley had stated that he could not hope to reach Khartûm under five weeks, *i.e.*, towards the middle of March, and by that time the hot season would have set in in all its severity. Thus, under a double foe, the Arab and the sun, for a mere *revanche* to have immolated the British Force in the "Grave of Armies" would have been madness. It had quite sufficient ordeal to endure, hutted on the banks of the Nile, during so many scorching months. Lord Wolseley shows a much more correct appreciation of the position in his despatch :—

"Lord Wolseley has declared that he can advance and take Khartoum, and we believe that he could be as good as his word. But, at the same time, he has warned the Government that the troops will be exposed to great losses, and that they cannot remain in Khartoum without paying a heavy penalty to the climate, which in a few weeks will become excessively enervating and malarious. Well! gloomy as that prospect is, there can be, we think, but one conclusion to all argument on that point. Khartoum must be taken and held, and that end can only be attained by an immediate advance of every man now available under Lord Wolseley's orders. It is a dreadful ordeal—toilsome marches over a burning desert, wearisome contention with the headlong river, day after day, with the consciousness that the original aim of the expedition has been missed, and that new purposes and objects must be substituted for the unique object of the expedition, with an illimitable *vista* of inglorious warfare."

This is not the place to depict the anguish of heart and rage of the soldiery, the crushing disappointment to every member of the Expedition, from the Commander-in-Chief downwards, when it was fully realised that their ardent anticipations had been for ever blasted, and that a most heroic deed of arms, eliciting the admiration not of Europe only, but of the civilised world, had been suddenly bereft of the only guerdon worthy of toils and dangers, so unsurpassed.

Effected by a deed of treachery, deemed startling for its atrocity even in the chosen home of treachery and deceit, the results, in so far as related to the Relief Expedition, are thus clearly summed up by Lord Wolseley, in his despatch of February 9th, 1885, to the Marquis of Hartington, then Minister at War :—

"I shall not attempt to disguise from your Lordship how deeply the reported fall of Khartoum is felt by all ranks in the army under my command. If it be literally true—and it is difficult to disbelieve it—the mission of this force, which was the relief of Khartoum, falls to the ground.

"The strength and composition of this little army was calculated for the relief, not the siege and capture, of Khartoum ; the two operations being entirely different in character and magnitude.

"The former meant one or more engagements in the open with an enemy who, owing to the geographical position of Khartoum, could not concentrate his forces without raising the siege ; and who, in order to concentrate, would have had to pass his troops, guns, ammunition, etc., over two unfordable rivers of considerable breadth, in the face of General Gordon's steamers.

"If he opposed my advance along the right bank of the Nile upon Khartoum, he must have fought in a position where defeat would have been his destruction.

"I think I may say that, as long as Khartoum held out, he could not have prevented my entering it, although he might afterwards have awaited my attack in a selected position on the left bank of the White Nile, to the south or south-west of the city.

"With Khartoum in the enemy's possession the whole conditions are reversed, and the Mahdi—strengthened by the large number of rifles, guns, ammunition, etc., taken in that place, and by the captured troops who would certainly fight on his side—could concentrate an overwhelming force to oppose my advance ; and, if defeated, could still fall back upon the city, the siege and capture of which, situated as it is in the fork of two unfordable rivers, would be an impossible operation for the little army under my command, more especially as it would then be encumbered by a large number of wounded men.

"As I have already said, the force under my command was not intended for any operation of that magnitude, nor was such an operation even contemplated in the instructions I received from Her Majesty's Government.

"Khartoum, in the hands of the enemy, cannot be retaken until the force under my command has been largely augmented in numbers and in artillery."[1]

When once, during its five months' progress up the Nile, communications were broken off between the Expedition and its Base in Lower Egypt, like a balloon no longer captive but sailing away into space, the British Force was entirely *en l'air*, dependent exclusively on its own resources; and the farther it slowly toiled up the Father of rivers, with increased liability to accident and a position more perilous and uncertain, the less hope was there of any possible aid reaching it from beneath. Not only for the safety of General Gordon, and those he had so long protected, but for that of the Expedition itself, it was essential that it should acquire a new *point d'appui*, a secure Base of Operations, in its objective Khartûm. To carry out the simile, the influence by which the Expedition was upborne in its far-off voyage—the gas inflating the balloon—was that happy-go-lucky optimism, ever dreaming that for the British Government the chapter of accidents would assuredly turn up prizes and no blanks, and all be well in the end. All was not well; and the little vanguard of the Force got within reach of the coveted goal only to find the tables completely turned—all they had wished to save destroyed, and the stronghold itself, with all its resources, in possession not of friends, but of a savage and triumphant enemy. With all that gave it buoyancy gone, for what remained of the balloon, no resource was left save to find its way back to mother earth as best it could; and so with effective strength reduced and Transport crippled, the Expedition retraced its footsteps down the Nile.

[1] *Parliamentary Papers*, Egypt, No. 9 (1885), No. 36.

Under circumstances such as these a renewal of the Campaign of 1884 on the Red Sea Littoral was determined on. Although only a sequel to that on the Nile, it became in many respects an absolute necessity. The Madhist successes in the Central Sûdan were exercising a dangerous influence on the eastern tribes. Osman Digna, once more on the war-path, and eager for another tournament with the Kaffirs from beyond the sea, was becoming more threatening and aggressive; while, with a view to ulterior operations, it was essential that the Suâkin-Berber route should be kept open, and any risk of Lord Wolseley's communications being interfered with, averted.

To return, however, to the episode with which we are more immediately concerned. About twelve minutes past three the main struggle at Tofrek was over, and General Graham's first despatch is timed 5.20 P.M. According to the *Daily Telegraph*, however, a message must have been wired from Suâkin to London at 4.10 P.M., and the first special Sunday edition of that paper which had been issued for many years appeared at 4.30, London time. Heralded by flaming posters, and hundreds of vociferous throats, the sale was enormous, copies going at six times the ordinary price immediately outside the publishing office, and rising to nine times that figure in the suburbs. To the twenty minutes elapsing between 4.10 and 4.30 P.M. must of course be added nearly two hours and a half for difference of time in east longitude between London and Suâkin. Still, even with this allowance, four hours from the cessation of an important conflict on the Red Sea Littoral, till the dissemination of the intelligence broadcast over the British metropolis in full-fledged newspaper form, was a remarkable feat of commercial and journalistic enterprise.

Let us glance for a moment at what was transpiring at the further extremity of the electric "Line of Communication." The variation of time in east longitude for half-past four in London gives about seven o'clock at Suâkin. The sun has just set behind the barren mountains, rising in rugged and forbidding masses against the western sky; the brief twilight of the tropics has faded away, and the dense gloom of a deeply-clouded night shrouds the blood-stained battlefield of Tofrek. The bivouac for the night is on the bare ground, under the open canopy of Heaven, in the midst of an East African desert, the savage enemy kept at bay only by the undaunted courage with which the previous assault had been repelled, and absolute certainty its renewal would again entail condign punishment. Worn out with incessant toil from earliest morning under a blazing sun, fully armed and accoutred, lying down in ranks two deep, as if in order of battle, the troops line the various defences. Deep silence is settling down over the scene of fierce conflict, and the two hours' watch in alternate ranks has just begun, the entire Force being on the *qui vive*, and ready at a moment's notice to repel the renewed assault, for aught they know, ever imminent.

Time and distance so minimised, between the great centre of civilisation and the barbaric *entourage* in which the British troops were placed, thus suddenly and for a brief moment so sharply confronted, how strange a contrast![1]   And to what purpose was a feat like this performed? For the remainder of the evening the *Daily Telegraph* played the *rôle* of News-pilot without competitor. Next morning the entire British Press spread the intelligence of that afternoon's doings over the length and breadth of the land, while post and telegraph alike secured its transmission to every quarter of the civilised world. We again ask to what purpose was this done? Did the information so conveyed in any degree represent the facts as they are now known, or as in the heart of that African bush

---

[1] In the previous campaign we find the same idea very pertinently expressed on the eve of the battle of Tamai :—

"No greater contrast can be conceived than that between the everyday surroundings of our English life, and the conditions under which the English Force has to advance to the encounter in the Egyptian desert. The suddenness, the completeness of the transition enhances the effect. The picture drawn by our Correspondent is vivid in its simplicity. . . . The nation is conscious of much more than a vague sympathy with those who are fighting its battles; it shares the emotions of the camp, and becomes almost a spectator of the combat. While the conflict, which we trust will prove decisive, is in all probability proceeding, we are admitted to a view of the battlefield, and can almost watch through the night with the expectant soldiers."—*Standard*, March 13th, 1884.

they really were? Most assuredly not. That a most determined attack had been successfully repelled was admitted; but there had been a dreadful surprise, the casualties were unduly heavy, the destruction of Transport enormous, and a narrow escape made from one of those crowning disasters like Maiwand or Isandlana, casting occasionally such a lurid gleam even over our "little wars," while defeat and annihilation had been averted "more by chance than by good guidance," all these evils being carefully credited to one origin.

Based on a want of information, but very slightly removed from that of the general Public it was desired to enlighten, although aimed chiefly at the General in Command, the animadversions, so unsparingly administered, embraced within their comprehensive sweep every superior Officer, down at least to the Colonels of Regiments. Tofrek was a brainless and invertebrate battle, where the upper grades of the Army, if they had any heads at all, had fairly lost them. The Force had been taken to a very bad place, entrapped amongst "dense, dark, thorny coverts," and *pari passu* with his march out, the General had forgotten to burn the bush. Of ordinary military precautions there were next to none. If the Cavalry were out at all it was only at a short distance from the main body, while the outpost and picket arrangements were of the most perfunctory character. That the troops were in any defensive formation was by implication stoutly denied; at the best it was a point on which the critic was completely silent, for the very good reason he could not know. One thing certain, they were dining, they were cutting bush, they had their coats off, their belts off, they were away from their arms, everything was topsy-turvy. From the General to the private, all alike were careless and *nonchalant;* as busy at their ordinary affairs and heedless of danger as the Antediluvians when "the flood came and took them all away."

Discounted on the ready plea *s'excuser, s'accuser,* reclamations by the Authorities, either at Suâkin or at home, were received only with snubs and ill grace. Carefully fanned by sensational newsmongers, so high rose the tide of obloquy that it invaded both

Houses of Parliament, and in the absence of any effectual or authoritative contradiction, instead of that sense of gratulation and relief usually accompanying a most effective victory, for several months there seemed to hang over the country the shadow of a grave military disaster! Before the inexorable logic of facts slowly the veil began to lift and events to be seen in their true proportions. There were no more fights of any importance on the Red Sea Littoral; the Army had to expend its energies on military promenades, flying columns, and, above all, the abortive railway. Whatever came of this, the second great object of the campaign, it was clear that for the time being the first had been fully accomplished. The "brilliant success," desiderated as a counterfoil to the fall of Khartûm achieved, and, in the words of Lord Wolseley, the power of Osman Digna crushed in the "hard-fought action of March 22nd," thanks to the politician all the rest was "leather and prunella," in men, money, and toil, of a very costly kind. The retention of the Expedition at Suâkin only served to confront it with a foe more dangerous than the Arab, a foe not waning but waxing, and with every day's advance of the sun from *Gemini* into *Taurus* in an ever increasing ratio of death and sickness, the old adage was forcibly illustrated, "War cannot be kept at a set diet."

Well may we ask then, whether, under such circumstances, in a mode of procedure like that just referred to, there was a single strain of the brave heroic blood, which, after a brief but most determined conflict, finally quelling the might of the enemy, had stood victorious on the field? Again, the answer must be, not a trace of it; on the contrary, with very few exceptions,[1] from first to last it was a voice cowardly and craven, the result not of calm dispassionate judgment, but of panic, prejudice, and fear.

Once resolved on, General Graham had lost no time in opening the

[1] It is deserving of mention that the only paper courageous enough to enter an effective protest against the senseless clamour of its contemporaries was the *Glasgow* now the *Scottish News*, which, in its issue of March 26th, with special reference to the reports then circulated, had a long and trenchant article on the action at Tofrek, headed "Unthinking Censure." *Vide*, Appendix VIII.

campaign.   After a fortnight spent in making the necessary preparations, and in collecting and organising the Expeditionary *matériel*, active measures were commenced on the 19th of March with a Reconnaissance in force towards Hashin, about eight miles due west from Suâkin, at the foot of the Waratab range of mountains; on the 20th, Dihilbat Hill was captured, and a zeriba established in a fortified position in its immediate vicinity.   Both these operations were carried into effect with all the resources of a well-appointed Army, every precaution requisite in dealing with a wily and uncertain foe being adopted.   More especially was this the case with regard to the Mounted troops, the entire available Cavalry Force, comprising two Squadrons of the 5th Lancers, and of the 20th Hussars, and the 9th Bengal Cavalry, being out on duty.   Brigaded with these were also the Mounted Infantry, a most important branch of the service, who both on this and other occasions proved themselves invaluable. Limited to reconnoitring duty, on the 19th this Cavalry Force was accompanied as supports by the Indian contingent—15th Sikhs, 28th Bombay, and 17th Bengal Native Infantry, and also a Battery of the Royal Horse Artillery.

With the exception of a single Regiment left in charge of the camp, on the 20th the entire strength of the Expedition was called out, and formed up in one vast half mile-broad Square.   In front marched the second Brigade—Berkshire, East Surrey, and Royal Marine Light Infantry, under Sir John M'Neill; on the right the Guards— Grenadier, Scots, and Coldstream, under General Fremantle; and on the left the Indian Contingent, under General Hudson.   The rear was left open, the interior of the Square being occupied by Transport of various kinds—water, rations, ammunition, and other army requirements, partly for use on the current day, partly for the force to be left in the contemplated position.   Taking camels and mules together, these stores were carried or drawn by from 1400 to 1500 animals, representing a proportion of beasts of burden and draught to fighting men of about one to five and two-thirds.

Covering this great array both on front and flank, sweeping far

ahead, searching every square yard of the ground, and gradually
feeling their way like the ever-active antennæ of the army, was the
fore-cited Cavalry Brigade and Mounted Infantry, followed in rear
by a Battery of the Royal Horse Artillery.

So marshalled under the personal Command of Lieutenant-
General Sir Gerald Graham, a fighting Force over eight thousand
strong, thoroughly prepared at every point, as if about to engage in
great tactical operations, with an equally well-equipped and civilised
foe, the Expedition of 1885 moved out for its first real trial of
strength toward the Arab stronghold.

That the results were at all commensurate with these great preparations, will scarcely be admitted. Not without severe loss, owing
to defective strategy, it is true that considerable damage was inflicted on the enemy and a fortified position established, garrisoned by
a Regiment, and protected by four guns. But, *cui bono?* Dihilbat
Hill, the real strength, as the Arabs deemed it, after being most
gallantly won, over difficult ground and a most exposed position,
by the Berkshire and Royal Marines under Sir John M'Neill, with
only two men wounded, in the advance and retirement, was shortly
afterwards vacated, and, being at once re-occupied by the enemy,
he might well be excused for thinking that with him lay the fruits
of victory. As to the fortified post, in the paragraph in which it
is referred to in General Graham's despatch, three reasons are
given for its formation :—

The position proposed for occupation was required in order to protect
my right flank in the impending advance on Tamai, to obtain a post of observation near to the mountains, and to assist in overawing the tribes.[1]

To what extent any one of these three objects was met, may be
judged from the fact, that, the influence it may have had in arrest-
ing the night attacks excepted, without having served any useful
purpose, save that of entailing harassing convoy duty, the Force left
was withdrawn, and in the words of the official " Diary of the Suakin
Expedition, 1885 "[2]—" The zerebas were dismantled and abandoned,"

---

[1] *Parliamentary Papers*, Egypt, No. 13 (1885), p. 19   [2] Page 25.

just five days after they were established,—the curious thing being
that the despatch quoted was written just four days prior to this
voluntary destruction of the zeriba and its redoubts, and twelve days
before the anticipated advance on Tamai, which proved really to be
an unopposed and all but bloodless promenade.[1] In its bearing then
on the fortunes of the campaign, both as to moral effect and tactical
result, the outcome of this day's work on the 20th of March, with all
its toil and bloodshed, proved to be practically useless.

Save for such preparations as might, during the latter part of
the day, be necessary for a renewed advance on the morrow, the
21st of March brought to the troops complete repose. Reverting
to the same attitude of guarded self-defence, which had preceded
the Reconnaissance of the 19th, no external movement of any kind
took place, a fact which the reader will find commented on in a
subsequent chapter.[2]

Opportunity was however taken to pay the last rites to such of
the "ne'er returning brave" as had fallen the previous day in the
conflict at Hashin. Foremost amongst these was Lieutenant Maxi-
milian Dudley Digges Dalison, of the Scots Guards, who was shot
through the heart during the hot fire to which the Guards' Square
was subjected as it fell slowly back from Dihilbat Hill, encumbered
with the baggage, Cavalry, and Artillery, to which it had afforded
refuge. Descended from an old English family, one of whose members had fallen fighting under the Royal Standard at the battle of
Naseby, of the gallant Guardsman it is recorded—"He was a soldier
of high courage and splendid *physique*, whose stately bearing and
grand countenance told of chivalrous honour and tender purity.
He will long be missed and mourned, not only by his own family,
but by the service of which he was an ornament, and the comrades
to whom he was dear."[3] Thus cut off in the prime of life, every
honour the occasion permitted was paid to the deceased. The
coffin, wrapped in the Union Jack, was conveyed by boat across the

---

[1] One man killed by mistake; one officer,
fourteen men, and one follower wounded.

[2] *Vide postea.*

[3] *Illustrated London News,* April 4, 1885.

harbour to the European cemetery. The flags of all the vessels flew at half-mast, and headed by Lord Abinger, late Colonel of the Scots Guards, the Officers of the Guards Regiments were largely represented.[1] Although Lieutenant Dalison was the only Officer actually killed at Hashin, before the afternoon closed another name was added to its death-roll, in that of Surgeon-Major Lane, who had gone scatheless through the campaigns of 1882 and 1884. The place where these and other brethren in arms are interred, is an unenclosed part of the desert, far removed from the bustle of the town, yet close to the north side of the long reef-fringed entrance to the harbour. Parched sand overlying coral reef, with a few mimosa bushes scattered here and there, the graves marked Arab-fashion by rows of stones set round about them ; such was the scene where many a gallant soldier was yet to find his " last long home." To it as well as to many another spot in the wastes of the Sûdan, and notably on the banks of the Nile, may fitly be applied the words used by Lucan with reference to the desert tomb of Cato—

> " Sacrum parvo nomen clausura sepulcro."
> " Destined in a humble grave to enclose an honoured name."
> *Pharsalia*, Book ix. 409.

Writing in 1878, Mrs. Speedy thus describes what was then a comparatively undistinguished desert " garden of unheedful death " :—

" There is a curious long strip of land at the other side of the harbour, which is used as a burying-ground for Europeans. We rowed across to it one evening, and wandered for a bit among the monuments and tombstones. They were mostly the graves of those who had died on the voyage home from distant countries; and this island cemetery, in the midst of the

---

[1] " Lieut. Dalison was probably better known to the rising generation of officers than any other officer in the Service. Very few of those who have been at Hythe during the last five years have failed to carry away some valuable hints on the subject of musketry training which he was always so ready and willing to impart."— *Admiralty and Horse Guards Gazette*, 4th April 1885.

sea, on the border of a most desolate country, struck a feeling of mournful desolation to my heart."[1]

Three years previously, in May 1875, while as yet, in Egyptian affairs, " No war, nor battle's sound," disturbed the ear of Europe, all unwittingly " seisin " had been taken of this desert shore by a young Officer of the Grenadier Guards, Thomas, fourth Earl of Ranfurly. In December 1874 he joined several brother Officers on a sporting tour in the Southern Sûdan, and taken seriously ill during the excursion returned to Suâkin only to die. The various circumstances connected with the mournful event have been fully detailed by Surgeon-Major Myers, in his *Life with the Hamran Arabs*, where it is mentioned : [2]—

" Our first idea was to bring poor Ranfurly's remains to England, but we found that this was impossible from the means not being at hand ; and we have therefore consented to their being laid in some ground on an island near the ship's anchorage, which has been set apart for the burial of Europeans, of whom a few already rest there."

In so painful an exigence in a foreign land, the Earl's friends were fortunate in finding Al-ed-Deen Bey, then Governor of Suâkin, latterly of Khartûm, a man worthy of his office :—

" Our utmost thanks are due to Alli Addeen Bey for the promptitude with which he has come to our aid. He has taken all the necessary arrangements for the burial entirely into his own hands, and by having about fifty men at work all night a grave was dug out of a bed of chalk, and walled in by this morning. In fact, though a perfect stranger to us, he has not only given us every assistance in his official capacity, but has also made us feel that his heart, as that of a true friend, has been in the work, and from which he never rested until, after heading the procession to the grave, and remaining there till the service was completed, he shook hands with us and bade us farewell, whilst we attempted as best we could to thank him for all he had done for us. Ranfurly's head rests on his favourite pillow, which is covered with black satin, and the tomb is situated next to one bearing the name of Dr. Simpson on a stone slab, and as a temporary measure a stone cross will be erected over it.

[1] *My Wanderings in the Soudan*, vol. ii. p. 261.   [2] Page 342.

"It is a curious coincidence that it was on this small island that Ranfurly first set foot on arriving in this country. How little could he have thought that over the ground upon which he then stood his lifeless body would so soon be carried!"

A remark, alas! only too applicable to many who, during the subsequent campaigns, have landed on this fateful shore.

This digression will, I trust, be excused, seeing that this representative of an ancient Scottish family seems to have been the first member of the British Army interred at Suâkin. The kind and sympathetic attitude of the Governor, who, as the coadjutor of Hicks Pasha in the most unfortunate Expedition of 1883, was destined to be yet more widely known, also shows that, like Tewfik Pasha and others, there were men of genuine worth even in the too frequently venal and corrupt Egyptian service.

By the operations carried into effect on the 19th and 20th, a demonstration having been thus made towards Hashin, the next venture selected was Tamai, Osman Digna's reputed Head-Quarters and stronghold. Situated about fourteen miles to the south-west of Suâkin, amid the outlying spurs of the rugged granitic mountains, culminating in Jebel Erkowit, the distance was too great to be traversed in one day's march. It became necessary then, as on previous occasions, to establish an intermediate position in which as an Advanced Camp, or Secondary Base of Operations, the usual stores of water, rations, and ammunition, might be accumulated.

SÛDAN ALMANAC

FOR

Lat. of Suâkin = 19° 2′ N.
Long. „ = 37° 30′ E.

MARCH 1885.

Time = mean time at Suâkin.

Phases of the Moon.

		H.	M.
On 1st, Full Moon	.. ..	6	30 A.M.
„ 8th, *Last Quarter*	.. ..	9	24 P.M.
„ 16th, New Moon	.. ..	8	6 P.M.
„ 23rd, *First Quarter*	.. ..	7	53 P.M.
„ 30th, Full Moon	.. ..	7	10 P.M.

Greek, 1885.	Coptic, 1601.	Arabic, 1302.	March.		Moon. Rises.	Moon. Sets.	Sun. Rises.	Sun. Sets.	Remarks.
17	23	14	1	S	P.M. 6.31	A.M. 6.14	A.M. 6.16	P.M. 5.52	* Eclipse of the Sun, on the 16th invisible in the Sûdan.
18	24	15	2	M	7.28	7.0			
19	25	16	3	TU	8.22				† Partial eclipse of the Moon on the 30th, visible in the Sûdan, beginning about 5 p.m. and ending about 8.30 p.m. The moon is in the *penumbra* of the earth's shadow till about 9.30 p.m., but the effect of this is hardly noticeable. The magnitude of the eclipse (at the middle) is 0·88, the moon's diameter being taken as 1·0, and the moon's light is consequently very much reduced. The obscuration of light in the earth's shadow is, however, very variable, according to the cloudy or clear state of the atmosphere through which the sun's rays pass towards the eclipsed moon.
20	26	17	4	W	9.16				
21	27	18	5	TH	10.7				
22	28	19	6	F	11.1				
23	29	20	7	S	11.50				
24	30	21	8	S	A.M. 12.39		6.13	5.55	
25	1	22	9	M	1.25				
26	2	23	10	TU	2.13				
27	3	24	11	W	2.58				
28	4	25	12	TH	3.42				
1	5	26	13	F	4.23				
2	6	27	14	S	5.4				
3	7	28	15	S	5.46		6.11	5.58	
4	8	29	16	M		P.M. 6.1	*		
5	9	30	17	TU		6.55			
6	10	1	18	W		7.51			
7	11	2	19	TH		8.49			
8	12	3	20	F		9.48			
9	13	4	21	S		10.46			
10	14	5	22	S		11.46	6.14	6.1	
11	15	6	23	M		A.M. 12.44			
12	16	7	24	TU		1.39			
13	17	8	25	W		2.32			
14	18	9	26	TH		3.21			
15	19	10	27	F		4.8			
16	20	11	28	S		4.53			
17	21	12	29	S	P.M. 4.53	5.36	6.5	6.4	
18	22	13	30	M	†6.9				
19	23	14	31	TU	7.3				

Greek column groups: rows 1–12 *Februarios*, rows 13–31 *Martios*.
Coptic column groups: rows 1–8 *Amshir*, rows 9–31 *Baramhât*.
Arabic column groups: rows 1–17 *Gemâd el-Awwel*, rows 18–31 *Gemâd et-Tâni (6th month)*.

Prepared at the Intelligence Department, War Office.

CHAPTER II.

THE INSTRUCTIONS.

"ἐπὶ μὰν βαίνει τι καὶ λάθας ἀτέκμαρτα ν΄φος,
καὶ παρέλκει πραγμάτων ὀρθὰν ὁδὸν
ἔξω φρενῶν."

"Yet oft before the wariest eyes
Mists of forgetfulness arise,
And unexpectedly betray
The wandering purpose from its way."
PINDAR's *Odes*, Olympia VII., Antistrophe III.

S a prelude to the second great movement of the campaign—the projected advance upon Tamai—during the course of the afternoon of Saturday the 21st of March, written Instructions to the following effect were issued from the Head-Quarters at Suâkin to Major-General Sir John Carstairs M'Neill, V.C., K.C.B., K.C.M.G.

In view of the grave questions to which the day's proceedings gave rise, it ought to be distinctly understood that, as to the subordinate ranks so to the General in Command, these Instructions conveyed the first clear and authoritative information regarding the duties he was called upon to discharge. In the Camp no doubt many rumours were flying about and guesses indulged in, but so long as Head-Quarters "gave no sign" these could be of no practical value. Under the peculiar circumstances in which the British Army was placed at Suâkin, with the surrounding district held in force by an enemy watchful, alert, keenly alive to the value of intelligence, with spies having no doubt free access to and inter-communication with the town's people,[1] the imperative necessity for strict reticence as to all prospective manœuvres must be clearly recognised. Still, even secrecy has its limits; and unless, by a combination rare in history, a General possess the genius, self-reliance, and resource of a Napoleon or a Wellington, to confide in a chosen and responsible few is just as essential as to distrust and keep at arm's length the irresponsible many.

In conferring upon any one a Command-in-Chief, a Govern-ment is just as unable to endow him *ex officio* with omniscience as with omnipotence. All it can do is to place him authoritatively in certain co-operative relations with the Force selected for the work in hand, and of the materials at disposal trust the best use will be made. In providing the thews and sinews, the bone and muscle of the body-corporate prepared for War, the Authorities at Home also supply the brain, the nervous system, and varied organs necessary to inspire that body with vigour, intelligence, and efficiency. In addition to the great bulk of the Army with its Regimental Officers, for general purposes a Head-Quarters Staff is constituted, with most important duties apportioned among its various members; while Brigade and other General Officers carry into effect the plans decided on.

It is evident that the complete success of any operation the Army may be engaged in depends to a great extent on the maintenance of perfect harmony between these great directing and motor powers, and the manner in which the skill, experience, and ability at command are utilised and turned to account. According to Lord Wolseley, "Orders for the March" should first of all be prefaced by a statement as to the "general direction and

---

[1] Whatever Osman Digna may have been ignorant of, he seems to have fully appreci-ated the value of the advice given by Lord Wolseley in his *Soldiers' Pocket Book* (p. 159): "A General who has the means of always learning the enemy's movements and intentions, is certain to annihilate an adversary to whom his doings are unknown, all other things being equal." On the latter points the wily Arab would be care-ful to give himself "the benefit of the doubt."

object of the march, giving a brief outline of the military situation and condition of affairs, so as to secure on the part of all Officers Commanding Columns an intelligent conformity with the views, wishes, and intentions of the Commander-in-Chief."[1] Conversely, as these provisions clearly indicate, if an Officer so placed is not to be a mere automaton, and be a man at all worthy of his position, it is evident no one can be more interested in, likely to give useful suggestions regarding, or entitled to be consulted in any particular movement, than the General to whom its execution is committed.

More especially may it well be doubted whether, charged as he was with a mission of the highest delicacy and importance, in the entire exclusion of the responsible Chief of an Expedition like that which moved out from Suâkin on the 22nd, from the preliminary consultations and interchange of ideas which must necessarily have taken place between the various members of the Head-Quarters Staff, secrecy was not being carried to an extent positively dangerous.

With a distinguished record and special experience in bush-fighting, on the personal staff of Sir Edward Lugard during the Jûgdespore jungle operations in 1858; on that of Sir Duncan Cameron in the war with the Maoris in 1861; Military Secretary to Lord Lisgar while Governor-General of Canada, and on the Staff of the Red River Expedition; until unfortunately disabled by a severe wound, Chief of the Staff and Second in Command under Sir Garnet Wolseley during the Ashanti War,—it may safely be said there was not an Officer at Suâkin better fitted by his antecedents to advise, or more entitled to be consulted, regarding a service such as that in which he was to be personally engaged than Sir John M'Neill.

Be this as it may, one thing is certain, the facts above mentioned have a most important and undeniable bearing upon the INCIDENCE OF RESPONSIBILITY. With all questions relating to the composition of the Force, the duties it was expected to perform within a given time, the amount of Transport under convoy, and

---

[1] *Soldiers' Pocket Book*, p. 307.

the direction in which the movement was to be made, definitely fixed in Orders, issued without the slightest reference to those charged with their execution, it is clearly evident that on Head-Quarters only must devolve whatever responsibilities might arise from miscalculation or misarrangement on these important points.

It may indeed be argued that as a mere preliminary, embracing only one day's operations—an eight mile march out of camp, the formation of two zeribas and the conveyance of so much Transport —the movement was eminently pacific. "No fighting was antici-pated;" and, if the Arabs would only be good enough *pro tempore* to suspend hostilities, sleeping dogs were to be let alone and no attempt was to be made to beat them up. Under such circum-stances, circumspection and precautionary punctilios might very well be dispensed with. Perhaps so; we shall see.

War is not only a "terrible game of chance";[1] like a quarrel, it requires two to make it, ourselves and *nos amis les ennemis*. In the present case this fact too much forgotten, need it be wondered that Head-Quarters, gambling with the Arab for the chance of his napping, completely lost the throw.

Instructions issued from Head-Quarters at Suâkin, March 21st, 1885.

I.

Sir J. M'Neill will proceed to No. 2 zeriba, eight miles off on Tamai Road, at daylight to-morrow, 22nd March.

Force—
        1 Squadron British Cavalry.
           „   Mounted Infantry.
       Company Royal Engineers.
         Gardner guns.
         Berkshire.
         Marines.
    3 Battalions Native Infantry.
    1 Company Madras Sappers.

---

[1] *Vide* Appendix V.

Strike tents to-night, and place under charge of Shropshire. All heavy baggage to be sent to Base Depot.

Regiments to carry thirty rounds of ammunition in regimental reserve. Greatcoats. One day's rations. Care to be taken that water-bottles are filled, and water-carts accompany Column.

[The Force to stop at 8th (eighth) mile, and to construct zeriba No. 2.]

Cavalry.
Mounted Infantry.
Gardners.
2 British Battalions.
1 Indian Battalion.
1 Company Royal Engineers.

Proceed eight miles and construct zeriba.

This zeriba to have interior space sufficient for all our camels, and to have two flanking redoubts for garrison.

As soon as zeriba is completed, all transport animals and water conveyance in tins to be sent back in charge of Cavalry, Mounted Infantry, and Indian Battalion.

The Force to stop at 5th (fifth) mile, and to construct zeriba [No. 1.]

This will consist of two Battalions Indian Infantry, one Company Madras Sappers.

This party will construct zeriba for a Battalion, with an interior redoubt for a company.

This zeriba will be held for the night by the Battalion of Indian Infantry and Madras Sappers which returns from No. 2 (*sic*).[1] The

---

[1] A company of Royal Engineers only were to advance to zeriba No. 2, the Madras Sappers halting at No. 1, *vide antea*.

other two Battalions Native Infantry, with the Transport, Cavalry [and] Mounted Infantry will return to camp.

The Commissariat have orders to send to No. 2 zeriba three days' rations and water for the garrison, and as much rations and water for the whole force as there is conveyance for. *Water to be placed under sentries, and issued as rations.*[1] Only the water for the garrison to be touched by the garrison.

Regiments to carry on men 70 rounds per man, and 30 by regimental reserve, and ordnance will carry 50 rounds per rifle.[2]

Details of sickly men, etc., of Berkshire and Marines to be attached to Shropshire Regiment.

G. GREAVES,

21/3/85.   C. of S.[3]

II.

The Cavalry and the Indian Battalion to be sent back as early as possible with the Transport.

The Indian Infantry Battalion to hold zeriba No. 1 for the night.

The other two Battalions to return to camp with the Transport and Cavalry.

Next morning (Monday) the two Indian Battalions and a squadron of 9th Bengal Cavalry will conduct a convoy to No. 1 zeriba. The Infantry will halt there while the garrison and Cavalry go on to zeriba No. 2, and so on.

G. G.

21/3.

[1] Italics are original.   [2] Thus giving a total of 150 rounds per rifle.   [3] Chief of Staff.

III.

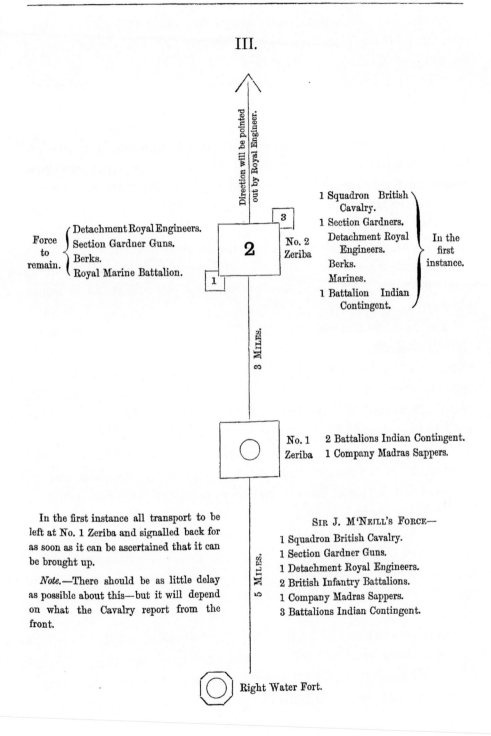

Direction will be pointed out by Royal Engineer.

Force to remain. { Detachment Royal Engineers.
Section Gardner Guns.
Berks.
Royal Marine Battalion. }

No. 2 Zeriba

3

2

1

1 Squadron British Cavalry.
1 Section Gardners.
Detachment Royal Engineers.
Berks.
Marines.
1 Battalion Indian Contingent. } In the first instance.

3 MILES.

No. 1 Zeriba   2 Battalions Indian Contingent.
1 Company Madras Sappers.

In the first instance all transport to be left at No. 1 Zeriba and signalled back for as soon as it can be ascertained that it can be brought up.

Note.—There should be as little delay as possible about this—but it will depend on what the Cavalry report from the front.

5 MILES.

SIR J. M'NEILL'S FORCE—

1 Squadron British Cavalry.
1 Section Gardner Guns.
1 Detachment Royal Engineers.
2 British Infantry Battalions.
1 Company Madras Sappers.
3 Battalions Indian Contingent.

Right Water Fort.

Such, then, were the first Instructions announced and delivered in writing on the preceding day, for the now memorable advance on the 22nd of March.

The point being one of considerable importance, it is extremely desirable that the reader should have a clear and unmistakable idea what the duties of the Column so organised really were.

Although started nominally under one Command, in the duties to be performed, it was arranged in two independent Sections. Following the order of time, the first of these Sections, viz. the two Battalions of the Indian Contingent, and the Madras Sappers, together with the whole of the Transport, were to halt five miles out on the Tamai road, and there to employ themselves in constructing zeriba No. 1, with its central redoubt, the Transport meanwhile waiting further orders from the front as to when it might with safety advance.

The second Section, including the Cavalry, Mounted Infantry, Berkshire Regiment, Royal Marine Light Infantry, Royal Engineers, Gardner guns, and one Indian Battalion, was to go on to the eight mile distance, construct zeriba No. 2, with its flanking redoubts, and if the Mounted Force found the bush clear of the enemy, orders were to be signalled back for the Transport Train to advance.

The instructions make no provision for the convoy of the Transport Train between the two zeribas, but, having delivered its stores at No. 2, it was then to return in company with the Battalion of the Native Infantry, Cavalry, and Mounted Infantry, and leaving the Indian Battalion—presumably the Sikhs—which had returned from zeriba No. 2 to garrison No. 1, the two Battalions and Madras Sappers, who had been engaged in constructing zeriba No. 1, were then to return with the Transport Train and Mounted Escort to Suâkin.

Even as enumerated in the above Instructions, it will be noticed that on three vital points the composition of the Force differed essentially from that which had twice previously engaged the enemy.

First, and most significant of all, is the disparity in the

Cavalry arm.   Instead of four Squadrons of British, and a Regiment of Bengal Cavalry, with the whole of the Mounted Infantry, one Squadron of the 5th Lancers, and a Company of the Mounted Infantry only were detailed for scouting duty.

Second, There is an entire absence of the Royal Horse Artillery. True, there were four Gardner or machine guns, but they could be of no service in shelling the enemy or inflicting that damage at long ranges, to the moral effect of which upon the Arabs General Graham has himself borne witness.

Third, The Expedition of the 22nd, while thus crippled in two most vital points, differed still further from those which had preceded it, in the inordinate amount of Transport committed to its charge.   We have seen from the Instructions that, in addition to the rations for the current day carried regimentally, the Commissariat had orders to send to zeriba No. 2 not only "three days' rations and water for the garrison," but also "AS MUCH RATIONS AND WATER FOR THE WHOLE FORCE AS THERE IS CONVEYANCE FOR."   That is to say, the amount of Transport was to be limited only by the number of beasts of burden and draught then procurable at Suâkin, all available conveyance being requisitioned for the day's work.

While in marked contrast with the elaborate precautions adopted when General Graham was personally in Command, on the one hand, the mounted and more mobile part of the fighting force was thus depleted down to its lowest possible minimum, —a Squadron of Lancers, and a Company of the Mounted Infantry, —to its more cumbrous portion, the Transport Train, there was superadded *carte blanche* for everything that could possibly go on legs or run on wheels.   In immediate presence of an enemy, whose strength, intentions, and position were very inadequately known, the marked weakness, in the most essential points noted, of the present as compared with previous Expeditions, was of itself a most serious and fatal mistake,—but worse was to follow.

When at daylight of the 22nd the parade took place, it was found that, without any intimation being given, the written Instructions

E

of the previous day had been altered, and various important changes made, which could not fail to act most detrimentally on the day's proceedings. In the *First* place the Mounted Infantry had been withdrawn, or, at least, either by intention or neglect, had not been detailed for duty. This Corps, composed of volunteers from various Regiments, took the place of the Rifle Regiments under the old *régime,*—differing chiefly in this that they were mounted instead of being on foot. It was their duty, advancing in open order, to engage the enemy from any convenient distance up to four hundred yards, and within that range to fall back upon the main body. Under the peculiar circumstances of Sûdanese warfare such aid was invaluable, as combining the musketry fire of Infantry with the mobility of Cavalry, with their hardy little mounts they could cover any ground, advance or retreat with equal facility, and so feel for and give timely warning of the foe's approach. *Secondly,* A noteworthy change was made in the plan of operations for the day. We have seen from the written Instructions of the 21st that, by the division of the Force into two Sections, zeriba No. 1 was to be commenced as soon as the five mile distance was reached; the Transport Train also waiting at that point until it could be ascertained that the ground ahead was clear of the enemy.

Both these arrangements showed at least some appreciation of the arduous nature of the duties to be performed, of the time they would necessarily occupy, and also of the danger which might possibly be incurred by the immense mass of Transport thus hurriedly and on the shortest notice sent out from Suâkin.

At whose bidding we know not, these gleams of common sense were now withdrawn. Not only had the Mounted Accompaniment been cut down to a single Squadron of Lancers, but the order in which the zeribas were to have been constructed was inverted. The halt at the fifth mile of the two battalions of Indian Infantry, the Madras Sappers, and the Transport Train was countermanded, and the entire Force, with its convoy, sent on to meet whatever fortune might have in store for it in the trackless and untraversed jungle, eight miles off.   Only when this point had been reached were the proper labours of the day to begin, and zeriba No. 2, with its flanking redoubts, to be constructed.   Meanwhile the Transport Train was to proceed with unloading ; and when these operations were completed the Lancers, Indian Infantry, and empty Transport, now released, were to return, stop at the five mile distance, construct zeriba No. 1, and, leaving it garrisoned by the 15th Sikhs, go back to Suâkin.

It is evident that this alteration on the original plan, had the fates not ordained the impossibility of its being carried into effect, would have involved a most serious and unnecessary detention and loss of time, especially to the Transport, which, in the rapidly waning day, would have had to await operations with which it was in no way really connected.   As we shall afterwards find, the consecutive instead of the simultaneous formation of the zeribas would within the time allotted have been in any case an impossible task.

Even in their original form, as issued on the afternoon of the 21st, the Instructions were severely criticised in the evening at the Brigade-Mess, and it is specially to be noted that it would be impossible to gather from the published despatches, that any other intentions had been entertained, or instructions given, than those which took effect on the 22nd.[1]

Such is a brief glance at the Instructions, which, with all their nice adjustments of mutual reliefs, marching and counter-marching, zeriba-building and storing, were destined to be so rudely torn up and stultified within the course of the next few hours.   Head-Quarters proposed, but Providence, in the shape of the Arab and circumstances over which to the Force sent out there was no possibility of control, disposed.

---

[1] Although its significance passed no doubt without comment, the only instance I am aware of, in which an approximate reference to the Instructions of the 21st was made in public, occurs in the *Daily News*, for March 23rd 1885 :—

"SOUAKIM, *Sunday*, 11.50 A.M.

"The 2nd Brigade, consisting of the Shropshire, Berkshire, and Marines, and also a portion of the Indian contingent, left this morning to form zarebas.   One will be five miles distant, in the direction of Tamai. Another will be eight miles.   The first zareba will be occupied by the Indian contingent, the second, eight miles away, by the 2nd Brigade."

CHAPTER III.

THE PARADE AND MARCH OUT.

" Vadimus in campos steriles, exustaque mundi,
Qua nimius Titan, et raræ in fontibus undæ,
Siccaque letiferis squalent serpentibus arva."

" We are going unto sterile plains and scorched regions of the world, where are excessive
heat of the sun and scanty water in the springs, and the parched fields are horrid
with deadly serpents,[1] a toilsome march."

Cato's *Address to his troops on entering the Libyan Desert.*
Pharsalia, Book ix. 382-384.

UÂKIN, lying only nineteen degrees and two minutes
north of the equator, has, in brief dawn and twilight,
all the peculiarities of the tropical day, with a variation
in its length amounting to little more than a couple of
hours between the summer and the winter solstice. Midway
between these lies the date in question, the sun on the 22nd
of March, according to the Almanac for the Sûdan, issued by the
Intelligence Department, rising at 6.14 A.M. and setting at 6.1 P.M.

Long ere daylight, however, the fighting Force, seriously shorn
of its most important safeguards, and the overgrown and cumbrous
mass of Transport, were being assembled on the parade ground near
the Left Water Fort, preparatory to the advance.

---

[1] The reference here is to certain exaggerated and mythical ideas the Romans entertained regarding the dangerous character of the *reptilia*, supposed specially to haunt the desert fountains (cf. *Phar.* B. ix. 607-941). If, however, for the genus *Ophis* we substitute that of *Homo*, the line remains by no means inapplicable to the situation in the Sûdan.

As if to crown the errors already committed, I must now ask the attention of the reader to certain circumstances affecting most materially the fortunes of the day.

The Instructions stating that the zeriba was to be constructed "8 miles off, on the Tamai Road," the troops were naturally "fronted" by Lieut.-Colonel W. F. Kelly, the Brigade-Major, upon whom the duty devolved, so as to march by the well-known route to that locality. As clearly indicated on the maps of the district recently issued by the Intelligence Department, for the first six miles this route follows the road to Kassala, therein designated "Kassala Road, a wide track," running due south through the open country towards the coast. It must not however be imagined that, even when occurring on an Intelligence Department map, the term "road" has the same meaning in the Eastern Sûdan it would naturally have in a civilised country. In this sense, indeed, there are no roads in these desert regions. Between the various localities there are more or less frequented and long established routes, owing little or nothing to human art, but marked only by such traces as persistent use, human or bestial, may have impressed upon them, their characters necessarily varying according to the natural features of the districts through which they run. The most important is that between Kassala, the great emporium of the Southern, and Suâkin, the only seaport of the Eastern Sûdan. For generation after generation it has been traversed by great caravans of camels, until recent times too often of slaves,[1] bearing ivory, gum arabic, coffee, senna, wheat, ostrich feathers, and all the multi-

---

[1] In spite of every effort both of the British and Egyptian Governments for its suppression, this nefarious traffic has been carried on until very recent times indeed. Referring to the state of matters which prevailed at Suâkin in December 1881, Mr. F. L. James states :—"We saw very little of the *Wakeel* [Deputy-governor of the town] Achmed Effendi, and did not hear at all a good report of him. We were told that he was doing anything but discouraging the slave trade ; that, on the contrary, he took a bribe of two Napoleons for every slave that he permitted to leave the port, and that the chief of police took one in addition. Some slaves had been lately seized, and a great to-do made about them ; but this was because the hush-money was not forthcoming."—*The Wild Tribes of the Soudan*, p. 11.

farious products of a tropical clime, for shipment at Suâkin, while in
return various articles of European manufacture, notably Manchester
cotton goods, find their way into the interior. Lying well down
towards the sea coast the route is comparatively open, with, at
intervals, ample space for the hungry camels to spread themselves
over the plain, and gather what sustenance they can from the herbage, parched or green. It is indeed one of the best and most
frequented caravan-routes in the Sûdan. A line of telegraph stations,
with watering facilities at each, divide the 280 miles of distance into
a twelve days' march. The portion of the route chiefly concerning
us is that lying nearest to Suâkin ; and, according to the united
testimony of travellers, under no circumstances and at no season of
the year does it present special difficulties other than those due to
climatic influences. Surgeon-Major Myers, who, with the Guards'
Officers previously mentioned, traversed this route at the close of
December 1874, thus records his experience :—

"At last we have commenced the desert journey, and have halted for the
night about eight miles from Souakim, *on a vast sandy plain*, freely studded
with stunted mimosas, now merely a mass of dry thorny branches, with here
and there the skeleton of a camel." [1]

Mr. F. L. James, following the same route in the middle of
December 1881, in consequence of the unusually humid character of
the season had a still more pleasant experience. Leaving Suâkin
on the 15th, he encamped "In a regular African deluge, and wet
to the skin," an hour and a half's march, or about four miles, out of
the town. The tents were pitched on the wide plain, and as if to
atone for the temporary inconvenience, Nature at once responding
to the life-giving showers, was seen arrayed in her choicest garb :—

"The desert was carpeted with a most beautiful grass of a very vivid
green ; the dwarf mimosa bushes, of which there were plenty, were bursting
into leaf ; and the plain was covered with cattle, goats, and sheep, while
numbers of camels wandered from bush to bush, or grazed on the fresh grass,
a rare treat to all animals in these regions." [2]

[1] *Life with the Hamran Arabs*, p. 18.   [2] *The Wild Tribes of the Soudan*, p. 23.

This delightful verdure, due to the very casual and intermittent coast rains, continued for about twenty or thirty miles on the road to Kassala.   Leaving this "road" to Kassala at the six mile distance, the "road" to Tamai turns to the right and, after a gradual ascent of under three miles, reaches the site of Baker's zeriba, Tamai lying six or seven miles farther on.   This was not only the route followed in the campaign of 1884, but in all previous advances towards Tamai,[1] and it might very reasonably be assumed that the same mode of approach would be adhered to now.   When, on the morning of the 22nd, General Graham rode up to inspect the troops and see them started, dissatisfied with this arrangement and acting apparently on an unannounced but preconcerted intention, he personally ordered a change of front from south to south-west, the Squares being accordingly wheeled round in that direction.   The only conceivable reason for such an alteration seems to be that given by General Graham in his despatch of May 30th to Lord Wolseley, where, referring to the zeriba in question, he states—

"The position of this post was selected with a view to making it a depot for operations against either Tamanieb or Tamai, according to circumstances."[2]

Whatever the motive, the change was made by General Graham in person, and, as tested by results, I think the reader will admit the alteration proved to be most unfortunate.

It must first of all be remarked that there is one statement in the paragraph just quoted, viz., that referring to the selection of the post, which is extremely misleading.   A military post is usually "selected" upon some other datum than that of a mere compass-bearing, yet such seems to have been the only principle followed in the present case.   A line, supposed to be equi-distant between two places like Tamai and Tamanieb, is run through a tract of wild country covered with dense bush and with very slight variation in point of level; eight miles is fixed upon as a convenient distance for an advanced Depôt or Secondary Base of operations; and this

[1] *Vide postea.*
[2] Supp. to *London Gazette*, Aug. 25, 1885.

is called "selecting a post," although it may be in every other respect utterly unfit for a military position.

This extraordinary method of striking out a road *de novo* for a heavy mass of troops and Transport, is rendered all the more incomprehensible when looked at in the light of the local topography. In addition to the road to Tamai just described, the Intelligence Department Map shows the road to Tamanieb running almost in a straight line from Suâkin, and, like the Kassala Road, it is designated "Wide track from Suakin to Tamanieb."

This route was also traversed in the campaign of 1884, and is marked by two zeribas,[1] respectively ten and fourteen-and-a-half miles from Suâkin. After the road to Tamai diverges from the Kassala Road, it runs almost exactly parallel with the road to Tamanieb, leaving between the two a space of just four-and-a-half miles in breadth, forming the trackless jungle or dense bush through which General Graham chose to run his ideal line equi-distant between the two alternative strategic points—Tamai and Tamanieb—although the truth is, it falls much nearer the one route than the other, being only a mile and-a-half south of the Tamanieb Road.

Yet another remark ere for the present we quit this subject. It is a recognised principle in civilised, and even in savage, warfare, that posts shall be "selected" with the widest possible outlook over all their approaches and with the least possible cover for the enemy to take advantage of. In the present case, so far as the Generals in Command were concerned, these principles were compulsorily violated; they were sent out with their Commands into a tract of country so uniform in its character that there were no vantage points from which to choose, and so densely covered with bush that, instead of being able to secure a tract of ground free from cover for the enemy, it was difficult to find a clearing large enough for their own operations.

It must be remembered that neither Generals M'Neill nor Hudson knew anything as to the direction to be followed beyond what was

---

[1] Nos. 4 and 5, occupied March 27, 1884.

stated in the Instructions, each of them having been only about a fortnight at Suâkin,[1] and during that period fully occupied with the duties entailed by their respective Commands.

The only one really cognisant of Head-Quarter intentions was Lieut.-Colonel Elliot Wood, the Officer of Engineers, who, with two or three natives to aid him, was sent to act as guide, and upon whom, as the sole depositary of Head-Quarter information, lay the responsibility of directing the march and selecting the site where the zeribas were to be constructed. Colonel Wood, who had been at Suâkin since the previous campaign, was presumably by this time well acquainted with the district. Yet, so far as can be judged, this great belt of country, extending from Suâkin right up to the mountains, and skirted on either side by two well-known routes, both traversed by the British troops in 1884, seems to have been a *terra incognita* even to him. It is possible that this want of familiarity with a tract of ground, after all only a few miles distant from the town, may be accounted for by the state of siege in which Suâkin was held by the Arabs during the interval between the two campaigns. If this was the case, then the regret must be all the greater that the experience of the previous year was entirely set aside in favour of a new and most unfortunate venture.

Selected on abstract grounds, and for strategical reasons only, apart altogether from its suitability as a road either to Tamai or anywhere else, this line of advance on a "position" still entirely *en l'air*, was an experiment—an uncalled for and hazardous experiment, carried out under the most dangerous and difficult circumstances. No wonder then that, through failure adequately to allow for the "unconsidered trifle" *nos amis les ennemis*, as already remarked, Head-Quarter plans, with all their nicely projected strategy, were doomed to be completely stultified; while in the heart of this dense bush, where all the advantages lay with the enemy and all the disadvantages with the British Force, the critical battle of the campaign was fought. Thanks to the skilful dispositions and

---

[1] General Hudson arrived at Suâkin on the 5th, General M'Neill on the 8th of March.

F

ready resource of the Generals on the spot, the promptitude and presence of mind of the Regimental Officers, and the steady and stubborn courage of the troops, what in feebler hands might have proved a crushing defeat, resulting in a most decisive victory.

Parade had been ordered at daylight, but, owing to delays chiefly connected with the unmanageable convoy with which the Force was encumbered, the change of direction already mentioned, and various other causes, it was nearly an hour later before the start was actually made. Ahead and on the flanks went the small detachment of Lancers scouting. Next marched the British Regiments formed up in Square two deep with a double-company front, under Command of Major-General Sir John C. M'Neill. The 1st Battalion Berkshire Regiment, under Lieut.-Colonel Huyshe, led the way. The Royal Marine Light Infantry, under Lieut.-Colonel Ozzard, brought up the rear in similar order. As at first arranged, the detachment of Royal Engineers, under Lieut.-Colonel Leach, were placed by General M'Neill in sections on either side as supports, but General Graham desiring that a place should be found for them in the exterior line, they were moved accordingly into the flank faces.

Sole representatives of the Artillery arm with which the Force was favoured, within the Square were the four Gardner guns, each drawn by four mules, with their ammunition-waggons and complement of sailors under Captain Domville, and a detachment of the Royal Marine Artillery under Lieutenant Herbert Slessor, also reserve ammunition, and water-carts, while ten or twelve two-horsed carts carried various implements used by the Royal Engineers.

As at first drawn up, there was also included within the Square a number of camels carrying the regimental baggage of the Berkshire and Royal Marine Light Infantry, with the entrenching tools of the Royal Engineers. General Graham however insisted that all the camel-borne baggage should be transferred from the British to the Indian Square, which was accordingly done. A little later the General inquiring of the Engineers whether they had their entrenching tools with them, was informed that they were carried on some of the camels just ordered to the Indian Square, when a retransfer had to be made.

Outside the British Square, but close to its left flank, moved the Field Telegraph Waggon and party, who kept unrolling the telegraph wire and covering it with loose soil as they went on,—so maintaining the means of communication with Suâkin throughout the entire advance.

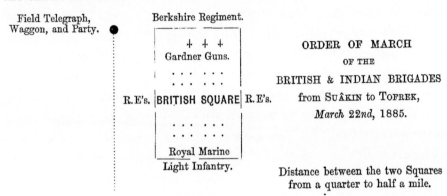

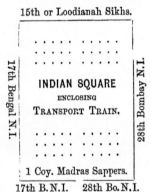

Formed up in a still larger Square, a short distance in rear of the right flank, the Indian Contingent marched in echelon under Command of Brigadier-General Hudson, C.B.[1] The 15th or Loodianah Sikhs, under the Command of Colonel Geo. R. Hennessey, formed the front face, and a small portion of the flanks. The remainder of the right flank and one half of rear face was formed by the 28th Bombay Native Infantry, under Colonel F. C. Singleton. The 17th Bengal Native Infantry, in absence of the Colonel, under Wing Commander Major J. M. W. von Beverhoudt, occupied a similar position on the left flank, and rear face. In reserve, immediately within the rear face, marched the Company of Madras Sappers, under Captain C. B. Wilkieson, R.E. Within this Square were

---

[1] Now Major-General Sir John Hudson, K.C.B.

enclosed the vast and miscellaneous array of laden camels, mules, carts, and conveyances of various kinds already mentioned. In a land where not an ounce of water was to be obtained except what was carried for the daily necessities both of man and beast, amounting to many thousand gallons: this alone formed a large and indispensable item of transport. For water-carriage about 580 camels were told off, furnished with "*suletahs*," strong coir or rope-work nettings, like large bags, suspended on either side of the animal, in which the vessels containing the precious fluid were slung. These vessels were of various kinds and very unequal quality.[1]

First, Galvanised iron water-tins three feet long, eighteen inches deep, and eight inches broad, holding about twelve gallons and-a-half, and with water weighing 155 pounds. These water-tins were closed by screw-stoppers, only to be opened by a special key. There were also eight and ten gallon tins.

Second, Barrels or kegs, some of equal capacity with these water-tins, others smaller.

Third, Water-skins, known by the Indian name of "mussocks," in Arabic *zemzemiyeh*.

Fourth, Indiarubber bags, which proved a complete failure.

All the latter modes of conveyance were liable to constant leakage, especially the skins, the water also becoming in time tainted and undrinkable. The water-supply was originally obtained entirely by condensation from steam-vessels anchored for convenience close to the quays.[2] The source was harbour-water, the receptacle of all kinds of nameless filth, garbage, and abomination, from which, as well as from the marine salts, the water was supposed to be purified by distillation. For the ultimate storage

[1] *Vide* Appendix IV.

[2] "In these operations the transport and distribution of water was the heaviest portion of the Commissariat and Transport work.

"The country was absolutely without water fit for Europeans to drink, and the whole supply was obtained from the Harbour of Suakin, where condensing ships, under the charge of the Royal Navy, were at work night and day.

"Reservoirs, constructed by the Royal Engineers, were supplied by pipe from these vessels, and the water for the Force was obtained thence."—*Report by the Senior Commissariat Officer, Suakin Expeditionary Force*, p. 13.

of this water at the zeriba large galvanised iron tanks were
provided, about four feet cube, requiring ten men to raise them to,
or remove them from, the two mule carts in which they were
conveyed, and containing about sixty-four gallons of water. In
addition there were large tanks made of waterproofed canvas,
every means being adopted by which a permanent supply of the
precious fluid could possibly be secured. Had the foresight and
precaution adopted in this respect been equally observed in not
less essential matters there would have been little ground for complaint. As the case stood, the Transport was completely overdone,
the preparations seeming rather those of an army in motion for
some distant scene than for an eight-mile march out of camp.

To convey these immense *impedimenta*, designed not so much for
present as for prospective use, and with a view to ulterior operations
which might or might not be carried into effect, there was requisitioned, in terms of the Commissariat Order, all the available
Transport at Suâkin, consisting of camels and mules, the latter for
use either as beasts of burden or draught. The great bulk of the
Transport-animals, together with their drivers, were entirely new
arrivals, daily pouring in from all quarters. Of these importations,
both men and animals were to a large extent Indian ; Arabia and
the Delta adding their quotas.

A motley gathering it was, replete with varied costumes and
tongues, diverse yet chiefly tropical. There were Soumalis from Aden,
with coal-black skins and negro type of features. Hindoos and
Mussulmans alike, from Scinde, Lahore, Mooltan, and other parts of
the Punjaub, by peculiarity of costume or feature all capable of
being picked out and discriminated by the experienced eye. Well
managed and duly organised, such *matériel* was no doubt fitted to
do good service in the arduous and responsible duties connected
with the Transport Train. As yet, however, it was in a state crude
and inchoate, compared with what it afterwards became. Both men
and animals were for the most part fresh from long sea voyages.
The great mass of the men were, of course, recent enlistments, new

to the position, to each other, and to the animals; and, no slight factor in such a convoy, the animals were equally so to the men.

In addition to this fertile source of trouble, there was yet another. It was the afternoon of the 21st when Instructions were issued from Head-Quarters as to the Transport preparations to be made for the advance on the morrow. These preparations were necessarily extended all through the night, and it was indeed only during the very late or rather early hours that the actual work of loading up the Transport animals could be effected. The moon, then in her first quarter, lit up the scene all the earlier part of the night, but, setting at 10.46 P.M., save for a certain amount of assistance afforded by the electric light from some of the ships of war, left the most important hours for preparation in total darkness,—to those who experienced it truly an Egyptian darkness, a darkness that could be felt. The result may easily be imagined. Every operation in this miscellaneous assemblage was carried on under disadvantage, and by the sense of touch rather than that of sight. Loads were unequally adjusted, and in many cases the baggage-animals carelessly overladen, straps and fastenings inadequately secured, and a foundation laid for all the mischiefs which were to tell with redoubled force on the morrow's march.[1]

As with the Commissariat and Transport so was it with the Regiments detailed for active duty on the 22nd, who got their orders for the "March out" about 4 P.M., and the various camps became at once a scene of bustle and preparation. In accordance with the Instructions the tents were first of all struck, and placed under charge of the Shropshire Regiment in their camp close to the Right Water Fort, while all valises and heavy baggage went to the Base Depôt. Simple as these operations appear on paper, to

[1] "On the 21st March orders were issued to prepare for an advance towards Tamai on the following day. *Again an all night working was necessary.*

"During the period over which the operations [in general] extended, much hard and harassing work had to be done, involving, particularly in the filling of water tins and the loading of transport animals, a great deal of night duty."—*Report by the Senior Commissariat Officer, Suakin Expeditionary Force*, pp. 4 and 5.

the various Regiments interested they involved a large amount of hard fatigue duty extending far into the night. For the transference of the tents and baggage, camels had to be obtained, loaded up, and looked after, and their burdens safely deposited in store, and every preparation made for a prolonged absence from camp.

For conveyance of all regimental baggage, blankets, and other materials necessarily accompanying the troops for their distant bivouac, another set of camels was provided, arriving about 9 P.M. These had all to be got in readiness, and every preparation made for an early start, so that really very little time was left for snatching a brief repose upon the sand under the open canopy of heaven.

Another noteworthy fact is that, contrary to all general practice on such occasions, the General in Command was never furnished with a Report as to what he was called on to protect, and, on making application afterwards to the Commissariat and Transport Department at Suâkin, found that no record had been kept or could be furnished. Notwithstanding every inquiry, it was found absolutely impossible to obtain from official sources any information as to the number of animals which had been collected and sent out. According to the most reliable calculations there could not be less than from 1,000 to 1,200 camels,[1] of which 550 were required for water-transport only, besides mules and horses, so that it is a very moderate estimate to say that there were in all 1,500 animals, the probability being that it rose considerably above this number.

We have seen that on the 20th the proportion of Transport animals to fighting men was about 1 to $5\frac{2}{3}$.[2] Now, let it be assumed that the combined British and Indian Force on the 22nd numbered 3,300 men, which is perhaps rather over than under the mark, and that the transport animals numbered only 1,500, this gives a ratio

---

[1] These figures show the range within which estimates varied. In Colonel Robertson's *Report* the number of camels is given at 1,080, "carrying water and supplies," the British Regimental Transport, being of course over and above, which would add one or two hundred camels to the quota. The Indian Regimental Transport was carried entirely by mules.

[2] *Vide* p. 11.

of animals to fighting men of just one to $2\frac{1}{5}$; but the number is very likely to have been higher, and had it run up only to 1,650, or the strength of the Force stood at 3,000,[1] it would have been in the ratio of one to two, a very great difference indeed from the balance of animals to combatants on the 20th.

There is yet another aspect in which this question may be looked at. On the 20th the entire Transport was enclosed, or understood to be enclosed, in the combined British and Indian Square, although, owing to this Square marching with an open rear, there can be no doubt that a large part of the Transport fell behind at its own "sweet will" on the march out and was practically defenceless. On the 22nd however, by distinct Orders from General Graham, the Force was drawn up in Brigade Squares, the British and Indians being independent. By the same Orders, to the Indian Brigade Square was assigned all the Transport; and, unlike the Force on the 20th, it marched with a closed rear. Assuming the Indian Force to number about 2,000, at 1,500 animals the ratio of protected to protectors would be as 1 to $1\frac{1}{3}$, falling, of course, if the number of Transport-animals be increased, or that of Indians lessened.

There is yet another thing which must be taken into account in striking the balance between the protectors and the protected, the combatant and non-combatant elements, that is the camp followers, drivers, or attendants, whose numbers increase of course in the same ratio as the Transport-animals. Unfortunately there are no returns of these for the 22nd, any more than of the Transport-animals, so that accurate comparison is difficult. The "Diary of the Suakin Expedition, 1885," gives, exclusive of Water Transport, the numbers for the 20th as follows :—

Camels and mules	949
Followers	317
Total Transport-animals and attendants .	1266

[1] As the strength of the Force falls, or the numbers of the animals rise, so does the ratio between the two approach equality, and *vice versa*.

Allowing for the 22nd the same proportion ($\frac{1}{3}$) attendants to animals, 1,500 of the latter, would give a total of 2,000, or just an equipoise between protectors and protected in the Indian Brigade Square. On the 20th the proportion was 1 to $5\frac{2}{3}$, or with attendants say 1 to 4. Facts like these lend additional emphasis to the remonstrance of General Hudson, that he had much more Transport under charge than he really had troops wherewith to enclose it, the cumbrous array frequently breaking bounds, and bulging out at various points in the most dangerous and annoying manner. Add to this, that it was only by the active exertions of the troops, many of whom had to be detailed as camel drivers and for other purposes, that the Transport Train was kept in order and got forward at all.

General Graham, and Sir George Greaves, the Chief of the Staff, rode out a short distance with the troops, but seem to have turned back before the real difficulties of the march began. Sir George Greaves in parting with Sir John M‘Neill, warned him to " Look out for an attack," adding the caution not to ride outside his Square ; a piece of friendly advice with which it was found impossible to comply, it being necessary for the General in Command to keep an eye on both Squares.

Beyond this casual reference to the possibility of an attack, a very likely thing to take place in such a locality under any circumstances, no official information was given to Sir John M‘Neill as to the probable movements or intentions of the enemy. This is all the more extraordinary, from the fact that the Intelligence Department at Suâkin was provided with a regular system of spies, who were constantly bringing in whatever information they could glean on this important subject. The whole tendency of their intelligence, as afterwards ascertained, went to show that the Arabs were in an aggressive mood and meant fighting.

On 14th February Ali Adam, of the Housab-Amaras, reports :—

" If the English come out (from Souakin) they (the enemy) will not wait as before, but attack them in their zeriba."

On 22nd February Barfuri Ahmed Ali states that the

G

"Rebels all say they will attack the English in their enclosure."

4th March.—A tribesman of the Amaras states :—

"If the troops encamp on way to either place (Tamai or Hashin), they are to be suddenly attacked during the night."

The following day, 5th March, a most important piece of news was communicated to Mr. Brewster by a native spy, to this effect:—

"If a zeriba is formed on the way to either of Osman Digna's positions, he has given orders to have it attacked. He will not make the mistake, which caused his losses last year, of letting the British attack him."

Again, on 8th March, Mahmoud Takir and Ahmed Ali report,

"On the day the English leave Souakin they (the enemy) are to rush the camp suddenly, and not to allow them to make a zeriba."

On 12th March Zeniab Ali, a woman, makes a similar statement. And on 13th March Tasein also reports that

"Osman has given orders that if the army leaves here (Souakin) they are to attack it before it has time to unload or settle down."

It will be noticed that all these reports are of precisely the same tenor, pointing only in one direction, viz., that the Arabs were resolved to assume the offensive, and attack whatever Force might be sent out towards their strongholds. Information to the same effect was continued up to the 22nd of March, and thus accumulating for over a month, subsequent events proved that it was thoroughly accurate and trustworthy. It would naturally be imagined then that the Commanding Officer of an Expedition like that sent out on the 22nd of March would have been made cognisant of all these facts, so that being thus "forewarned" he might also be "forearmed." Save the casual and off-hand remark already mentioned, no such communication however was made, or even the slightest approach to it, the information remaining bottled up at Head-Quarters, where it could serve no purpose, instead of being placed at the disposal of those to whom it would have been of the most vital consequence. The above information only became known to Sir John M'Neill by the intervention of a friend, a considerable time after the action had taken place—an extraordinary fact, deserving to be placed on record, as illustrating the secretive system then in vogue at Suâkin, and which told so mischievously against the interests of the Service.

As a further illustration of this most unaccountable state of matters, it may be mentioned that ten days after the action, in presence of Lord Wiltshire,[1] General M‘Neill's Aide-de-Camp, Lieut.-Colonel Kelly, the Brigade-Major, and Major now Lieut.-Colonel R. C. d'Esterre Spottiswoode of the 10th Hussars, Mr. Brewster told Sir John that, at half-past six on the morning of the 22nd, he had sent word to the Intelligence Department that a spy had just come in with news that the Force then going out was to be attacked by 5000 Arabs.[2]   Had this intelligence been conveyed to Sir John M‘Neill in time, he would at once have sent back the greater part of the camel-convoy with an Indian Regiment, and moved on disencumbered.

In the most interesting and impartial narrative of Major De Cosson, entitled *Days and Nights of Service,* in allusion to this incident it is stated [3]—

"I am bound to say, however, that I have ascertained on excellent authority that the only telegram that reached the Intelligence Department was one sent at 8.10 A.M., on the morning of the 22nd March, to say that, according to the report of a spy, 8000 Arabs were at Deberet, about one and a half miles from the Surrey Regiment at Hasheen."

With reference to these remarks, I will only say I am not aware that the medium of communication was necessarily telegraphic, and may also mention that on the back of the excerpt containing the spy-information just given, there is a holograph note written at the time, to the following effect :—

"Mr. Brewster, Interpreter to the Intelligence Department, told me 10

---

[1] Now Marquis of Winchester, Coldstream Guards.

[2] Whether referring to the same incident or not, it was reported on good authority that on the evening of the 21st, or morning of the 22nd, an old Arab sheikh went to Mr. Brewster and warned him not to accompany the Force about to go out, as it was certain to be attacked, and that by a large body of the enemy.

[3] P. 140.

days after the action, that at 6.30 on the morning of the 22nd, the day I marched out, he had sent word to the Intelligence Department that a spy had come in with news that my force was to be attacked by 5000 Arabs.

" Had this news been sent in time I should at once have sent back two-thirds of my camels with a Native Regiment, and moved on with a fighting Force.

"(Signed)   J. C. M‘NEILL."

The whole tenor of this note seems to imply that the message referred to was quite distinct from that mentioned by Major De Cosson. The one refers to an actual massing of the Arab forces in a particular locality, viz., Hashin, which may have been ascertained by observation ; while the other refers to a settled purpose and determination, of which this concentration was a very likely result. The informants were probably different individuals, adopting separate methods ; so that the one reports specific and settled intentions with regard to the Force about to start, the other a simple fact, irrespective of any particular destination.   Taken together, the messages bear out, what seems pretty certain on other grounds, that in addition to a special and selected attacking force there was also a powerful reserve, ready in the event of success, to take advantage of it, and operate in other directions.

The warnings of imminent danger, thus to no purpose placed at the disposal of Head-Quarters, received corroboration from other sources as the day advanced. The Officers of the Hospital ship " Ganges," afterwards stated that, from their look-out, a large body of camel-men could be seen all the forenoon, gradually closing round the Force, buried in the dense bush, and busily at work on its appointed task. From such vantage points as the neighbour-hood of Suâkin, owing to the gradual elevation of the plains towards the mountains, the entire surrounding district was placed under survey ; and with so important a movement on foot surely it was not too much to expect that the Intelligence Department would have been all eyes and ears, taking note of every circumstance which could in any way affect the welfare of the Expedition.

Very shortly after leaving Suâkin the Expedition entered the bush which, in the direction followed, stretches with ever-increasing density and height until the mountains are approached. During the entire progress of the march communication was kept up without intermission between the Brigade Generals by means of the Staff Officers, and General M'Neill was very early apprised that the anticipated difficulties of the advance had begun. The rate of progress between the two Squares was naturally very different, owing to the numerous obstacles connected with the Transport Train; the constant tendency of the second Square being to lag behind. As being under convoy, it was the duty of General Hudson to call a halt or order an advance as the exigencies of his charge required; and as the Force got into the bush the halts became always more frequent, and the delays more imperative.

Notwithstanding the *désagréments* just mentioned the march out had its lighter and more humorous side. To guard in some measure against the ills which, under such circumstances, flesh is very apt to become heir to, the War Office had provided a variety of minor comforts which a good many of the troops were inclined to regard as savouring too much of the Christmas-tree style of soldiering. The dust-veils were generally worn like puggarees round the helmets, while the goggles were just as often stuck up in front, like specs off duty. The spine protectors, long pads worn vertically up the small of the back, were also at a discount; and on the whole it must be admitted that, even at the risk of blistered skin, sore eyes, swollen lips, and sunstroke on the spine, Tommy Atkins showed himself rather unappreciative of these refined methods by which a paternal Government sought to promote his welfare. Of course, for this state of matters, the clear remedy was to have taken time by the forelock and sent the troops out at a time suitable for campaigning, instead of the very close of the season. But this was precisely what the Home Government would not do.

We have seen under what circumstances the Transport Train had been accumulated and loaded-up. Now, according to the testimony of General Hudson, it was found that the thick and prickly mimosa bushes impeded the movements of the animals and loosened their burdens, which were being constantly thrown, while the drivers, with their clothes torn and their bodies lacerated by this prickly scrub, tempted to seek a passage by some devious path, were always breaking the line of march.

To those who had been in India, a country thus densely covered with vegetation recalled the jungles of that tropical clime, and we find this characteristic term frequently employed both in reports and narratives. But there is a great difference between a jungle in India and anything to which that term may be applied in an African desert, for desert it still remains in spite of this abundant growth. In India, a jungle generally implies a rank and luxuriant vegetation springing up from a rich, deep, well-watered soil. But here all the soft herbaceous plants forming such a feature in less arid climes are entirely awanting. Under foot there is nothing, especially in the " khors " or dry shallow water-courses frequently crossing the line of march, save deep soft sand, burning hot to the touch and toilsome to traverse, varied here and there with hard gravelly patches of similar temperature, and, as in all such desert marches, the solar radiation from this highly heated surface glowing like a furnace, greatly inconvenienced both men and animals, aggravated as it was by the clouds of dust incessantly set in motion by the marching host.

Out of this parched and arid soil spring the mimosa bushes, forming so prominent a feature of these East African deserts, their straight horizontal branches well armed with prickly thorns ; the whole plant hard, repellant, holding its own against all comers in an almost grim aggressive way. No grateful shade could it cast on that scorched ground, or afford shelter to humbler forms of vegetation. A desert in the ordinary sense of the word, would at least have given freedom and unimpeded motion, but here it was a desert with the way barred on every hand by a thorny armature of the most annoying kind.[1] Overhead was the torrid sun, this 22nd of March being a perfectly still, windless, roasting day, with

[1] For a further account of this mimosa bush *vide* Appendix XII.

the air untempered by the lightest breeze,—one of those days on which the vertical sun of the tropics, shining out of a cloudless sky, has it all his own way to broil and bake. No wonder, then, that a great miscellaneous assemblage like that crowding the interior of the Indian Square found progress to be an arduous and difficult task, while every load thrown or requiring readjustment meant stoppage and delay, not to one Square only, but to both.

As the Force advanced, the Lancers began to report that parties of the enemy were hovering about. Uncertain what their intentions might be, between eight and nine o'clock General M'Neill sent Lord Wiltshire, his extra Aide-de-Camp, to inquire whether General Hudson considered himself able to protect the Transport in the event of an attack being made. To this inquiry General Hudson, fully alive to the difficulties of the position, replied—"You tell Sir John M'Neill that I will do my best, more I cannot do." Sir John also took the precaution of ordering the Lancers to keep farther out, and not to ride so close to the Infantry.

After proceeding about five miles, and the bush becoming thicker as the Force advanced, General Hudson requested Sir John M'Neill to come and learn for himself the state of the Transport Train, on the ground that so large a proportion of the Indian Troops were being necessarily detailed to act as drivers and in other capacities, declining at the same time to be any longer responsible for its defence, and stating that it was utterly impossible, under existing conditions, for this disorganised mass of animals to struggle on to the eight-mile distance laid down in the Instructions. With this view Sir John M'Neill heartily concurred, at the same time requesting General Hudson to persevere for half an hour longer, and promising that at the expiration of that time he would desire Colonel Wood to halt at the first place he considered suitable for a zeriba.

At this time, *i.e.* about ten o'clock, it was calculated by the two Generals that, if the plan of operations laid down by Head-Quarters were fully adhered to, allowing time for the construction of the zeribas Nos. 1 and 2, with their redoubts, and the return journey, it would be well on towards midnight before the Indian Brigade and Transport Train could possibly get back to Suâkin. The truth is that, so long as the operations existed only on paper, the time requisite to carry the Head-Quarters' scheme into effect seems never to have been thought of, or at least the practical difficulties in the way of its fulfilment, never really faced. With every obstacle encountered trenching upon the fleeting hours, from the rate of progress achieved, it was evident that the eight-mile distance could not be reached before mid-day, and that with a disorganised and exhausted Transport Train. Allowing time for unloading and for getting zeriba No. 2, with its redoubts, into a defensible state, the return journey could not have been commenced until late in the afternoon; sundown, as we have seen, took place at six o'clock, and, although the moon was above the horizon, it so happened that the evening of the 22nd was dark and deeply clouded, and, had the attempt been made to struggle on to the distance designated in the Instructions, it would have been impossible for any human fore-sight to divine what might have happened, especially under the ever-imminent risk of an attack.

With its many elusive elements of uncertainty, War must ever be a game of chance. To reduce these chances to the lowest possible minimum, to make them as much as possible the objects of calculation, and bring them under strict control, to plan operations on such a basis so to previse that this plan shall be found workable, and that within the allotted time, is the first duty of a Commander-in-Chief, the prime object and *raison d'être* of a well-appointed Head-Quarter Staff, the great test of whose efficiency must certainly be the practicability of the plans it lays down, and for which its members are in various degrees responsible. To Head-Quarters at Suâkin went all information acquired either on reconnaissance or by spies. Provided with very special and very expensive means for its acquisition, it was the depository of all information affecting the well-being of the Force and the success of the operations in which it was engaged. To the Army it occupied the place of a local Providence; its authority was supreme; and from the General of Brigade, through every rank, down to the private soldier, all were bound to carry out its decisions and to obey its behests.

It may reasonably then be asked, how, at this initial stage of the day's proceedings, with the enemy as yet appearing only in stray parties, retiring as they were approached, and with the force still engaged in the endeavour to reach the scene of anticipated operations, so great a discrepancy between Instructions formulated and the possibility of their being carried into effect at once presents itself. In the Report drawn up by Lieut.-Colonel Robertson, Senior Commissariat Officer at Suâkin, and recently issued by the War Office, we are informed that " The camel should never be hurried or hustled, and *the pace of the column always regulated by that of the slowest camel* " ![1] Instead of being based on this lucid principle, it would seem as if the Instructions had been calculated for the rate of progress attainable by a Force either disencumbered from Transport altogether, or at least not impeded by that variable and uncertain element "the slowest camel," operating under conditions most trying and adverse to its carrying capacities, and under which the entire Transport Train was compelled ultimately to succumb.

It is just possible that had the written Instructions issued on the 21st been adhered to, the zeribas simultaneously constructed, and the Transport Train allowed the option of remaining at zeriba No. 1, and only advancing on No. 2 if no difficulties arising from the presence of the enemy were encountered, Head-Quarters' scheme *might* have been carried into effect. The *viva voce* emendations, however, seem to have been determined on without any thought of time, or of what it was practicable to accomplish in a day which gave no lingering twilight, and on which, if the moon happened to

[1] P. 12. All questions relating to the Transport Train having a most important bearing on the state of matters on the 22nd of March, I have thought it right to give liberal extracts from this carefully drawn-up and authoritative Report. *Vide* Appendix IV.

H

be obscured, sundown meant sudden darkness. The difficulties
of the day thus began neither with General M'Neill, with General
Hudson, or the combatant Force, but with the Transport Train
only; and that under circumstances in which, if the attempt had
been made to carry out Orders, these difficulties were irremediable,
even although no hostile movements had taken place, and no duty
remained to be discharged other than the formation of the two zeribas
and conveyance of the *impedimenta* to the prescribed distance.

Having thus arranged with General Hudson that the Transport
Train should advance a little further, General M'Neill requested
Colonel Wood to look out for, and stop at, the first place he might
consider suitable for the final halt. This Colonel Wood promised to
do, at the same time distinctly stating that he would select a place
where the bush was dense, and materials for constructing the zeriba
and its redoubts easily acquired.

The open space selected by Colonel Wood as the site of the
zeriba was reached about 10.30 A.M. It formed a large oblong of
very irregular outlines, presenting an area in the clearest portion
about half a square mile in extent. With a hard gravelly surface it
formed merely a slight rise of the ground between two of the wide
shallow "khors," or water-courses, by means of which the heavy
autumnal rains escape from the mountains to the Red Sea, and in
which the bush naturally grows with greater luxuriance.

When the ground was reached, General M'Neill telegraphed
to Head-Quarters the change the state of the Transport Train had
necessitated on the Orders given. The reply was, "Go on if you
can, and if not zeriba; and as you have stopped at the six mile
instead of the eight mile distance, no zeriba will be required at
the five mile point as previously ordered." With this slender
appreciation of the difficulties encountered, by mutual consent and
imperative necessity the duties involved in the preliminary part of
the Instructions came to an end.

"Go on if you can!" Save for the difficulties thus brought to
our knowledge, there is no reason why you should not. All spy

reports, rumours, etc., that might create alarm, modify our Instructions, or induce caution, we discount and ignore. "Go on if you can!" if the camels will drive, or bush permit, short of the distance designated these are the only checks we recognise, and certainly did not anticipate. "Go on if you can!"—the enemy expects you eight miles off;—harassed and disorganised from a heavy march, you will walk an easy prey straight into the jaws of the lion, couched and ready for you, who will otherwise have to crawl noiselessly, stealthily, over the two intervening miles before making his final spring. "Go on if you can."

So far as can be judged, the spy reports as to the Arab ambush of the 22nd at the eight mile distance were just as true as that relating to the gathering in the ravine near Tamai in 1884; and, encumbered with Transport, entangled in dense bush, at the end of a toilsome march, without note of warning or time given for defensive preparations, we ask the reader to judge whether the chances of the two Brigades at Tofrek in 1885 would have been at all equal to those of the two Brigades at Tamai in 1884. Certainly not. At Tamai it was the fault of the British that there was any mishap, who,—instead of remaining steady as rocks, and permitting the enemy to "charge the Squares,"—rushed into danger; while in 1885, the circumstances were such that the premature breakdown of the Transport Train can only be regarded as a most merciful interposition of Providence.

CHAPTER IV.

THE ZERIBA.

"Arm, warriors—arm for fight! the foe at hand,
   Whom fled we thought, will save us long pursuit
This day: fear not his flight; so thick a cloud
He comes, and settled in his face I see
Stern resolution, and secure. . . . This day will pour down,
   If I conjecture aught, no drizzling shower,
But rattling storm of arrows barbed with fire."
                    Paradise Lost, Book VI., 537 *seq.*

E have now brought the two Brigades, and especially the Transport Train, to the *terminus ad quem* of their harassing march. Before proceeding farther, we will glance for a few moments at the plans meantime being resolved on for the efficient discharge of the work in hand.

As may easily be imagined, the ultimate arrangements for the day were to the General in Command the objects of the most anxious care and deliberation, and above all else there were one or two guiding principles never for a moment lost sight of.

In presence of such an enemy as the Sûdanese had proved themselves to be—cruel, bloodthirsty, ferocious, and inspired with an utter contempt for death—it was evident that the first and most paramount of all duties incumbent on the Expedition was that of its own self-preservation, and the making such disposition of the resources at command as might most effectually conduce to that end. Unless this object were secured all was lost; as, with such a brave but ruthless foe as might at any moment be encountered, any material error meant the virtual destruction of the entire Force.[1]

Safety thus provided for, there followed the duties this Force had been sent out to discharge ; constructing the zeriba and its redoubts, unloading and storing the Transport, etc., and all to be arranged for in the most orderly and expeditious manner ;—in all these operations there being yet another imperative necessity, rapidity, promptitude, dispatch—to have the whole arranged with as little delay as possible in order to the safe return to camp of the Indian Brigade and Transport Train before sundown. As the sun would set at six o'clock, and including the formation of zeriba No. 1, three hours at least must be allowed for the return journey, there would be little more than four hours left in which to complete the various operations connected with zeriba No. 2 and its redoubts.

The first idea entertained by General M'Neill was to form the troops, both British and Indian, into one great Square, within which the entire work of making zeribas, and unloading, storing, and arranging the Transport might be carried on. To this arrangement the main objection was that, in event of any part of this large Transport-burdened Square being broken, either by the enemy from without, or a possible stampede among the animals from within, the Arab, following his favourite tactics, would have the game all his own way. Such complicated operations as forming zeribas, collecting the materials, unloading stores, and arranging Transport, would also be very much hampered in so confined a space.

Another alternative thought of was, after having the zeriba with its redoubts marked out, to apportion the Force accordingly, and let each Division work at that part of the defences where its special interest lay. The Berkshires would thus have had the south redoubt committed to their charge *ab initio;* the Royal Marines

---

[1] "The slightest mistake on our part would have been almost irretrievable, nothing but immense care, activity, and secrecy could have ensured the great success which was achieved, and which gives ample cause for pride on the part of the country, the general, his staff, and the troops engaged." — "The Battle of Tamai." By a Soldier. *United Service Magazine,* 1884, part I. p. 700.

that on the north; while the Indian Brigade would have the central zeriba in which to store the loads, and surround it with an adequate defence. Both these arrangements were, however, rejected in favour of the modification which actually took effect. The Indian troops were still to form three sides of a great inclosing or covering Square, but on the fourth side the British Force was to be retained in its concentrated square formation as an independent rallying point,—a living redoubt, a citadel, within which might be protected all that was vital to the Expedition— Gardner guns, Reserve ammunition, Telegraph waggon, etc.

All that now remained was to carry these ideas into effect: and the site for the zeriba fixed upon, no time was lost in making the necessary dispositions. The troops marched upon the ground in the same order in which they had advanced, and the British Square being the first to emerge upon the open, turning a little to the left, halted in its original formation, taking up a position on the north-eastern side of the great open space. Past it streamed the Indian Brigade with the Transport Train under its charge, General Hudson being instructed so to dispose his troops as to cover on the three remaining sides the whole ground necessary for the coming operations and facing toward the probable point of attack. On the side opposite to the British Square were accordingly posted in line the 15th Sikhs, to the right the 28th Bombay Native Infantry, and on the left the 17th Bengal Native Infantry. The bush in front of the 28th being very dense, and comparatively open in front of the 17th, two Companies of the latter were moved across, and placed on the right of the 28th Bombay Infantry, in order to strengthen and prolong this face, and more effectually to cover the working-parties engaged in collecting materials for the north-eastern redoubt.

In order to protect the front of these various lines of infantry small pickets, of from four to five men each, taken from the flanks of the companies of regiments, were thrown forward about 150 yards to the front. With special reference to the close nature of the country and the known tactics of the Arabs, General Hudson considered these small groups preferable to one large picket from each regiment, and the event proved that he was correct.

A quarter of a mile or so farther out, in front of these pickets, were the Lancers, arranged in Cossack posts of four men each, viz., one vedette and three men in reserve, and, according to the testimony of Captain H. L. Jones, the Officer in Command, covering in all over three miles of frontage. Another Cossack post, also of four men, was used as a connecting link, the remainder constituting the picket and visiting patrols. Every precaution was thus adopted which the number of the Mounted Force at disposal would admit of. That these arrangements took place under circumstances which rendered every precaution nugatory was certainly not the fault of General M'Neill, or of those under his Command.

To a small portion of the Squadron a melancholy interest is attached. Early in the day Lieutenant Richardson[1] with three

[1] Lieutenant James Bernard Richardson was the eldest son of David Richardson, Esq., of Hartfield House, Cove, Dumbartonshire, N.B., and was born 2nd June 1860. Receiving his preliminary education at Harrow, where he was head boy of his house, in 1879 he passed into the University College, Oxford. After prosecuting his studies with marked success, in Feb. 1882, at the top of the list of University candidates, he entered the Royal Military College at Sandhurst.

Embracing the profession of arms for his vocation in life, *con amore*, he adopted every means that might lay a foundation for after usefulness, becoming especially an accomplished linguist, and adding a knowledge of the Russian language to his other acquisitions. A skilful swordsman, and expert with the revolver, in whatever form

death at the hands of the Arab may have come to him there is no doubt he would sell his life dearly.

His commission of Lieutenancy in the 5th Royal Irish Lancers dating 10th March 1883, he had just been two years in the Army when, at the early age of 23 he was thus cut off in the very opening of a promising career. During one of Lieut. Richardson's visits to Russia, where he went with a view to improvement in the language, he married a Russian lady, who, when informed of her husband's death, took it so much to heart that she only survived him about six weeks.

A search made in the bush for traces of the missing Party resulted in the silver whistle used by Lieut. Richardson being found at a spot amid the bush five or six miles distant from Suâkin, and a mile or two

men was detached on patrol duty to the left of the line of advance. After being so engaged for some hours, his horse getting knocked up he rode into Suâkin about the middle of the day, and, changing his mount, returned to his patrol duties, neither himself nor the men under his Command being again heard of. They were no doubt cut off and slain by the Arabs in the course of the afternoon.

Such was the double cordon, first of Infantry, second of Cavalry, established round the Force concentrated at Tofrek. In proportion to the ground to be covered, it must be admitted that the exterior line was extremely weak. Cossack posts distributed on a three mile frontage stationed at the distance apart say of a post and vedette for each quarter of a mile, gives certainly but an open mesh for a dense bush, within which an enemy might freely operate unperceived within very short distances. It is also evident that to have extended the radius of observation would, by widening the distances between the posts, only have made matters worse, while to have patrolled the bush, or to have carried out observations two or three miles from the main Force, would have been practically impossible to such a handful of troopers. Even if, after the experience of the 20th, it had been advisable to introduce Cavalry into the bush at all, it would require to have been in much greater strength than a Squadron of Lancers. A Regiment would have been all too little, especially when we remember that in the advance on Tamai in 1884 the Cavalry were over seven times the strength of those out on the 22nd, and that on the 19th and 20th the entire Cavalry Brigade was at the front. It is too evident that the whole question as to the employment of Cavalry, in great numbers

south of the zeriba. This whistle, now in the possession of his family, was distinctly marked with a spear thrust and encrusted with blood ; and it is only too evident that having advanced on patrol duty to the same distance as the zeriba but farther to the left, the small party had been caught in the great Arab wave sweeping down from Tamai on the British Force and killed to a man.

The only other traces found were at the capture and destruction of Tamai on the 3rd of April, when, on searching the huts, a scabbard and saddle belonging to two of the missing Lancers were discovered.

or in small, whether used in scouting or vedette work, or for direct encounter with the enemy, had received but scant attention, and of this failure to comprehend the true conditions of a most important problem the arrangements for the 22nd had the full benefit.   With regard to outpost duty under such circumstances one thing is clear, that neither a vedette nor a sentry can be held to be responsible or efficient farther than his eyes can see or his ears hear, and to surround either the one or the other with a dense screen, behind which, so long as he be stealthy and catlike, the enemy can operate with perfect impunity, is to stultify every military precaution and jeopardise the man's life to no purpose. Yet this is exactly what took place at Tofrek, without any possibility of remedy if the ordinary regulations of the Service were to be observed.   After the capture of Dihilbat Hill on the 20th, Sir John M'Neill had an excellent opportunity of studying the tactics employed by the Arabs in dealing with men on outpost duty. From the top of the hill a bird's eye view could be got of the whole surrounding district.   In the bush below were several detached files of the 9th Bengal Cavalry.   As seen by Sir John M'Neill, two of these at least were run in upon by the enemy and killed.   Under cover of the bush an Arab would present himself and engage the trooper's attention in front; while thus occupied in playing his lance at the enemy before him, other two Arabs, equally stealthy in their approach, would spring upon the man from behind, drag him off his horse, and stab him to death in a few moments.   From the summit of Dihilbat Hill, 828 feet in altitude, and extremely steep, the plain below looked as if dotted with tufts of herbage, amid which the movements of friend and foe could be followed with the utmost ease.   Yet, when the descent was made it was impossible to see more than a short distance, regarding which General Graham in his despatch relative to the Reconnaissance on the 19th states :—

"The whole country is covered with dense mimosa scrub, from 6 feet to 8 feet in height. Beyond the first hills, A, B, C, D, and up the Hasheen

I

Valley, this scrub is even more thick. *This scrub renders it impossible to follow the movements of an enemy on foot, who can conceal himself perfectly within a short distance of our vedettes."* [1]

Well, on the 20th, the Bengal Cavalry, sent into a tract of ground like this, found themselves absolutely helpless, without the power of making an effective charge, liable only to be stalked and cut up in detail, and, as further stated in the despatch just quoted, "Charged by the enemy in considerable strength, retired with loss on the Square formed by the Guards at the foot of the Dihilbat Hill."

If the impression conveyed by this state of matters was not lost on a Commanding Officer like Sir John M'Neill, still less was it likely to be so on the troops themselves; and there can be little doubt that the adverse experiences of the 20th had a most important bearing on the action of the Cavalry on the 22nd. But we are anticipating, and must refer the reader to a subsequent *résumé* of this question in Chapter VII.

From this Cavalry cordon, weak and inefficient, through inadequate numbers as the logic of facts unfortunately proved, we revert again to the main body. For a notice of the gross misrepresentations indulged in regarding it, the persistent attempts to depict the ensuing struggle, not as a well-organised combat where victory declared itself on the side of sound organisation and discipline, but as a brainless and invertebrate battle, we must refer the reader to the Chapter dealing with "The Press and the Battle."

Meantime, in addition to what has been said as to the formation of the troops, I would only make one or two remarks as to their constant preparedness for any eventuality that might befall, and that throughout the entire day, say from 10.30 or 11 A.M., till the moment of the attack. While the real question at issue is,—"were these preparations *effective?"* to the careless, incurious, or non-military eye they might not look at all *impressive,* and it is undoubtedly in the distinction to be drawn between these terms that the entire

[1] *Parliamentary Papers,* Egypt, No. 13 (1885), p. 19.

mischief has originated. On arrival we have seen that the British troops piled their arms, and after their quota of fatigue and covering parties had been detailed, the remainder were ordered to lie down and rest themselves as well as they could. Seeing that the men had been toiling most of the previous night in making preparations necessary for the new movement, and, after snatching a few hours' repose, astir from four or five o'clock in the morning and on the march since seven—judged by military economics this was certainly a very judicious thing to do, but at the same time a very bad and a careless thing from the outsiders' point of view, who would no doubt have kept the men standing to their arms in review order until they dropped from sheer exhaustion. The truth is, that to trained and disciplined men the difference of time in preparedness for attack between the two arrangements amounted only to a few seconds, while the boon to the worn and wearied troops under the blazing sun of the tropics was simply incalculable. The exaggerated importance given to the distinction between the Service ideas of what was *effective*, and the outsider's idea of what to the careless and unthinking observer would have been *impressive*, may excuse a little detail as to " Piled Arms."

Troops can " pile arms " in any two-deep formation, and the piles of arms, each containing four rifles, accurately mark the alignment of the ranks. Thus, if a bird's-eye view be taken of the piled arms of a battalion of four companies in open column they would appear thus :—

```
        ×          ×          ×          ×
        ×          ×          ×          ×
        ×          ×          ×          ×
        ×          ×          ×          ×
        ×          ×          ×          ×
```

in close column thus :—

```
              ×   ×   ×   ×
              ×   ×   ×   ×
              ×   ×   ×   ×
              ×   ×   ×   ×
              ×   ×   ×   ×
```

in square of two ranks thus :—

```
× × × × × × × × ×
×               ×
×               ×
×               ×
×               ×
× × × × × × × × ×
```

Without bringing it to the ground no pile can be disturbed unless the men are in their places ready to take their rifles, and, by practice, they can find their positions almost as quickly as they run in. A battalion may thus be dispersed from quarter-distance column, *i.e.,* column at quarter-company interval ; the men smoking, lying down, etc., over a radius of 50 yards ; the bugle sounds the "assembly," on the word "stand-to" they will be in their ranks, the word "unpile arms" follows in about 20 seconds, and they will be ready to "shoulder" and move off certainly within the half minute. So that, as the left wing of the Berkshire, at the time of attack, were mostly lying *inside* the square of piles, they would be in their places within at most 30 seconds, and with their "faces" quite sufficiently "dressed" (*i.e.* aligned) for fighting purposes.

But piled arms, especially in square, do not *look* regular to anyone on their level, and to a non-military observer they look most irregular; this was, no doubt, one of the stumbling-blocks of such specials as happened to be on the spot. Men lying down, some inside some outside, and arms apparently anyhow. Precisely the same remarks apply to the Indian Contingent, who were not lying down but standing to their arms, and whose arrangements were so thoroughly ignored by the Press, that they were assumed to have been practically *non-existent.* All the world has heard of Sir Colin Campbell's thin red line, the gallant 93rd, which, armed only with muzzle-loading Enfields, so thoroughly discomfited the Russian Cavalry that they never got to within 250 yards of it. Well, that line was at least *red,* and would have caught even the eye of a special. Like the British troops the Indians were in dust-coloured khakee, and although standing to their arms with bayonets fixed, these arms were not " shouldered " but " ordered," and the men " at ease," in style thoroughly *effective* if not *impressive*.   These thin dust-coloured lines had however an immense advantage over even the Crimean heroes.   They were armed with breech-loading Sniders, and could cover a " zone of fire " with a leaden hail, from the rapidity with which it was delivered immeasurably more destructive than that of the Enfield.   What of it ? not a special seemed to be aware that there were Indian lines at all, and as a wink is as good as a nod to a blind horse, they might have been armed with antiquated matchlocks or old Brown Besses for all he knew or cared.

The Indian troops thus remained standing to their arms the whole time in lines two deep, with fixed bayonets, and cartridges loose in the ball-bags ready for action.   Every precaution was adopted which the *matériel* at command could possibly supply to guard against surprise or misadventure, and Sir John M'Neill's idea was thus fully realised of making the Indian troops one great covering party enclosing the space where the operations of the day were to be carried on, the British Regiments meantime forming a Rallying Square to which all might turn as a citadel of strength.

Habituated to savage warfare, and keenly alive to the necessities of the position, the troops were no sooner on the ground than General M'Neill had the Engineers out measuring and pegging off the site of the future zeriba and its redoubts, and the place for stores fixed on.   With equal promptitude working and covering parties were organised for cutting down the bush and dragging it into position. The chief work of construction fell, of course, upon the Royal Engineers and the Madras Sappers, but to expedite the work fatigue parties were drawn both from the British and Indian troops.   In the case of the Indian Regiments these were furnished by taking the alternate ranks of alternate sections, thus preserving a front rank always intact.   The British Regiments had of course to furnish their quota of working and covering parties, fatigue parties for unloading stores, and Officers' guard for water and other duties.   The remainder of the British Square were ordered to pile their arms, place sentries over them, and then to lie down in square, with the object of saving the men as much as possible.   The heat told much more heavily on the British than on the Indians, who were to return to Suâkin that afternoon; whereas, in the event of an attack, the British would have to bear the brunt of it, and be in any case saddled with the arduous task of keeping a constant night watch.

The laborious task of collecting materials and forming the zeriba had now commenced.   Zeriba is a native term for an enclosure like the laager of South Africa, capable of being rapidly improvised and fenced in on every side not with waggons but with the thorny mimosa bushes growing so abundantly in this desert land.   The height of the mimosa scrub, of course, varies very much, averaging from six up to eight or ten feet—so high, indeed, as to obstruct the view even of a man on horse- or camel-back.   The oldest and largest of these trees are cut down and laid with the thorny heads outwards, the stems inwards; and so, closely packed and with the interstices filled in with smaller plants and branches, a breast-high fence is formed, until supplemented by entrenchments, useless against shot yet very effective against direct attack.   The British troops in forming their zeribas also took the precaution of wireing together the mimosa stems, so that they could not be dragged out or shifted in any way.   In cutting down these trees, owing to the horizontal spread of their straight thorny branches, the men had often to go down upon their knees to hack and hew at the stems.   For this purpose a variety of implements had been supplied, axes, long-handled and short-handled billhooks, etc.   Unfortunately, at the very moment when they were most required, these tools proved to be of the very worst description. They failed in the handles and edges at once, the latter especially splintering out, till the tools looked like saws rather than cutting implements.[1]

[1] At the close of the campaign, when the stores were being entirely withdrawn, it was decided by a Board of Officers sitting at Handoub, that 400 of these implements, axes, bill-hooks, etc., should be broken up and buried in the sand.   General M'Neill, seeing that such a store of metal if got hold of might be useful to the Arabs, advised their being carried down per rail to Suâkin and there flung into the harbour or otherwise disposed of, which was accordingly done.

PLATE I

Rough Sketch to Illustrate Sir John McNeills Zareba
as Altered 30th March 1885.
(*Diary of the Suakin Expedition p.32.*)

To Suakin

45 Yds.

Redt 20 dia.

45 Yds

Redt 20 dia.
30 Men

Water
Stores

Mules

Hay Traverse
9' High

100 Yds.

100 Yds.

Redt with Ditch.
20' dia. 30 Men.

Signal Station.
Redt with Ditch
15 yds sq.
80 Men

a Water Depot
b Commis. Stores

Thick Bush

Rough Sketch to Illustrate Attack
made upon Sir John McNeills Zareba
22nd March 1885.

To accompany my despatch
dated 28th March 1885.

Gerald Graham
Lieut Genl
Comg Suakin Field Force.

To Suakin

R.N.

R.M.L.I.

R.M.L.I.

R.M.L.I.

R.M.L.I.

75 Yds

45 Yds

½ Battn Berks

Camels
Mules
etc.

120 Yds.

Water Casks
Biscuit Boxes

120 Yards

28th Bombay

15 Br Sikhs

R.N. Berks

Berks

Berks

65 Yds.

65 Yds.

65 Yds.

6 Cos 17th N.I.

Thick Bush

The accompanying plate will enable the reader to form an accurate idea how zeriba No. 2 was arranged at two distinct stages in its formation.

First, As it was laid out and constructed on the 22nd, and so remained during the rest of the week, with accommodation for two Battalions in the respective redoubts both of equal dimensions. The reader will see at once the object in so constructing this great Depôt or Secondary Base of operations. Although attached by and communicating at their angles, the three squares are placed diagonally, or, as it is termed, in echelon, the large square intended to contain the stores, non-combatants, and animals, being placed in the centre. By this arrangement every side of this central zeriba was capable of being swept by a flanking fire from the defensive works at the angles, thus, however large it might otherwise be, completely protecting it from hostile approach.

Second, As it was modified on the 30th of March, in order that it might be held safely by only one Battalion accommodated in the northern redoubt, each of the three remaining angles of the central Depôt having a small defensible work attached to it. This alteration was effected with great skill and promptitude, by Colonel Leach and the Royal Engineers, and the zeriba rendered equally serviceable with a much smaller garrison.

While the zeriba and its redoubts were thus in course of formation, busy hands were at work unloading the camels, etc., in the central space, and arranging the various stores in orderly fashion. Biscuit boxes, preserved meat cases, all the multifarious requirements for camp life present and in prospect, were being carefully massed together under superintendence of the proper Officers. Of these, one item especially bulked largely in the expenditure of time and care it required. Ἄριστον μὲν ὕδωρ, "Water the first of elements we hold." So commence the *Odes* of Pindar,[1] and from first to last the sentiment might well have been re-echoed by the Suâkin Expedition. One half of the

---

[1] *Olympia* I., Strophe 1.

Transport Train on the 22nd was devoted to the carriage of water, and the orders being that all empty tins were to be returned with the convoy, the emptying of all the smaller vessels into the large receptacles provided formed one of the most pressing necessities of the day. The large iron and waterproof canvas tanks were first of all got into position in close proximity to the redoubt occupied by the Royal Marines. Then commenced the tedious and troublesome operation of transferring into these the water carried out in skins, barrels, and tins. The latter had to be unscrewed with their special key, and the water allowed slowly to trickle out— a nice business when time is pressing, hurry the order of the day, and the attack of a horde of savages ever imminent. Over all these arrangements an Officer's Guard had to be stationed to prevent the water from being purloined. The troops were all parched and mad with thirst, their water bottles long since empty, and even the store in the Regimental water-carts mayhap exhausted. Under circumstances like these need it be wondered that the men were always trying to thrust in their tins to get a few drops of the precious fluid, and that it was only by the strong hand that what was intended to be kept " for many days " was not used right off in supplying present needs.

In pursuance of a Brigade Order addressed verbally to the Adjutant of the Regiment, about half-past twelve the Royal Marines had their rations served out, dining by half companies; the right half companies first, the left half companies afterwards, and cooks preparing the rations by sections. The men were not allowed to take their belts off.

At one o'clock Major Frank Graves, of the 20th Hussars, rode up to Sir John M'Neill and stated that he had been sent from General Graham with a squadron of the 20th to communicate with him. He brought no information from Head-Quarters; and on being questioned as to what had occurred on the way out, he reported having seen in his front stray parties of the enemy, who retired before the Cavalry, and did not come into collision. From this Sir John judged that if an attack took place it would come not from the Suâkin but from the Tamai direction, facing which were the three Indian Regiments standing to their arms with bayonets fixed. Major Graves had got his orders at 10 A.M. to take his Squadron, numbering ninety of all ranks, but raised at his request to one hundred and ten, and, following the line of telegraph, to obtain and keep up communication with the Force under General M'Neill. On receiving a despatch from Sir John for the Chief of the Staff, to the effect that matters were progressing satisfactorily, he started on his return journey at 1.30 P.M.

As the most vital part of the defences, and the earliest intended for occupation, attention had been first of all directed to the formation of the redoubts which at first took the form of small zeribas. Both of these were pushed on with the utmost expedition, but, as we have seen, the bush being thickest on the north side, in front of the 28th Bombay Infantry, the redoubt at this angle was in a more advanced state. It was completed shortly after two o'clock; and the salient, with its trench and sand-bag parapet, having been finished, the two Gardner guns, under command of Lieutenant Alfred W. Paget, R.N., designed for it, were got into position. The Battalion of the Royal Marine Light Infantry, hitherto forming part of the British Square, were now transferred to this redoubt, together with the reserve ammunition and the Telegraph Waggon, and communication was thereby kept up constantly with Suâkin until about 6.30 P.M., when either the Arabs or some chance accident severed the wire, which was never again repaired, the limelight by night and heliograph by day doing duty instead. With this transfer of the Royal Marines the Berkshire Battalion was contracted so as to form a smaller Square.

The south redoubt was also being rapidly completed, and at this time Colonel Huyshe represented to General M'Neill that the men of his Regiment had eaten nothing since four o'clock in the morning, and that as they were feeling the sun very much, it was desirable to serve out food and water. General M'Neill agreed to this,

K

on the understanding that the regiment should have their food by half battalions, and as soon as the first half battalion had finished it should move into the south redoubt, now nearly ready. Rations and water were accordingly served out, and when this half battalion had finished it was marched by Colonel Huyshe into the south redoubt, very soon after the Marines had occupied that on the north. The time was now getting on towards half-past two, and shortly after the half battalion had gone into the redoubt the men piled their arms inside, part of them going out in front of the Sikhs to cut bush in order to complete the defences. The salient for the guns, with its trench and sand-bag parapet, was so far advanced that the remaining two Gardner guns had been brought up ready to be placed in position. The great object in retaining the remaining half battalion of the Berkshire in its original position, instead of moving it at once into the zeriba, was to guard the rear of the camels against the possibility of an Arab attack and also to prevent them straying into the bush. Whenever the Transport had been collected, and General Hudson able to move off, it was intended that the half battalion should join its companion in the south redoubt.

When the change thus mentioned in the dispositions had been effected, General M'Neill rode into the centre zeriba where the Transport Corps and fatigue parties were engaged in unloading the numerous animals and arranging the stores. This work was so far advanced that about half-past two General M'Neill, being anxious the start should not be made later than three o'clock, so as to ensure the camp being reached before sunset, requested General Hudson to get the empty Transport collected together in the unoccupied space to the south-east of the zeriba, preparatory to returning to Suâkin. General M'Neill then left General Hudson with these words, " Come to me again at three and I will tell you how matters stand, meantime be getting everything in readiness to move off."

GROUP OF MADHIST DERVISHES.

CHAPTER V.

THE BATTLE.

"All at once, as at a signal given,
    We heard the *Tecbir*,[1] so these Arabs call
    Their shouts of onset, when with loud appeal
    They challenge Heaven, as if demanding conquest.
    The battle joined, and through the barbarous host,
Fight, fight, and Paradise ! was all the cry."
               Siege of Damascus, Act II. Scene 1,
               By John Hughes, A.D. 1677-1720.

IMMEDIATELY after this conversation with General Hudson, Sir John M'Neill returned to the southern redoubt occupied by the half battalion of the Berkshire Regiment. As yet no note of warning had been given that special danger was imminent, and it seemed as if the labours

[1] The *Takbīr*, the well-known invocation *Allāhu Akbar*, God is Most Great, introduced as a prominent feature in all Mahometan prayers. Quadrupled it forms the *Takbīr-i-Tahrīmah*, which precedes both the *Azan* or Muezzin's call to prayer, and the *Salat*, or liturgical prayer, recited five times a day by all devout Mahometans. The *Takbīr-i-Tahrīmah* is pronounced standing, with the thumbs touching the lobes of the ears, and the hands open on each side of the face ; and after its recital attention must be entirely concentrated on the worship. As a probable survival of the ideas entertained in ancient times that even the killing of an animal for food is in some sense a religious or sacrificial act, amongst Mahometans the ejaculatory repetition of the *Takbīr* precedes any such slaughter. A similar idea probably inspires the Arab robber who, before cutting his victim's throat, will first offer up a prayer himself, and requires the trembling wretch to do the same. As the Romans on certain occasions dedicated their enemies to the Infernal gods, so may it be no matter of surprise to find this great ascription used in consecrating the slaughter in battle of the *Kaffir*, the infidel, the unbeliever in the sole Divinity of Allah and the prophetic mission of his servant Mahomet.

of the day, which had now been progressing satisfactorily for four hours, would be carried on to their completion without disturbance from the enemy.

Suddenly, and with the lapse of not more than a few minutes since he had parted from the Indian Brigadier, one of the Lancers rode up and informed Sir John M'Neill that the enemy was gathering in front and advancing rapidly, and was immediately followed by a second Lancer with similar intelligence.

General M'Neill instantly told Lieutenant-Colonel Kelly, the Brigade-Major, to have the working and covering parties called in, and ordered the troops to stand to their arms. While these instructions were being carried into effect, the Cavalry were to be seen galloping in on every side with the Arabs close at their heels. The Indian Infantry pickets, also running in on the flanks of their Companies, quickly cleared the front, and left the troops ranked up in line, free to open fire.

The Arabs were now surging onwards, chiefly from south and west, not in any regular formation, but with their usual tendency to advance in little knots and groups, yet forming by sheer weight of numbers one vast impetuous mass, enveloped in clouds of dust, filling the air with a pandemonium of shouts and yells, and making frantic efforts to storm the position. The Berkshire and Royal Marines, the Sikhs, and Bombay Infantry, faced the fierce rush with undaunted bravery. The Bengalees alone quailed before the shock, and, with some of their Companies thrown into partial disorder from the Cavalry riding through them, had just time to fire a wild and scattered volley towards the enemy, when, overborne by the resistless torrent, they turned and fled for such cover as the zeriba might afford. Every effort was made by their own Regimental Officers and Sir John M'Neill to rally the panic-stricken fugitives, and the General actually got a large number within the south redoubt, where about a hundred and twenty men, standing up to the southern fence, again fired a scattered, and, in all probability, an aimless and ineffective volley towards the swarthy and surging horde, but on the Arabs delivering their assault, repeating the previous scene, again broke and fled.

The Arabs now crowded in by the uncompleted salient, where the guns were not yet in position, killing Lieutenant Seymour and six sailors while gallantly defending their charge.   Captain Domville, who was with the party, had several narrow escapes, killing several of the enemy with his own hand, and shooting down an Arab who was on the point of spearing Lieut.-Colonel Kelly, the Brigade Major. At this angle also Capt. Romilly and Lieut. Newman were killed.

Meantime General M'Neill, seeing how matters went, had instantly ordered the rear-rank of the Berkshire half battalion, then engaged in defending the western face of the redoubt, to face about and occupy the vacated position through which the Arabs were now pouring.   This they at once did, and meeting the enemy half way, quickly despatched every Arab who had entered, one hundred and twelve dead bodies being afterwards counted as having fallen within the limits of this redoubt alone.   It is only right to mention that in this gallant repulse the Berkshires were assisted by some of the Bengalees, rallied by Captain Percy Henry Noel Lake of the Intelligence Department temporarily attached to the Brigade Staff, and who as Assistant Field Engineer with the Southern Afghanistan Field Force, had gone through the Afghan War of 1878-79.   A considerable number also rallied within the centre zeriba, and lining its southern and eastern defences, seem to have fought well, and kept the enemy off.   There was on this part of the defences no violent attack, but the Arabs getting behind the camels tried to stampede them upon the central square.

During this determined assault on the southern redoubt an interesting episode befell Colonel Huyshe of the Berkshires, who, sitting on horseback close to his Regiment when the attack took place, was suddenly confronted by an Arab of gigantic size and most ferocious demeanour, appearing from behind a camel, brandishing an enormous spear, and evidently bent on slaughter.   Their eyes met, and, seeing the Colonel's revolver levelled at his head, the expression on the countenance of the savage suddenly changed from triumph to horror. The Colonel fired, and, with the upper part of his head blown away, the Arab fell a ghastly wreck of the "noble savage." It was indeed no time for mincing matters. The stern necessity on every hand was kill or be killed, and it required a steady eye, a cool head, and unfaltering courage for a man to hold his own amid such a carnival of death. This is forcibly illustrated in the fate which befell Lieutenant Swinton,[1] a young Officer of the Berkshires, in charge of the Regimental transport. When the action was over he had gone outside their redoubt alone to look for his pony, lost sight of in the confusion, and, walking along by the central zeriba, without paying any attention to him, passed a wounded Arab, who sprang up, and throwing his spear with a sudden effort, drove it into the back of the unfortunate Officer. The Arab was immediately killed and Lieutenant Swinton attended to, but his wound proved to be mortal. No further serious attack was made upon this redoubt, the bulk of the enemy sweeping down on the disloaded Transport Train.

The first brief moments of uncertainty over, the troops were all on the *qui vive,* and the enemy was being repelled at every point. No sound could now be heard save that of the steady and sustained roar of musketry, in volley after volley repeated, with all the rapidity and precision of clockwork. With unflinching firmness the troops, both British and Indian, had thoroughly settled to their work, and the mighty engine of destruction embodied in the fire of from two to three thousand breechloaders, Martini-Henry's and Snider's, steadily, unceasingly delivered, was in full and disciplined operation. Sweeping every front as with a solid sheet of lead, within its range nothing lived, and if, at the hand of the *Kaffir,* the Moslem fanatic sought a royal road to Paradise for once he found

---

[1] Lieutenant George Sholto Swinton, was the eldest son of the late Major William Bentinck Swinton, of the 8th Madras Light Cavalry, a descendant of the old Scottish Border family, the Swintons of Swinton, Berwickshire. Lieutenant Swinton was educated at Sandhurst College, and got his commission in the 1st Battalion of the Berkshire Regiment in 1882, thus falling prematurely in his twenty-third year.

To these ferocious banditti their self-elected battlefield had
·ed an Aceldama, on which they fell "thick as autumnal
es that strew the brooks in Vallombrosa." On the com-
d British and Indian Force, with a tornado's overwhelming
ıgth on a ship at sea, the storm had suddenly burst in all
ury, but the gallant ship was ready, with her yards all tightly
ed, her sails in perfect trim, and—save for the blind unreason-
mass she had in tow and the faint hearts among her crew
ıoroughly obedient to the helm, she met .the storm without
iver.

Repelled by a torrent of leaden hail from every defended front
;he position, the Arabs swept round by the great mass of
ısport animals gathering together for the return journey to
ɪin. It was to cover this part of the ground on its southern
that the 17th Bengal Infantry had been drawn up in line, and,
rding to the distinct testimony of their Brigadier, General
ɪson, if they had stood their ground as did the 15th Sikhs and
28th Bombay Infantry, the Arabs would never have got to the
els or followers at all, and the losses incurred in that respect
ld have been trifling. When, for a particular purpose, a General
a Force placed under his Command, it is only reasonable
ɜxpect that it will do its duty, and on this assumption dis-
tions are made. So was it with this Indian Regiment. The task
mitted to it was not more arduous than that of its brigaded

1 " Hear all !—Prepare ye now for boldest deeds,
And know, the prophet will reward your valour.
Think that we will to certain triumph move ;
Who falls in fight yet meets the prize above.
There, in the gardens of eternal spring,
While birds of Paradise around you sing,
Each, with his blooming beauty by his side,
Shall drink rich wines that in full rivers glide
Breathe fragrant gales o'er fields of spice that blow,
And gather fruits immortal as they grow ;
· Ecstatic bliss shall your whole powers employ,
And every sense be lost in every joy."
Siege of Damascus, Act III.

battalions, but, although the Commanding Officer, Major Beverhoudt,[1] sacrificed his life in the endeavour to recall the men to such sense of duty as would at once have ensured their own safety and that of the Transport Train they were stationed to protect, the effort was in vain. True, a large proportion of the Regiment remained on the scene of action, and contributed more or less effectually to the subsequent defence. Failing, however, to retain the original formation, the primary duty for which it had been detailed remained entirely undischarged, and, once out of hand, much mischief was done by wild and reckless firing. The Regiment had evidently too few British Officers, and was no doubt put to rather severe a test by seeing the British Cavalry beating a hasty retreat upon its lines.

This unfortunate collapse gave the Arabs an opportunity they were not slow in turning to advantage. With a wild and indescribable howl peculiarly alarming to the camel, they rushed upon the panic-stricken and helpless mass, with the object of stampeding it upon the vigorously defended works, and so at once to secure cover for themselves from the withering fire, and to overpower the defenders by the blind unreasoning avalanche hurled upon them. Nor did the Arab content himself with frightful yells. His innate savagery and thirst for blood revelled in inflicting all the mischief he could on the unresisting non-combatant

[1] Major James Mandeville Wood von Beverhoudt, youngest son of Major Adam von Beverhoudt, formerly of the 58th Rutlandshire Regiment, born March 1844. Receiving his military education at Sandhurst, he was Gazetted ensign in the 90th Regiment in 1864. In 1869 he entered the Bengal Staff Corps, and was appointed to the 17th Bengal Native Infantry, and, generally on the Staff, retained his connection with this Regiment till the time of his death, a period of sixteen years. He became Captain in 1876, and served with the Regiment during the Afghan Campaign of 1879-80. Became Wing Commander 8th June 1880. On his return from Afghanistan he was placed on the Staff of the Commander-in-Chief as Deputy-Assistant Adjutant-General. Became Major in 1884 ; and on the selection of the 17th Bengal Native Infantry for service at Suâkin, Colonel Thompson being at the time invalided, although absent in England on furlough, on rejoining he was placed in Command, and gallantly fell at Tofrek while vainly endeavouring to keep the Regiment to its duty. He is stated to have been "an excellent and zealous officer, devoted to his profession, and a general favourite in his Regiment."—*Illustrated London News*, May 16th, 1885.

crowd of men and animals. Plying lance and sword with keen avidity, cutting, stabbing, hacking, hewing, ham-stringing the quadrupeds, and slaughtering their drivers, the tribesmen of the Sûdan secured what they wanted, a terror-stricken crowd to whom fear lent wings, moved only by one uncontrollable impulse,—to fly from the awful doom which in the blazing heat of this torrid land had so suddenly swooped upon it like a wild beast out of its lair, or a horde of incarnate fiends suddenly broke loose out of the deep abyss of hell. For a moment it might well seem as if the ghastly memories of the past were about to be anew illustrated—Sinkat, El Teb, or those other scenes of slaughter, a few miles off on the Sinkat and Tamai roads, where the bleached bones of Egyptian troops were yet whitening the ground, the Army engulphed on the march to Obeid, and last, not least, Khartûm; all so many milestones, marking successive stages in the ever-mismanaged Sûdan affairs. The great question then hanging in the balance was, will the *ruse* of the quick-witted Arab succeed, and British squares and Indian lines be alike overborne and trodden down by the sheer momentum of this unreasoning mass, wild with fear, heedless of everything except just to fly, onward, anywhere opening up a pathway of escape from the Angel of Death all too surely pursuing it?

So driven, the Transport Train broke up and scattered itself in various directions. Impelled by the Arabs, part of it bore down upon the redoubts held by the Berkshire and Royal Marines, and part on the centre zeriba. Mixed up as they were with the charging enemy, many of these animals were unavoidably shot down by the troops as a matter of self-preservation. The same thing happened in the attack made on the half battalion of the Berkshire, yet in square; but, pursued relentlessly by the Arabs, the great bulk must have gone off towards Suâkin and the sea, stopped, and surrounded by the Cavalry under Major Frank Graves, a considerable number being recovered after the fight and brought into the zeriba.

After the southern redoubt, the two main points of attack were the northern redoubt, as held by the Battalion of the Royal Marines, and the left wing or half Battalion of the Berkshire Regiment still formed up as the last remnant of the original British or Rallying Square. Both of these positions lay in the direct line of the camel-stampede, and their occupants were thereby placed at great disadvantage. In spite of its completed mimosa-fences, trampling their way over all intervening obstacles, a mass of the terror-stricken animals, streaming in full flight Suâkinwards, tore right through the northern redoubt, for the time seriously disorganising the defence. As stated by Colonel Way, an eye-witness well qualified to judge, "Everything seemed to come at once, camels, Transport of all kinds, including water-carts, ammunition mules, 17th Native Infantry, Madras Sappers, sick-bearers, Transport Corps, Cavalry, and Arabs fighting in the midst. All these passed close by me and went out on the other side of the zeriba, carrying away with them a number of the Marines and some Officers, who eventually got together and returned. The dust raised by this crowd was so great that I could not see anything beyond our zeriba for a minute or two, and it was impossible to see who was standing or what was likely to happen. The men behaved splendidly, and stood quite still. It was about the highest test of discipline I shall ever see, as in my opinion nothing could beat it."

In addition to this display of steadiness and good discipline, one great reason for the Royal Marines so rapidly recovering their formation was no doubt the number and excellent quality of their Officers. The Battalion was Officered to its full complement, and, regardless of their own lives, they rallied the men, so that after the living avalanche had swept past, Officers were to be seen everywhere in the redoubt with small knots of men gathered round them, who were quickly brought into regular order so as to line the various faces. Prominent amongst the Officers who thus distinguished themselves were Lieutenant-Colonel Nowell Fitzupton Way, C.B., Major Alston, Captains Kitching, Pyne, Woods, and Bridge the Adjutant of the Regiment. Notwithstanding the rush of Transport which had passed through it, comparatively few Arabs seem to have penetrated this redoubt, only twelve bodies being afterwards found in it. Outside the dead were much more numerous, the position having been attacked on various sides; but the men behaved with the greatest coolness, and were well in hand during the entire struggle, as was shown by the deadly fire, and the relatively small amount of ammunition expended. Out of a strength of about 460 all ranks, there were only 9 killed and 18 wounded. Amongst other incidents, it may be mentioned that at the commencement of the struggle, one of the Marines who happened to be outside the zeriba was knocked down by an Arab, who was about to kill him, when another Marine rushed out and saved his comrade by despatching the Arab with his own knife.

The Royal Marines were no doubt well seasoned to the arduous duties they were called to engage in at Tofrek. Since the previous campaign they had garrisoned Suâkin, passing 1,500 men through the ranks to maintain a strength of 500, such was the unhealthy character of the climate, especially during the intense heats of summer. Owing to the constant night attacks they had been more than 300 times under fire. In consequence of the constant guards requiring to be maintained both Officers and men were well practised in sleeping on the ground *sub cœlo*, fully armed and accoutred, and with no other protection than a greatcoat.

More fortunate than their companions in the south redoubt the Naval Detachment, under Lieutenant Alfred W. Paget, R.N., had the Gardner guns in action from the first, discharging at least 400 rounds, and doing great execution.

The left wing or half Battalion of the Berkshires, still remaining formed up on the site occupied by the Rallying Square at a distance of about 250 yards east of the zeriba, had also a severe time of it. Falling in at once and standing to their arms they made a most successful defence against the heavy attacks made upon them. It was afterwards found that 200 of the enemy had fallen before their rifle-fire, amongst the defenders there being only one slight casualty.

About three o'clock, during a momentary lull in the combat at this point, while the Arabs, trying to make up their minds for another rush, were yet clustering in large numbers on the fringe of the bush, a Mahdist standard was most gallantly captured in the immediate vicinity of the redoubt occupied by the Royal Marines. The leading facts of the incident are thus noticed in the *Daily Chronicle* of March 23rd :—

"The Marines held their own, when engaged hand-to-hand with the Arabs, and gained their formation as speedily as any. They had a few minutes of hot work. A desperate Sheikh, waving a banner, was right upon them with a horde of followers before the square was formed. But the Marines were equal to the emergency, and bayonet and bullet proved too much for the Arabs. The ground was cleared, and the Sheikh scorning to fly, died fighting with his last gasp. The banner was secured by the Marines, and was afterwards borne into the redoubt as a trophy."

The precise details of the capture were as follows:—Immediately after the repulse of the main attack one of the Royal Engineers directed the attention of Captain (now Major) Thos. F. Dunscomb Bridge, Adjutant of the Royal Marine Light Infantry Battalion, to a Sheikh about fifty yards off who, with two men lying down beside him, was waving a standard and gesticulating in the vain effort to induce his followers to advance. The Adjutant's horse having been injured or carried off in the camel-stampede, he mounted that of Colonel Ozzard, and called on some of the Marines to accompany him. Three men responded, but the cry being raised that the Arabs were again advancing, two of them fell back, the third, Private Bayley, kept to his officer, who, riding forward, with a well-aimed shot from his revolver sent the Arab rolling in the dust. He then called on Private Bayley to hand him up the standard, and, waiting until he saw the Marine safely out of harm's way, returned with it to the zeriba. The two Arabs who seemed at first to be lying down beside their chief were found to be dead. The Sheikh himself, who was a fine powerful man, was dressed in a magnificent tunic, elaborately decorated, more like the tabard of a herald than the ordinary

FIG. I.—MAHDIST FLAG, CAPTURED AT TOFREK

PLUG

FIG. III.—SNUFF BOX.

FIG. II.—CHARM BOX. WORN ON LEFT ARM

Mahdist uniform.   Unlike some of those encountered by the Nile Expedition, especially at Abu Klea, he was armed, and meant to fight, kneeling down as the Adjutant approached, but the revolver well handled prevented him from doing any mischief.   Firing was still going on at both the redoubts, and a renewal of the attack seemed to be imminent.   There was, of course, no means of ascertaining who the Sheikh was, although it is evident he must have been a man of consequence.   It was reported after the fight that Faggiah, one of Osman Digna's leading emirs, had been killed at Tofrek, and his identification with the subject of this episode would have been interesting.

In from fifteen to twenty minutes the short fierce crisis of the attack was over, and, in spite of the most reckless and fanatical daring, the enemy, thoroughly beaten, were forced to recoil at every point before the deadly hail.   It became evident to Sir John M'Neill that the weight of the attack was gradually slackening. The enemy would still form up in companies as if to encourage each other for a renewed assault, but, without effecting anything, they gradually melted away before the relentless fire.   Individual Arabs would come forward, throw up their arms above their heads, and face the rifles as if bent on suicide, and courting the death they soon received.   As nearly as can be judged, it was just eight minutes to three when the *melée* began, and the attack thus gradually dying off, it was about twelve minutes after it when, by the General's orders, the bugles rang out the "Cease firing," and the toiling but serried ranks had time to breathe.

A dreadful spectacle now presented itself.   The dead bodies of friend and foe lay thickly scattered throughout the enclosures. Everywhere were wounded and slaughtered men and animals, with all the ghastly accessories of blood eagerly absorbed by the parched and burning soil, while groans and cries filled the not less sultry and torrid air.   Strewn about the ground were arms, equipage and accoutrements of every kind, with all the usual accompaniments of a fierce and sanguinary conflict—in a form more concentrated and terrific than even the prophet of old could have ventured to conceive : a "Battle of the warrior with confused noise, and garments rolled in blood ;" ay, "with burning and fuel of fire." [1] This stretch of open ground in the dense Tofrek jungle, which for so many hours previously had been associated only with watchful attention, and patient, steady toil, now looked as if a very cyclone of human passion had swept over the scene with its devastating breath. Strange survival of a once wide-wasting warrior-creed. After the lapse of centuries in these half-barbarian tribesmen of the Sûdan, there had been revived, happily in vain, all the ferocious instincts and relentless bigotry of the early Mohammedan conquests.

Although the tremendous fusillade, which for twenty minutes had rendered the zeribas absolutely unapproachable, was now over, there was no relaxation in the attitude of watchful vigilance maintained by their defenders. The Arabs were still thronging the bush, deterred from renewing their " rushes " only by the certainty of destruction the moment they entered the " zone of fire " engirdling the British Force. At the same time, as opportunity offered or the attitude of the enemy seemed to require, a partial and desultory fire was still maintained from the more important points of the position.

Towards half-past three an exceptionally large gathering presented itself to the south-east of the zeribas. This being the quarter whence the camel-stampede had been originally effected, the Arabs may have had the notion that from this direction a renewed assault would be most likely to meet with success. The state of matters had become so threatening that Sir John M'Neill resolved to assume the offensive, and make a sortie so as to disperse if possible the sable horde. Riding up to the redoubt held by the Royal Marines he requested that a detachment might be paraded in order to go with him on this service. This was accordingly done ; a couple of Companies under Captains [2] Coffin and M'Kechnie, and commanded by Colonel Way, were formed up, and, with Sir John M'Neill, still mounted on his gray Arab, went straight for the

---

[1] Isaiah ix. 5.   [2] Now Majors.

enemy.   As they advanced the little force was soon in front of the dusky foe.   Fire was at once opened and the ground cleared, and, although the men were more than anxious to have charged into the bush with the bayonet, the demonstration having served its purpose, and the enemy showing they deemed discretion the better part of valour, the troops were withdrawn, but kept engaged in searching the battlefield.   It was admitted by all those who witnessed it, that this counter-attack of Sir John M'Neill's with the Marines, had a most important effect on the *morale* both of the British and Indian troops, and not less on the Arabs.   As throughout the entire conflict, so in this particular incident, Sir John showed the utmost coolness and judgment, leading the men on with a courage oblivious of danger, and it was only when, either informed or ascertaining he was "masking fire," that he rode clear and left the men free to use their rifles.   The enemy hung about in force for a short while afterwards, but, finding that the alert and vigilant watch kept up at every point left them not the slightest prospect of success, they finally withdrew about 4.15 P.M.

Towards four o'clock Major Frank Graves again rode into the zeriba and reported himself to Sir John M'Neill.   After having gone two miles on his return to Suâkin, he had just met his relief, a squadron of the 9th Bengal Cavalry, one hundred and fifty strong, under Lieutenant Peyton, when hearing heavy firing at the zeriba he took command of the two Squadrons and hastened back.

About a mile from the zeriba he came upon a number of camel drivers, native infantry, and a few English soldiers, together with a number of camels, mules, etc., in full retreat for Suâkin, closely pursued by the enemy, who were in much greater force, and were cutting them down and killing them in large numbers.   He at once formed his men in line, and, changing front to right, cut into the line of pursuit, and the enemy checking, he dismounted every available carbine and fired several volleys, which stopped the pursuit. The men remounted, he pressed on, and halting within three hundred yards of the enemy, fired several more volleys.

These were so well delivered that the enemy turned and retreated towards the zeriba, leaving a number of dead and wounded, together with some who had lain down to escape the bullets. Pressing on, these last jumped up, but were all killed hand to hand, to the number of about fifteen. Major Graves having gone out in front with his trumpeter, two of the Arabs who had lain down suddenly sprang up and rushed at him. Before the Major could disable him, one of them succeeded in wounding Troop Sergeant-Major Mobbs, who was riding at this assailant. He fell before the revolver, and, pinned to the ground by one of the 9th Bengal Cavalry, was promptly killed. Captain Bellasis, noticing the incident, bore down on the second Arab, who, turning, threw his spear at his assailant, when Major Graves fortunately shot him down. Captain Bellasis very narrowly escaped, the spear passing within an inch of his neck.

This skirmish over, Major Graves noticed that the enemy were trying to turn his left flank towards the sea, with the object no doubt of again falling upon the Transport, and ordered Lieutenant Peyton to take a troop of the 9th Bengal Cavalry and intercept them. This he did most effectually, bringing some twenty wounded and stragglers safe to Suâkin. When Major Graves saw that his flank was safe, and being joined by a troop of the 5th Lancers, under Lieutenant Goodair, to the number of forty, he brought up his left flank and, pursuing on, drove the enemy by dismounted fire in front of the left or sea face of the zeriba, from which they were enfiladed so effectually that they dispersed towards the sea and did not again assemble in any numbers.

He then formed a strong cordon round the Transport and baggage, and, sending out some patrols, came into the zeriba and reported his return. The casualties in the five troops under his Command were one Non-Commissioned Officer wounded and one horse killed. Of the enemy, forty or more were counted lying dead in the direct line of the Cavalry's advance and fire, in addition to those killed fighting hand to hand. Some twenty or more wounded, and others, who took refuge behind the Cavalry, got safe back to the zeriba.   Like the much larger Force which had traversed this district in the morning, Major Graves found the bush extremely close, and the ground very bad.   This rendered it impossible for the Cavalry to keep their formation and charge the enemy as they would otherwise have done, the only resource being to adopt infantry tactics, and drive them off by dismounted fire.

When there was time to look around, the first thought of those who were scatheless was for the wounded and the fallen, and one of the first duties attended to was to call for returns from the various Regiments as to the numbers of killed, wounded, and missing. While the action was still in progress the Medical Staff had set to work with great promptitude, and were busily engaged attending to the most urgent cases.   When some measure of quiet was restored, improvised Field-hospitals were at once established in the two redoubts.   Their sides were formed out of piled biscuit-boxes and cases of various kinds, and although no tents were pitched, the walls of tents were stretched out so as to form shades or awnings from the pitiless rays of the now declining sun.   To these Field-hospitals the wounded were carefully brought in, and their wants attended to as well as the resources of a battlefield would permit.

When the open ground surrounding the zeriba was sufficiently clear of the enemy to admit of its being patrolled, by Sir John M'Neill's directions Colonel Way took the two Companies of the Royal Marines already outside the zeriba to try and save the remaining camels.   Several Arabs feigning death were lying about and sprang up at once when approached.   There were still numbers of them in the bush, and others were prowling about, even in the open, watching their chance for mischief with sullen demeanour, and

> " Baleful eyes,
> That witnessed huge affliction and dismay,
> Mixed with obdurate pride and steadfast hate." [1]

But very soon these were either killed or took themselves off. With reference to this period of the day the following remarks

[1] *Paradise Lost*, I. 56-58.

M

occur in the *Times*, and, as very accurately depicting the situation, are deserving of record.

"The Arabs seem to be more like wild beasts than human beings. Even women and children fight in their ranks; and when our men sought to afford aid to some of the enemy who could not walk, the latter crawled towards them with their spears between their teeth, striving even yet to slay a Kaffir. These traits somewhat diminish the sympathy which we should otherwise feel for such brave antagonists. Were their ferocity shown in the heat of the battle it would be excusable, but these wretches hours after were animated by a fiendish desire to injure those who sought to relieve their sufferings. Even the nobler animals have some idea of gratitude, and Arabs must henceforth be regarded in the light of the most savage of the worst description of beasts of prey. The fact is they are maddened into brutality by fanaticism." [1]

As a good deal has been said about this question of self-defence against wounded Arabs, it may not be inappropriate to quote the following remarks by General Gordon, based as they are on the undeniable experience of one as distinguished for his humanity as for his generosity to a foe :—

"It must be remembered that in all these engagements in the Soudan no quarter on either side has been given, so it must not be expected that the Soudan troops will give it now if you come; also with respect to the wounded Arabs, if you go and help them they will (like the Afghans) try and kill your men who make the effort; they are very treacherous, and, worked up by religious frenzy, they think—1. That you only pretend to help them in order to kill them afterwards; 2. That, being desperate, they think to enter Paradise if they kill an infidel. It seems rather cold-blooded to write this, but such is the character of those whom you are to fight." [2]

Such, then, was the ruling passion, strong even in death, of those whom General Graham terms "the desperate fanatics of the Mahdi, whose great desire was to get killed after slaying an enemy." [3] The influence for good and for evil exercised by Mohammedanism over barbarous or semi-barbarous races like the Sûdanese, is very well exemplified in the following extract from a well-known writer :—

[1] *Times*, March 25th, 1885.   [2] *Journals*, Book V., *sub* October 25, 1884.
[3] *Journal of the Royal United Service Institution.* Vol. xxx. p. 235.

" When Islam penetrates to countries lower in the scale of humanity than were the Arabs of Muhammad's day, it suffices to elevate them to that level. But it does so at a tremendous cost. It reproduces in its new converts the characteristics of its first—their impenetrable self-esteem, their unintelligent scorn, and blind hatred of all other creeds. And thus the capacity for all further advance is destroyed; the mind is obdurately shut to the entrance of any purer light. . . . There are to be found in Muhammadan history all the elements of greatness, faith, courage, endurance, self-sacrifice; but, closed within the narrow walls of a rude theology and barbarous polity, from which the capacity to grow and the liberty to modify have been sternly cut off, they work no deliverance upon the earth. They are strong only for destruction. When that work is over they either prey upon each other or beat themselves to death against the bars of their prison-house. No permanent dwelling-place can be erected on a foundation of sand; and no durable or humanising polity upon a foundation of fatalism, despotism, polygamy, and slavery. When Muhammadan States cease to be racked by revolution they succumb to the poison diffused by a corrupt moral atmosphere. A Darwesh ejaculating ' Allah !' and revolving in a series of rapid gyrations until he drops senseless, is an exact image of the course of their history." [1]

To return, however, to the Royal Marines. Colonel Way found it extremely difficult to deal with the camels, tied together as they were in threes. Many of them though still on their legs were badly wounded, and all seemed completely stupified by the ordeal passed through. To attempt to bring them into the zeriba was found an almost impossible task, as they would not move, especially before the gentle ministering of Tommy Atkins. Generally, when thus tied up in line, if the leading camel be got in motion the others will follow, but in the present case they would not budge. They appeared to be not Egyptian, but chiefly from India or Aden, and missed their native drivers. To pull on their headropes, either on foot or horse-back, was found equally useless, and many of them strayed into the bush, which was full of them, especially on the south.

In addition to these duties the zeribas had to be cleared of their encumbrances, dead Arabs and animals, and the British and Indian fallen brought in and suitably arranged. The defences had also to be completed and strengthened, and every preparation made for the possibility of a night attack. So gradually closed for the troops this long, busy, and eventful day, its various experiences no doubt indelibly engraven for life in the memory of everyone whose fortune it was to have passed through it.

To the furious fusillade, the tumult and fierce strife of the afternoon, there had now succeeded a profound but watchful silence. Reserving twelve feet within the thorn fences for the sentries to pace their rounds, the Indian Regiments in the centre zeriba, the Berks and Royal Marines in their respective redoubts, were ranged all round the defences two deep, as if on parade—one rank to lie down and sleep, the other, with bayonets fixed, keeping two hours' watch, all fully armed and accoutred ready for the foe, if, under cover of darkness, he should attempt to renew the assault. Not a tent was pitched, not a voice heard, or light shown, nothing permitted that might in the slightest degree attract notice, or in any way draw or direct the enemy's fire. A false alarm during the earlier part of the night in an instant surrounding the works with a storm of leaden hail, showed that even in repose the entire Force was on the alert.

It was most unfortunate that, at the close of the battle, owing to the entire absence of suitable Artillery, not a shell could be sent after the retreating Arabs, either to quicken their retreat or warn them of too near approach. Within the range of the rifles and the Gardners all was safe, but beyond it the enemy had the undisturbed freedom of the bush. This rendered the night-watch all the more harassing. With dense bush closing everywhere around them, none knew how near the stealthy foe might be. The tension must have been severe, the watch constant. Formed up within the zeriba and redoubts in order of battle, the soldiers sleeping and watching by alternate ranks, after a brief glimpse of moonlight so passed the long and tedious hours, waiting for a foe that never came, but for aught that was known might do so at any moment.

The experiences of the day might indeed well induce watchful-

ness, for the Arabs had shown not only the most daring courage in
their attacks but the greatest cunning and astuteness; and the
means used both by the hale and the wounded to get within.
striking distance of the foe were most pertinacious.

Among various mischievous devices resorted to may be noted that
of an Arab armed with a rifle who, during the attack, managed to
creep close up to the mimosa fence of the south redoubt. Thus
sheltered under its cover, whenever a befitting chance occurred,
rising to the occasion, he contrived in succession to shoot first one
and then another of the Berkshires, and though fired at was missed.
His third shot was directed at Major C. B. Bogue, who was on duty
inside the redoubt, and narrowly escaped a severe if not fatal
wound, the charge carrying away his trousers' pocket and part of
his coat; and not till then was the Arab shot. Another trick
the Arabs had was to bring hides, and throwing these on the top of
the thorny bushes forming the fence, they would spring on to them,
and then leaping down into the zeriba run-*amok*[1] like the Afghan
Ghazis and other Eastern fanatics.

Various sensational accounts having appeared of the imminent
risks run by Sir John M'Neill, it may be mentioned that he never
was in any personal danger other than that common to all those
engaged in the conflict. During his preliminary efforts to rally the
Poorbeahs, General M'Neill, mounted on his gray Arab, found
himself outside the defences, with the enemy streaming on full in
front. Strange to say, he seemed to be entirely unnoticed.
Bending forward, with eyes fixed, and attention riveted as if on
some object in the distance, the swarthy foe, advancing at a trot,
held right on for the zeriba. Having no wish unnecessarily to
attract attention, with revolver in hand ready to despatch any one
who might venture too near, Sir John quietly turned his horse, and
found no difficulty in making him cross the fence.

Of the unfortunate incident also which befell Lieut. the Hon. A. D.

---

[1] Derived from the Malay *Amok*, killing; a race among whom this state of homicidal
frenzy is very prevalent, and *amok, amok, amok*, the warning cry, heralding the murderer.

Charteris, Aide-de-Camp to Sir John M'Neill, various versions have appeared; the real facts, however, seem to have been as follows :—

A short time previous to the attack, the half dozen camels detailed to carry the camp equipage of the General and Staff had been led within the Berkshire redoubt, and made to kneel down preparatory to being unloaded. Lieutenant Charteris, dismounted, was busy superintending this operation, when, owing to the partial exposure of the redoubt owing to the flight of the Poorbeahs, an old Arab accompanied by a boy, advancing to the mimosa fence, flung the boy over into the interior and then leaped in himself. Lieutenant Charteris, with the object apparently of capturing the boy alive, ran after him, when the old savage, rushing forward, with his lance inflicted a most formidable wound on the Lieutenant, driving the blade through the palm of the left hand and severing several of the arteries and tendons of the arm. At the close of the fight, Sir John M'Neill, having missed his Aide-de-Camp, sent Lord Wiltshire, extra A.D.C., to see what had become of him. His Lordship found him lying in the Berkshire redoubt, pale and covered with blood; beside him stood Subadar Goordit Singh, of the D Company of Sikhs, and a Sergeant attached to the Medical Corps was binding up his wounds.

At the moment of attack the Indian servants attached to the Staff were engaged in preparing the first meal that had taken place since breakfast at 4 A.M. At the close of the *melée* the cook was found shot dead at the post of duty, and the table riddled with several bullets. The *bheestie* or water-carrier was also amissing, and it was feared he had met with a like tragic fate. The next day, however, he reappeared with General Graham's Convoy bearing a mussock full of fresh water, when the following curious conversation took place. On seeing the man supposed to have been killed, with a suggestive smile some of his fellow-servants said to the General—

Khodawund dekho bheestie ata hye. [Lord of the Universe, behold the water-carrier is coming.]

To whom the said Lord remarked—

Haram zadah kahan se aye ho? [Worker of evil, whence have you come?]

As if nothing out of the way had occurred, the *bheestie* very composedly made his salaam, and said—

Main Suâkin Sahib se aya hoon kuhan panee ke waste gaya. [I am come from Suâkin, Sir, where I have been for water.]

Burradoor gie ho panee kewaste. [You have gone a long way for water.]

Han. Sahib burradoor. [Yes, Sir, a long way.]

In contrast to the timorous disposition of the Bombay *bheestie,* an act of bravery that may be cited, was that of a young syce from Bhurtpore, still in his teens. His particular care happened to be the pony or cob from the same place, on which the General had ridden out from Suâkin. In the wild firing which ensued on the Arabs getting mixed up with the Transport, this pony was shot through the neck, and the young syce was so enraged at the injury inflicted on his favourite charge that, picking up a native sword that had been dropped, in revenge he rushed upon two Arabs in succession and killed both of them.

In conclusion, as an illustration of the invaluable qualities of courage and steadiness, and as a set-off against the outcry made about the number of casualties which unfortunately took place in this conflict, a fact specially to be noted is the small number of such casualties occurring in the Regiments which really did their duty. This was conspicuously exemplified in the half battalion of the Berkshires, still remaining on the site of the original Rallying Square. Although, owing to the camel stampede bearing down upon it, attacked under most disadvantageous circumstances, it successfully repelled the enemy without losing a man, at the same time killing two hundred of its assailants, that number of dead Arabs being afterwards found lying opposite the position. Owing to the collapse of the 17th Bengal Infantry, and the position in which it was placed by the influx of the Arabs into the southern redoubt, the other half battalion suffered more severely; but the death of Lieutenant Swinton, the only Officer either killed or wounded, took place after the affray was over. Although extended in line, and sustaining the brunt of the attack on the western front, the 15th Sikhs, out of an effective strength of about six hundred and fifty engaged, lost only seven men, with two missing, and eleven wounded. The losses of the 28th Bombay Native Infantry were also very small, having only one man killed, and two officers and nine men wounded and six missing.

The 17th Bengal Native Infantry shows the heaviest list. Their gallant Commander, Major Beverhoudt, fell at the very beginning of the action when endeavouring to recall his men to their duty. They had also two Officers wounded, and over fifty of the rank and file killed and wounded.

Owing to their duties requiring them to be at work in the bush at the time of the attack, in proportion to their numbers the losses of the Engineer detachments, British and Indian, were also severe; but this does not affect the general question that safety lies in steady courage, in strict discipline, and the maintenance of an unbroken formation.

Nowhere does history repeat itself more significantly than in War, and facts like those just mentioned carry us back at once to the days of Tyrtæus and ancient Sparta, seven centuries B.C. The following lines, which might be adopted as a poetic description of the fight at Tofrek, only express an experience universal amongst contending forces :—

> "Of those who dare, a strong compacted band,
>   Firm for the fight their warrior-spirits link,
> And grapple with the foeman, hand to hand,
>   How few, through deadly wounds expiring, sink !
>
> "They, foremost in the ranks of battle, guard
>   The inglorious multitude that march behind ;
> While shrinking fears the coward's step retard,
>   And dies each virtue in the feeble mind.

" But 'tis not in the force of words to paint
    What varied ills attend the ignoble troop,
Who trembling on the scene of glory faint,
    Or wound the fugitives that breathless droop.

" Basely the soldier stabs, with hurried thrust,
    The unresisting wretch, that shieldless flies!
At his last gasp dishonoured in the dust
    (His back transfixed with spears) the dastard lies!" [1]

Early on the 23rd, the dead were interred in large trenches, the Berks burying to the west, and the Royal Marines to the north, of their redoubts. It was troublesome work, as the bush swarmed with Arabs, and twice before 9 A.M. the troops had to suspend operations and stand to their arms. It was an occasion when a few shells, or even rockets, would have been extremely useful, and compelled the enemy to keep at a respectful distance. When finished, the graves were marked off in native style. In the burial of their dead the Arabs, as might be expected, dig a comparatively shallow grave. When this is filled in, they set stones all round the edges, covering over the central space also, using, when it can be got, white quartz, and preferably parti-coloured stones, as more attractive. The trenches for the British dead were dug much deeper, out of the hard gravelly subsoil; but when completed, the only way of distinguishing them was, in Arab fashion, to have them set round about, and covered on the top with stones.

When Lord Wolseley inspected the battlefield on May 10th, the graves were found intact, and on the 15th a Cavalry patrol, under Major James, interred the remains of eight British and twenty-five native soldiers, who, owing probably to their having fallen in the bush, had been left unburied. Two of the 19th Hussars, who had been killed in the affray with the Arabs at Handoûb on February 5th, having also been found, were buried near the zeriba, as a last contribution to the gallant dead.

---

[1] *The War Songs of Tyrtæus*, ii. Translated by the Rev. R. Polwhele.

N

CHAPTER VI.

THE INDIAN CONTINGENT.

" From India, and the Golden Chersonese,
    And utmost Indian isle Taprobane,
    Dusk faces with white silken turbans wreathed."
                    Paradise Regained, IV. 74-76.

" Mislike me not for my complexion,
    The shadow'd livery of the burnish'd sun,
    To whom I am a neighbour, and near bred."
                    Merchant of Venice, II. 1.

E cannot close this account of the active operations of the 22nd, without making more special reference to the gallant body of troops, who, from India, joining the Expedition to the Eastern Sûdan, at once raised it to the rank of an Imperial Force.

The mere fact of their presence so far west, was of itself significant, and cannot but call to remembrance the outcry made, both in Parliament and throughout the kingdom, when, during the Russo-Turkish war in 1878, another small, but well selected Indian Contingent, was ordered to the Mediterranean.

In the light of subsequent events, it seems scarcely credible that so much dust could have been raised around a measure, merely intended to bring Russia to her senses, by supplementing Britain at her weakest point in the eyes of Europe—a restricted Army supply. No sooner was the fact announced than a perfect storm of party obloquy and opposition swept over the country. The Contingent was stigmatised as a body of " foreign troops "; the Ministry of the day—as " a false and evil Government, determined for war, and resolved to injure the liberties of the country "—the Prime Minister, Lord Beaconsfield, being characterised as " that fearful Mephistopheles " ! The movement itself was denounced in the severest terms by all the leading members of the Opposition. At a meeting of Liberal delegates, held at Manchester on the 30th of April, Mr. Bright spoke as follows :—

" Lord Derby thought this calling out of the Reserves was an important matter, followed, as it was to be, by other measures which he was not then at liberty to indicate, but with which he was acquainted. We now come to the day when Parliament separated, on the 16th—that is, a fortnight ago. I was in the House that day, and heard the leader of the House say, again in the same tone, ' There was not the least danger of anything; did not apprehend anything ; things did not really look a bit worse than they had been some time ago ;' and there was a general feeling of some sort of comfort in that sometimes disturbed, but always in matters of this kind credulous, assembly (Laughter). But what happened the very next day, the moment the door of the house was shut and the key turned in the lock ? On the very next day, I believe it was, you had that *amazing and alarming telegram from Calcutta or Bombay* that I know not how many—now a few thousands, but we are promised it may be scores of thousands—Mohamedan soldiers from Calcutta are to be brought to Europe for the purpose, I presume, of fighting, it may be, against the Christian nation of Russia (' Shame !'). But when we asked them a short time ago to lessen their military expenses in India for the purpose of enabling them, by a greater economy, to abolish the duties on your manufactures (hear), the reduction of the armaments was impossible ; but now to follow up this policy, this blind and wicked policy (hear, hear)—*that is being done, for to-day or yesterday some of the troops were to leave Bombay. That had been done—was being done—which has never been boldly or daringly contemplated by any Prime Minister in past times.*" [1]

And, at a similar meeting at Hawarden, on the 8th of May, Mr. Gladstone thus referred to the same subject :—

" The announcement was a surprise to everybody—I will not call it a deception—but undoubtedly it was a measure of a most surprising and

[1] *Times*, May 1, 1878.

astonishing description, with no sort of precedent of any kind to support or suggest it. Therefore they are coming at this peculiar time, and to a limit of which we know nothing. The whole Indian Army is entirely at the disposal of Her Majesty's Government; a body of two to three hundred thousand men, including 100,000 English troops, are entirely at the disposal of the Executive; and it is a body not organised by Parliament, but of which they assumed the power to make use." [1]

At the bare idea of Indian troops appearing in the Mediterranean, after four years' tenure of Office, Lord Derby resigned the Foreign Secretaryship, while in the heated political atmosphere of the time, this simple event, seemed purposely designed to threaten the very bases of the British Constitution and of personal freedom! In the address just quoted, the following remarks occur on this point :—

"That opens to you another question which seems to me extremely grave. Something was said to-day about the present position of English liberty. (Hear, hear.) I will go so far as to say that it is in an unexampled position, but whether it is in danger or not at this moment I will not say; but I will say that it requires a great watchfulness. This proceeding with the Indian troops is itself a proof that if you care for your liberties you must be watchful over them. . . . What has now been done I cannot tell; what is intended I cannot tell; but this I will say, that to our liberties it is time to look." [2]

While language at once so enigmatical and intemperate, was freely used by leading politicians, it is little wonder that the bugbear was paraded of 70,000 or 80,000 Indian troops being landed in London, in order to coerce the free-born British subject.[3] It required three days' acrimonious debate in the House of Commons, and a division, heavily on the side of the Government, before such phantoms could be laid, and the 7000 orderly and well-conducted men, who represented the potential might of India, to aid the mother country in her threatened struggle with the Colossus of the North, be permitted quietly to settle down in Maltese cantonments.

This extraordinary episode in the political history of the country has been recalled, because it illustrates in a striking manner the

[1] *Times,* May 9, 1878.
[2] *Ibid.*

[3] Speech in the House of Commons by Mr. Fawcett, May 6th, 1878.

distinction between the parochial and the Imperial aspects and tendencies of British statemanship. On so slender a basis did the noisy phillipics of the day rest, that only four years after these stormy discussions, precisely the same expedient was unhesitatingly adopted by a Ministry composed of the very men who had most vigorously denounced the employment of Indian troops beyond their own frontiers. It was, however, no gigantic war, no overwhelming odds, which now called into requisition the Imperial resources. It was rather military operations undertaken in a country, and at seasons most dangerous and destructive to the health of uninured European troops, as the entire course of the subsequent campaigns fully proved.

With regard to that most ridiculous of all arguments, used by Mr. Bright with reference to the "Christian nation of Russia!" the truth is that all the earlier Expeditions the Indian Forces were engaged in beyond the sea, were directed not against Pagan or Mohammedan but so-called "Christian" Powers, for, notwithstanding its temporary aberration, in this category France must be included. The most notable of them all, that of 1801, had for its object the restoration of the native Mohammedan authority in Egypt, menaced and for the time overturned by the ambitious projects of Napoleon. Then, as in 1878, the question was political and in no respect religious, the outcry raised on this score at the latter date being a mere subterfuge of unscrupulous partisanship.

Although slighted by the Opposition, these Expeditions were admirably conducted, and, in their measure, eminently successful. Owing to the wars with Hyder Ali and Tippoo Saïb, India itself had been the theatre of great events, and the Army was thoroughly efficient and well commanded. Only the state of his health prevented the Expedition of 1801 being commanded by the future Duke of Wellington, then Colonel Wellesley, in person, while in Sir David Baird it found for the time a not less renowned and able leader. The place it held in connection with the Expedition from Britain under Sir Ralph Abercrombie, has been recorded by Sir Robert

Wilson,[1] and Captain Walsh,[2] who were both present in Egypt with Sir Ralph's Force, and wrote from official sources.

As due to an Officer actually serving with the Indian Contingent, the most interesting account of its experiences is that written by a French *emigré*, M. le Comte de Noé,[3] who, at the close of last century, finding the prospect of an early return to his native land by no means encouraging, exchanged from the 81st Foot for a Lieutenantcy in the 10th or North Lincolnshire Regiment, in consequence of the War with Tippoo Saïb, then under orders for India. The capture of Seringapatam and death of Tippoo rendering their co-operation unnecessary, a concentration of British and Indian troops was ordered at Trincomalee, with a view to a descent on Batavia, war being then waged with another " Christian " Power—Holland.

The change of destination to Egypt necessarily brought the author into collision with his own countrymen, and the value of the narrative lies in the testimony borne by an unprejudiced Frenchman, loyal to the Flag under which he served, to the admirable management and condition of the Army maintained by the East India Company. On this point the author states :—

"Les troupes de la compagnie sont on ne peut pas mieux disciplinées et equipées : le matériel est aussi magnifique qu'immense. Toujours prête à entrer en campagne, son armée, composée de naturels exercés à l'Européene, rivalise avec les troupes d'Europe pour la précision des manœuvres, le courage et le sang-froid dans les mouvemens militaires ; elle est d'ailleurs fort attachée

[1] *History of the British Expedition to Egypt*, by Lieut.-Colonel Sir Robert Wilson. London, 1802, pp. 161–168, Appendix, pp. 297–299.

[2] *Journal of the late Campaign in Egypt*, by Thomas Walsh, Capt. 93rd Foot. London, 1803, pp. 187–196.

[3] Louis-Pantaleon Jude Amédée, Comte de Noé, was born in the château de *l'Isle de Noé*, Gers, Oct. 28, 1777, and emigrated with his father in 1791, returning to France on the overthrow of Napoleon. At his father's death in 1816 he succeeded to the title, became a Peer of France, Gentleman of the Chamber, and Grand Officer of the Legion of Honour. While still in the British Army he married an English lady, Miss Caroline Halliday, and by her had two sons, one of whom, Amédée Noé, by a scriptural pun on his parental patronymic, adopting the *nom de plume* of Cham, became a celebrated draughtsman and caricaturist. Our author the Comte de Noé, who was also endowed with high artistic talent, died at Paris 6th February 1858.

au gouvernement qui la paye avec exactitude, et qui va jusqu'à prendre soin, lorsqu'il fait franchir la frontière à quelque corps d'armée, des familles des soldats absens. Ces troupes sont exclusivement commandées par des officiers Européens." [1]

In the various points enumerated, the regular pay, and the attention paid to the comfort and well-being of the soldier and his family, when on active service, the writer would seem to draw a contrast between the service with which he was connected, and that under which his less-favoured fellow-countrymen were compelled to be content. These favourable opinions were only enhanced by subsequent experience with these troops amid the actual toils and dangers of the field. With reference to the journey across the desert of the Thebaid the writer remarks :—

"Ces mêmes détachmens se hasardèrent dans le désert pour découvrir des sources et creuser des puits sur la route que nous devions parcourir, et pour tâcher d'ouvrir des communications avec le Nil. Ce furent les Cipayes de Bombay qu'on employa à ce service. Ils s'en acquittèrent au mieux et déployèrent un zèle et une intelligence dignes des plus grand éloges." [2]

And in a note appended to this passage, the following statement is made :—

"En parlant de l'intelligence des soldats Cipayes, je ne puis me refuser à l'éloge de l'excellent esprit qui les anime. Les Cipayes ont un fonds d'honneur vraiment admirable, et une émulation surprenante à rivaliser de sang-froid et de bravoure avec les Européens dans toutes les occasions périlleuses : il ne leur faut que des chefs. Aussi inspirent-ils à leurs officiers une estime qui leur vaut d'en être fort bien traités, et leur condition au service est des plus douces." [3]

The march across the desert from Kosseir to Keneh, a distance of 140 miles, was led by Lord afterwards Marshal Beresford, with the 88th or Connaught Rangers, of which he was the Colonel, and a Detachment of Bengal Sepoys. To their gallant Commander Sir James M'Grigor refers in the following terms :—

[1] *Memoires relatifs a l'Expedition Anglaise,* par M. le Comte de Noé, p. 20.

[2] *Ibid.* p. 139.

[3] Note, p. 139.

"To Brigadier-General Beresford the army owes very much. It is not my business to say how much all were indebted to the man who, under circumstances the most discouraging, led the advance over the desert." [1]

Then followed the 10th Foot.

At the first station a singular discovery was made. The bodies of five or six Royal Marines were found dried up by the sun, being probably part of the troops debarked by H.M.S. "Fox," at Kosseir, and hotly received by the French, who occupied the town from 1798 to 1801. The several stations being determined by the occurrence of wells, they had probably struggled thus far in hopes of being able to reach the Nile, perishing in the attempt. During the remainder of the march the troops were much annoyed with sandstorms, but at last reached Keneh, the ancient Coptos, where, in the fertile valley of the Nile they found an abundant supply of all the necessaries of life. The purchasing value of a piastre was one sheep, 600 eggs, three dozen chickens, or a dozen of geese. A horse was procurable at from 20 to 30 piastres, a camel from 25 to 30, an ass 4; wages rated at a half piastre per month, the labourer providing for himself. As elsewhere on the Nile, the natives, at the instigation of Morad Bey, Chief of the Mamelukes, eagerly supplied the wants of those whom they regarded as their allies, and with whom the rule was compensation and not pillage.

Arrived at Keneh, the first object was to procure boats in order to effect the descent of the Nile. With this view detachments were sent up the river to Thebes, Luxor, and the Cataracts; a sufficient number, however, do not seem to have been obtainable, as it was only on marching down to Girgeh that the entire body of troops embarked on djerms, and so reached the island of Rhoda, where an encampment was formed. Here they were attacked by a malarial fever, which raised the sick-list to an alarming extent. After a short stay the journey down the Nile was continued, the British and Turkish Forces, with the French who had surrendered at Cairo, having preceded them a month previously. According to the terms

[1] *Medical Sketches of the Expedition to Egypt*, p. 3.

of General Belliard's capitulation the latter were shipped off for their native country, and Alexandria having been besieged and taken, the British Expedition left soon afterwards, the Indian Contingent remaining in garrison at Alexandria, Rosetta, and Damietta. The plague made its appearance in September, and before its cessation had carried off four per cent of the entire Force, nearly one-fourth of the total death-list being due to it only. In the succeeding spring the Contingent reascended the Nile to Cairo, crossed the desert to Suez, and without further trouble save that of quarantine, returned to India early in June.

Although, unfortunately, owing to the prevalence of adverse winds in the Red Sea,[1] and the collapse of the French resistance, the Indian Contingent was not in time to participate in any of the warlike operations in Lower Egypt, its appearance in the Thebaid had a most important effect in threatening the possible line of French retreat into the upper and more inaccessible districts of the country. Sir Robert Wilson states that on the 1st of June the British Army having moved forward to Mishlei, General Hutchinson, who had succeeded to the Command on the death of Sir Ralph Abercrombie, now saw two objects of his march secured, viz., a union with the Turkish Army under the Grand Vizier, and also with the Mamelukes, while at the same time

"Intelligence having also been received that Colonel Murray had landed at Cossir with a few hundred men, and that he entertained the momentary expectation of the remainder of the army joining, the General was relieved from the fear of Gen. Belliard's retiring into Upper Egypt, a movement which would have been most disastrous to the English, as pursuit there was almost impracticable from the sickly state of the troops."[2]

[1] As an illustration of the way in which the tedious navigation of these days affected military operations, it may be mentioned that Admiral Blanquet, with a small Force intended to dislodge the French from Suez, was nearly three months, or from the beginning of February to the latter end of April, beating up from Jeddah to that port, a distance of 800 miles, or about three days' steaming. With the care and accuracy distinguishing his work, the Comte de Noé gives a map showing the track of the Expedition in the Red Sea up to Kosseir, and it is an extraordinary example of a *voyage en zigzag.*

[2] *History of the British Expedition to*

O

These facts were fully recognised by Major-General the Earl of Cavan, who, in his report to the Marquis of Wellesley, rendered at the close of the Expedition, states :—

"Their excellent discipline and obedience, and their patience under great fatigue and hardship, have been equalled by their highly exemplary conduct in the correct and regular discharge of every duty of soldiers; and though they may lament that circumstances rendered it impossible for them to have taken part in the brilliant actions of their country during the last campaign, it must be a satisfaction for them to know that their services in Egypt have been as important and as essential to their country as those of their brother soldiers that gained such distinguished victories in it." [1]

This Expedition also gave occasion for a most interesting and instructive Report being drawn up and published [2] on the medical aspects of the Campaign, by the late Sir James M'Grigor, Bart., K.C.B., for thirty-five years Director-General of the Army Medical Department. Like M. le Comte de Noé, Sir James went out to India, at the close of 1798, with the 88th or Connaught Rangers, of which Regiment he was Surgeon. The 88th forming part of the Expedition to Egypt, by recommendation of the Bombay Medical Board he was appointed Head of the Medical Staff, and through many trying circumstances, due chiefly to the endemic diseases of Egypt, discharged the duties of this position with unwearying zeal and efficiency. This Report, which in its published form he modestly calls his "first and last work," [3] was drawn up by request of the Court of Directors, of whom he states :—

"The India government has ever been peculiarly anxious about everything that related to the health of their troops, zealous in collecting any fact and circumstance touching the causes of diseases or the means of obviating them, and most liberal in everything that regarded the health of the sick soldier." [4]

Egypt, by Lieut.-Colonel Sir Robt. Thos. Wilson. London, 1802. P. 122.

[1] *The Military History of the Duke of Wellington in India.* London, 1852. P. 70.

[2] *Medical Sketches of the Expedition to Egypt from India.* By James M'Grigor, A.M. London, 1804.

[3] *The Autobiography and Services of Sir James M'Grigor, Bart.* London, 1861, p. 154.

[4] *Medical Sketches*, p. 2. *Vide* also pp. 89-91.

While its *cure* lies with the Medical Officer, viewing the *prevention* of disease as usually the province and mostly within the power of the Military Officer, he further states :—

"In no army, perhaps, was the health of every soldier in it more the care of every officer, from the general downwards, than in the Indian army."[1]

And of Sir David Baird it is remarked :

"His extreme attention to everything which regarded the health and comfort of the soldier, I must mention, was a principal cause of the degree of health enjoyed by the army."[2]

The change of destination from Batavia or the Isle of France to Egypt, was hailed with delight by the army.

"Our destination was changed from Batavia to the Red Sea; and now all was joy—for fighting and promotion were considered the certain result of an expedition to that quarter."[3]

Of the march from Kosseir to Keneh, Sir James M'Grigor gives an interesting account. The route was almost identical with that traversed in 1769 by Bruce the celebrated traveller. The marches were always performed at night, and with comparatively inconsiderable loss the troops reached the Nile in a very healthy state. Of this earliest attempt in modern history to carry an Army across from the Red Sea Littoral to the Nile Valley, Sir James remarks :—

"The route which we took from India to Egypt is remarkable for having been that by which, in the earliest ages, the commerce of Asia—its spices, its gums, its perfumes, and all the luxuries of the East—was conveyed to Tyre, Sidon, Carthage, Rome, Marseilles, and, in a word, to all the coasts of the Mediterranean, from Egypt, a country rendered extremely interesting by various recollections. The situation of the army from India has accordingly excited no common share of interest. It penetrated Egypt by a route over the desert of Thebes, a route unattempted by any army for perhaps two or three thousand years."[4]

[1] *Medical Sketches*, p. 3. *Vide* also p. 94.

[2] *Ibid.*

[3] *The Autobiography and Services of Sir James M'Grigor, Bart.*, p. 105.

[4] *Medical Sketches*, p. 4.

Notwithstanding the *désagréments* of sandstorms, scarcity and bad quality of water, and the scorching midsummer sun, that the march was not devoid of amenities is clear from the following statement :—

"Much had been said by our brethren of the King's army from England, whom we here met,[1] of the luxury in which the Indian army had traversed the desert; and not without reason. They jeered us much, and called us the army of Darius; for besides many articles of apparel, and other things, which were unknown in the English army, several officers carried with them a stock of wine, such as hock, claret, etc., besides various luxuries for the table."[2]

Making every allowance for the statement made by Sir James M'Grigor that "The fatigue on the march has perhaps never been exceeded in any army,"[3] the troops under Sir David Baird must indeed have been well off compared with the small detachment of 200 men of the 86th under Colonel Lloyd, whose march from Suez to El Khanah, a distance of 50, prolonged by a detour to 70 miles, on the 7th-9th of June, with a temperature rising to 140°, and the *Khamsin* blowing, was specially notable for the sufferings endured.

According to the narrative of Captain Walsh :—

"The intense heat, the intolerable reflection of the sun from the burning sands, the excessive thirst and the general want of water, most of the men having imprudently expended their small store, rendered this march more painful and distressing than can well be conceived. To ease the camels the officers cut off the baggage from their backs, and the wearied soldiers threw away their knapsacks and other encumbrances about their persons."[4]

Of those aspects of the campaign more immediately concerning a Medical Superintendent, Sir James states :—

"During an uncommonly long voyage, in a march over extensive deserts, and in a country and climate described as the most inimical to the human race, the Indian army enjoyed a considerable degree of health, and suffered but a small mortality."[5]

According to a carefully-compiled statistical table, from a

---

[1] Rosetta.

[2] *The Autobiography and Services of Sir James M'Grigor, Bart.*, p. 114.

[3] *Medical Sketches*, p. 10.

[4] *Journal of the late Campaign in Egypt*, p. 172. [5] *Medical Sketches*, p. 2.

medical point of view the native portion of the Contingent had the worst of it. The effective strength was in all 3,759 Europeans and 4,127 Indians; the total European deaths being 309, and the Indian 700. Of these, the most fatal complaint—dysentery, claimed 148 Europeans, against 195 Indians; and the plague 38 against 165. In sunstroke the cases were equal, two and two. The winter at Alexandria told with considerable severity on the children of the tropics, and brought on rheumatic and bronchial complaints, as stated by Sir James M'Grigor in his *Medical Sketches :—*

"At this period the weather in Egypt became so immoderately cold as not only to destroy the comfort of the native troops in the army, but seriously to endanger their lives. General Baird found it necessary to equip them with bedding and warm clothing, even to greatcoats, and to increase their provisions."

The northerly winds rendering a winter's residence in Egypt so agreeable to the European, presented a very different aspect to the natives of India, by whom these and other privations of the campaign seem, however, to have been cheerfully borne.

Although the entire currency of the present century has elapsed since the date of this Expedition, it still holds an honoured place in military annals. In its commencement it was associated with one who, then a simple Colonel, resigning its Command with regret, in a series of victories from Assaye to Waterloo, was destined in the brief space of fifteen years to rise to the highest pinnacle of military renown. While ill-health was the ostensible reason for Colonel Wellesley's supersession, it is evident that the post itself was the object of keen but in so far friendly rivalry between himself and Sir David Baird. At this distance of time it is curious to learn, from a letter written at the time to his brother Henry, how the great Captain of his day felt on the matter :—

23rd March 1801.

" This supersession has ruined all my prospects, founded upon any services that I may have rendered. . . . It must have been occasioned either by my own misconduct, or by an alteration of the sentiments of the Governor-General. I have not been guilty of robbery or murder, and he has certainly changed his mind; but the world, which is always good-natured towards those whose affairs do not exactly prosper, will not, or rather does not, fail to suspect both or worse, have been the occasion of my being banished, like General Kray, to my estate in Hungary." [1]

Another glimpse behind the scenes is given in a letter of date 11th April, 1800, written to Colonel Champagne, his *interim* successor in the Command :—

"I am entirely ignorant of the circumstances which have caused my removal from the command of the troops ; but I conclude that the Governor-General found that he could not resist the claims that General Baird had to be employed. I believe you know that I always thought that General Baird had not been well used, when I was called to the command. But I do not think it was proper that I should be disappointed more than he was, in order that he might not have reason to complain. However, this is a matter of little consequence to anybody but myself, therefore I say no more on the subject." [2]

In a letter written three days previously, regarding his own work in the earlier and preparatory stages of preparation, he states :—

"I have been a slave to it till this moment, notwithstanding I was sick ; and now they have only to take care of what they have got until the operations on shore commence." [3]

Colonel Wellesley was in so far identified with the future conduct of the Expedition that he drew up a memorandum, dated April 9th, 1801, on the Red Sea operations, addressed to Major-General Baird,[4] in which the desert route by Kosseir and Keneh was sketched out by the future " Iron Duke." Those of Wellington and Sir David Baird, were not the only historic names connected with the Contingent. Lieutenant-General William Carr, Lord Beresford, to be afterwards so well known in connection with the Peninsular War, in addition to being Colonel of the 88th, commanded one of the Brigades, and, as we have seen, led the advance across the desert

[1] *Wellington Despatches*, vol. i. p. 306.
[2] *Ibid.* p. 321.
[3] *Ibid.* p. 312.
[4] *Ibid.* pp. 314-19.

from Kosseir to Keneh, and was also Commandant of Alexandria, and remained until the evacuation of Egypt.

The Quartermaster-General was Lieutenant-General Sir John Murray, Bart., who highly distinguished himself in the wars with Scindiah and Holkar. He also commanded the King's German Legion under Sir John Moore, and during the Peninsular War.

The Adjutant-General was Lieutenant-General Sir Samuel Auchmuty, K.B., who in 1811 commanded the Expedition against Java, and captured Batavia. These, and other names associated with the Force sent out from India, with that despatched from the British shores, thus form a roll of honour of which any nation might well be proud.

Such was the first precedent for the utilisation of Indian troops beyond their own frontiers, and, so far as circumstances permitted, it proved in every way successful. If there was, happily, less fighting than might have been anticipated, it was due entirely to the French, who were heartily sick of the country, and gladly seized the opportunity of returning to their native land. It would have been well in many respects had the political results of the British intervention been more important. A long train of interminable complications might have been summarily nipped in the bud, and the question of supremacy in Egypt permanently settled. How fortunate such a solution would have been for that country itself was fully recognised at the time, as the following remarks of Sir Robert Wilson's clearly indicate :—

"England, when she undertook the expedition against Egypt, disclaimed the intention of appropriating the conquest to her possessions, but happier would have been that country, and more advantageous might the arrangement have been made for Turkey, if Egypt had been constituted as an Indian colony. Egypt is necessary to England for security, not as an acquisition of wealth or aggrandizement." [1]

The opportunity was, however, allowed to slip, while the Turk and the Mameluke resumed their sway, until, with the destruction

[1] *History of the British Expedition to Egypt*, p. 241.

of the latter body, and the vigorous and ambitious rule of Mehemet Ali, the modern history of Egypt may be said to have commenced. At the same time, it must be admitted that the movement we have so briefly sketched, instead of being scouted in 1878 as a forgotten episode in the history of the country, might well have been considered as forming a most honourable precedent for any future Expedition.

That the Egyptian Expedition of 1801 was associated with such a galaxy of military renown was due to the great wars then in progress both in Europe and in India. At the Battle of Aboukir Sir Ralph Abercrombie closed his honourable career, while Wellington was just on the threshold of that half century of public life, during which he filled a foremost place in Europe, and stood acknowledged as the greatest Captain of his age. Sir David Baird received his appointment as the meed of twenty years arduous service—from the disastrous field of Perambankum and imprisonment in the dungeons of Hyder Ali, to the capture of Seringapatam, and the death of Tippoo Saïb; while Lord Beresford and Generals Moore and Murray were to leave names indelibly associated with the Peninsular War. If not so exceptionally brilliant, succeeding expeditions from the shores of India show a record of varied and useful service,—the capture of the Mauritius, known formerly as the Isle of France, the descent on Batavia, the Burmese, Chinese, and Persian Wars, all bore witness to the gallantry and devotion of Indian troops.

On the outbreak of the Maori War in New Zealand in 1863, Sir George Grey, then Governor of that colony, was extremely anxious that Sikh troops should be sent from India, and communicated with the Home Government to that effect. Lord Palmerston, who was then Prime Minister, fully supported the request, but a debate arising in the House of Commons, and Mr. W. E. Forster strongly objecting to the proposal, it was ultimately abandoned.

The Expedition rendered necessary by the outbreak of the Abyssinian War in 1867-68 was not only organised in, and conducted from, India as a Base, but was largely composed of native troops, and commanded by one of the most distinguished Generals the Indian Army has produced. The admirable series of narratives, official and private, in which the history of this most interesting war is embodied, bear ample testimony to the high qualities and efficiency of the Indian Service in all its departments. The initial blunders characterising the Transport arrangements, and proving a source both of disaster and delay, illustrate this still further. From the first Sir Robert Napier had advocated the Transport being placed under the control of the Quarter-Master-General, and so subjected to military organisation and discipline. The Bombay Government thought otherwise, and the results were most deplorable. Recruited chiefly from the Mediterranean seaports and commercial towns of the East, as Captain Hozier tells us, the enlistments for the Transport Service "were the sweepings of the Eastern world, and yet over them the Government declined to place any effective supervision." [1] The complete disorganisation which followed compelled a return to the original proposal, and, after the loss of three months, under the personal superintendence of Sir Robert Napier, the Transport was completely reorganised. The Levantine and Egyptian muleteers and drivers were almost entirely replaced by natives of India, with the most satisfactory results. In the Official *Record of the Expedition,* compiled by orders of the Secretary of State for War, their services are thus mentioned in the most complimentary terms :—

" Several levies of Punjab muleteers and many camelmen were afterwards engaged and sent to Abyssinia, under the command of selected officers, for duty in the Transport Train generally, and to replace the Egyptian and Turkish drivers.

The good and cheerful services of the Punjabees employed as muleteers during the expedition, the readiness with which they took service, their desire to be regarded as a military body, the facility with which they learned their work, and acquired a military organisation, were in marked contrast with the

[1] *British Expedition to Abyssinia,* p. 68.

P

qualities of the men who engaged themselves as muleteers in Egypt, Syria, Turkey, Arabia, Persia, and other countries not under British rule. . . . The natural aptitude of these men for a military life, their perfect obedience and desire to please, made their organisation and discipline a comparatively easy task. . . . The good conduct of the men was attributable to their natural dispositions, and to the influence which the Native Officers exercised over them for their good. The Jemadars were an excellent body of men."[1]

Captain Hozier also renders his meed of praise to the efficiency of the new arrangements :—

"A considerable proportion of the new muleteers were Punjabees who had acquired experience in the mule trains of Lahore and Rawul Pindee, and were disciplined and armed, while for the others native arms were bought, which placed them on equality at least with the Abyssinians. It was derived from the experience of this campaign that it is of great importance that the drivers of a land Transport Train should be sufficiently under discipline and control to be trusted with arms, as they are then enabled to dispense to a great extent with escorts, especially when the animals are sent out to graze, and the side-arms are also available for cutting grass."[2]

Rightly to estimate the importance of the change, it must be remembered that in carrying an Army into a hostile, inaccessible, and mountainous country like Abyssinia, a properly-conducted Transport Train was of the most paramount importance, as upon it depended not only the success but even the safety of the Expedition. The native troops were drawn from the Bengal and Bombay Presidencies, and to these were added a Belochee Regiment of picked men. The Bengal Sappers and Miners were highly useful in the formation of roads and other operations necessary to render the mountain gorges traversible by an Army. There was no fighting until Magdala was reached, and the operations resulting in the capture of that formidable stronghold are noteworthy, as being the first in which breechloading rifles were used by a British Force.

With a series of precedents like those enumerated, extending over a period of seventy years, it might naturally be supposed that

[1] *Record of the Expedition to Abyssinia,* vol. ii. p. 228.

[2] *The British Expedition to Abyssinia,* by Captain H. M. Hozier, p. 159.

no imaginable basis existed for an outcry like that raised in 1878. If the pleas then urged deserved to be held in any degree valid, the Christianity of Abyssinia was not, surely, so far behind that of Russia, as to entitle the Pagan and the Mohammedan, on hostile errand bent, to desecrate its soil without protest.   Was not the war also directly due to the arrogant line of action adopted by Earl Russell towards King Theodore?   Poor Theodore, the "Christian" Monarch, insulted beyond endurance by an equally "Christian" Premier, and then, driven to bay by Belochee and Bengali, perishing at last by his own hand; yet, all the while, without one reclaiming word, silence broods over the benches of the Opposition!   Even Mahomet held the Abyssinians in special favour, as Consul Zohrab, when writing in 1883 on the Mahdi's mission, informs Earl Granville :—

"It is on record that the curse of Mohamet would fall on all Mussulmans who attacked the Abyssinians, and that then the political power of the Mahommedans would decline and fall.

"The Abyssinians were attacked by Mehemet Ali, and from his time the power and prestige of the Sultans has rapidly declined; this has not passed unnoticed or unfelt, and the revival of religious enthusiasm or fanaticism in the East is, I think, a certain indication that the fear of extinction is awakened."[1]

Happily, in 1878, the demonstration effected by the Expedition from India, like that of the Fleet in the Dardanelles, proved sufficient.   Showing that Britain was thoroughly in earnest, and had her resources well in hand, all clamour notwithstanding, it constituted a powerful factor in the settlement of political affairs in Europe.

Four years elapsed, and with the Opposition again in power, in the teeth of all previous arguments and resolutions, precisely the same measures were adopted—the imported troops stopping short at Ismailia, instead of proceeding to Malta; and so, for the combined Imperial Forces opened the recent Egyptian Campaigns.   For a very brief account of the Indian Contingent despatched to Suâkin in 1885 the best introduction will be the following Memorandum, kindly drawn up by Major-General Sir John Hudson, K.C.B.—

[1] *Parliamentary Papers*, Egypt, No. 5 (1884), p. 11.

MEMORANDUM

RELATIVE TO THE

INDIAN CONTINGENT AT SUAKIN

BY

MAJOR-GENERAL SIR JOHN HUDSON, K.C.B.

On the 14th February 1885, the following Government of India General Order was issued by the Military Department in Calcutta, for the despatch of an Indian Contingent for service at Suâkin :—

GENERAL ORDER.

MILITARY DEPARTMENT.

Fort William, the 14th February, 1885.[1]

FIELD OPERATIONS.

No. 88.—Under instructions from Her Majesty's Government, the Right Hon'ble the Governor General in Council has been pleased to direct that a force, as detailed below, be despatched for service at Suakim :—

Strength of the Force.

1 Regiment Native Cavalry.
3 Regiments Native Infantry.
1 Company Sappers and Miners.

Detailed as follows.

9th Bengal Cavalry.
15th Bengal Infantry (Loodhiana Sikhs).
17th Bengal Infantry (Loyal Poorbeahs).
28th Bombay Infantry.
1 Company Madras Sappers and Miners.

[1] Also published in the Gazette of India of the 21st February 1885.

The appointments herein made will have effect from the dates on which the officers named may enter upon the duties thereof :—

Colonel J. Hudson, C.B., Bengal Staff Corps . . . . Commanding.

Captain C. W. Muir, Bengal Staff Corps Aide-de-Camp.

Major R. McG. Stewart, Royal Artillery . . . . Assistant Adjutant - General and Quartermaster-General.

Major N. R. Stewart, Bengal Staff Corps . . . . Deputy Assistant Adjutant and Quartermaster-General.

Major A. J. Pearson, Royal Artillery Deputy Assistant - Adjutant and Quartermaster - General (for Intelligence).

Major J. Cook, Bengal Staff Corps . Brigade-Major.

Medical Department.

Brigade-Surgeon J. H. Thornton, M.B., Bengal Medical Service,—Principal Medical Officer.

Brigade-Surgeon J. C. Morice, Bengal Medical Service.

Surgeon G. A. Emerson, Bengal Medical Service.

Surgeon J. F. MacLaren, M.B., Bengal Medical Service.

Surgeon W. A. Sykes, Bengal Medical Service.

Surgeon W. G. P. Alpin, Bengal Medical Service.

Military Accounts Department.

Lieutenant H. F. S. Ramsden, Madras Staff Corps . Field Paymaster.

Commissariat Department.

Lieutenant - Colonel E. S. Walcott, Bombay General List, Infantry Senior Commissariat Officer.

Captain H. C. E. Lucas, Bombay Staff Corps . . . . Sub Assistant Commissary-General.

Captain G. B. E. Radcliffe, Bombay Staff Corps . . . Sub Assistant Commissary-General.

[*Transport Department.*

Major G. R. Shakespear, 12th B.C. . Assistant Commissary - General for Transport.]

Provost Establishment.

Captain H. R. L. Holmes, Bengal Staff Corps . . Provost Marshal,

The following regulations are laid down for the guidance of all concerned :—

1. Native regiments will go as far as possible on their full established strength of 550 of all ranks for cavalry, and 832 for infantry, *minus* the depot establishment.

2. Commanding officers will be held responsible that none but officers, men, and followers in every way fit for field service accompany the regiment. After eliminating sickly men they will complete with volunteers from other regiments. Regiments giving volunteers will recruit to complete establishment.

3. Each Native regiment will be completed to its full establishment of eight British officers, including those who may be recalled from furlough, and who may be expected to join.

4. Followers, servants, baggage, camp equipage, and kit for staff and departmental officers will be according to the Kabul scale, but without grass-cutters, except as hereinafter laid down for the cavalry. Regiments will be completed with full establishments in their respective presidencies. Each regiment to take field mule transport. Entrenching tools to be taken according to Kabul scale.

5. Depots for regiments will be formed under the orders of the Commander-in-Chief in India and of the Governments of Madras and Bombay, in accordance with G. O. No. 39 of 1884.

6. Mule *puckals*[1] will be supplied as follows :—

    8 per company, with 10 spare *mussucks*.[2]

    Chaguls[3]—1 per man for cavalry, to be supplied by the Commissariat Department.

7. Native Infantry will draw extra batta; and free rations will be allowed to all ranks of cavalry and infantry while on foreign service.

Troops not provided by the State with carriage will draw extra batta from date of marching. Non-batta drawing regiments will draw extra batta from date of embarkation.

8. Each Native commissioned officer of the cavalry will be required to keep up one pony and one attendant as syce and grass-cutter, whether he takes one or two horses; and the non-com-

[1] These are large skins for the carriage of water on mules.
[2] Small goat skins for carrying water.
[3] Still smaller skins in which water is carried under the horse's belly by Native Cavalry.

missioned officers and privates to maintain one pony and one grass-cutter for every two horses.

9. Compensation at the rate of R5 per mensem will be allowed to the Native officers for each bargheer[1] sanctioned by existing regulations, if maintained by them, out of which sum they will pay the share of the grass-cutter's wages and provide the stable gear. A similar amount will be deducted from the pay of the bargheer sowars.

10. As during a sea voyage the officers, non-commissioned officers, and sowars of the cavalry would be unable to make the requisite provision for the forage of their horses, whilst difficulty might be experienced in this respect during a portion of their service on land, the forage of the horses and of the mules or ponies accompanying will be undertaken by the Commissariat, with such assistance as the regiments and followers may be enabled to render after landing.

11. All ranks will be required, as at present, to maintain one efficient horse; but the Native commissioned officers will be allowed forage for two horses each, if they desire to take a second charger.

12. The grass-cutters will be paid by the troops as usual; but the ponies will receive grain, and, when necessary, hay, free of cost. Both grass-cutters and animals will be employed to procure forage when obtainable, and must be held disposable for all purposes.

13. The Native commissioned and non-commissioned officers of cavalry will continue to subscribe to the regimental funds to such extent as commanding officers may deem necessary within the limits prescribed by regulations.

14. They will continue to supply themselves with the ordinary clothing, equipment, saddlery, and stable gear for their horses, but articles of extra clothing which may be necessitated by any speciality of climate or service will be issued free of cost.

15. All casualties of horses or ponies arising from neglect or from causes evidently unconnected with the particular nature of the service must, as usual, be replaced by the regiments concerned. Each troop will be allowed to embark and maintain two chunda horses,[2] to meet casualties, which will be rationed free of cost.

---

[1] A trooper whose horse is supplied by the State, instead of being his own property.

[2] Horses provided from the Regimental subscription fund, as distinct from those purchased privately.

16. All casualties among horses or ponies fairly attributable to, or connected with, the service, including those from accident on boardship or during embarkation or disembarkation, will, if there has been no proved neglect, be replaced by Government, or compensation will be allowed under the rules in Army Regulations for India, Volume II.

17. During the continuance of the arrangement under which the supply of grain and forage to the cavalry is undertaken by the State, the pay of the several grades will be as follows :—

Bengal Cavalry.

		Rates of pay.		
		R	a.	p.
1 Ressalder, 1st[1] class	. . . . .	300	0	0
1 „ 2nd „	. . . .	250	0	0
1 „ 3rd „	. . . .	200	0	0
1 Ressaidar,[2] 1st „	. . . .	150	0	0
1 „ 2nd „	. . . .	135	0	0
1 „ 3rd „	. . . .	120	0	0
1 Woordie Major[3]	. . . .	150	0	0
2 Jemadars,[4] 1st class	. . . .	80	0	0
2 „ 2nd „	. . . .	70	0	0
2 „ 3rd „	. . . .	60	0	0
Duffadars[5]	. . . .	30	0	0
Trumpeters	. . . .	25	0	0
Sowars[6] .	. . . .	20	0	0

18. Public followers, except those engaged on salaries specifically laid down for the occasion, will receive an addition of 50 per cent on pay and batta,[7] in addition to free rations, while on foreign service.

19. The sanctioned followers paid by the troops will receive from Government free rations and such extra pay as may be necessary to put them on a par with the public followers of a similar class.

20. The scale of rations for Native troops on shore will be that laid down in Article 533, Army Regulations, India, Volume V.,

---

[1] *Risáldár*, from *risálah*, a troop of horse, and *dar* a holder, the Native Officer commanding a troop of Cavalry.

[2] The next in rank to a Ressalder.

[3] Native Adjutant.

[4] Troop Subalterns.

[5] Native Sergeants.

[6] Ordinary Troopers.

[7] Allowance for provisions when on active service.

extracted in the margin.[1] An allowance of 1 lb. of meat per man weekly is also authorised.

The scale of rations for followers will be as follows :—

Wheat flour, or rice	1½ lbs.
Dhal	4 oz.
Ghee	1 „
Salt	⅔ „

21. On land the forage allowance for each horse will be 8 lbs. of such grain as may be procurable, with 14 lbs. of hay when green forage is not procurable, or otherwise as may be ordered. The allowance for ponies will be one-half of the forage ration of a horse.

22. British officers will be allowed to draw rations for themselves, servants, and horses from the Commissariat Department, payment being made as laid down in Article 1677, Army Regulations, India, Volume V.—

Officers—

	R.	a.	p.
Rations for themselves, daily, exclusive of rum or extra supplies .	0	8	0
Rations for their servants, monthly	2	8	0
Rations for each horse, daily	0	8	0

23. Transport will be charged for at the rates laid down for the Afghan war, namely, 8 annas and 7 annas per diem for camels and mules, respectively.

[1] Atta, 2 lbs., or rice	1½ lbs.
Dhal	4 oz.
Ghee	2 „
Salt	⅔ „
Onions	1 „
Pepper	⅙ „
Chillies	⅙ „
Turmeric	⅙ „

When meat, even on special occasions, is issued, the ration of atta or rice is to be reduced one-half.

No claim for pecuniary compensation can be admitted, if through accident any part of the above authorised scale of rations is not forthcoming.

The issue of tea and sugar should be confined to the cases of sick and wounded for whom medical officers may authorise it, and for the rest of the troops on special occasions of fatigue, exposure, or bad climate, when recommended by the principal medical officer. On such occasions 2 oz. of sugar and ½ oz. of tea per man may be issued.

Tobacco can only be issued on payment at the rate of 1 oz. per man per diem, the price charged being the first cost to Government, without any addition on account of carriage or losses.

Q

24. The officer of the Military Account Department with the force will act as Field Paymaster, and have charge of the treasure chest.

25. Pay lists of Native troops will be forwarded, as soon after the first of each month as may be possible, through the Field Paymaster, to the Pay Examiner of the presidency to which the troops belong. Officers commanding regiments will draw monthly from the field pay office such sums as may be required for the pay of themselves and their men, after making provision to meet family allotments and remittances, fund subscriptions, etc., the amount of which allotments, etc., they will debit themselves with in their general states.

26. The pay bills of all staff and departmental officers will be adjusted by the Field Paymaster.

27. All payments to Native troops will be made in the coinage of the country or British money, their pay and allowances being converted into that coinage, under the orders of the General Commanding, at the rates of exchange current in Egypt.

28. Officers commanding Native regiments and detachments detailed for service are directed to at once draw and distribute three months' pay in advance to their respective corps.

29. Staff and departmental establishments may receive similar advances, not including command, contract, office and staff allowances.

30. The family remittances of Native troops will be arranged for, as usual, by officers commanding regiments. Officers and non-commissioned officers, requiring remittances to India, may remit the whole or any part of their pay to India at par on paying the amount to the Field Paymaster, who is authorised to grant transfer remittance receipts on any treasury in India. As an alternative arrangement, officers may leave with the Presidency Paymaster, Bombay, an allotment roll stating the amount they wish to be paid monthly, and the person to whom it should be remitted. That officer will then make the necessary remittance monthly and he will furnish the Field Paymaster with a list of the sums thus allotted, to enable the latter to make the necessary deduction from officers' pay bills. Remittances to England for the benefit of their families may be made through the Field Paymaster at the official rate of exchange, to the extent of one-half of an officer's clear receipts, exclusive of office and contingent allowances.

31. Officers of the expeditionary force should recover from the pay of followers serving under them the amount that each man may desire to be paid to his family in India, and send to the Controller of Military Accounts, Accounts Branch, Bombay, in time to reach him not later than the 20th of each month, a statement * of such

* Form attached.

recoveries, according to which the families will be paid under instructions to be issued by that officer. The amount thus recovered should be paid to the Field Paymaster, whose receipt should be entered on, or attached to, the statement.

32. Every care should be taken to fill in the statements correctly from the tickets given to the men on engagement and the records in the field. Where the information is not available, owing to the loss of the tickets or any other cause, immediate application should be made to the depot commanding or departmental officers concerned.

33. Clothing and equipment on the following scales will be issued to troops and followers :—

Native Troops.

Waterproof sheet	1
Jerseys	2
Shoes (Native), pair	1
Putties [1]	1
Blanket (country)	1
Canvas frock, for boardship	1
Flannel belts	2

Followers.

Waterproof sheet	1
Banians or jerseys	2
Shoes (Native), pair	1
Blanket	1
Lascar or follower's coat	1
Flannel belt	1
Pyjamahs (cotton)	2
Tin canteen	1
Haversack	1

Waterproof sheets for troops and followers to be held in Com-

[1] Gaiters made from a strip of cloth rolled up the leg from the ankle to the calf.

missariat charge and to be issued under the orders of the Gen
Officer Commanding as required.

34. In addition to the above, the regulated service kit for
troops will be maintained complete. Regiments are to take tl
colours, and officers and men the whole of their uniform exc
full-dress uniform.

35. Ten per cent of field service clothing for the whole f(
will be held in store by the Commissariat and issued as required.

36. Tulwars[1] will be provided for 50 per cent of followers
issue should the General Officer Commanding deem fit.

37. The following amount of ammunition will be taken :—

> 500 rounds per rifle, 200 in regimental charge ; and
> rounds per carbine, of which 100 will be in regime)
> charge.

38. All the arrangements special to this service will have ef
from the date of embarkation, and continue in force until the (
of return.

39. The embarkation and all subsidiary arrangements will t
place under the orders of the Commander-in-Chief in India.

Statements of Recoveries on account of Family Payments of Followers, etc.,
Field Service during the Month of   188 .

FOLLOWERS, ETC.				FAMILY CERTIFICATES.				
1 Designation.	2 Name.	3 Where enlisted.	4 Corps or Depart-ment to which attached.	No. of ticket.	To whom payable, and relationship to followers.	Amount recovered.	Period for which re-covered.	By whom and where payment is to be made.

[1] *Talwár,* from Sanscrit *tarwári,* a sword.

APPOINTMENTS.

No. 89.—BRIGADE—

With reference to G. G. O. No. 88 of this date, Colonel J. Hudson, C.B., Bengal Staff Corps, Commandant, 28th Bengal Infantry, will have the temporary rank of Brigadier-General, 2nd class, while employed in the command of the troops proceeding to Suakim.

G. CHESNEY,

Secretary to the Government of India.

The Company of Sappers detailed for this duty was the F Company of the Queen's Own Madras Sappers and Miners. It was at the time stationed at Bangalore, the Head-Quarters of the Corps of Sappers and Miners. It was commanded by Captain C. B. Wilkieson, Royal Engineers, and to it were attached Captain Romilly and Lieut. Newman of the Royal Engineers.

The Corps of Madras Sappers has been employed in almost all the wars and expeditions in which the Indian Army has been engaged during the last fifty years, and has done excellent service on all occasions. As Military Artificers the Madras Sappers are active, intelligent, and handy men, though their physique may perhaps not be quite equal to that of the Bengal Corps.

The 9th Bengal Cavalry, selected for service at Suâkin, had been formerly one of the Regiments of Hodson's Horse, and had done good service in the Mutiny Campaign of 1857-58. For the service on which it was now to be employed it was decided to arm the Regiment with lances, in addition to the carbines with which it was already armed. The Regiment was under the Command of Colonel A. P. Palmer, an Officer who had seen much active service as a Staff and Regimental Officer; a man possessing most of the qualifications hoped for in a leader of Cavalry—dash, enterprise, and a fine physique.

The Regiment was mostly composed of men from the Punjaub and Northern India—Sikhs, Dogras, Pathans, and Punjabi Mohammedans. The Order for service reached the Regiment on its march from Peshawur to Umballa.

The 15th Bengal Infantry, or Loodiana Regiment of Sikhs, recruited from the Loodiana and other adjacent districts in the Punjaub. In order to raise the Corps to its service strength it received some sixty volunteers from the 45th or Rattray's Sikhs, and the Battalion thus completed presented a magnificent appearance; and when it embarked at Bombay on the 22nd February excited the admiration of His Excellency General Sir Arthur Hardinge, Commander-in-Chief of the Bombay Army, and all who witnessed its departure. In size, appearance, and soldierly bearing, the men of this Battalion would have compared favourably with any Regiment in any Army in Europe or India. Its traditions, too, were most honourable, for it had taken part in many Indian Campaigns, and had recently distinguished itself in the late Afghan War, under its present Commander, Colonel George Henessey, an Officer of proved ability in the field.

The next Regiment was the 17th Bengal Infantry, or Loyal Poorbeah Regiment, composed of Hindustanis—about five hundred Hindus, Brahmins, and Rajpoots, and some three hundred Hindustani Mohammedans, all drawn from the north-west Provinces, Oude, and Bengal.

The Regiment had not previously seen much field service, having been employed towards the close of the late Afghan War at and near Kandahar. It was Commanded by Major von Beverhoudt, a comparatively young Officer, who, although he had been some years in the Regiment, only succeeded to the Command when it embarked at Bombay for Suâkin.

The fourth Regiment was the 28th Bombay Infantry, a Corps composed for the most part of Mahrattas and others, recruited from Provinces in the Bombay Presidency, but having a few Sikhs and men from Northern India in its ranks.

The men were strong, active, well set-up fellows, intelligent, and able under their Officers to turn their hand to any work that should be required of them. The Regiment had done good service at Kandahar in the last Afghan War. It was Commanded by Colonel F. C. Singleton, and had an exceptionally good body of Officers with it. It was considered one of the best Regiments in the Bombay Army.

Each Regiment or Detachment which embarked at Bombay, took with it in the Transport a proportion of mules, ammunition, entrenching tools, tents, commissariat and hospital stores, so that on landing it might be ready at once to take the field, and march in any direction and on any service.

Each Regiment had its own Transport. The Cavalry had, in addition to its 245 grass-cutters' ponies, 192 mules.

An Infantry Regiment had 502 mules. The Company of Sappers had 148 mules, making a total of nearly 2000 mules, of which 150 were kept in reserve as "spare."

In addition to this "Regimental" Transport, the Officer of this Department attached to the Indian Contingent, Major G. R. Shakespear, Assistant Commissary-General for Transport, had 150 Transport carts, drawn by 150 pairs of fine strong Indian bullocks.

He had also under his orders an Ambulance Corps, consisting of—

        8 Sirdars (Supervisors).

        15 Mates.

        927 Doolie-bearers.

From these the Base and Field Hospitals, and each Regiment in the Contingent, was furnished with its prescribed complement.

Major Shakespear had an Assistant, and a Staff of Warrant and Non-Commissioned Officers to work the Department.

The Medical Department for the service of the Base and Field Hospitals was under the direction of Brigade-Surgeon J. H. Thornton, Indian Medical Service. He had two Brigade-Surgeons and five Surgeons, in addition to the Medical Officers attached to the Regiments, to assist him.

There was a wooden ship of the Indian Marine, the "Czarewitch," fitted up and anchored in Suâkin harbour, as a Base Hospital Ship. She was fitted up in a most comfortable manner; and to secure ventilation a plank had been removed from her side all round, thus affording a free circulation of air at all times.

The Commissariat Department had been detailed entirely from Officers and subordinates of that Department in the Bombay Presidency, and was presided over by Lieutenant-Colonel E. S. Walcott of the Bombay Army.

There was a small Ordnance Depôt and Field Park, from the Bombay Ordnance Department, in charge of Conductor Whiffen.

A Field Paymaster was attached to the Contingent.

First Class Veterinary-Surgeon Rayment, A.V.D., was attached to the Force, and afforded professional assistance and supervision to all horses and Transport animals in the Contingent. His services were also made use of by the Commissariat and Transport Department of the British Force, so soon as the large number of camels employed by that Force arrived.

The first Detachment of troops embarked at Bombay on the 22nd February, and with such energy and expedition was the work carried on, and so admirably were all the arrangements made, that by the 14th March the whole Indian Contingent had landed at Suâkin.

Nothing could exceed the zeal and activity displayed by the Indian troops in the work of disembarking; and, as an instance, it may be mentioned that the Indian Marine Troopship " Clive," with the Head-Quarters' Staff and the 17th Bengal Infantry on board, reached Suâkin at 2 P.M. on the 5th March, and that by noon of the 6th she was steaming out of the harbour on her way back to India, having in twenty-two hours, with the help of her own boats and ship's company, assisted by the troops on board, disembarked and landed all their baggage and stores of every kind.

The Naval Transport Department was at the time hard worked, and gladly permitted the work of disembarkation to be carried out by the troops and ship's company, and on its conclusion expressed admiration for the zeal and energy which had been displayed.

On arrival the Indian Contingent was encamped on the open plain south-east of Suâkin, its right front resting on Fort Foullah, its right rear on the harbour, its front stretching in an easterly direction, with the left slightly refused[1] towards Graham's point at the entrance to the harbour. The front of the camp was protected by a series of small entrenched circular picquet redoubts, capable of holding eight to twelve men each.

(Signed)   J. HUDSON, Brigade-General.

---

[1] *i.e.* Drawn back, retired. This peculiar rendering of the term, seldom included in the ordinary English dictionary, is aptly illustrated in General Hutchinson's despatch of April 5th, 1801, relative to the battle, near Alexandria, of March 21st, in which Sir Ralph Abercrombie was mortally wounded. Describing the dispositions of the French Army, he states that "The French, during the whole of the action, *refused* their right."—(*London Gazette*, 1801, p. 530). Cf. also Sir Robert Wilson's *Hist. of the Expedition to Egypt*, p. 42.

Major-General Sir John Hudson, K.C.B., who, as General of Brigade, Commanded the Indian Contingent at Suâkin, has, during nearly thirty-five years service, distinguished himself in many an arduous campaign, and hard fought field.

As Adjutant of H. M. 64th Regiment, he went through the Persian war of 1856-57. Brigaded with the 20th Bombay Native Infantry, the 64th formed part of the first Division under Major-General Stalker, which preceded the rest of the Force, and landed at Hallila Bay, in the Persian Gulf, in the beginning of December 1856. General Hudson was thus present at the storm and capture of the old Dutch fort of Reshire, on the 9th of that month, and at the bombardment and surrender of Bushire, on the following day. After these exploits, the Division forming an entrenched camp outside the latter town, awaited the arrival of Sir James Outram, who held supreme Command, with the rest of the troops under Sir Henry Havelock. This event took place at the end of January 1857; and a forward movement having been arranged on February 7th, the Persians made their celebrated night attack, resulting, on the morning of the 8th, in the battle of Kooshab, when the British Force scored a brilliant victory. A strong concentration of Persian troops having taken place, and extensive fortifications been thrown up, at Mohumrah, a town situated at the confluence of the Euphrates and the Karoon, three days' sail from Bushire, the two Divisions were conveyed thither, and on March 26th, although confronted with 13,000 Persian troops, and formidable batteries, the town was bombarded and captured. Sir John Hudson was present at all these engagements, and for his services in this campaign received the Persian medal and clasp.

Like Sir John M'Neill, Sir John Hudson took an active and distinguished part in the Indian Mutiny of 1857-58, being present especially in all those complicated operations, of which Cawnpore and Lucknow were the two great centres. As Adjutant of his Regiment, in the advance upon Cawnpore, under Sir Henry Havelock, he was present in the action at Futtehpore, gained 12th July 1857,

R

without the loss of a British soldier, through the skilful use of artillery, and the fear inspired by the long range and accurate aim of the Enfield rifle, a hundred riflemen of the 64th being especially serviceable; also in the action at the village of Aoung, and at the stream called Pandoo Nuddee, about twenty miles from Cawnpore, both fought on the 15th, a fiercely hot July day. It was on the passage of this river by the relieving Force, that Nana Sahib ordered the slaughter of all the captives, still alive at Cawnpore. The next day the battle of Cawnpore was fought, the rebels being driven in succession from the various villages in which they were posted. At the close of this action the 64th was especially distinguished by the capture of a 24-pounder gun, so posted on the cantonment road as to be extremely annoying. The advance, straight upon the muzzle of the gun, was led by Major Stirling on foot, Sir Henry Havelock's son, who was acting as his father's A.D.C., also leading on horseback. For this gallant action he received the V.C., although the fact was afterwards severely commented on by Sir Colin Campbell, as involving a breach of military etiquette, the Lieutenant being sent not to take the place due to the Regimental Officers, but simply to convey a message. The next day Cawnpore was entered, and the dreadful circumstances attending the massacre fully ascertained. Vengeance, however, was on the murderer's track, an immediate advance being made on Bithoor, where Nana Sahib's palace was sacked and burnt to the ground.

General Neill having arrived with some troops from Allahabad, now took over the Command of Cawnpore, leaving Sir Henry Havelock free to attempt, if possible, the relief of Lucknow. The Ganges was accordingly crossed on the 23rd of July, and an advance made into the Province of Oude. At Mungulwar, a plan of Lucknow and important information was received from Brigadier-General Inglis. On the 29th July two battles were fought against the enemy, strongly posted, first in the town of Oonao, and second in that of Busseerut-Gunge. From both of these positions the rebels were driven by the small Force with the utmost gallantry, the

64th especially, at Busseerut-Gunge, making a flank movement to the left, and so cutting off the communications with the town. Notwithstanding these successes, to such an extent had not only battle, but disease, and the season then at its hottest, told upon the extremely limited British strength, that it was found absolutely necessary to fall back upon Mungulwar, and sending his sick and wounded into Cawnpore, Sir Henry Havelock determined there to await reinforcements.

A very few men arriving from Cawnpore in the beginning of August, an advance was again made on Busseerut-Gunge, and the rebels being found still very strongly posted, a second battle was fought and the enemy successfully driven from the town. Their strength, and the difficulties of the enterprise was however so great, that no alternative remained save again to retire on Mungulwar.

A powerful concentration of the enemy now took place at the scene of the two previous battles, with the view of cutting off the British line of retreat towards the Ganges. To defeat this intention, on August 12th, the battle of Boorbeakechowkee was successfully fought, the British again falling back, and recrossing the Ganges without opposition the following day. Ere rest however could be obtained at Cawnpore, another battle had to be fought. Nana Sahib had strongly entrenched himself at his old seat at Bithoor, and on August 16th, Sir Henry Havelock, with about 1,300 men,—the entire Force he had at command,—after a most obstinate resistance, drove the rebel chief from all his positions. So ended the first attempt to relieve Lucknow, from the 12th of July to the 16th of August, ten battles having been fought under circumstances which tried to the very utmost the resource, courage, and endurance of every Officer and man engaged in this most arduous but unsuccessful effort, with a mere handful of troops, to raise the siege of Lucknow, and withdraw its beleaguered garrison. Just a month afterwards, the long looked-for reinforcements arrived with Sir James Outram. Thus augmented, and still under the Command of Sir Henry Havelock, the British Force recrossed the Ganges on the 19th of September, and at its old halting-place, fought the battle of Mungulwar, on the 23rd, after a fierce struggle capturing the Alumbagh, which from this date was never again lost to the British. The Alumbagh secured as a permanent stronghold, Lucknow itself was at once attacked, and there followed that famous advance upon the Residency, and relief of the beleaguered garrison, on the 25th, which is for ever indelibly engraved as one of the brightest and most affecting pages in the military annals of Great Britain.

In all the battles enumerated, Sir John Hudson bore a gallant part, under circumstances of the most difficult and trying character, which can possibly fall to the lot of the military man, faithfully discharging his onerous Regimental duties. During the second advance to Lucknow he was also on the Staff of General Havelock as Deputy-Assistant Adjutant-General to the Oude Field Force; and, in recognition of these varied and important services, rendered in the hour of his country's need, was specially mentioned in despatches,[1] and thanked by the Governor-General in Council.[2]

The Residency was relieved, but to the relievers in turn it became a prison. For two months, in the very heart of Lucknow, and four miles off, at the Alumbagh, the British Force, with those for whose relief it had so gallantly fought, were closely invested by a seething mass of cruel and bloodthirsty foes. Of the two divisions thus effectually separated, those imprisoned in the Residency had the hardest lot, and stood in the greatest danger. The Alumbagh was well stored, had great capabilities of defence, and its surroundings were comparatively open. On the 3rd of October 300 men of the 64th Regiment, and various subsequent Convoys, reached it safely from Cawnpore.

With the Residency, however, there was no such possibility of communication. The history of these two months is a narrative of incessant struggle. The enemy never wearied of the siege so persistently maintained from the previous June. To the besieged

[1] Both by Sir James Outram and Sir Henry Havelock.
[2] *London Gazette*, February 17th, 1858.

it involved harassing duty, with continual hazard and exposure, varied by sorties, now to dislodge parties of the enemy only too well posted, now to capture guns, or demolish buildings.[1] During this prolonged period of uncertainty and suspense, in these various duties, Sir John Hudson was actively engaged.

On November 17th, a day scarce less memorable than that of September 25th, Sir Colin Campbell effected a junction with Generals Havelock and Outram. The Residency was finally relieved, but only to be for the time abandoned. On the night of the 22nd, with the most admirable precautions and perfect order, the evacuation, of what for five months had proved an ark of safety, took place; in silence and secrecy, without a shot being fired, or the slightest alarm given, the great convoy of non-combatants, two thousand in number, embracing women and children, sick and wounded, were carefully withdrawn, first to the Dil Koosha and then to the Alumbagh, and so by Cawnpore and Allahabad, safely to reach Calcutta. Just two days after this final relief died their gallant deliverer, Sir Henry Havelock, who only survived long enough to witness the completion of his great enterprise.

For the soldier hard work yet remained to be done. As Adjutant of the 64th, in December 1857, Sir John Hudson was engaged in the defence of Cawnpore, threatened by the Gwalior mutineers, and in their defeat. The first days of 1858 saw him, under Sir Adrian Hope, securing the iron suspension bridge over the Kallee Nudee,

[1] In his despatch of November 27th, 1857, Sir James Outram thus refers to the privations and conduct of the garrison during this second period of the siege :—

"I cannot conclude this report without expressing to his Excellency my intense admiration of the noble spirit displayed by all ranks and grades of the force since we entered Lucknow. Themselves placed in a state of siege—suddenly reduced to scanty and unsavoury rations—denied all the little luxuries (such as tea, sugar, rum, and tobacco), which by constant use had be- come to them almost the necessaries of life —smitten, in many cases, by the same scorbutic affections and other evidences of debility, which prevailed amongst the original garrison—compelled to engage in laborious operations—exposed to constant danger, and kept ever on the alert, their spirits and cheerfulness, and zeal and dis- cipline, seemed to rise with the occasion. Never could there have been a force more free from grumblers, more cheerful, more willing, or more earnest."— *London Gazette*, February 17th, 1858.

and fighting in the action there, and at Futtehghur. On the 1st of May, he was at the Battle of Kerkeroulie, where General Penny fell, the only Officer killed, and five days afterwards at the Battle of Bareilly, fought under Sir Colin Campbell.

As a most interesting association connected with his arduous and gallant services rendered under Sir Henry Havelock, it may also be mentioned that in 1859 General Hudson married his niece, Isabel, daughter of the late General Charles Frederick Havelock.

As Brigade-Major, in General Taylor's Brigade, Sir John Hudson was also engaged in the actions at Burnai, Mohumdi, and Shadabad. In the last Afghan War he was second in Command of the 21st Bengal Native Infantry, taking part in the operations in the Khost Valley, and the affair at Matoon. He was also with Sir Frederick Roberts's Division in the advance on Cabul in 1879, and with Brigadier-General Macpherson's Brigade in the engagement at Charasiah, and from January 1881 Commanded the Brigade, holding the Khyber Pass until the final withdrawal of the British Force.

Trained in the hardest school of war, habituated to heroic deeds, such was the General Commanding the Indian Brigade at Tofrek.

When, on the evening of the memorable 25th of September 1857, in spite of the most obstinate resistance, the Oude Field Force, had penetrated to the Fhureed Buksh, the swift darkness of the tropics coming on, Sir James Outram proposed to suspend operations till the following day. Sir Henry Havelock, unwilling to keep the " gallant and enduring garrison " even for a night longer in an agony of suspense, or defer the joy of deliverance, ordered the 78th Highlanders, and the Ferozepore Sikhs, to form a Column of attack. To use the words of the despatch, " This Column rushed on with a desperate gallantry, through streets of flat-roofed, loopholed houses, from which a perpetual fire was kept up, and overcoming every obstacle, established itself within the enclosure of the Residency." At the head of this heroic band, and the first to reach the long beleaguered gates, were four Officers, Sir James Outram, Sir Henry Havelock, Lieutenants Hudson and Hargood![1]

The best type of a British Officer, a man in whom unswerving truthfulness and integrity are combined with the calm, efficient, and successful discharge of important duty, amid the egregious mis-representations, for months darkening as with a dust storm from the desert all the doings of the 22nd, General Hudson stood a rallying point, and witness to the fact, that the Battle of Tofrek was not the panic-stricken, brainless, and invertebrate scrimmage the public were led to believe, but, on dispositions carefully thought out, and wisely arranged, a well-fought and thoroughly successful battle—a battle of which, amid many others, the great lesson is, that Victory is not necessarily chained to the chariot-wheels of the strategist, but con-fers her laurels as the reward of Duty effectually discharged, where-ever you can find your enemy; or, what is equally, or perhaps *more to the point*, WHEREVER YOUR ENEMY CAN FIND YOU.

While, as the General in Command, the full burden of what we can only term a strictly VICARIOUS RESPONSIBILITY, was unscrupulously laid on Sir John M'Neill,—whose lips were, at the same time, in duty and in honour practically sealed,—the testimony of Sir John Hudson became of paramount importance.

Although, it may be, not the first to protest, as charged with the duties of Convoy, it was General Hudson who was first compelled practically to realise both the difficulties connected with the route, and the peculiar composition of the overweighted Force sent out on the 22nd, and the impracticable nature of the Instructions drawn up for its guidance.

When the tide of clamour, invading both Houses of Parliament, rendered a personal visit by Lord Wolseley to Tofrek incumbent, it was General Hudson who, on the spot, explained to his Lordship the exact dispositions, and various circumstances, both in their weakness and their strength, under which the battle was fought.

[1] Despatches by Sir Henry Havelock, of date September 30th, 1857.—*London* *Gazette*, December 15th, 1857, and Feb-ruary 17th, 1858.

When the most calumnious charges were made as to the assumed neglect of all ordinary military precautions, and other matters affecting the fortunes of the day, the one standard of appeal was that Report of General Hudson which, although its substance be well known, has never yet formally seen the light of day.

Finally, when relieved from garrison duty at Suâkin, he was free to visit England, it was General Hudson who gave in person to Her Majesty, and to the Commander-in-Chief, the explanations he had previously given to Lord Wolseley.

In behalf of his coadjutor in Command, under these various circumstances, Sir John Hudson was ever distinguished by the most loyal and steadfast maintenance of what he knew to be the actual facts of the case. It was not, indeed, the first time they had been mutually concerned in important operations.

In that darkest hour of Britain's Empire in India, when her power to protect from torture, outrage, and death, even the worthiest and most faithful of her children, was passing through a deep and a blood-stained eclipse—the two Generals at Tofrek were still in the very opening of their respective military careers. During this period both alike had been most intimately and most honourably associated with men and with events, whose remembrance their country will never " willingly let die."

We have briefly sketched the part taken by Sir John Hudson in the various movements connected with the first relief, and subsequent defence, of the Residency at Lucknow, under Sir Henry Havelock. As Aide-de-Camp to Brigadier-General Sir Edward Lugard, K.C.B., who Commanded the second Division of Infantry under Sir Colin Campbell, Sir John M'Neill performed a not less important part in the final storm and capture of the great centre and focus of the rebellion in Oude. To the second Division fell some of the hardest work in that memorable capture. The storming of La Martiniére on the 7th of March, and the operations on the 11th against the Begum Kotee, when that "attack of a very desperate character" took place, of which Sir Colin says, " This was the sternest struggle which occurred during the siege,"[1] were carried out under the immediate directions of Sir Edward Lugard. The services of his Aide-de-Camp, Lieutenant M'Neill, then of the 12th Bengal Native Infantry, the *Kelat-i-Ghilzai*, rendered during these arduous and critical operations, are thus referred to in the Roll of Officers serving under Sir Edward "who are deemed deserving of honourable mention"; "A most intelligent and meritorious Officer, has given me great aid."[2]

Lucknow taken, to Sir Edward Lugard was committed the task of destroying the power of Koer or Kunwár Singh, a most dangerous rebel, whose bands were infesting the districts round Azimgurh, and especially the Jûgdespore jungles, where his chief stronghold lay, and threatening even Benares. During these trying and difficult operations, and until at the end of June the state of his health compelled Sir Edward Lugard to resign his Command, Sir John M'Neill continued to act in the same capacity he had previously done, and was mentioned by his chief in the following complimentary terms:—

"Lieutenant M'Neill, my Aide-de-Camp, with Captain Middleton, extra Aide-de-Camp, deserve my best thanks; they are both very intelligent and active Staff Officers, and have rendered me much assistance."[3]

After the lapse of twenty-eight years, the two Officers in question were called upon to confront an enemy, not more cruel, treacherous, or bloodthirsty, than their old foes, but certainly much braver, and much better endowed with those very qualities which enabled Britain to reconquer in India her lost ground—an indomitable courage ready to face any odds, and meet death itself with unfaltering resolution.

In the Campaign of 1885, of these qualities, the most determined display was that made at Tofrek; and we may be certain

---

[1] Despatches by Sir Colin Campbell, March 22nd, 1858.—*London Gazette*, May 25th, 1858.   [2] *Ibid.*

[3] Despatches by Sir Edward Lugard.— *London Gazette*, August 21st, 1858.

that, on the spur of the moment, and in from fifteen to twenty minutes, finally and effectually to defeat a Contingent of Mahdist Dervishes, flushed with the assurance of Victory, inspired by the most deadly and fanatical hatred, presupposes a thoroughly organised system of defence, and the exercise of every quality a sound Generalship can possibly demand. That such was indeed the case we are assured on unimpeachable authority. Whom, then, are we to believe? Those who at the first notes of alarm fled incontinently, and filled the world with their panic and their clamour; or those who, well inured to "War's wild alarms," bravely stood their ground, did their duty, and, as their reward, gained a most signal Victory?

> "Majestic Danger calls but for the Brave;
> Trusts not the dastard's arm." [1]

By all who came in contact with them, the Staff Officers were acknowledged to be men of exceptional excellence, and ability in the discharge of their varied and important duties, and, like General Hudson himself, had, without exception, taken part in the Afghan War of 1878-80.

Captain Charles Wemyss Muir, of the Bengal Staff Corps, and Commandant of the Governor-General's Body-Guard, a son of Sir William Muir, the eminent Oriental scholar, and Principal of Edinburgh University, acted as Aide-de-Camp. He had seen eighteen years' service, and taken part in the Afghan Campaign in 1880.

Major, now Colonel, Robert M'Gregor Stewart, R.A., the Assistant Adjutant-General, and Quartermaster-General, with twenty-seven years' service, as Adjutant in the Royal Artillery, had served in the Hazara Campaign of 1868 against the tribes on the Black Mountain; and in the Afghan Campaign had been Assistant Quartermaster-General to the 2nd Division of the Candahar Field Force, and is now one of Her Majesty's Aides-de-Camp.

[1] Pindar's *Odes*, Olympia I., Ep. iii.

Major, now Lieut.-Colonel, Norman Robert Stewart, of the Bengal Staff Corps, Deputy-Assistant Adjutant and Quartermaster-General, with sixteen years' service, during the Afghan Campaign, had been present in the engagements at Ahmed Kheyl and Urzoo, near Ghuznee, and had also served with the Nile Expedition 1884-85.

Major Arthur James Pearson, R.A., Deputy-Assistant Adjutant, and Quartermaster-General, for Intelligence duties, with twenty-four years' service, had also gone through the Hazara Campaign of 1868, and the entire Afghan War of 1878-80.

Major, now Brevet Lieut.-Colonel, James Cook, of the Bengal Staff Corps, the Brigade-Major, had served in the Campaign on the North-West frontier of India in 1863, and was present at the capture of Umbeyla, and in the War in Afghanistan; was present at the attack and capture of Ali Musjid, and was also with the first Expedition into the Bazar Valley under Lieut.-General Maude, and in the Mahsood Muzeeree Expedition in 1881.

Lieut.-Colonel, now Colonel, Edmund Scopoli Walcott, C.B., the Senior Commissariat Officer, had served in the war against the Taepings, near Shanghai, in 1862, and was present at the attack and capture of the entrenched camp at Wangkaza, the town of Tseerpoo, etc.; and in the war in Afghanistan had taken part in the defence of Candahar, and battle there.

Major, now Lieut.-Colonel, George Robert James Shakespear, of the Bengal Staff Corps, Senior Transport Officer, had seen over twenty-five years of service, and is now Assistant Commissary-General, Transport Branch.

In addition to the interesting information given by General Hudson, it may be mentioned, that of the Regiments selected for service in the Eastern Sûdan, the 9th Bengal Cavalry, known originally as the 1st Hodson's Horse, were formally enrolled August 26th, 1858.

While still an Irregular Cavalry, among the many good services referred to by Sir John Hudson, performed during the eventful period in which the Regiment took its rise, one of the most famous of their exploits was the capture of the King of Delhi, and various members of his family, effected by the dauntless courage and magnificent daring of their leader, September 21st, 1857, at the Tomb of the Emperor Humayoon, where, with a large following, he had taken refuge. A few days afterwards, several of the princes, chief instigators of the cruel massacres at Delhi, richly deserving their fate, died in an attempted rescue, by Hodson's own hand.

The full-dress uniform of the 9th Bengal Cavalry is blue with white facings, and their honours "Delhi," "Lucknow, relief and capture," and now "Suâkin, 1885."

Their Colonel, Arthur Power Palmer, C.B., of the Bengal Staff Corps, went through the Indian Mutiny 1857-9, raising a Sikh Regiment, 600 strong, for service in Oude, in March 1858. He joined Hodson's Horse at Lucknow in June of that year, and was present with them in the Oude Campaign until its close on the Nepaul frontier. He was also engaged in the campaign on the North-West frontier in 1863-4, was Adjutant of the 10th Bengal Lancers in the Abyssinian war, served in the Afghan war of 1878-80, being present at the capture of the Peiwar Kotal, and with the Expedition to the Khost Valley.

The 9th Bengal Lancers was one of the Cavalry Regiments selected for the Expedition of 1878, and were referred to at the time in the following complimentary terms :—

"If cavalry be the eyes and ears of an army, it would be difficult to find in any European fighting body sharper eyes or ears than would be supplied by the Indian Cavalry. The Bengal Cavalry in particular is in a highly efficient state, well-drilled, well mounted, and perfectly equipped."[1]

So also, in 1885, their soldierly qualities are thus referred to :—

"The 9th Bengal Cavalry are all expert in the use of their weapons, and if the spearmen encounter them the Punjabi will prove more than a match for the Arab."[2]

[1] *Times*, April 8th, 1878.   [2] *Daily Telegraph*, March 16th, 1885.

Throughout the Campaign they did good service both in direct conflict with the enemy and in scouting duty. They were specially serviceable in this respect during the progress of the railway, and in the night raid of May 5th on the stronghold of Mohammed Adam Sardoun at Thakool, when they scouted in the hill-country, and brought off the cattle in most effective style, also capturing a standard, which was afterwards presented to Sir Gerald Graham.

The 15th Bengal Native Infantry, otherwise known as the Loodianah Sikhs, were raised on the 30th July 1846, their honours being "China, 1860-62," "Ahmed Kheyl," "Kandahar, 1880," "Afghanistan, 1878-80;" and now "Suakin, 1885" and "Tofrek." Their Colonel, George Robertson Hennessey, C.B., of the Bengal Staff Corps, served during the Indian Mutiny with the 93rd Highlanders, and was present in the various actions preceding the relief of Lucknow under Sir Colin Campbell. With the 75th or Gordon Highlanders he served with Sir James Outram during his occupation of the Alumbagh, being present in the action fought December 22nd at Guillie, three miles from the Alumbagh on the Dilkoosha road; also at the very severe actions on the 12th and 16th January 1858, when the Lucknow rebels to the number of 30,000 attempted the capture of the Alumbagh. Colonel Hennessey was also engaged in the Bundelcund campaign of 1859-60, and commanded the 15th Sikhs in the Afghan War of 1878-80, taking part with Sir Donald Stewart's Division in the advance on and occupation of Kandahar, and in the actions at Ahmed Kheyl and Urzoo near Guznee; and was also with Sir Frederick Roberts in his march to Kandahar in August 1880, and fought in the subsequent battle.

Throughout these various complicated and arduous operations during the Afghan War, the 15th Sikhs did excellent service, their selection for the campaign in the Eastern Sûdan being no doubt due to the soldierly qualities and effective condition, borne witness to in such flattering terms by General Hudson. As the first of the Regiments leaving India for the Eastern Sûdan, the following description of their embarkation at Bombay from the local Press will be perused with interest, and in the popular enthusiasm evoked, recalls similar scenes then being enacted on the British shores.

" A few days ago the first of the regiments composing the Indian contingent for service in the Soudan embarked at the Prince's Dock and was despatched to Souakim. This was the 15th Loodhiana Sikhs. Their arrival took place at daybreak, and the arrangements for their reception were so forward that the majority of the men had left Bombay by the next high tide. Few of them saw anything of the city of Bombay, for the troop trains were run down into the dock and there unloaded. In and around the jetty shed, along which the transports for the regiment were lying, a scene of the busiest activity was presented. Inside the troops piled their arms and relieved themselves of their accoutrements for a time, cleared the baggage and the animals from the railway waggons, and then proceeded to pic-nic in the shade. Everyone was in the highest spirits, and to the many visitors who found their way during the morning to the place of embarkation freely expressed their delight at the prospect of being actively engaged in fighting.

" Reminding their hearers that they were a warlike race, and proudly exhibiting the marks of distinction on their khaki[1] tunics—mementoes of campaigning in China, during the Mutiny, and in Afghanistan—they laughingly declared their intention of not permitting the present campaign to end without winning for themselves further laurels. Not that all are veterans. Two-thirds will see active service for the first time in Egypt, and still more cross the *bara kala pani*[2] for the first time. Yet these were in no way less eager for the opportunity of distinction, nor were they inferior to their older comrades in promising appearance and fine military bearing.

" The regiment looked, indeed, a splendid body of men as they were drawn up in line during the morning for medical inspection. This duty was performed by Brigade-Surgeon Thornton. Most of the men appeared veritable sons of Anak, and their magnificent physique commanded unstinted admiration. Their arms had been burnished until they shone like silver, and the picturesque appearance of the sepoys was heightened by the glittering halo formed round their puggarees by the steel quoit which becomes in the hands of the Sikh such a terrible weapon at close quarters. Altogether the regiment

[1] *Kháki*, Hindustani, from the Persian *Khák*, ashes, the colour of dust or ashes.

[2] *Barā*, great, *kālā*, black, *pānī*, water, the name given by the Hindus to the boundless expanse of the Indian Ocean, the symbol to them of banishment beyond the sea !

mustered within a dozen of 900 strong, the places of some fifty sick having been filled by volunteers from the 45th Sikhs at Agra. This little band of volunteers consisted solely of men who have just returned from the Zhob Valley Expedition, and included 1 subadar,[1] 5 havildars,[2] 4 naiks,[3] 1 bugler, and 46 sepoys. These men of Rattray's Sikhs wished it recorded, in the hope that it may reach the Sirkar, that they were *bara kushi*[4] at the acceptance of their proffered services. A request of such a character, made with their own peculiar earnestness and simplicity, it was impossible to refuse. Some idea of the height of the men composing this batch may be gathered from the fact that the regimental average is 5 ft. 9 in.

"At noon the bugle sounded, and the first allotment marched on board the British India steamer *Madura*, the transport that is to lead the way to Souakim. As the gangway was cleared and the vessel began to move from the bunder,[5] the cheers of the men on board were answered by their comrades ashore, the spectators joining heartily with the latter in the farewell. The parting salutation between the Sikhs was peculiarly impressive. '*Bhaurji-ka-Khalsa, Bhaurji-ka-Fatta*'[6] they shouted as they waved their quoits over their heads; and this appeal to their faith, with the exhibition of its holy symbol, was by no means devoid of solemnity. Even before they left Lucknow their last act was to collect and transmit to their guru a few hundred rupees as an earnest of their hope that good fortune might attend their enterprise.

"Among the transports were goats for the flesh-eating portion of the regiment, rice for those whose caste rules permitted them to cook it during the passage, and gram and parched rice for those belonging to the Brahmin caste, who would on no account light a fire for culinary purposes in the midst of what they regarded to be impure associations. With but a few exceptions, stalwart and fine-looking fellows every one of them, these Sikhs were not at all afraid of crossing the *kala-pani* to be landed in a distant, and to them even now, it is to be presumed, an unknown part of the world. They held themselves fortunate in having been selected for active service, and there is no doubt that, with their quoits and their lances, as well as with their arms of precision, they will give a good account of the enemy. Along with the troops came their *guru* or spiritual adviser, but he did not proceed to the scene of war in charge of the souls of his flock.[7] When asked why he, too,

[1] Native captain.
[2] Native sergeant.
[3] Native corporal.
[4] Greatly delighted.   [5] Quay.
[6] Another form of invocation among the

Sikhs is—"*Wâh! Wâh! Gúrû-ji! Fatteh!*"
"Bravo! Bravo! O, Gúrú! Victory!"
[7] This statement refers to the older *guru* connected with the Regiment; there was a younger man who really did go.

did not proceed to the Soudan, he gave a reply which was, perhaps, more curious than pertinent. He said that if he went there he would not come back alive. He would spurn all manner of protection, charge right against the enemy wherever he found him, and die on the battle-field. The general appearance of this 'fighting parson,' with the quoit gleaming from the folds of his turban, as well as the deep earnestness with which he uttered these sentiments, showed that his deeds would not belie his words."

Defending, as they did, a front of the position, forming a special object of the Arab attack, the Sikh fire necessarily did great execution, opposite the left or D Company alone there being found ninety-two dead bodies. If the same proportion obtained in the other Companies, nearly half the estimated numbers of the enemy slain would fall to their share. So closely at times were they pressed by the Arabs, that several times the bayonets had to be lowered for the charge to repel those who had escaped the searching fire of the Sniders.

Among other deeds of gallantry performed, that of Subadar Goordit Singh, the Native Officer Commanding this left or D Company of Sikhs, especially deserves mention. At the first alarm, when the pickets and working parties were running in, two or three of the Berkshire men with Captain Jamieson, who had been out in the bush on the west side of the clearing, were seen making their way back to the redoubt, hotly pursued by several Arabs. The Berkshire men were likely to have the worst of it, when the Subadar of the Company on whose front the little episode was taking place, rushed forward, and with three passes of his sword delivered in rapid succession, cut down as many Arabs, the weapon unfortunately breaking on the neck-bone of the third. The lives of the Berkshire men at all events were saved, and a deed of gallantry like this, performed in presence of the enemy, could not go unrecognised. Steps were at once taken for having this brave act brought to the knowledge of the Authorities, with a view to the Order of Merit being conferred upon the Subadar. One of the regulations necessary for the candidate to comply with is that he be afterwards personally identified by those whose lives he has been instrumental in saving. Six weeks having elapsed since the date of the battle, and the troops getting scattered along the line of railway, in the present case this became a matter of some difficulty. Lord Wiltshire, Aide-de-Camp to Sir John M'Neill, went with the Subadar in search of the saved men. After many fruitless efforts, the task had been almost given up in despair, when it was recollected there was a small water-guard over a well at Handūb yet unvisited. Thither the two Officers went, and found at last the objects of their quest. The Subadar not only got his well-deserved decoration, but, in recognition of his distinguished bravery, was presented with a sword of honour by Lord Wolseley when he visited Suâkin, and mentioned in his despatch of June 15th, 1885.[1]

As forcibly illustrating Lord Wolseley's statement as to individual Arabs being able in spite of the most deadly fire to reach the Squares,[2] it may be stated that of the seven Sikhs killed one presented a peculiarly ghastly spectacle. From the position in which the body lay it was evident that he had been attacked outside by one of the Arabs, who had managed in spite of the withering fire to reach the fighting line. Under penalty of losing their caste, it is the custom of the Sikhs never to poll their hair from earliest infancy, but to keep it coiled up in a great mass under the turban. Attacked by the Arab, armed probably with one of the long heavy swords they so dexterously wield with both hands, the Sikh's head had been struck right off his shoulders, and lay on the ground inside the zeriba, with the magnificent black hair bespattered with blood, escaping in great dishevelled masses ; while outside lay the headless trunk, with the clubbed rifle still tightly grasped in the clenched hands.

As an interesting illustration not only of a peculiar rite, but, under the circumstances, an extremely sensible proceeding, it may be mentioned that when the Sikhs were about to return with

[1] *London Gazette*, August 25th, 1885.
[2] *Vide* Chapter VII. p. 213.

T

General Graham's convoy, Sir John M'Neill asked General Hudson what they were going to do with their dead. "O don't you bother about that; they have arranged the whole thing themselves," said the General. Presently there was to be seen a little fire burning just outside the zeriba. With such wood as could readily be obtained a funeral pyre had been constructed, the bodies of the dead warriors disposed upon it, liberally covered with ghee, and, with the fire kindled, in a short time nothing remained save a little white dust.

This incident brings out in a striking manner the contrast between the Sikh and ordinary Mohammedan forms of belief. Both by religious precept and common practice the *interment* of the dead is universal in Moslem countries, and is held to have received Divine sanction, when, as related in the Koran, God sent a crow to scratch the earth, and show Cain how his brother's body should be concealed.[1] On the same authority it is strictly forbidden to burn the living. "Punish not with God's punishment,[2] for it is not fit for any one to punish with fire but God." At the same time, even in death the body is supposed to retain consciousness of pain, as the Mishkat says, "The breaking the bones of a corpse is the same as doing it in life;" hence, inferentially, the same restriction against the destruction of the body by fire during life applies after death.

In the disposal of the dead, however, the Sikh follows not Mohammedan but Hindu custom. This point is curiously illustrated in a narrative of the circumstances said to have taken place at the death of Nānak, the founder and first Guru of the Sikh religion,[3] from a manuscript preserved in the India Office, London :—

[1] Cain having slain Abel, "*He knew not what to do with him; for he was the first dead person upon the face of the earth of the sons of Adam. So he carried him upon his back.* And God sent a raven, which scratched up the earth *with its bill and its talons and raised it over a dead raven that was with it until it hid it,* to show him how he should hide the corpse of his brother.

He said, O my disgrace! Am I unable to be like this raven, and to hide the corpse of my brother? And he became of [the number of] the repentant. *And he digged* [a grave] *for him and hid him.*"—*Selections from the Kur-án,* Sūrah v. By Edward W. Lane (Trübner's Oriental Series), p. 54.

[2] *i.e.* Fire.

[3] H. H. The Maharajah Dhuleep Singh,

"The final incident in the life of this enlightened teacher is in precise accord with all that has been said of his former career. Nānak came to the bank of the Rāvī to die—in conformity with Hindū custom—by the side of a natural stream of water. It is expressly said that both Hindūs and Muslims accompanied him. He then seated himself at the foot of a Sarīh tree, and his Assembly of the faithful (*Sangat*) stood around him . . . Then the Hindūs and Musalmāns who were firm in the name (of God), began to express themselves (thus): the Musalmāns said 'We will bury (him);' and the Hindūs said, 'We will burn (him).' Then the Bābā[1] said, 'Place flowers on both sides; on the right side those of the Hindūs, on the left side those of the Musalmāns, (that we may perceive) whose will continue green to-morrow. If those of the Hindūs keep green, then burn (me); and if those of the Musalmāns keep green, then bury (me).' Then the Bābā ordered the Assembly to repeat the praises (of God); and the Assembly began to repeat the praises accordingly. [After a few verses had been recited] he laid down his head. When the sheet (which had been stretched over him) was raised, there was nothing under it; and the flowers of both (sides) remained green. The Hindūs took away theirs; and the Musalmāns took away theirs. The entire Assembly fell to their feet."—(Indian Office MS., 1728, fol. 239, 240.) *Dictionary of Islam.* By Thos. P. Hughes, p. 588, *sub* Sikhism.

The 28th Bombay Native Infantry were raised 21st January, 1846, their honours being "Kandahar, 1880," "Afghanistan, 1879-80;" and now "Suakin, 1885," and "Tofrek."

Their Commandant, the late Brevet Lieutenant-Colonel Francis Corbet Singleton, C.B., carried the regiment through the Afghan War, taking part in the defence of Candahar, and in the engagement at Kokeran. He died at sea, on his way home from India on sick

in recently announcing to the Sikhs the intention to renounce Christianity and return to his ancestral faith, is reported to have written—"In returning to the faith of my ancestors you must clearly understand, Khalsea Jea, that I have no intention of conforming to the errors introduced into Sikhism by those who were not true Sikhs—such, for instance, as wretched caste observance, or abstinence from meats and drinks which Sutgooroo has ordained should be received with thankfulness by all mankind; but to worship in the pure and beautiful tenets of Baba Nānuk and obey the commands of the Gooroo Govind Singh." [Govind Singh, who died A.D. 1708, was the last of the ten great Gooroos recognised by the Sikhs; he was largely instrumental in giving a military and political character to the Sikh religion, uniting his disciples and giving to each the name of *Singh* or lion.]

[1] *i.e.* The Teacher, Nānak himself.

leave, in the autumn of 1886: was brother of Captain Singleton of the 92nd Highlanders, who died of wounds received in the attack on Majuba Hill; and of Captain Singleton, R.N., who commanded the "Jumna" at Suâkin in 1884. On the embarkation of the regiment for Suâkin, the *Times of India* gave the following notice of the event :—

"The 28th Bombay Native Infantry Regiment was formed in 1846, and since that time has taken part in the Persian Expedition,[1] and in the last Afghan Campaign, distinguishing itself in the defence and battle of Kandahar. It was recently, greatly to the gratification of the men composing it, selected for service in the Soudan, and on Friday night it left its quarters at Poona, where it has lately been stationed, amidst the good wishes of the citizens and the regiments in garrison in Bombay.

"It arrived in the docks early on Saturday morning. The men do not look so imposing as their more stalwart companions in arms from Bengal, but although less in stature, they look lithe and active, and capable of undergoing a great deal of fatigue and privation, and to be highly adapted for offensive purposes in a quarter like Egypt."[2]

Several of the Bombay Regiments having taken part in the Abyssinian Campaign, a few remarks by Captain Hozier on their capabilities for foreign service will be read with interest :—

"In the Presidency of Bombay is quartered the least prejudiced and not the least faithful portion of the Indian army of Britain. The sepoys of Bombay object less to cross the ocean than do those of Bengal or Madras. Their caste is less tenacious of its rites and diet. They had already proved high capability of foreign service in the Persian war. Affghanistan, Sind, Beloochistan, Central India, and the Punjab, had borne testimony to their prowess in the field."[3]

With a still wider reference, the following remarks by Colonel Wilkins, suggested by the same Campaign, deserve quotation :—

"From the days of Clive downwards, our Indian armies have been accustomed to encounter war without long lapses or intervals of time. Their enemies have never suffered them to grow rusty; they are consequently always prepared for war, and engage in it without any fuss or confusion. The im-

---

[1] The Light Company.
[2] *The Times of India*, March 2nd, 1885.
[3] The *British Expedition to Abyssinia*, by Captain Hozier, p. 50.

portant branches of Commissariat and Transport conduct their operations in India, owing to its vast area and resources, much in the same manner during peace as in times of war. India is one vast Chobham or Aldershot, with the advantage of being a real camp instead of a mock one." [1]

Nor is this high state of organisation the growth of modern reforms or recent times. At a period when the Duke of Wellington's description of the miserable condition of the British soldier was only too true, Sir Robert Wilson gives us a glimpse into a very different state of things in the Indian Army; and we have already seen that Sir James M'Grigor, and M. le Comte de Noé, fully corroborate his statements :—

"The Indian army, in very fine order, disembarked and encamped near Aboumandour.[2] Whilst at Rhoda, this army had attracted much surprise and admiration. The Turks were astonished at the novel spectacle of men of colour being so well disciplined and trained; indeed, the general magnificence of the establishment of the Indian army was so different from what they had been accustomed to see in General Hutchinson's, that the contrast could not fail of being striking. But General Baird proved to them also that his troops were not enfeebled, or himself rendered inactive by these superior comforts. Every morning at daylight he manoeuvred his army for several hours, and in the evening again formed his parade. Never were finer men seen than those which composed this force, and no soldiers could possibly be in higher order." [3]

The Madras Sappers and Miners well deserve the encomiums bestowed upon them by Sir John Hudson. Their list of honours goes back into the last century, commencing with " Seringapatam "; then, for services beyond sea, " Bourbon," " Java," " Egypt " (with the Sphinx); in India, " Mahidpore," " Nagpore," " Ava," " Lucknow," " Central India," " Afghanistan, 1878-80 "; and again for foreign service—" Egypt, 1882," " Tel-el-Kebir ;" and now " Suakin, 1885 " and " Tofrek." Field-Marshal H.R.H. the Prince of Wales is the Honorary Colonel, and in token of distinction as the " Queen's Own " bear as their cognizance the Royal Cypher within the Garter.

---

[1] *Reconnoitring in Abyssinia,* by Colonel H. St. Clair Wilkins, p. 340.

[2] On the Nile, near Rosetta.

[3] *History of the British Expedition to Egypt,* London, 1803, p. 207.

At the moment of the assault, a party of the Madras Sappers and Miners were engaged preparing the salient of the Berks' redoubt, for the reception of the Gardner guns. At this point Captain Romilly and Lieutenant Newman were killed, while superintending its formation, and must have been among the first who were attacked. Their bodies, with that of Quartermaster Eastmead, of the Ordnance Department, by some means unknown, had been conveyed to the north redoubt. Next morning, when the bodies were uncovered, no one knew who they were, and Colonel Way forbade their removal until recognised. The Royal Engineers ultimately took charge of the Engineer Officers, and the Royal Marines buried the Quartermaster, in the grave they had dug on the northern side of their redoubt.

As the 15th Sikhs were the first of the Indian Contingent to leave for Suâkin so were the Madras Sappers and Miners the last, and the following notice of their departure may be read with interest :—

"The last detachment of the Indian Contingent, that supplied by the Madras Sappers and Miners, left for Suakim yesterday in the Indian Government steamer *Tanasserim*, Captain Hotham. The officers and men, with their followers, were brought from Poona, where they had stopped *en route*, yesterday morning, by two special trains, which were, as before, run into the dock.

"The strength of the detachment is four officers, Captains Wilkieson and Romilly, Lieutenant Newman, and Surgeon Smith, 173 men, 196 followers, 4 horses, and 158 mules and ponies. The *Tanasserim* had also on board some members of the Staff, viz. Major Shakspear and Major N. Stewart, and a medical officer, Brigade-Surgeon Morris, with 12 followers and 4 horses." [1]

In Chapter III., the various difficulties connected with the march to Tofrek, especially as they affected the Indian Brigade, have been pretty fully described. This Brigade especially being charged with the immediate convoy of an inordinate amount of Transport, a few further remarks, in addition to what has been already stated, may not be out of place.

[1] *Bombay Gazette*, March 3rd, 1885.

In terms, very curiously displaying the weakness both of the strategy pursued in 1885, and of the convoy, as distinct from the fighting Square, in his Lecture on "Infantry Tactics," General Graham has told us that—

"The real reason for our adopting Square formations was the dense impenetrable character of the belts of bush in the desert, which paralyzed effective Cavalry action, while allowing the fearless active Arabs, who move with all the rapidity of Cavalry, to approach unseen."[1]

These remarks, at first sight, seem applicable alike to the fighting and the convoy Squares, but, from what is stated further on, General Graham seems specially to refer to the latter :—

"Our object in the Square was to cover the baggage animals, and we generally found we had not any men to spare after doing it. Camels and baggage animals are apt to straggle, and their loads break down; the result is, the Squares get extended, and you find you never have men enough to do the work of keeping a complete guard all round your baggage animals. We did not consider the Square as a fighting formation, but as a defensive formation for the convoy."[2]

Referring to the succeeding Chapter for a more detailed comparison of the routes pursued in 1884 and 1885, the first idea that occurs on perusing this passage is, Why go to the "dense impenetrable belts of bush"? Why give the Arabs such undoubted advantages, and place your Transport, especially, in such danger? In 1884 there was not a convoy Square formed,—only fighting Squares. The convoys went almost continuously between Suâkin and Baker's Zeriba, with scarce even an escort, and encountered no "dense impenetrable belts of bush," and certainly without disturbance from the Arabs.

These statements by General Graham also bring very forcibly to remembrance the fact that it was not while being disloaded at the zeriba that the Transport stood in the greatest or most imminent danger. It so happened that the Arab attack took place then, but if "loot," not decisive victory, had been the object of the enemy,

---

[1] *Journal of the Royal United Service Institution,* Vol. xxx. p. 233.
[2] *Ibid* p. 270.

it might with equal probability have taken place during the march out ; and, with still greater likelihood, on the return journey.

In the first case, the relations between the fighting and the convoy Squares, would have been put to a very severe test.   Without disputing the advantage of the square formation either for fighting or convoy work, in presence of an enemy like the Sûdanese Arabs, it must at the same time be admitted that in the present instance, especially by reason of the excessive Transport, the arrangement of the Brigade Squares was undoubtedly liable to very grave objections.   While the British or fighting Square was practically invulnerable, in the event of attack, the Indian or convoy Square would be placed in an extremely difficult and perilous position.   With every possible element of weakness eliminated in the one case ; in the other, owing to the large non-combatant mass it was necessary to defend, weakness was unfortunately in excess.   It will be said, of course, that the one Square had the support of the other, and that, by marching in echelon, they were mutually protected by their flanking fires, so that an attack made upon at least two faces of either Square, supposing the enemy to be foolish enough to do so, would infallibly subject him to punishment from both.

It was no doubt also expected, and not without reason, by those who planned this arrangement, that the brunt of any attack would necessarily be borne by the British Square.   These ideas, however, although all very fine in theory, would have been found by no means so feasible in practice.   The mutual flanking fires presuppose that the Squares are acting on tolerably open ground, able to see each other and the enemy, and to keep their due relative positions in echelon.   Now this was the very thing, on the morning of the 22nd, that the Squares could not do.   They were marching over a level sandy plain, with dense bush closing in everywhere around them. During the course of the march the opinion was distinctly expressed by General Hudson that owing to the density of the jungle the view of the Squares was impeded, and if attacked they would be in danger of firing not into the enemy but into each other ; that is to say, that instead of retaining their exact relative positions in echelon, or angle to angle, the one Square was "masking" or overlapping the other's front.[1]

The success of the second idea depends entirely upon the disposition of the enemy. If, instead of hurling himself upon the British bayonets, he chose to shun their environment of withering fire for the more promising "loot" of the weakly defended camel-convoy, who could blame, or even say him nay? and that this would undoubtedly have been his tactics may easily be inferred from the mode of attack followed in the afternoon. It only required an attack, as resolute as that made at the zeriba, with the same collapse of one of the Indian Regiments, to produce a disaster a great deal more serious, and one which the British Square would in all probability have been powerless to prevent. It could not, without imminent risk to itself, have quitted the Square formation; and to move in the dense bush in all the sudden exigence of an attack would have been practically impossible. It is well that the double Brigade formation was never tested; but its having by mere chance escaped should not blind us to the fact of the undoubted risk to which it stood continually exposed.

What would have happened in the second case, viz., that of an attack on the return journey, we leave to the imagination of the reader. In an entrenched position, and with its stores safe, the fighting Square would have been all right. The convoy Square, with scarce "men enough" to keep "a complete guard all round," and no exterior aid, would have been in a bad way. If, for such an amount of Transport a separate fighting Force was necessary for the outward journey, it was not less so on its return. Happily, the attack did take place at the last moment, when the combined Force

---

[1] On this point, in the Lecture referred to, General Graham states :—

"The objection to having separate bodies in echelon, either in line or square, in bush or broken ground, where the enemy can get in between, is, that the separated portions of the troops are liable to fire into one another. This actually happened at Tamai, in March 1884, when the two brigades were in separate formations, but happily without serious results."—*Journal of the United Service Institution*, Vol. xxx., p. 233.

U

was still intact, and we know the result; still, as just stated, this should not blind us to the undoubted risk to which the Transport was *continually exposed.*

With regard to the formation of the Indian Brigade Square during the march out, also the dispositions at the zeriba, and various other matters affecting the Indian troops, I have much pleasure in giving the following extracts from a letter Sir John Hudson has kindly favoured me with. They are of special interest, entering as they do into various details, explanatory of points on which misconceptions had been entertained.

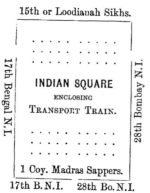

15th or Loodianah Sikhs.

17th Bengal N.I. — INDIAN SQUARE ENCLOSING TRANSPORT TRAIN. — 28th Bombay N.I.

1 Coy. Madras Sappers.

17th B.N.I. 28th Bo. N.I.

"The Square which escorted the Transport on the march of the Force from Suâkin to the Zeribah on the 22nd March was formed thus:—

"*i.e.* the 15th Sikhs formed the front face, and a small part of the side faces; the 28th Bombay Infantry the right face and part of the rear face; the 17th Bengal Infantry similarly formed the left, and part of the rear face; the Madras Sappers were in reserve in the interior of the Square.

"Next, the positions of the three Indian Infantry Regiments at the Zeribah, at the moment when the Arabs delivered their attack, were thus:—

"*i.e.* the 15th Sikhs were in front, the 17th Bengal Infantry on the left, the 28th Bombay Infantry on the right, and early in the day, two Companies of the 17th Bengal Infantry were detached from the flank of that Regiment on the left, and placed on the right of the 28th, where the bush was very close and ᐟthick, so as to afford more effectual cover to the parties engaged on the construction of the Marines' redoubt.

"The Madras Sappers were employed in assisting in the construction of the Zeribah, and had no position in the covering lines.

"In regard to the time at which the Indian troops had luncheon,

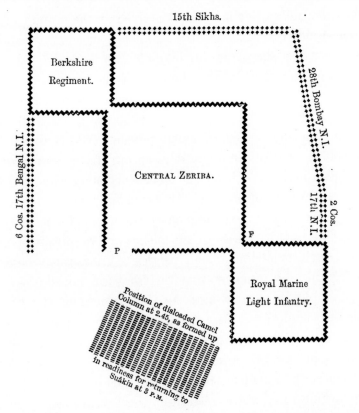

Plan, showing dispositions of Indian Brigade at Tofrek, March 22nd, 1885. This diagram also shows the position of the disloaded Camel Column at moment of attack, *vide* p. 150.

I should state that the men made no regular meal, they had some dry food, and *chuppatties* (cakes) in their haversacks, and as they stood in their ranks they eat these as they felt inclined.[1]

[1] In curious contrast to General Hudson's remarks, the *Daily News*, of March 23rd 1885, states : " The English soldiers quietly sat down to their luncheon, and their Indian comrades to their 'tiffin.' An Indian *khana*, with its punctilious observances, often of a religious character, is a somewhat absorbing process, even among gallant Sepoys and Sowars, but we do not know whether this had anything to do with what followed. The Arabs, who were supposed to have disappeared, were only biding their time—and there could be no better time than luncheon time, when the men were hungry and tired after four hours'[1] incessant work in the blazing sun."

[1] If this very thoughtful and conscientious editor had stated *eight* hours' work and *eleven* hours' fast he would have been nearer the mark, for certainly the march out was just as tasking and the sun as hot in the earlier part of the day as during the period he is pleased to recognise as that of labour proper.

"When the Indian Regiments first arrived on the ground on which it had been decided to construct the Zeribah, I had them disposed in lines two deep, as shewn in my Sketch No. II., and, with their bayonets fixed, they remained in these positions throughout the day. Small picquets of four or six men were thrown out from the right of each Company about 150 yards to the front, so as to watch the front. I preferred adopting a line of small picquets, which could, in the event of attack, readily run in and clear our front, to a few large picquets, which under those circumstances probably cloud the front, and delay the opening of fire, and the event fully bore out my view.

"During the day it was frequently necessary for some of the Infantry in line to assist in dragging bushes and scrub into position, but, whenever this was done, small parties of men were taken from alternate sections and ranks, so that the front was never broken, and the men so employed worked close to their places in the line, and with their rifles slung over their shoulders. However at the moment of attack no men of the Indian Infantry were so employed, all were in their places in line, and awaiting the order to retire and form a Square to escort the unladen Transport animals back to Suâkin."

The following brief notes, recording the actual experience of an Officer occupying a responsible position in the Brigade, will, I have no doubt, be perused with interest, conveying as they do, a very truthful idea of the difficulties previously mentioned.

"I have been trying to think of any incidents out of the common that befell us that day on the march out, but I cannot call to mind anything out of the way. One had such a lot of convoying duty up in Afghanistan, where, on account of the narrowness of the roads, the progress was always slow, that there was nothing impressed one except the intense boredom of the whole thing, and we had not the excitement of an expected fight to keep us going. On the 22nd it was simply one continuous series of short advances of the Square, and continuous halts to put on the loads of the camels which had been thrown, these casualties principally occurring from defective packing on the part of unskilled drivers, and also from the animals being so packed together that they rubbed off each others unwieldy loads. You can easily understand that, as all the loading of a camel is done by balance, any slight disarrangement of the disposal of the weight on one side causes a total collapse of the whole load.

"After the attack at Tofrek the Contingent lined the central Zariba thus :—

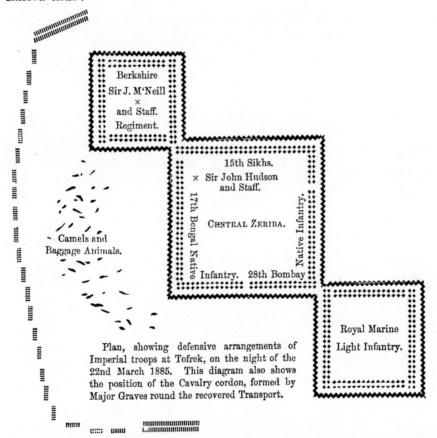

Plan, showing defensive arrangements of Imperial troops at Tofrek, on the night of the 22nd March 1885. This diagram also shows the position of the Cavalry cordon, formed by Major Graves round the recovered Transport.

"As far as I can remember the troops lay in double rank all round, with sentries standing at intervals, who were relieved as usual. There was one alarm about 8.30, but after that there was nothing, and barring the *intense cold* I never spent a better night."

It must be remembered, as mentioned at page 84, that in order to avoid attracting the attention of the enemy, no tents were pitched, or lights permitted; nothing, in fact, that could in any way " draw fire," hence, all ranks bivouacked alike in the open air. From the diagrams just given it will be seen that the relative positions of the Indian Regiments were never varied—the 15th Sikhs being always disposed on the front, the 28th Bombay Native Infantry on the right, and the 17th Bengal Native Infantry on the left,— whether acting as Convoy to the Transport Train, as covering lines to the operations at the zeriba, or lining the defences at night.

I have occasion elsewhere [1] to remark that the Transport Train formed the Hamlet of the march out. This character it always retained, and never more so than at the time of the attack, the state of affairs at that particular moment being as follows: [2] When the Transport had been safely convoyed by the Indian Brigade to the site selected for the zeriba, it was there kept collected together, while the defences grew up around it, and the stores were being gradually removed from the Transport animals and placed in proper order. As the camels were unloaded they were led out by a service-opening left at the south-east angle of the zeriba at P, and then, made to lie down, were knee-lashed as close outside as was convenient. As the time drew on when the Transport Train, having been nearly all disloaded, and preparations were being made for the return journey, under directions of Lieutenant C. G. Sinclair, Acting D.A.C.G., the camels were roused, and formed into a close column of companies facing towards Suâkin, all ready for the return journey. This was effected in a very short time, and the report was just being conveyed to Sir John M'Neill that the column was ready to start, when the first shot was fired, and the attack commenced, of which the stampede already mentioned was the immediate result.

It will easily be seen that the state of matters at this particular juncture greatly favoured the success of the Arab *ruse*. The camels were almost all on their legs; with them were many pack-animals, and mules with carts, ready to start on the homeward

[1] *Vide* p. 271.   [2] *Vide* diagram, p. 147.

rney. The entire mass was in that prepared and expectant dition in which an alarm would operate with redoubled force. came from the rear, and once communicated to the vast and wieldy column, with an uncontrollable impetus it rushed forward, great bulk taking the road for Suâkin, part going through the yal Marines' redoubt, and a small portion into the central zeriba ough a temporary service-gap left at the angle F; Captain W. Pollock, D.A.C.G, in charge of the Commissariat Convoy, ng driven before this portion of the derelict mass with part of his npany, but, by making a short detour, got safely into the redoubt upied by the Royal Marines.

A stampede like this, effected at the very moment when a mn of Transport animals was ready for the march, may be said have been inevitable. It is easy enough to protect or control els which, after being made to lie down, have been knee-lashed; when on their legs, and formed up in a column ready to move it is a different story. If the reader will turn to Appendix X. will find some interesting illustrations, not only of the sustibility of the camel to drill, but of its imperturbable indifference erious alarm. On the Nile, when stationed at Korti, the entire iment of the 19th Hussars, cheering and yelling, charged the e-lashed camelry. The only result was that one camel out of lot struggled to his feet, looked round, and knelt down again. haps the range and *timbre* of the British voice may not be al to those savage notes the Arab so freely commands; but Korti episode forms a curious commentary on the Tofrek pede. In military operations it is, of course, just as impossible ys to have your camels knee-lashed as it is with a large unt of fatigue-duty to be discharged, *always* to keep your iers standing to their arms; but the circumstance tells with ubled force against that entire absence of warning as to the concentration forming so unfortunate an element in the day's eedings. We have already seen, at page 44, what Sir John eill would have done had such warning been communicated, and that, instead of going on to Tofrek two-thirds of the Transport Train would have been sent back safely to Suâkin.

Such then is the latest occasion on which, in words used in 1878, "The Army of the Queen has been gallantly aided by the Army of the Empress of India."[1] For a very long term of years, they have indeed "fought side by side on many fields," but never were encomiums better deserved than those bestowed on the Indian Contingent of 1885, both when reviewed by General Viscount Wolseley at Suâkin, and in his despatch to the Secretary of State for War, of date June 15th, 1885,[2] wherein it is stated:—

"The Indian Contingent, under Brigadier-General Hudson, C.B., showed high soldier-like qualities, and was of the utmost value in the operations round Suakin."[3]

To the same tenor in a Special General Order, dated at Suâkin, May 16th, 1885, General Graham states:—

"The Indian Contingent came to the Soudan admirably equipped and organised, and has fully justified all that was expected of such a force, and whether in fighting, in marching, or in camp, it could not be surpassed in conduct and appearance or in discipline and efficiency."[4]

In his despatch to Lord Wolseley dated at Alexandria, May 30th, 1885, it is also stated:—

"The Indian Contingent was most efficient. The 9th Bengal Cavalry, 15th Sikhs, and 28th Bombay Infantry, were conspicuous for their gallantry in the field, and smartness on parade, while the 17th Bengal Infantry did good service in garrison at Suâkin. The Queen's Own Madras Sappers and Miners again proved themselves first-rate troops, whether for fighting or for work. Brigadier-General Hudson commanded the Indian Contingent. He is a thorough soldier, with great coolness and marked capacity for command, and from his long experience is thoroughly well qualified for the command of Indian troops."[5]

[1] Rear-Admiral Sir John Hay, Debate in House of Commons, May 6th, 1878.
[2] Supp. *London Gazette*, August 25th, 1885.
[3] *Ibid.*, June 15th, 1885.
[4] *London Gazette*, May 29th, 1885.
[5] *Ibid.*, August 25th, 1885.

CHAPTER VII.

RETROSPECTIVE.

"ὅ τι γὰρ πολύ καὶ πολλᾷ ῥέπει,
ὀρθᾷ διακρίνειν φρενὶ μὴ παρὰ καιρόν,
δυσπαλές."

"Hard it is
Where interests clash and contests rise
To meet th' occasion, yet with judgment pure
The scales of right sustain."
PINDAR's *Odes*, Olympia VIII. Strophe II.

E have now briefly, but, we hope, truthfully, placed before the reader the Battle of Tofrek in all its main features. In view of the persistent and unscrupulous misrepresentations both at the time and subsequently made regarding it, in so far as not already touched upon, it only remains with equal brevity to summarise the various circumstances exerting an adverse influence on the fortunes of the day, more especially in their bearing upon the INCIDENCE OF RESPONSIBILITY. This could not have been done previously without unduly interrupting the course of the narrative, the only resource that remained being to relegate such discussion to a separate Chapter.

Recalling to the reader's recollection a previous allusion, we would, first of all, remark that war is not only a "terrible game of chance"—by chance, meaning circumstances or eventualities lying entirely outside all human foresight or control—yet of sufficient importance seriously to affect carefully preconcerted plans and arrangements.   War is much more than this—it is not by "chance," but deliberately, and, as one of its normal characteristics, a game of the deadliest cross purposes—where the great aim is, by superior strategy, strength, or intelligence, to take an adversary unawares or at a disadvantage, and thereby inflict upon him some crushing misfortune or defeat.   More especially is this the case in savage states of society, where war is to be seen in all its undisguised and native barbarity, and where cunning, craft and stratagem form its indispensable elements.

While still retaining too many of the harsh features inseparable from War, the great tendency of civilisation is to raise it into a region immeasurably above its rude and barbarous beginnings, as these are to be seen still practised amongst savage races.   Deeply seated amid the passions which animate the human breast, as admirably expressed in the lines of the poet—

> " I grant that men, continuing what they are,
> Fierce, avaricious, proud, there must be war." [1]

The study of this great Art is essential to the stability—to the social and political welfare of every civilised community.   War in itself, one of the most difficult and intricate of the Sciences, has laid under contribution for its service every department of human knowledge, until, under the fostering influence of modern discovery, it has gradually become what we see it in our own day—one of the mightiest monuments of Applied Science, requiring a long and arduous training, a special education, not of the body only but yet more of the mind.   For the low artifices, the untutored expedients of the savage, there have been substituted far-seeing sagacity, reason, judgment,—all the higher faculties of man in their loftiest exercise, rising in special instances into genius the most commanding.

War thus prosecuted, on principles well understood by all civilised nations fully cognisant of their mutual strength and resources, like the game of chess between two adequately instructed players, comes to be mainly a trial of skill, wherein, if one player errs or fails

[1] "Table Talk," 9. 10.   By William Cowper.

adequately to cope with his antagonist, he does so with his eyes open, and in full view of all that is being done. With a savage foe the case is entirely different. Except in their immediate practical results, tactical operations are to him mere *caviare*, while it becomes extremely difficult and often quite impossible to obtain correct information on, it may be, all-important points. A General is thus compelled to conduct his operations almost entirely in the dark, and while fully aware of his own intentions and resources, as to those of the enemy he may be in a great degree ignorant. It must be admitted that this was the case in the Eastern Sûdan to a much greater extent than was at all desirable. All the ordinary means of acquiring information between two civilised but hostile armies were either entirely awanting or impracticable. Any European attempting to act as scout or spy would have paid instant forfeit with his life; while, if we may judge by certain notable instances, the reports of the native spy or "friendly" seem to have been to every practical intent thoroughly discredited. In so far then as the British Army was concerned, the hiatus between the two contending forces was much greater than could possibly be the case in almost any civilised country. The invader was completely "out of touch" with his antagonist. With combined land and maritime forces he held his Base of operations in unassailable strength; but beyond this he could move, make reconnaissances, and acquire serviceable or trustworthy information only in Force, and this within a comparatively limited range. For all preliminary and tentative purposes, the real strongholds of the enemy, and consequent knowledge as to the strength in which they were held, and the disposition of his forces, were absolutely inaccessible.

And, as with the General, so was it with the private soldier. Except for his arms of precision, as a civilised man he found himself positively at a disadvantage in presence of his savage foe. The Arab was as thoroughly adapted to his environment as if he had been one of the *feræ*, and this an environment above all others hostile to the uninured and civilised inhabitant of a temperate clime. The civilised man required heavy and very special impedimenta, ammunition, rations, and above all water. The savage troubled himself with nothing of the sort. Movement to the one was slow and toilsome; the other had all the lithe activity of the wild beast. He could cover ground and effect dispositions with a certainty and speed impossible to his antagonist. The same qualities placed him on a still more dangerous level in a hand-to-hand encounter. With troops in close formation, and able to maintain an effective " zone of fire," the breechloader might well dispose of any numbers; but this magic *cordon* once broken, man for man, or in overwhelming numbers, the chances were that the contest became very unequal. Past masters in the use of thoroughly serviceable weapons, the same lithe activity, the same resolute and reckless courage which marked their advance, lent murderous precision to every blow.

> " Each at the head
> Levelled his deadly aim; their fatal hands
> No second stroke intend."[1]

Need we wonder, then, that the British Army found the Sûdanese a foe with whom no tricks were to be played, no negligence to be indulged in with impunity.

No one was more thoroughly alive to facts like these than the ever brave yet guarded and watchful General Gordon. It is on this account we have prefaced our opening chapter with the extract from his journals bearing on this question, and trust that the importance of the subject will excuse its repetition.

"The wretched peasant, with that filthy cloth, which you see, is a determined warrior, who can undergo thirst and privation, who no more cares for pain or death than if he were of stone. The young fellows even have a game by which they test who will bear the lash of the hippopotamus whip best. They are in their own land; the pains of war are their ordinary life; and they are supported by religion of a fanatical kind, influenced by the memory of years of suffering at the hands of an effete set of Bashi Basouks.

---

[1] *Paradise Lost*, ii. 711-13.

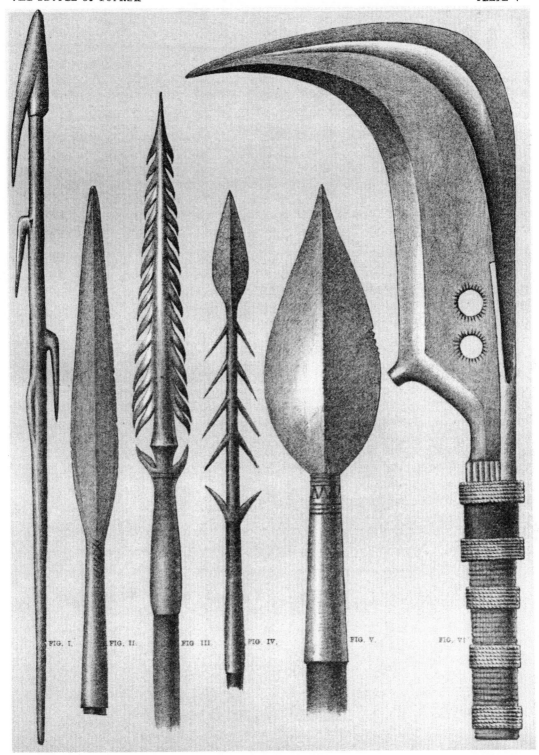

FIG. I.   FIG. II.   FIG III.   FIG. IV.   FIG. V.   FIG. VI.

SUDANESE WEAPONS.

No; if our Kentish or Yorkshire boys are to come up to help me, it is not with my wish, UNLESS WITH THE GREATEST PRECAUTION." [1]

"WITH THE GREATEST PRECAUTION." It is no exaggeration to say that these pregnant and well-weighed words, written by one thoroughly cognisant of all the circumstances, contain the gist of the whole question as between the British troops and the Sûdanese Arabs. According to a favourite maxim of Napoleon Buonaparte, "The chief art of War consists in being the strongest on a given point." And in military matters the principle has a much wider application than that of strategical combinations. It is with this object, the being "strongest on a given point," that every cannon is fired, every rifle discharged, every weapon thrust; and in formulating this axiom Napoleon simply meant that in manœuvring the forces at his disposal a Commander should make it his aim so to concentrate his available strength on some given point, that as with bomb or bullet he might pierce with fatal effect the defensive arrangements of his antagonist, disorganise his army, and shatter his combinations.

So much for the offensive; conversely, on the defensive, to present an effective resistance to hostile encroachment is the object with which every fortress is constructed, every ironclad armour-plated, and all those elaborate precautions adopted whether by land or sea which may enable the defence to be strong enough on all vital points to thwart or turn aside every adverse blow. Although in its perfection very rarely, and only under special circumstances, attainable, the antithetical proposition then to the Napoleonic maxim just quoted would be that, as its one condition of impregnable security, the defence ought to be the strongest, not on some given or selected point, but at all times and everywhere.

Falling back on that ordinary but wise and skilful conduct of war, to which Napoleon intended his maxim primarily to apply, in the *beau ideal* of what a well-managed campaign ought to be, two objects would require to be fully met and harmonised.

[1] *General Gordon's Journals: sub* 24th September 1884.

First, On the defensive, to be strong enough at all times, and at every point to be so thoroughly guarded, as to present an effective resistance to the hostile efforts of an antagonist.

Second, On the offensive, to have the resources at disposal so arranged that they might be concentrated with crushing effect on some carefully selected point, some chink in the defensive arrangements of the enemy.

Had these simple principles been invariably observed at Suâkin in 1885, with a conflict, it may be, not less severe, nothing would have been heard on the 22nd of surprise or disaster. As the case stood in the Eastern Sûdan, of the objects just mentioned by far the most important was the first. We have seen that the Arabs under the leadership of Osman Digna were in a most " dangerous and aggressive mood,"[1] and meant fighting, and suitable opportunity being afforded there was little doubt that to assume the offensive would not be left to the invader. Besides, to the British Force the real strongholds of the Arabs were practically inaccessible. Haunting places like Hashin, Tamai, or Tamanieb, with a difficulty and loss of life, proportioned to the vigour of the defence, might be occupied; but spots like these were the mere outposts of the mountainous territory amid which it lay at the option of the enemy to retire. If Osman Digna had been a wise and judicious leader, instead of an overweening, hot-headed, and revengeful fanatic, instead of urging on the tribes to be slaughtered in thousands, his true policy would have been, while keeping up a harassing guerilla war, to withdraw the main body of his forces to the mountains, and for the few weeks intervening between the intense heats of summer leave the invader uselessly to expend his energies on the only field open to him, the parched and burning plains of the Red Sea Littoral. Thus resorting to a waiting and defensive attitude, instead of turning his adherents into so much food for hyænas, vultures, and jackals, with undiminished strength, and Nature on his side, the Expedition, after effecting comparatively little, might

---

[1] *Antea*, p. 2.

have been compelled to suspend operations and retire baffled and stultified to more temperate climes and befitting occasion. Osman Digna's position, however, compelled him to be not a mere politic Chief but an active and aggressive belligerent; and if this fact brought down upon the British Army a troublesome foe, it saved it an untold amount of bootless toil.[1]

In addition to this failure to appreciate the necessity of maintaining a watchful and well-guarded defence, invulnerable *at every point*, there was combined a failure to recognise what we may well call the belligerent rights of the Arab,—the fact that he had a strategy of his own, and had it at his option to decline or to offer battle, as he deemed most expedient. In the combined movements of the 19th and 20th the intention of Head-Quarters was, if possible, to bring on an engagement, and for this eventuality they were fully prepared. With exception, however, of harassing the invader by every means in their power, and watching any chance of mischief that might arise, whatever their reasons were for refusing to be drawn, the Arabs positively declined the combat, as evidenced in the complaint of General Graham that they " refused to charge his squares." On the 22nd of March, as we have already seen, all unwitting if not to the Head-Quarters at Suâkin, at least to the Force at Tofrek, in the full exercise of his belligerent rights, the Arab determined that what to him should be the pitched battle of the campaign was to be fought. Thus staking his all he lost, and within twenty minutes from the commencement of this most determined and murderous fight, within the half-mile radius surrounding the zeriba at Tofrek, thoroughly crushed and beaten into the dust lay the flower of Osman Digna's following, the heart of the rebellion in the Eastern Sûdan, a mass of mortality, to be burned, buried out of sight, or devoured by wild animals, but never again to lift sword or spear, to slake an insatiate thirst in the blood of the stranger, or

---

[1] In the Chapter on " The Press and the Battle " are given various newspaper comments penned after the Battle of Tofrek, forcibly illustrating the difficulties of a prolonged campaign in the interior, *if such had been necessary. Vide* pp. 240 *seq.,* 256 *seq.*

respond to the wild appeals of an intolerant fanaticism. Save for the discredited or at least neglected reports of the spies, this event befell entirely outside the anticipations, and certainly the precautionary measures adopted, by Head-Quarters at Suâkin; and the mere fact that it should so happen, enforces with startling emphasis the remarks already made as to the necessity of being equally safeguarded at all points, and of fully recognising the belligerent rights of the enemy.

Without intimation given, Head-Quarters elected to have two Field-days on the 19th and 20th. It piped, but the Arab failing to dance, on both occasions the British Force fell back on its Base, leaving to the enemy, in a possession yet undisturbed, the undisputed honours of the day. On precisely the same terms, but with much more deadly intent, the Arab elected to have not a Field-day but a pitched and resolute Battle on the 22nd, and the invader had to dance whether he was adequately prepared and liked it or not. If this determination to return to the British Force, with interest paid in full, a Roland for its Oliver, was not the assertion of belligerent rights on the part of a people who deemed themselves in creed, in politics, and in war, immeasurably superior to their antagonists, I do not know what is. Our business, however, is with those on whom, deprived of essential safeguards and heavily overburdened, like men set to swim for their lives in a stormy sea, THE FULL WEIGHT OF THE RETALIATORY BLOW FELL.

Among the various influences adversely affecting the fortunes of the day on the 22nd of March, the first place must be given to the change from the old and well established approach to Tamai. Seeing that the occasion for an advance on Tamanieb never arose, it would serve no purpose to enquire whether any advantage would have accrued from the possession of an Advanced Depôt equally serviceable for Tamai or Tamanieb. The object in selecting a new route was to kill two birds with one stone. Only one bird required to be hit, and we need not trouble ourselves as to the other, which was in any case a mere eventuality. In 1884 the British Force seems to have been none the worse for having to march upon Tamai and Tamanieb by two distinct and separate routes. The marching in any case would be not a yard the less; any possible gain being merely a matter of storage and an intermediate *point d'appui.* It is more to the purpose to say that, as a line of approach to Tamai, no worse route could have been selected. In saying this I have no wish to be misunderstood. As a piece of wild country approaching the mountains, there might be little or nothing to choose between the tracts of ground lying respectively between Tamai and either the Tofrek or Baker's zeribas. That is not the question. The distance between either of these places was only intended to be covered by a fighting Force, disencumbered of everything not actually necessary for the immediate operations. For an Advanced Depôt or Secondary Base, beyond all question the most important part of the road was that which lay between it and the Primary Base, and which had to be constantly traversed by heavily-laden convoys and *impedimenta* of all kinds.

It is the character of the ground then, and its suitability for a Line of Communications between the Primary and the Secondary Base, which, in a case like the present, forms the real criterion of any particular route; and in this respect, as tested by results, the route selected in 1885 stands utterly condemned. The enormous difficulties to which it gave rise need not be mentioned here, they are matter of history, and have been quite sufficiently dealt with in the previous pages. It will be more advantageous to fall back on 1884, and enquire whether any similar difficulties were then experienced. Reference to all available sources of information only serves to show that, to use a well-worn phrase, these difficulties were " conspicuous by their absence." The character of the route between Suâkin and Baker's zeriba has been already described in Chapter III., and need not be recapitulated. Suffice it to say, that in every record referring to the Expedition of 1884, if we except an Arab scare on the part of the Egyptian camel-drivers, there is no reference to one solitary hitch in the matter of Transport—certainly none arising from the character of the route, which could scarcely be, seeing it was simply part of the ordinary well-traversed though certainly unmade and natural desert-road between Suâkin and Kassala. On this score as little mention is made of difficulties as a man blessed with a sound digestion has got to tell of dyspepsia.

This diversity of route being a point of considerable importance, we may be excused for quoting some contemporary notices. After the Battle of El Teb and advance on Tokar, the Force being again concentrated at Suâkin, on the 9th of March by a Cavalry reconnaissance the first steps were taken towards the new movements on Tamai.

"At eight o'clock this morning [9th March] a squadron of the 10th Hussars, under Major Gough, Colonel Stuart and others going with them, scouted to the south-west as far as Baker's zereba, eight miles out, but saw no signs of the enemy. They went a mile and a half beyond, towards the mountain range, without entering the defiles, and selected the zereba for an advanced camp. It is square, has 100 yards of front, and is enclosed by two feet of earthen mound and brush. Osman's camp is in the valley, nine miles to the westward of the zereba. The cavalry found the country tolerably open, though there is some mimosa nearer to the hills, yet clear ground suitable to cavalry." [1]

Reports being thus favourable, on the morning of the 10th the Black Watch were sent out to take possession of Baker's zeriba, and make such alterations as might be necessary in turning it into an Advance Depôt. No difficulties seem to have been encountered other than those originating in the intensely hot and oppressive character of the day. Many of the men fell out, and it was only after a toilsome march, due to this cause, that the entrenchments were reached.[2] They were immediately followed by a convoy laden with ammunition, provisions, and water, and had not been ten

[1] *Daily Telegraph*, March 10th, 1884.

[2] They were to have gone out on the evening of the 9th, but had to stay behind and receive a wigging from General Graham for alleged wild firing, and being out of hand at El Teb. The canteen was also closed, and the Regiment informed that it would occupy an advanced position on the morrow, when it was trusted the good name forfeited at El Teb would be retrieved.

minutes in the zeriba before they were at work unloading the camels, storing the ammunition and provisions. Duties like these lasted about three hours, when the reparation of the zeriba next claimed attention. Although they could do little injury to the entrenchments, the Arabs seem to have burned the mimosa fencing. To get materials for a new one it was necessary to go a mile or more from the zeriba, the bushes when cut being dragged back by camels, etc., or by the men themselves. While thus occupied there was an alarm, due to the approach of about a thousand of the enemy. The men stood to their arms for over an hour, but in the meantime some of the Artillery happily arriving, the enemy took themselves off to the hills. Resuming their labours, by 5 P.M. a zeriba had been fenced in of such dimensions that next day General Graham condemned it as being too large, and it had to be considerably reduced.

The useful character of this zeriba in 1884, and what we cannot but regard as its most unfortunate abandonment in 1885, may excuse our noting a few facts as to its history. In the *Daily Telegraph* of March 10th, 1884, we are told— .

"The zereba referred to got its name from the fact that it had been constructed by General Baker's force, when they advanced on reconnaissance from Suakim. It is far more substantially built than most of the British soldiers' work of the same kind, and the addition of the low mound of earth all round affords perfect security against rifle fire, as the country is quite flat there."

The reader will notice in the closing sentence of this paragraph several important admissions. In 1884, at the farther extremity of what, for a desert route, was a very easy Line of Communications, the British Force advancing on Tamai had for its Secondary Base not a mere thorn-fenced enclosure, but a regularly constructed and, when topped anew with mimosa, a thoroughly serviceable earthwork, carefully selected with a view to defence against hostile approach, and, we may add, for the *status quo* at the time of its formation, an admirable strategical position, commanding as it did the group of desert-routes running south and south-west by Tokar, Kassala, Tamai, Sinkat, etc.

It is a well-known fact that, while not to be relied on for facing an enemy in the open, owing to their practice in river and canal banking in the Delta, the Egyptian soldiery were adepts at constructing Fieldworks, and while the Arabs were very chary in attacking, the fellaheen might be expected to be a little more resolute in defending such works. This zeriba showed then a good deal of skill on the part of General Baker, as well as industry on that of the Egyptians.

A letter, dated January 16th—only one of a very good series, in the columns of the *Standard* of February 5th, 1884—throws some light on the tactics being adopted by General Baker at the commencement of the year :—

"Meantime General Baker continues to drill his troops incessantly. During the last few days we have had route marching, the whole force moving out into the bush for a few miles, accompanied by all the transport available. The General surrounds the column with a cordon of cavalry scouts. We move, as it were, in the centre of a vast square of vedettes, so that a surprise is impossible. The enemy would be discovered, notwithstanding the thick bush, a full mile before he could approach the infantry. That would afford the latter ample time to get into formation for resisting attack, while the cavalry, concentrating, would endeavour to hang on the enemy's flanks and rear.

"Every night we shall form a sereebah or laager of brushwood. The black troops are particularly clever from long practice in running up these, and the Egyptians and Turks are quickly learning the work. It is reassuring to know that in no instance in African warfare has a sereebah been successfully attacked. The brushwood is simply impenetrable to human beings, and the triangular-shaped banquettes in the centre of each side of the square will permit of a flanking fire being delivered. The inner laager will contain the cavalry horses and baggage animals, so as to prevent a sudden stampede, carrying confusion amongst the infantry."

Although, when put to the test in the field with an Arab foe, too often the Egyptian troops could only show "how not to do it;"

admirably exemplifying as they do the remarks already made as to the wisdom of such a mode of procedure, the reverse was certainly the case with their General's precautionary measures; and we cannot but reflect how differently matters would have turned out had like watchful care been invariably observed in 1885.

The actual construction of the zeriba in question seems to have taken place during that most distressing period prior to the movement from Trinkitat when, like an enraged but outmanœuvred and overmastered lion, General Baker was exerting every means in his power to relieve the long death agony at Sinkat, doomed to end at last in so tragic a *finale*. Powerless to awaken from their torpor the British and Cairene authorities, unable with the miserable *matériel* provided to risk breaking the savage *cordon* investing the imprisoned but gallant Tewfik and his brave garrison,[1] he seems to

---

[1] Although only 35 miles from Suâkin, 11 hours' travel according to Consul Moncrieff, and 2½ days by the War Office Report, the great difficulty of any attempt to relieve Sinkat lay in the mountainous character of the district intervening between it and Suâkin, and through which any route that might be selected necessarily ran. The nature of the ravines through which it must be approached may be judged from the fact that it is situated 2500 feet above the sea level, and forms a favourite retreat of the Suâkinis during the heats of summer and the rainy season. As stated by Consul Moncrieff, hostile approach would be extremely difficult "against numbers, however poorly armed, on account of the passes, *which could be held by a mob with stones*" (*Parl. Paper*, Egypt, No. 1 (1884), p. 14). It was in these formidable ravines that the various detachments sent to reinforce Sinkat were destroyed, and these facts had no doubt an important influence in determining Baker Pasha's plan of operations. It must also be remembered that so late as Jan. 9, 1884, or just a month before the fall of Sinkat, Sir Evelyn Wood writes to General Baker—

"If it is absolutely necessary to use force in order to extricate the garrisons of Sinkat and Tokar you can do so, *provided you consider your force is sufficient and that you may reasonably count on success.*

"The enforced submission of the men who have been holding out at these two places would be very painful to His Highness the Khedive ; *but even such a sacrifice is better in his opinion than that you and your troops should attempt a task which you cannot reckon fairly to be within your power*" (*Parl. Paper*, Egypt, No. 7 (1884), p. 1).

With only the most untrustworthy fellaheen levies and a few black troops at disposal, and Earl Granville, with reference to the Soudan under date Nov. 30, 1883, telegraphing : "We cannot lend English or Indian troops"; and again, Dec. 13 : "Her Majesty's Government have no intention of employing British or Indian troops in that province" (*Parl. Paper*, Egypt, No. 1 (1884), pp. 93, 131), there was thus slight hope for Tewfik and his brave garrison. Tewfik

have been uncertain whether to beat about and make a diversion for the partial relief of the beleaguered town by land or by sea. If the siege could not be raised, some good might at least be done by engaging the attention of the Arabs elsewhere, and so in that truly forlorn hope, a desperate sortie, give Tewfik a better chance of escape. Accordingly, we are informed that, "On the 22nd January Baker Pasha moved out with four hundred Cavalry towards Osman Digna's camp fourteen miles off." And again, "On the 24th General Baker moved out with two thousand two hundred men. These threw up some slight entrenchments at a point commanding both the Sinkat and Tokar roads. They remained there all night."[1]

We know the sequel. Apparently deeming it imprudent to tempt the Arabs amid their rocky strongholds near Suâkin, and in hopes that an advance on Tokar might aid in relieving Sinkat, the Egyptian Force was embarked for Trinkitat, only to be completely cut up at El Teb on the 4th of February, Sinkat falling just a week afterwards. Truly, desperate diseases need desperate remedies!

Sentiment, however, goes for little in War, and no matter how interesting its associations, how admirably fitted for the requirements of 1884, if, in 1885, Baker's zeriba was not equally well adapted to meet a new set of circumstances it would be summarily discarded. Our averment is, that in a district like that round Suâkin, with little variety in the natural contours until the mountains are approached, few spots presenting exceptional advantages from a military point of view, and the chief obstacle to be considered, that intractable encumbrance the mimosa scrub, as a

---

Bey, Mohaffiz of Suâkin, on whose "courage and conduct," as far back as August 1883, Consul Moncrieff bestows the highest praise. "Tewfik—from whom no amount of modesty could hide the fact that he was the only available person capable of commanding efficiently in a crisis" (*Ibid.* p. 14), who, impelled only by a high sense of honour and duty threw himself into Sinkat, and even when urged, "hoping against hope," refused to retire. Truly, in that miserable time it was the gallant, the brave, the capable, who were sacrificed,— the scoundrels only escaped. But Nemesis was at hand, and as a sequel to the *non possumus* of 1883 came the Expedition of 1884 and that of the combined Imperial Forces in 1885, with the prolonged naval and military occupation of Suâkin.

[1] *Standard*, February 1st, 1884.

Secondary Base, to which a good convoy-route or Line of Communications was indispensable, entrenched as it was, and only requiring a few hours' reparations, Baker's zeriba was out of sight the best position for an advance on Tamai, and any departure from previous practice the result of a misleading and mischievous delusion. In proof of this we point to the known facts of the two advances in 1884 and 1885, and simply say, "Look on this picture and on that."

After the Black Watch had taken possession on the 10th, the principal business was the conveyance of stores. It was telegraphed on the 9th :—

"Whenever General Graham is able to get three days' supplies and water stored in the zereba, the whole force will move to attack Osman's command." [1]

And as the result of the same day's work at Suâkin, it is stated :—

"Camels and mules, conveying water and stores, have been passing out all day, and already there are 10,000 gallons of water and a large quantity of ammunition and food in store. Nine convoys went out, and to-morrow the number will be doubled." [2]

Successful work indeed for so short a time. Nine convoys one day, and eighteen in prospect for the next ! why, this means that the Transport Train must have been traversing almost uninterruptedly throughout the day [3] that south-going Line of Communications, and this apparently without any great armed escort. Three days' supplies for an advance, commencing on the 10th ending on the 15th, and resulting in a fierce battle and successful capture of Tamai, and this by a Force about equal in numbers to that which first moved out to Tofrek. Alluding to the final preparations for the advance on Tamai in 1885, what has the *Times* to say on the other side :—

"Ever since the fight on Sunday week, the troops had been incessantly

[1] *Daily Telegraph,* March 10th, 1884.
[2] *Daily Telegraph,* March 11th, 1884.
[3] And by night also. On the evening of the 11th a light visible only from the direction of Suâkin was affixed at the top of a stage-ladder or look-out, for the guidance of convoys.

occupied in pouring into the zareba convoys laden with the greatest and most essential of our necessities—water. *It is impossible to over estimate the enormous difficulties attending the formation of this zareba depôt in the bush.*[1]

At pages 309-10 of the Appendix, in the brief telegrams sent by General Graham to the War Minister, in "no news, good news," will be found the negative aspect of the route and convoy question in 1884; but in the detailed despatch of March 15th, as published in the *London Gazette*,[2] even the bald official despatch reads like a moonlit idyll, wherein

> " Heaven's ebon vault
> Studded with stars unutterably bright,
> Through which the moon's unclouded grandeur rolls,
> Seems like a canopy which love has spread
> To curtain her sleeping world." [3]

"At 6 P.M. on the 11th instant, the Artillery and Infantry advanced to Baker's zeriba, about 8½ miles, reaching it about 10.30 P.M.

"There was a bright moon, and the night air soft and pleasant, so that the march did not distress the men, although it was hard work for the Naval Brigade."

So the sailors, acting in the deep sand as beasts of draught to the guns, formed the only *drawback* to this delightful march. In the same despatch the convoy question is thus dealt with :—

"The convoy (under Major Turner) had advanced in rear of the force and halted at Baker's zeriba. Cavalry and Mounted Infantry sent back to bring it on; arrived 6.30, consisting of 245 camels carrying two days' supplies of war for men, 4,400 rations, forage for 1,200 horses, and reserve ammunition."

Other sources relieve the dryness of the official narrative, and let in light, not as to the *désagréments* but the amenities of this brief but successful expedition.

"The convoys with water and provisions arrived from zeriba at 6.15 P.M. The convoys were in charge of Lieut. Chamley Turner, who deserves the

---

[1] *Times*, April 1, 1885.   [2] Supplement, April 3rd, 1884.
[3] " Queen Mab," by Percy Bysshe Shelley.

highest praise for his activity and efficiency in discharging his duties, being always on the spot at the right moment." [1]

"The Commissariat and Transport, under Assistant-Commissary-General Nugent, was wonderfully good, and it is no wonder that the troops were pleased, since they were luxuriously supplied and never seemed to want for anything. . . . The Transport had magnificent mules and camels, splendidly equipped, and which, being lightly loaded, worked well to the end of the campaign." [2]

Combining together these fragmentary statements, it seems scarcely possible that they refer to an operation exactly equivalent to that carried into effect in the succeeding campaign under such widely contrasted circumstances. It must indeed be admitted that, relatively to the Force employed, there was more work done, and that of a more effective and soldierly character, in the first campaign than in the second, and with much less of "cross purpose" between the tactics of the two belligerents. This may have been in part due to the Arabs, who no doubt had learned caution in confronting the varied arms and multiplied resources of a civilised army, with which, in its totality, when well managed and made mutually supporting, they were themselves so ill fitted to cope. The range and destructive fire of a well-served Artillery, the prompt and effective checkmate of the Cavalry at Tamai, turning the tide of triumph at the very moment

> " When the fierce Foe hung on our broken rear
> Insulting, and pursued us. . . .
> With what compulsion and laborious flight : " [3]

may well have impressed the Arabs, especially when, in the latter case, despite its fiery hedge, they had got the Infantry comparatively at their mercy. Be that as it may, the leading facts of the two campaigns are before us, and it must be admitted that they present in many respects an undeniable and a startling contrast.

---

[1] *Times*, March 14th, 1884.   *United Service Magazine*, 1884, Part I.
[2] " The Battle of Tamai," by a Soldier.   p. 698.   [3] *Paradise Lost*, II. 78-80.

In 1885, to accomplish "The first and most pressing object of the campaign—the destruction of the power of Osman Digna,"[1] from 11,000 to 12,000 men were detailed and fully provided. Yet, most unexpectedly, this object was effectively achieved by a Force of just the same strength as that employed in 1884, with the very curious result, that the large body of men destined for the advance on Tamai had not only their work taken entirely out of their hands, but in their turn became a "white elephant," for whose anticipated necessities the most enormous preparations required to be made. An untold amount of trouble, and expenditure, both of time and money, and not a little life, was thus involved, and all for a purpose proving to be entirely superfluous and, assuming that the fact of the enemy's collapse had been known, much better dispensed with.

This "white elephant" then of a Force, and of operations ultimately found to be superfluous, not merely aggravated but was the direct cause of a great part of the mischiefs so loudly complained of. To make provision for its prospective wants the excessive Transport was sent out on the 22nd, and to the same end were the incessant convoys and storage of the next ten days; and it cannot be denied that much of the resulting difficulty was due to what, in military language, must euphemistically be called the "Line of Communications" between the Primary Base and Advanced Depôt. Why there should have been so wide a departure from previous experience in 1884 it is difficult to discover. It arose certainly from no great accretion to Osman Digna's power. His numbers were just as uncertain and hypothetical in the first campaign as in the second. He was just the same savage, semi-barbarian foe as ever. In the case of a civilised power many things might have occurred in a year to change the military situation. Allies might have been acquired, new armaments adopted, fortifications built, earthworks thrown up, but the Arab was the same in 1885 as he had been in 1884, *plus* a little more experience with a civilised antagonist.

With the facts now mentioned before him I must leave the

---

[1] *Parliamentary Papers*, Egypt, No. 9 (1884), p. 9.

reader to judge whether it would not have been much better to have followed the accustomed route by Baker's zeriba, in which direction the Brigades were drawn up at sunrise on the 22nd of March, instead of involving the entire Expedition in this new and unexplored line of approach to Tamai, *with the red herring of Tamanieb drawn across the trail.*

The plea advanced by General Graham for the changed direction on the 22nd, being that the position of the post it was desired to establish "was selected with a view to making it a depôt for operations against either Tamanieb or Tamai, according to circumstances,"[1] it may be of service to glance at the route followed to the alternative locality in 1884. The battle of Tamai fought, and the Expedition reconcentrated at Suâkin, great uncertainty seems to have prevailed as to the movements and intentions of the enemy. With the view of eliciting information and opening up the Berber route, a Secondary Base was formed at Handûb. Possession was taken by the Gordon Highlanders, Cavalry, Mounted Infantry, and two Batteries of Artillery, under General Stewart; a zeriba constructed, and reconnaissances made to Otao and Tambuk, and also in other directions, the only Arabs encountered being "friendlies." Owing especially to its water supply, Handûb formed a most serviceable position for a Secondary Base. Situated 320 feet above the sea level, it forms the first important stage on the Suâkin-Berber road, marking the point where that road turns the northern flank of the Waratab range of mountains. The hilly nature of the ground gave facilities for a strong position being selected for the zeriba, which is thus described :—

"The laager or zereba, which was formed at the base of the hill,[2] extending to within a few yards of the more permanent wells of water, was triangular shaped. The apex was at the hill top, the sides enclosing the west face of the hill, and the base line at the foot. The latter was protected by a wire entanglement and small iron spikes, called 'crows' feet.' "[3]

[1] Supp. to *London Gazette*, Aug. 25, 1885.   [2] 200 feet in height.
[3] *Desert Warfare*, p. 238.

And still further—

"The troops have encamped at the base of a hill, the top of which and an adjacent hill are held by a company of the Gordon Highlanders, who have built a low wall of stones on the summit, behind which they lie. At the base, covering the wells, a strong zereba has been constructed, within which the transport and baggage animals, as well as the rest of this force, are entrenched. The troops went forward by easy stages, and as a breeze was stirring the men stood the journey well, arriving in good order." [1]

The advantages presented by Handūb were enhanced by a water supply practically inexhaustible.

"There was an abundant supply of water at Handoub. The well in front of the zereba was simply a round hole 6 or 7 feet deep and as many wide, dug in the clayey shingle. There were always from 3 to 4 feet of water in it, and no amount of 'drawing' for the horses emptied it. If it was plied too industriously the water became muddy, but the supply was not affected. Several barrels and hogsheads were sunk in the plain at the foot of the hill, and in each of these there was also plenty of water. The natives, when they required water, went into the dry bed of the river or khor, and scraping away a foot or two of the loose sand and shingle, came upon the water. There were thus ample facilities for baths and morning 'tubs,' and we made the most of our opportunities in that direction. The troops were ordered to drink the condensed water carried up from the base at Suakin. This they did, but as their thirst was great they superadded to it refreshing draughts of the cool and slightly mineral-tasted water of Handoub. So far as we could see no one was any the worse because of this indulgence in good teetotal beverages." [2]

Nature and art thus combined to render Handūb an admirable centre of military activity for the district lying to the north-west of Suâkin ; but notwithstanding the most diligent Cavalry patrols, no enemy presenting himself in this quarter, it became requisite to renew the search for Osman Digna and his following in the more

[1] *Desert Warfare*, p. 239.

[2] *Ibid.*, p. 240. The account given in the *Times* is scarcely so favourable, although the inference is that in four of the wells at least there must have been a good supply.

"It is reported that there are five wells at Handoub. It was found that one was soon emptied ; and when necessary those using it have to wait until it is refilled. The water is brackish, and only fit for the horses, which, moreover, are only able to water very slowly."—*Times*, March 19, 1884.

rugged and formidable localities to the south-west, where, amid mountain fastnesses, favoured by a perennial water supply, at Tamanieb the Arab found a secure retreat. Handūb, unfortunately lying considerably to the north of the direct route from Suâkin to Tamanieb, a new movement became necessary. Accordingly, on March 21st, the Gordon Highlanders marched across from Handūb to the entrance of the Tamanieb valley, where they were joined by a Company of the 89th or Royal Irish Fusiliers, with entrenching tools, from Suâkin. At this point was formed the zeriba marked on the Intelligence Department Map as No. 4,[1] and referred to in the *Times* of March 27th as " Graham's zariba." It is situated about eleven miles south-west [2] of Suâkin, on the direct line of that " Wide track from Suâkin to Tamanieb," previously mentioned.[3] The official despatches for 1884 are unfortunately still more meagre than those for 1885, and such information as can be got must be

[1] Excluding those formed on the line or during the construction of the railway, in the district around Suâkin, eight principal zeribas were made or occupied by the British during the campaigns of 1884 and 1885.

1884.

No. 1. Baker's Zeriba, repaired and occupied March 10th-15th.

No. 2. Zeriba at New Tamai, formed March 12th and occupied till next day.

No. 3. Zeriba at Handūb, formed March 21st, etc., and occupied till the close of the campaign ; occupied again in 1885, from immediately after the advance on Tamai till the close of the campaign.

No. 4. Zeriba No. 4, in the *Times* of March 27th designated "Graham's zariba," formed March 23rd, on the " Wide track from Suâkin to Tamanib," and occupied as a Base for the advance on Tamanib till March 29th.

No. 5. Zeriba No. 5, " Buller's zariba," having been formed March 26th by

the Brigade under his command, four or five miles in advance of zeriba No. 4, and occupied until March 28th.

1885.

No. 6. Zeriba at Hashin, formed March 20th and occupied till the 25th, when it was " dismantled and abandoned." [1]

No. 7. M'Neill's zeriba, formed March 22nd and occupied till April 6th. Burned May 1st.

No. 8. Zeriba at Teselah Hill, formed April 2nd and occupied till next day.

In addition to the above there were also zeribas at Trinkitat and Tokar, and at Otao and Tambuk, on the line of Railway.

[2] In the *Daily Telegraph* and *Desert Warfare* the direction is given as " ten miles *nearly west by north* of Suâkin," an extraordinary variation from the Intelligence Department Map.

[3] *Vide* p. 32.

[1] *Diary of the Suâkin Expedition*, p. 25.

obtained from other sources. One thing is clear, no particular difficulty arose from the character of the route in its earlier stage, but in spite of a local supply, the great difficulty was the storage of an adequate stock of water.

On the 24th we are told that

"Convoys have been pressed forward all day with water and stores. Water is still the one great obstacle to rapid movement; and although men are put upon the shortest allowance, and the horses have to drink brackish well water,[1] the reserve increases slowly. The heat to-day has been intense."[2]

Notwithstanding this tedious accumulation of a prime necessity of existence, the Force destined for Tamanieb advanced in the afternoon of next day, March 25th, from Suâkin to zeriba No. 4. The heat made the march excessively trying, three to four hundred men falling out through exhaustion. For this result, however, the narrator gives a more prosaic reason than excessive heat. In war as in peace men must dine, and it is mildly suggested that much of the trouble was due to a *post-prandial* march. On the 26th we are informed—

"Yesterday the infantry carried fifty rounds per man only, and, perhaps, much of the falling out on the march was due in some degree to the fact that the men had dined, and that many had drunk copious draughts of canteen beer before starting, that beverage evidently overheating them."[3]

Troublesome question this of dinner to a field or fighting Force, especially when there are specials present to chronicle all the minutiæ of the British lions' "feeding time." These remarks are, however, harmless compared with those made regarding Tofrek, where, caught redhanded in the act, the entire Force was declared guilty of the enormity of "dining," "lunching," etc., at the very moment when the Arab made his sudden onslaught.

The Force concentrated at zeriba No. 4, the chief business of the 26th was a Cavalry reconnaissance in force under General Stewart, who pushed forward amongst the rocky gorges leading

---

[1] Water had been found in the immediate vicinity of the zeriba.

[2] *Desert Warfare*, p. 249.

[3] *Ibid.*, p. 255.

towards Tamanieb until further advance became impracticable for
Cavalry. Our chief interest of course lies in the character of the
route, regarding which we are informed—

"For the first four or five miles it was easy going along the plain through
mimosa sparsely growing, and occasionally over bare patches of sand, gravel,
and small stones.

"When we got to the foothills the ground became very rough, full of
sharp pieces of splintered gneiss, granite, and greenstone, making the horses
walk as gingerly as cats on a broken glass wall, and laming several, despite
the utmost care. It was the worst piece of ground we have as yet traversed
in the campaign." [1]

Although still more bloodless, two horses belonging to the
Mounted Infantry being the only victims, during these latter days
of March 1884, as in the earliest of April 1885, took place
one of those great military promenades, whose only result
was to show that the Arab most emphatically deeming discretion the better part of valour; the campaign for the time
being had come to an end. Baffled by an enemy more inexorable than the Sûdanese, within the next few days, in hot haste
the Expedition had vanished from the Red Sea Littoral. With
exception of the oppressive heat, so far at least as the entrance
on the mountain gorges, the march to and from Tamanieb presented
just as little difficulty as did that to Tamai. Both routes had been
thoroughly reconnoitred; and, in addition to this, if not by the
British at least by the natives they were old established and
frequently traversed routes. The mimosa sparsely growing and of
moderate size, seems to present no impediment, the principal
mischief being the excessive heat. Such, then, was the actual
experience of the Expedition of 1884 on the march to these
alternative localities, towards which an entirely new and unexplored
line of approach was sought to be established in 1885. In making
this rapid survey, what we plead for is that, according to the point

[1] *Desert Warfare*, p. 257.

of attack selected, one or other of the previously well known and frequented routes ought undoubtedly to have been followed, and if there were strategical reasons for adopting a new route its selection should have been due not to haphazard or compass bearing, but to well ascertained and unquestionable advantages.

As intimately connected with this mis-selection of a route, and, so far as ordinary military practice goes, the direct cause of all the mischiefs arising therefrom, must be noted the ENTIRE ABSENCE OF ANY PRELIMINARY RECONNAISSANCE. So far as we are aware, throughout both campaigns in the Eastern Sûdan, this march upon Tofrek was the only movement of any importance undertaken without some previous exploration of the locality destined to be the scene of critical and warlike operations. In 1884 the battle of El Teb was fought under circumstances which might well have precluded the idea of a British reconnaissance as being if not impracticable at least unnecessary. The enemy was in full occupation of the coast, and in force just five miles off. Baker Pasha was with the advance, and as the scene of recent conflict the ground was comparatively familiar, yet on February 26th, the day previous to the battle of El Teb, the 42nd Highlanders to the number of seven hundred men, and three hundred and fifty of the Royal Irish Fusiliers, with a Camel Battery and two Squadrons of the 19th Hussars, and Mounted Infantry, were sent forward on reconnaissance and took possession of Fort Baker, the Cavalry advancing a couple of miles inland until they came within sight of the enemy in strength, and only then, acting on orders, withdrew.

We have also seen previously,[1] how thoroughly, in 1884, the comparatively well-known route to Tamai by Baker's zeriba was reconnoitred preparatory to the advance resulting in the second great battle of the campaign. The same caution was observed in the subsequent movements towards Handûb and Tamanieb, no important operations being engaged in until both the local topography, and the whereabouts of the enemy were pretty well known.

[1] Page 162, *seq.*

In 1885, after ten months' enforced confinement within the camping lines, active operations were resumed on 1st February by a reconnaissance towards Hashin under Major-General Lyon-Fremantle, when Colonel Kelly's horse was killed, and his saddle, bridle, and field-glasses, lost. After the unfortunate episode[1] on the 3rd of February at Handūb, nothing further seems to have been done until the 19th of March, when Hashin was again reconnoitred in full force by General Graham. No such preparatory steps were taken for the Movement on the 22nd, although the circumstances were such as should have rendered similar measures even more imperative. The line of advance had apparently never been previously traversed, the various admissions subsequently made in the despatches, showing that its characteristics were entirely new and unknown even at Head-Quarters. In the telegraphic despatch of March 23rd the first recognition occurs : "The cavalry, 5th Lancers, did their best to give information, *but the ground being covered with bush it was impossible to see any distance."* [2] In the detailed despatch of 28th March this is still further amplified :—

"Sir J. M'Neill's convoy, *on its march through the dense scrub* [3] *which lies between Suakin and the hills, experienced much difficulty.* The great mass of Camels inclosed in the Indian Brigade square was continually getting into

---

[1] *Vide* p. 190.

[2] *Vide* Appendix II. p. 315.

[3] In the discussion which ensued at the close of General Graham's lecture on "Infantry Fire Tactics" delivered at the Royal United Service Institution, this term gave rise to some curious remarks. General Olpherts, Ⅴ.Ⓒ., referring to the expression used by General Graham at the opening of the lecture, had asked the question, how it was possible for a square to get through "impenetrable scrub." To this General Graham replied :—"He (General Olpherts) asked how we could manage to get through the 'impenetrable scrub' with a square. Well, I should say we could not, nor in any other way ; but I never used the ex-

pression, and therefore am not responsible for it. The scrub was not 'impenetrable' as we proved by getting through it ;" and in a note adds—"General Olpherts was, however, quite right. I *did* use the expression 'impenetrable.'—G. G." (*Journal of the Royal United Service Institution,* vol. xxx., 1886, p. 270.) The following remarks were subsequently made by General Olpherts : "With regard to what General Graham said concerning the phrase that I used of 'impenetrable scrub,' I beg leave to withdraw that phrase and to substitute for it Sir Gerald's own term 'dense scrub,' but I am still unable to understand how a large square could be moved through a 'dense, thorny scrub.'" (*Ibid.,* p. 272.)

2 A

disorder, *owing to the high prickly bushes through which it was obliged to force its way.*

"Thus frequent halts were necessary in order to get the Camels back into position, and restore the chain of defence with which it is necessary in such a country to surround the transport animals and non-combatants." [1]

In his final despatch to Lord Wolseley of 30th May 1885, in describing the physical characteristics of the district around Suâkin, General Graham also states :—

"In the immediate vicinity of Suakin, towards the north and west, the country is fairly open for a mile or two, but beyond this radius, *and south-west towards Tamai, the bush is thick.*

"The scrub is chiefly composed of the prickly mimosa bush, growing sometimes to a height of six or eight feet, and of a growth of small shrubs in belts, following the shallow beds of the numerous watercourses or 'khors,' which carry off (in a north-easterly direction) the water flowing to the sea from the mountains during the periodical summer and autumnal rains." [2]

In his lecture on "Infantry Fire Tactics," in defending the use of the square formation in the Sûdan, General Graham states :—

"The real reason for our adopting square formations was the *dense impenetrable character of the belts of bush in the desert,* which paralysed cavalry action while allowing the fearless active Arabs, who move with all the rapidity of cavalry, to approach unseen." [3]

Now, all this information is quite correct, and cannot be too carefully stated and understood, but the question at once arises, if the density and impenetrability of the bush "south-west towards Tamai" was so well known at Head-Quarters prior to the 22nd of March, why did this knowledge not exercise its legitimate influence on the arrangements for the advance? If, on the contrary, it was not known, but was entirely *ex post facto,* to the zeriba experiences, the neglect to reconnoitre ground, so soon to be the scene of important and troublesome operations, was a serious mistake.

[1] *Vide* Appendix II.
[2] Supp. to *London Gazette,* August 25th, 1885.
[3] *Journal of Royal United Service Institution,* 1886, p. 233.

Surely the Expedition was sent out to the Eastern Sûdan for some better purpose than to give occasion for an amusing play upon words, and enable a distinguished General to speak in paradoxical terms of "the dense scrub," "the dense and impenetrable character of the belts of bush in the desert," and then correct his phraseology by saying—"The scrub was not 'impenetrable' *as we proved by getting through it!*" As a mere feat of strength or of foolhardiness, with his clothes torn to shreds, and his body lacerated and bleeding, a man might force his way through a thorn-hedge, which any other sane person would carefully avoid. But when the alternative of a more open and convenient road lies close at hand, is it reasonable that he should do so? Certainly not. And yet, on the very grandest scale this is exactly what was done on the 22nd of March, and succeeding days. The contrast between the experiences in this respect of 1884 and 1885 could not be better expressed than by selections from General Graham's own despatches. In the earlier part of this chapter[1] we have seen, both from despatches and other sources, how successfully the advance on Tamai was performed the previous year, and, in addition to the extracts just given from the despatches of 1885, I need only further quote that of 30th May :—

"Looking upon all these operations merely as trying the qualities of the troops, it cannot be denied that they were severe tests, and that no troops could have stood them better. . . . The long marches and toilsome convoy duties under a tropical sun ; the repulse of the enemy's sudden charges in the bush ; the toilsome ten nights' watch in the zereba amid the carnage of a battlefield, are achievements of which any troops may be proud. As an instance of the high spirit that animated the whole force, I may mention that the 1st Battalion Berkshire Regiment, who bore so glorious a share in defeating the enemy's sudden and desperate onslaught of the 22nd March, continued to form part of the garrison of the zereba until the final advance, and, though suffering great hardship declined to be relieved."[2]

Under much more unfavourable circumstances, this is the advance and decisive battle of the previous year rolled into one ;

---

[1] *Vide* pp. 162-169.   [2] Supp. to *London Gazette*, Aug. 25, 1885.

with this difference, that the troops instead of at once leaving the field were compelled to remain on it, and also that while, up to a certain point, the one route was thoroughly known and reconnoitred, the other was not. The only mishap that took place in 1884 was due to inadequate acquaintance with the unreconnoitred *terrain*, leading to a mistake as to the exact position of the khor in which the ambush was laid.

In a pamphlet, published anonymously soon after the close of the Campaign, we find it mentioned : [1]—

"The 21st March was spent by the Cavalry in surveying the line of country for future advance, and by the other troops in preparing a large convoy, which was to be forwarded the following day, about seven miles through the bush." [2]

No movement having been made on the line of the projected railway before April 6th, or until after the return from Tamai, the first statement in the quotation, like the second, can only refer to the new line of approach to the Arab stronghold. This being, so far as I am aware, not only the solitary and unsupported assertion regarding any such surveying operations, but also as to any external movement having taken place at Suâkin on the 21st, I have been at some pains to test its accuracy, and am able to state upon the very highest authority, that of Brigadier-General Sir Henry P. Ewart, K.C.B., who Commanded the Cavalry Brigade, that beyond the usual camp-patrols, forming of course a daily duty, there was no Cavalry movement of any kind on the day cited, and certainly none partaking the character of a reconnaissance. The *Diary of the Expedition* is also entirely silent on the point; and as there was not even a convoy to Hashin, it may be taken for granted that, saving duties falling within the camp, the 21st was for the troops in every respect a much needed *dies non*.

For a writer who professes to "clear up some of the obscure points" of the "quaint campaign" of 1885, by giving the contents

[1] *Arab Warfare—Souakim*, 1885.   By a Combatant Officer.   Stanford, London, 1885.
[2] *Ibid.* p. 14.

of a carefully kept diary, *Arab Warfare* shows a strong tendency to the same inaccuracy, he very truly avers of the special as " certainly to be found in hurried notes, which are written, often under the excitement of an enemy's fire, and always against time." In the quotation already given, the author states that the 21st " *was spent* by the cavalry" in executing the imaginary survey, " *and by the other troops* in preparing a large convoy," etc. Now the instructions for the 22nd were not issued until late in the afternoon ; and it was more correctly the evening, and greater part of the succeeding night which were so spent. On the same page it is also stated—"The whole party safely reached, in the early *afternoon*, a position which *the commander approved*." The arrival really was in the early *forenoon;* and as to the approval, there was no option in the matter, consequent on the urgent necessities of the Transport Train, at the Commander's request to Colonel Elliot Wood, the site having been selected as the best that could be found.

On the next page we find the remark :—

" It is impossible in that district *to see any greater distance than* 300 *yards*, owing to the dense growth of thorn bushes, which are *as thick as apple-trees in an English orchard*." [1]

It must be a very sparsely planted orchard in which there is a clear view of nearly one sixth of a mile ! and one tenth of the amount stated would have been more correct. At page 10 also, " *eighteen miles* south-west from Souakim," is too high an estimate for the distance of Tamai, which does not exceed fourteen or fifteen miles, and errs as much one way, as the *Daily Telegraph* does the other. [2]

To return, however, to the reconnaissance. At first sight, it does seem quite reasonable to expect, that on an " off day " like the 21st, a Staff Officer with a Squadron or two of the large Cavalry Force which was to find very partial employment for the next ten days, might have been detached, in order to reconnoitre and report on the

[1] *Arab Warfare—Souakim*, 1885. P. 14.   [2] *Vide* p. 243.

proposed "direct line to Tamai" ere the Infantry and Transport Train were sent out on chance to seek for themselves an eight-mile distant "position." But the truth is, a reconnaissance so effected would have been strategically out of place, and a great deal too late, for the plain reason, that the route by Tofrek as alternative either to Tamai or Tamanieb, must have been determined on *prior to the commencement of active operations,* and therefore before any suitable reconnaissance had been or could be made. The first movement of the organised Force proceeded upon the selection of this route as a foregone conclusion. In 1884 operations were commenced in a common-sense way by reconnoitring the main line of advance, and selecting a definite and well-known position as a Secondary Base. In 1885 this was left, to use a cant phrase, entirely *en l'air,* to be prospected for, and discovered by the Infantry and Transport Train, while the great object of reconnaissance and of labour upon which the entire strength of the Expedition for two days was expended, was a supposed defensive, subordinate, and practically useless position, six miles off on the right flank, the formation of which, and operations necessarily connected with it, really precipitating the very evil it was designed to evade.

As has been already shown,[1] the leading peculiarity of the district immediately round Suâkin, is the presence of a dense and more luxuriant growth of mimosa bush in the khors and lower grounds, due to their retention of moisture, with a corresponding sparse and stunted growth on the elevations, however slight these may be. This necessarily makes for troops in close formation and heavy marching order, and for a loaded Transport Train, all the difference between an open and a seriously obstructed line of advance. These facts receive ample *ex post facto* recognition in the despatches, but the question of real moment is, why, in relation to the Tofrek route, were they not previously ascertained? These are matters appealing to common sense and ordinary experience, and no special insight is required in order to realise their significance.

[1] *Vide* p. 46.

It may be accepted then as an axiomatic truth, that there never was any intention specially to reconnoitre the main line selected for the advance on Tamai in 1885, its capabilities being taken for granted, and no expectation entertained that such difficulties would occur as those actually encountered. Both on this score and the ample cover afforded by so dense a bush for hostile approach, this was really a serious matter, more especially as between Hashin and the new route, Head-Quarters' ideas seem to have got into a vicious circle. The choice of the new route gave to Hashin an importance exaggerated beyond what it otherwise possessed, while, no fixed haunt of the Arabs lying on the "direct line to Tamai," it received no strategic attention. The very first efforts, and combined strength of the newly organised Expedition, were expended on the side issue —Hashin, with this disadvantage, that premature collision was precipitated rather than evaded. To this change of route from that by Baker's zeriba, the entire operations at Hashin were indeed a direct sequence. As General Graham informs us,[1] the enemy at first occupying "the line Tamai, Hasheen, Handoub," on the Arabs evacuating the latter "Hasheen became a place of some importance as it threatened the right flank of my advance on Tamai." So it was the new route which lent significance to, and made Hashin dangerous. Had the previous line of advance been adhered to, owing to its leading away from positions whose occupancy was chiefly due to the presence of water, with much less likelihood of attack by the enemy, the centre of reinforcement and concentration would probably have become not Hashin but Tamai, and whereas the best policy for Head-Quarters evidently was to get through preparations with as little preliminary fighting or interference as possible, that actually adopted proved to be a direct precipitation of the main issue.

Such then was the tangled skein in which the new departure involved the Expedition. Although not traced to their source in the altered route, the weak points of the strategy it involved were

[1] Despatch, May 30, 1885. Supp. *London Gazette*, Aug. 25, 1885.

promptly seen by the London Press. In its issue for the 23rd the *Times* comments as follows on the first movement of the campaign :—

"Since we last wrote we have received fuller information concerning the circumstances of the action at Hasheen, and here we take the opportunity of protesting against the use of such big phrases as 'desperate battle' and 'great victory' as inapplicable to the operations being carried on in the Soudan, and calculated to make us ridiculous in the eyes of foreign military critics. Was the action at Hasheen a victory, and why was it fought? It was a victory if Sir Gerald Graham accomplished his object. What was his object, and did he accomplish it? His object, as he himself stated it, was to establish himself in a strong position commanding Hasheen Valley, and protecting his right flank and line of communications during his contemplated advance on Tamai. In addition to this avowed object he probably hoped to deal such a crushing blow on what may be called Osman Digna's left arm, as to prevent its taking part in the coming struggle with the main body of the Arab forces. It is difficult without a detailed map of the ground to follow exactly the operations which took place or to realise what was accomplished. As far, however, as we can gather, the events of Friday may be summed up as follows : Sir Gerald Graham constructed a zariba and some redoubts on high ground facing the range forming the eastern edge of the valley, at the bottom of which are the Hasheen wells. It is possible that we may be wrong, and that there is no intervening ridge between the redoubts garrisoned by the Surrey Regiment—the 70th—and the Marine Artillery ; but it is pretty clear under any circumstances that at best we can only forbid the approach to the wells during the daylight by distant fire. At all events we do not actually hold the wells in question.

"But how can a single battalion cover Sir Gerald Graham's right flank and protect his line of advance to Tamai? The whole country is open to the movements of the Arabs, and they may either mask our redoubts or, by making a slight circuit, turn them. It is not as if the redoubts guarded the only pass leading from Hasheen wells to Suakin or Tamai. The 70th will be chained to the spot, and can at best but make demonstrations which the Arabs will know how to appreciate at their just value. That regiment cannot hold fast any number of the enemy, and we can only understand its being posted in its present position on the assumption that the redoubts are intended to protect the westernmost end of the first section of the railway. As to the unavowed, though obvious second object, viz., that of dealing the left wing of Osman Digna's army a crushing blow—that certainly was not accomplished. Our men behaved exceedingly well, and dislodged the Arabs from successive positions till the latter fell back to the hills west of the wells; the wells themselves were not held and can not be held unless we occupy the surrounding hills in force. When we reached the wells, finding it impossible to bring the Arabs to a decisive engagement, our troops were ordered to fall back, which they did in good order, but as soon as their faces were turned towards the redoubts the enemy haunted our steps and pelted us with rifle shots till we had quitted the valley of Hasheen.

"The Arabs certainly lost heavily, but there was nothing like panic observable among them, and it would seem as if they acted in pursuance of a regularly formed plan and previous instructions. Their tactics have decidedly altered. They seem to have trusted more to rifle fire than a charge, and they broke up into fragments, each fragment as soon as it got a chance trying to slip past our advanced troops and to fall on those in the second line. In fact, they made offensive returns repeatedly, and in various parts of the field. They also tried to get into our rear, and at one time some were actually between us and Suakin. We fail to observe any diminution of courage on their part. Our loss was heavier than it was first reported to be by Sir Gerald Graham, in killed alone being 21. Among the wounded was Surgeon-Major Lane, who died on the following day. The Bengal Lancers suffered very heavily, and no wonder, for they either were ordered or were led by their ardour to undertake a duty not suitable for their arm—viz., to charge into the bush. There they got separated from each other, and were baffled by the tricks of the Arabs, who cast themselves suddenly down and hamstrung the horses as they passed, afterwards mobbing and killing the dismounted riders. The Bengal Lancers were not prepared for this manœuvre, but next time will, being prepared, probably be able to baffle it. It seems to us that in this campaign the rear rank ought to follow at a distance of 20 yards from the front rank. If then any of the front rank were dismounted, they would be at once succoured by the comrades close in rear of them. It is remarked by those who were present that the Arabs showed a positive contempt for cavalry, actually, though on foot, charging them. The Arabs, whether we call the fight a victory or not, will certainly deem themselves the conquerors, for Sir Gerald Graham employed the whole of his force, save two battalions, against them, and, after advancing a short distance, retreated, marching back in the evening to Suakin."

2 B

Two days later the following remarks occur :—

"The Shropshire Regiment—the 53rd—who for their wonderful marching exploits and spare condition during the Indian Mutiny were called the Indian Greyhounds, escorted a convoy to the Hasheen redoubts yesterday, and were to return in the evening. These redoubts seem, by the way, likely to absorb a large number of men. A battalion constitutes its garrison, and on Sunday and again on Tuesday another battalion was sent to escort a convoy to the post. We have paid dearly for its establishment, and are paying, as we have shown, heavily for its retention, and, as we have asked before, of what good is it? General Graham said it was to protect his communications with Tamai; did it do so on Sunday? As we have pointed out, the garrison is chained to the spot and can be easily eluded. As it is not strong enough to venture outside its defences, we venture to think that it is too large. Two companies, if the works are strong and properly supplied with ditches, wire entanglements, and other obstacles, would suffice to protect the guns, and would be as effective as a whole battalion, whose services are much needed elsewhere. The price we paid for it was 64 casualties, of whom 20 are dead."[1]

The following day the abandonment of the fortifications is thus commented on :—

"Yesterday the Grenadier Guards brought in the garrison of the Hasheen redoubts. A few shots were interchanged with the enemy, but no one was hit on our side. The fact that the garrison could not return to Suakin without an escort proves what we said yesterday and previously, that the Surrey Regiment was chained to the spot and perfectly powerless to do anything but defend itself when behind the parapets. In short, the battalion was completely neutralized and might as well have been at Aldershot for all the influence it produced on the campaign."[2]

A false start for the campaign then, and bootless fighting, was the first price paid for the altered route. The most enduring result of the two days' operations—the fortifications—had to be abandoned within a few days; and while failing altogether to protect the " right flank and line of communications," the entire proceedings forced the fighting in a way Head-Quarters did not anticipate, and brought down prompt and unexpected retaliation. The second part of the

[1] *Times*, 25th March 1885.   [2] *Ibid.*, 26th March 1885.

bill then, was the action at Tofrek, with all these inevitable troubles the character of the bush in that locality necessarily involved.

If the operations on the 22nd of March were the first of any importance not preceded by a reconnaissance, it is pretty certain they were also the last. For the remainder of the campaign, escort and reconnoitring formed the principal duty of the Cavalry, the subsequent despatches being indeed to a great extent a catalogue of such "frequent and successful reconnaissances." [1]

The truth is that, in 1885, owing to the entire absence of information as to the intentions and dispositions of the enemy and difficulty of acquiring it, combined with the depreciation of spy information, to which in the earlier part of this chapter we have already referred,[2]—so great was the "hiatus between the two contending forces," and of which the action at Tofrek forms the most startling proof, that as a matter of necessity reconnaissances in one form or other may be said to have constituted the leading feature of the campaign. Even the advance on Hashin on the 20th is only redeemed from this category by the establishment of the short-lived and ineffective fortifications. Otherwise it was a reconnaissance in force, in the strictest sense of that term, for it only drew the enemy, partially engaged him, and then retired. The final advance upon Tamai, the object of such great preparations, and from which so much was expected, was nothing more than a more distinguished manoeuvre of the same kind, as was fully and promptly recognised by the London Press. In its issue on the following day, the *Standard* especially makes the following pertinent remarks :—

"Some eight thousand men advanced yesterday on Tamai, after great precautions against surprise on the march and immense previous exertions to

[1] Special Field Force Order, by General Graham, 16th May 1885; and in his despatch to General Lord Wolseley, of May 30th, referring to the "successful reconnaissances" effected on the line of railway, the following note is appended :—

"Reconnaissances.—To Otao, 13th April; to Khor and Abent, 15th April; to Tambouk, 17th April; to Khor and Abent, 18th April; towards Es Sibil, 24th April; to Khor and Adit, 29th April; surprise and attack of Thakool, 6th May."—Supp. *London Gazette*, August 25th, 1885.

[2] *Vide* p. 155.

bring up water and provisions for three days. There were Infantry, Cavalry, and guns ; the whole Force had lain the night before watching against attack and receiving a few shots from the enemy, which did little damage. Yesterday the eight thousand men advanced with all the pomp of war, and in a formation calculated at once for celerity of movement and for the repulse of forces overwhelming in numbers. They found practically no resistance, but as there was no water to speak of, they marched back again with fifty Arabs hanging on their flanks and trying to cut their communications. . . .

"The affair may be considered as a novelty in war. There are reconnaissances of various kinds.[1] The reconnoitring which is carried out by small groups of men; the reconnaissance by a squadron or two of cavalry, with perhaps a very small infantry support; and the reconnaissance in force, which means the advance of a body, generally including the three arms, sufficiently strong to make the enemy show himself in his full strength. In all these reconnaissances it is expected that there will be retirement, with or without fighting, as soon as information has been gained. The novelty of yesterday's affair is such as to require that a new term be introduced into tactical phraseology. It was a 'Reconnaissance in full force.' And our Correspondent says that the 'full force' is to return to Suakim, or at least the first zareba, and to begin to push out minor reconnaissances towards Tamanieb."[2]

So much for reconnaissances in 1885, and seeing there was so much of a good thing going, the only pity is that Tofrek did not get the benefit of the superfluity. Had even a reconnaissance in the humblest "minor" form, compatible with safety, been sent out on the 21st, on the ideal Line of Communications, to where the "position was selected" at the eight mile distance, it is possible the experience of the day might have resulted in the countermand of the crow-flight, the "line leading directly to Tamai."[3] A poor

[1] Reconnoitring, the most important of all duties for an army in the field, is subdivided as follows by Lord Wolseley :—

"Reconnaissances. — The most reliable method of obtaining information as to the enemy's movements is by reconnaissances, which may be divided into four classes.

"1st. Reconnaissances in force.

"2nd. Those made by a detachment of all arms, of sufficient strength to protect themselves and secure their retreat.

"3rd. Those made by Staff Officers, accompanied by a small cavalry detachment.

"4th. Those made continually by individual officers from the outposts.'
—Soldiers' Pocket Book, p. 289.

[2] Standard, 4th April, 1885.

[3] Despatch, 28th March 1885.

crow-flight or " direct line" at the best for the British Force, destined as it was by bitter experience to illustrate the truth of the old adage, " The more hurry the less speed."

Only second in importance to the absence of any reconnaissance stands the question of the Mounted Accompaniment. We have seen how, on the 19th and 20th, in the reconnaissance and advance upon Hashin the entire available Cavalry Force was brought into requisition. There was the *arme blanche* in both its forms— the lancer, British and Indian, and the swordsman in the 20th Hussars. In addition to these there was, for scouting and skirmishing work, the still more useful Mounted Infantry, who could pick off the enemy, and give him a wide berth, in a style impossible to those whose arms were only of service when engaged at close quarters. In Chapter II. we have also seen how limited, even in the written Instructions, was the mounted strength intended to go out on the 22nd, and that this was cut down to one half, and that, under the circumstances, the least useful half, of the detachments detailed on paper.

There is at the same time no use evading the fact that in the campaign of 1885, as compared with that of 1884, the Cavalry arrangements were seriously defective. In advocating an immediate advance on Berber in that year, we find the *Times* of 10th March stating—" We have at this present at Suakin exactly the sort of cavalry which is required—the 10th Hussars, acclimatized to India, and the 19th Hussars to Egypt."

The 10th Hussars had been in India since January 1873, eleven years, and in addition to other service had gone through the Afghan Campaign of 1878-80. They were just stopped in time on their voyage home, and having no horses with them took over those of the Egyptian Cavalry. The 19th Hussars had served in the Campaign of 1882 ; both Regiments were thus thoroughly effective, and inured to a tropical climate.

Now, if there was one place more than another where troops not only seasoned but thoroughly trained to active service were required, it was the Eastern Sûdan. Yet, in 1885, the idea seemed to be that Suâkin might be made serviceable chiefly as a drill ground. Mishaps began early. On the 3rd of February a composite Force of British and Egyptian Cavalry rode out towards Handub, and proceeded to burn the huts of the deserted Arab village. While so occupied a large body of camel-men and others emerging from the hills to the west, prepared an ambush in a khor two miles from Handûb, which was only discovered in time to prevent the retreat of the Cavalry on Suâkin from being completely cut off. As it was, they had a race for life, and with some loss both of men and horses,[1] had to gallop round the enemy's flank under a heavy fire. General Fremantle, then in Command at Suâkin, gives the following explanation of this unfortunate affair, at the same time stating that the "Officer commanding cavalry exceeded his instructions":—

"Reconnaissance of 3rd February was intended as short instruction in scouting for young soldiers; the operation at Handoub was quite beyond the scope of instructions to Apthorp. Such an operation, if desirable, should have been carried out differently.

"Apthorp understands, and regrets his error in judgment. The advance was carefully made, with every precaution taken as to scouts and flankers, but they were too far from, and too slow for, safety. Vedettes, whilst at Handoub, were well posted on heights, and, if more experienced, should have at least seen the camel-men getting in their rear; this would have avoided all loss."[2]

Two days previously the General had personally made a reconnaissance towards Hashin, of which he writes:—

"We found position very strong, and enemy very numerous and courageous on their own ground, coming on with loud yells. But they would not leave the khor and broken ground."[3]

Although this detachment of the 19th Hussars was subsequently

[1] Out of 80 sabres, half British, half Egyptian, the Hussars lost eight men and twelve horses, their allies three men and seven horses. The correspondent of the *Morning Post*, in giving an account of the affair, states—"The heavier loss on our side, compared to that sustained by the Egyptian cavalry, is to be attributed to our scouts—*mostly young soldiers of but one year's service*—not falling in properly, and to the fact of our men's horses, which have been but a short time here, not being in the same condition as those of the Egyptians."—(*Morning Post*, March 5th, 1885.)

[2] *Parl. Papers*, Egypt, No. 2 (1885), p. 5.
[3] *Ibid.* p. 1.

withdrawn, there was no improvement in the trained and seasoned quality of the troops sent out by the Home Government. In a letter appearing in the *Morning Post* on the inefficient and defective state of the Cavalry arm in general, owing to want of men, by Major-General Charles C. Fraser, the British Cavalry serving at Suâkin are thus referred to :—

"The Hussar regiment that last month formed two squadrons for the Soudan, the only cavalry regiment on the higher establishment of 600 men, and the first for service, had received 310 recruits in the last eighteen months; whilst between October 15, 1883, and October 14, 1884, 82 invaluable trained soldiers, of over five years service, but who had not completed their engagement, were permitted to leave the regiment for the reserves. The Lancer regiment on the lower establishment of 469 men, which also formed two squadrons for service, had received in the last 18 months 252 recruits." [1]

Facts like these speak for themselves. Here are two regiments first on the roster for foreign service, who within a year and a half previous to the date mentioned, had each received more than one half its own complement in new enlistments, at this rate the entire regiment being renewed in less than three years, or half the short service term! What kind of *matériel* was this to cope with the Sûdanese Arabs? What wonder that, without even such warning as would have been conveyed by a sputter all round of carbine-fire, a Cavalry stampede preceded that of the Transport?

It is, of course, no fault of young troops that they cannot do the work of seasoned veterans, the blame resting entirely with those who, without adequate acclimatisation or practice in the field, sent them out into immediate contact with an enemy acknowledged to be amongst savage races the most dangerous the British Army could possibly encounter.

To return, however, to the Cavalry Accompaniment sent out to Tofrek. Instead of the imposing spectacle presented on the mornings of the 19th and 20th, when the entire available Mounted Force, radiating over the plain in all directions like a

---

[1] *Morning Post*, March 10th, 1885.

great fan, rode on miles ahead, through every patch of broken ground and cover, searching, signalling, warning, there was now but a handful of Lancers, their very numbers matter of keen dispute.

On this point the lowest estimate I am aware of is that given by the special correspondent of the *Daily Chronicle*, whose statement runs as follows :—

"Not a man of us had any idea that thousands of rebels were quietly stretched amongst the scrub and behind boulders and hillocks, silently watching us as we innocently and jovially worked at our zarebas. A few pickets were out, and a squadron of cavalry scouts as well—I believe 18 all told—so we were content.

"Suddenly there was a great cry of alarm, rising loud above the din of the fatigue parties and the accompanying bustle of a great camp, and then hoarse cries from the officers—'Stand to your arms, men!' Never was word of command more promptly obeyed.

"But the men were scattered, many of them a considerable distance from their arms. The brave fellows did their best, however, to get into their allotted positions.

"As the squares formed, the 18 cavalry scouts came rushing in—crashing through our own lines—and then we saw and heard the leaping, roaring, fantastic, yet terrible-looking wave of black forms, which we knew was the enemy in strong—in overwhelming force." [1]

In its issue for the following day the *Times* also endorses this statement : —

"We are informed that there were 18 cavalry vedettes thrown out, and several infantry pickets. Cavalry were evidently out of place and useless in the bush." [2]

In the present case, the " 18 all told " seems very like a deduction from the 18 who " came rushing in," and the latter is certainly an under estimate. With special reference to this episode and to its bearing on the Cavalry strength, an eye-witness, well qualified to judge, writes as follows :—" The only collected party of them that I saw was when they came dashing in from the front, and for a moment formed up in the centre of the centre zeriba;

[1] *Daily Chronicle*, March 24th, 1885.   [2] *Times*, March 25th, 1885.

and certainly that party did not number more than 25 or 30 men. They only stayed there for a moment or so, and then luckily cleared out, as they would probably have been shot by the bullets which were flying pretty freely about."

At the same time, it must be admitted that even amongst those who were best informed an impression prevailed that the Squadron, if such it might be called, was extremely weak. Whatever the grounds were for this opinion, according to the general estimate, its strength did not exceed from 40 to 50 men. It must be remembered that owing to the nature of their duties, save, it may be, when the Lancers rode upon the ground at earliest parade, no opportunity of estimating their strength can possibly have occurred during the day, and, even then, lost amid the great array of Transport and fighting men, such a handful of Cavalry must have easily escaped observation.

So firmly indeed was the conviction referred to held by all the Superior Officers out on the 22nd, that on his return to England, after the withdrawal of the Indian garrison from Suâkin in the spring of 1886, in stating the facts connected with the action at Tofrek to H.R.H. the Duke of Cambridge, Sir John Hudson placed the Squadron strength at 43 men, which, with allowance for Officers, agrees very closely with the numbers stated by Sir John M'Neill. Similar opinions were widely prevalent at the Base, as well as at Tofrek. With special reference to this point the following re- marks made by an Officer connected with the Indian Contingent, but detained on duty at Suâkin on the day when the action was fought, may be quoted :—" Regarding the number of the 5th Lancers at the zareebah the 22nd March, I heard at the time, from whom I can't remember, that there were about 40 men out. This information, if I recollect right, was given to me as an answer to a question as to how the zareebah could have been so suddenly attacked if the proper number of vedettes and scouts had been out at the proper distance."

In a letter with which he has favoured me, alluding to this opinion, Sir John Hudson also states :—" I believe nine out of every

2 c

ten men in the Indian Contingent, and in the remainder of the Force assembled at Suâkin, shared the opinion expressed, viz., that there were not more than 40 men of the 5th Lancers ; and so firmly was I impressed with this idea, though I too could not now tell you whence, *i.e.* the precise authority from which I derived it, that I had no hesitation in stating it to H.R.H. the Duke of Cambridge, nor did I hesitate to state it publicly wherever I touched on the incidents of the action of the 22nd March. I may however mention, that ever since I heard of there being a doubt as to the correctness of the smaller number, I have, when alluding to the occurrences of that day, mentioned the doubt."

While for a considerable period these estimates were held in all good faith, as being approximately accurate, it appears from the Regimental Medal Roll and Casualty Returns of the 5th Lancers, that, including Lieutenant Richardson and the men who were with him, the number of those who, as being out on the 22nd, were either recipients of, or entitled to, the Tofrek clasp, are as follows, viz.—4 Officers, 20 Non-commissioned Officers, and 76 privates, raising the Squadron strength to 100 of all ranks. At the same time it may be mentioned that the number of Tofrek clasps on record at the War Office as issued to Officers and men of the 5th Lancers is 104.

We have already seen (at pp. 53, 54) how far even a Squadron fell short of the actual requirements of the 22nd, and also that, on the testimony of Captain Jones, the outposts covered over three miles of frontage, and this in a dense scrub. Taking the strength of the Squadron even at the most favourable estimate, an extract from the Instructions issued by the War Office will show how inadequate the numbers were for the duties to be discharged :—

"The strength of cavalry that will be required to cover any given front must evidently depend upon the nature of the country ; but on tolerably open ground a cavalry regiment of 400 sabres will safely watch ten miles of front. *For a close country a greater strength will be required.*"[1]

[1] *Instructions for Cavalry Outpost Duties*, p. 5.

"Tolerably open ground," of course means more or less absence of cover for the enemy, with corresponding freedom of outlook for the vedette. In the present case the watching was limited to a purview of the immediate surroundings, beyond these all hostile movements being concealed by a screen, open as a sieve below, impervious above. Every circumstance thus favouring the enemy, and rendering useless whatever precautions might be adopted, at Tofrek were realised the very worst conditions contemplated by military strategists in writing on this question. The best way to prove this will be to lay before the reader a few extracts from authorised and other manuals on the subject. We commence with those issued by the War Office for the guidance of the Cavalry in its field duties :—

"Vedettes are posted by the commander of the field-piquet, or by a non-commissioned officer specially detailed for that duty; they *should be in open country*, from 1000 to 1200 paces in front of the field-piquet, and at the most 1000 paces apart, but always near enough to prevent *anything being able to pass between them unseen.*

"Their position must, if possible, be selected so that the vedettes can *see far without themselves being seen.* For this reason they will be, when practicable, posted in concealed positions on high ground; thus, for example, in a small hollow, or near the crest of a ridge of hills, but so that their heads can see over it. Neighbouring vedettes must be able to see each other. Should it *exceptionally happen* that this cannot be arranged, they must the more frequently ride to positions from where they can do so." [1]

So also in the *Instructions for Cavalry Outpost Duties* already quoted :—

"In posting vedettes, the first object to be sought is an uninterrupted view of their front; and the second, a means of concealment to protect them from the enemy's notice." [2]

"Vedettes should see the vedettes on their right and left, and should command all the intermediate ground, and have a clear view to the front. They should be within sight of the sentry of the piquet." [3]

---

[1] *Cavalry Field Duty,* p. 52.   [2] *Instructions for Cavalry Outpost Duties,* 1876, p. 36.
[3] *Ibid.* 1870, p. 5.

While very pertinently illustrating the fact that :—

" The line of sentries . . . should be the eyes of the army, always peering forward to watch and report what the enemy is doing,"

Lord Wolseley lays down the following regulation :—

" Sentries should never be posted near any copse or cover from which a sudden rush might be made upon them; but all woods, ravines, etc., in the neighbourhood of the post must be watched, and occasionally visited by patrols, to prevent the enemy from assembling a body of troops unobserved in the vicinity." [1]

To the same effect, in his admirable work *A Chapter on Outposts*, in terms intended for Infantry, but equally applicable to Cavalry, Sir Edward B. Hamley states, in the section specially devoted to the " Adaptation of outposts to ground " :—

" The points which afford generally the clearest and farthest view to the front should be the posts of the sentries. So long as they observe *all the surrounding ground, and cannot be approached unawares*, they can in no case run any risk by day. . . .

" The most favourable circumstances for outposts will be those in which shelter from the view and fire of the enemy is afforded to the skirmishing line, with a good range to the front, and advantages for retreating under more or less cover past the next stand-point, occupied by the second line.

" The least favourable will be those where the view and range to the front are very contracted, while the retreat lies for a considerable distance over open ground.

" Next to being shut up in an enclosure, the worst case in which part of the outpost line could find itself would be facing a wood, within a short distance, where the enemy could approach it unseen and unmolested, and begin his attack with all the advantages of cover on his side. . . .

" The worst place possible for the outposts would be along the hither edge of the wood, and close to it, where they could see nothing, and would be shot down by an advancing enemy without the chance of injuring him in return, while he could mass or manœuvre there, to any extent, unseen.

" If the wood covers so large an area that the outpost line must traverse it, and the troops are unable to make the requisite clearing, the sentries must

---

[1] *Soldiers' Pocket Book.*—Sentries and Vedettes, pp. 293-94.

be very numerous, and very near the pickets, which must be numerous also; and the patrolling in front must be almost incessant." [1]

In the same work the *role* of the Arab on the 22nd is sketched very felicitously in the following paragraph :—

" Looking at the matter for the moment from the other [*i.e.* the attacking] side, it is manifestly the right policy for a general who intends to bring his antagonist to battle to drive in the outposts in such force, and with such determination, as will in any case reduce their resistance to a minimum, and which, if they are not thoroughly efficient and well handled, will allow of no mode of retreat on their part *except flight.* If they are merely brave troops, untrained in the business, he will be likely to capture many of them, to drive the rest on the line in disorder, and to advance with so little interruption that their function of setting the defender on his guard has been almost limited to the noise of the attack." [2]

So also Major-General Napier :—

" The great principle to be observed in placing a chain of outposts is, that every vedette, sentry, and picquet should be able to see and communicate with the next vedette, sentry, or picquet on either side, and that, while they should be able to observe the movements of the enemy, they should themselves be as little seen by him as possible. But this, like many other very good general rules, is easier laid down than followed." [3]

Numerous authorities might be cited to the same effect, all of them agreeing with General Jarry, where he states—

" If the chain [of outposts] were carried through a thick wood where the sentries could neither see nor stop spies and deserters, the first principle of outpost duty would be violated." [4]

" Each vedette also must be able to see the next vedette on his right and left; and one or other of two neighbouring vedettes *must be able to see the ground between them, so that nothing can pass without being seen and stopped.* This essential rule constitutes what may be called the principle of the formation of the chain." [5]

So also Major-General Von Mirus :—

" It may be said that the vedettes, flankers, and patrols, are the eyes of the

[1] *A Chapter on Outposts*, by Sir E. B. Hamley, Sect. V. pp. 28-32.

[2] *Ibid.* p. 38.

[3] *Military Reconnaissance*, p. 89.

[4] *Outpost Duty*, p. 6.

[5] *Ibid.* p. 7.

main body, they must see without being seen, they must carefully note every-thing relating to the enemy or of military importance. *It is absolutely indis-pensable carefully to examine every spot where it is possible that an enemy might be concealed.*" [1]

We have already seen (at pp. 54-56) that it was not only by rendering all ordinary outpost precautions futile that the bush proved to be in the highest degree disadvantageous. Not only did it prevent the Cavalryman from doing his duty in any effective manner, but it became to him especially a source of the most pre-eminent danger. This had been fully experienced only two days previously at Hashin. The dangers then encountered, and of whose serious nature the entire Cavalry Force must have been thoroughly impressed, befell troops in close formation, with all the advantage of mutual support and protection, and while in the very act of charging the enemy. If, against the peculiar tactics of the Arab, even under circumstances like these, the horseman found himself helpless, how much more so were solitary vedettes, or even Cossack posts,[2] quite stationary, and separated at wide intervals from all their comrades, whom theoretically, and according to regulations, they ought to have been able to see, but in the present case most assuredly could not. With the experiences of the 20th full in remembrance, instinctively realising that the position into which they were trapped, was that of individual and unsupported bush-fighting with the Arab, under the worst possible conditions, no wonder that on the 22nd, with two or three premonitory warnings, the entire Cavalry outpost-system suddenly collapsed. It was the logical result of men being posted under circumstances thus graphically described by General Graham in his despatch of March 28th :—

" This scrub renders it impossible to follow the movements of an enemy on foot, who can conceal himself perfectly within a short distance of our vedettes."

However hurried the retreat, and imperative in exact proportion

[1] *Cavalry Field-Duty,* p. 16.
[2] These " Cossack Posts " consisted of a vedette and three men in reserve. The great object of this arrangement being to

to its suddenness, there is at least one mode of alarm, by firing off carbine or musket, usually adopted by Cavalry or Infantry when on vedette or sentry duty, the absence of which in the present instance was most unfortunate.   Owing to the difficulty of taking accurate aim, and unsteadiness of the horse when it is most desirable it should be under control, firing from the saddle against the enemy becomes comparatively ineffective, and, accordingly, in the Eastern Sûdan was habitually discouraged.   When the Cavalry had to act under circumstances rendering a charge impracticable, dismounted fire was invariably adopted.   To fire however from the saddle against the enemy, and as a warning on the part of vedettes, are two different things ; and there seems to have been some misapprehension on the part of the Lancers that the regulation was to be held applicable to both duties.   With special reference to this point, the author of a pamphlet already quoted expresses the opinion—

"Had the Lancer vedettes *broken through their regimental tradition,* and fired at the enemy, sufficient time might perhaps have been available for the labouring infantry and pioneers to prepare to meet the coming onslaught." [1]

It is difficult to understand how any "regimental tradition" could be permitted to contravene either the standing regulations of the British Army or the practice of all armies, regular and

save the horses, by enabling all the men not actually on the look-out to dismount; if the regulations were acted on, this would be the case with all the reserves, and also the Picket, leaving only the reserves and visiting patrols mounted.   One or two extracts from well-known manuals will illustrate this point.

"In order to save the horses from unnecessary fatigue, Cossack posts, instead of double vedettes, may often be used in outpost duty.   Cossack posts are composed of two or three, or even a larger number of horsemen, of whom one remains mounted as a vedette, while the others, having dismounted, remain some little distance in rear, and assist their mounted comrade in keeping watch.   The advantage of these Cossack posts is, that they save in some degree the horses from fatigue."—(*Cavalry in Modern War,* by Colonel F. Chenevix Trench, p. 154.)

So also General von Schmidt in his *Instructions for Cavalry,* p. 215, states, regarding "Non-Commissioned Officers or so-called Cossack Posts":—

"These Cossack posts are much more useful than vedettes; the security of troops in camp is much more surely effected through them, and the horses are much less worked than when widely-extended chains of vedettes are employed.   The partiality for the latter is very general, but why have this expenditure of power?"

[1] *Arab Warfare,* p. 15.

irregular, possessed of firearms.   Among men, civilised and savage, so to burn powder, forms the most natural and effective, as well as the most universal method of conveying an alarm, under sudden and unexpected attacks, known to the military art.   Had but one carbine in each Cossack post been ready and discharged, of what value to the " labouring infantry and pioneers " would have been the ten or fifteen minutes so gained, but which were necessarily occupied in covering the distance between the outposts and the zeriba !

This preference for, or it may be unavoidable restriction to, the use of the *arme blanche,* at once raises the question as to the suitability of that arm for the special work of the day.   We have seen (at pp. 20, 21, 26, etc.) that, in the written Instructions issued on the 21st, a Detachment of Mounted Infantry, as well as of Cavalry, was included.   Why this arrangement was not carried out it is impossible to tell ; but one thing is clear, whatever omission there was, it ought not to have been the Mounted Infantry.   Where no fighting was anticipated there could be neither charging nor pursuit, and for scouting purposes the circumstances were precisely those under which that arm can be used with the greatest effect.   As Major Hutton, in his able article on " Mounted Infantry,"[1] tells us :—

"The most important *rôle* for which mounted infantry are required, and for which recent experience of the last twenty years of continuous small wars has shown the paramount necessity, *is that of scouting, and acting as covering parties to bodies of infantry moving through an unknown and savage country."*

Whether as footmen trained to act on horseback, or as horsemen trained to act on foot, it is by most effective services rendered under just such circumstances, that the idea of a Mounted Infantry has been winning its way to tardy recognition in the British Army.   The brilliant exploits of Hodson's Horse during the Indian Mutiny, of the Cape Mounted Rifles in the South African Wars, of the gallant little band under Sir Archibald Alison in 1882, and numerous other instances, prove that, combining as it does the two great desiderata—celerity of movement with arms of

---

[1] *Illustrated Naval and Military Magazine,* vol. i. p. 13.

precision—this special arm is destined to play a most important part in modern warfare; while the able article given in the Appendix,[1] shows that even the Colonies are alive to the vital interest of this question. Omitted on the 22nd, in addition to the 9th Bengal Cavalry, the Mounted Infantry accompanied General Graham on the 23rd, and arrived at the zeriba, proceeded to scout the surrounding bush. The quest for the enemy was of course fruitless. In war an opportunity once lost seldom or never recurs; and it is vain to expect that the neglect of one day can be remedied by any amount of care or watchfulness on the morrow.

While the means for exploring the district immediately surrounding the zeriba were thus totally inadequate, with no Cavalry Force strong enough to act as independent patrols, and the fringe of outposts debarred by some "tradition" from giving instant notice of hostile approach, as an effective method of exploring a most difficult country, of searching the bush, and detecting the movements of the enemy, at so critical a juncture, the absence of the Captive Balloon must always be a matter of regret.

The endeavour to enlist the aid of the aeronaut had been the object of experiment at Chatham for many years, and the Egyptian Campaigns had given it new impetus. Elaborate preparations had at last been brought to a successful issue, and even the gas necessary for inflation had been made at Chatham, stored in reservoirs, and sent out to Suâkin. Nothing was awanting save an occasion in active service worthy of such laborious and long-continued efforts; and for this purpose no more fitting day could have been found than the 22nd of March. Unlike the 2nd of April, it was calm and sultry, and without a breath of air stirring.[2] With atmospheric conditions so perfectly fitted for ballooning, and an exigency so unique, the 22nd might truly have been a red-letter day in British military aerostation. That honour was reserved

---

[1] *Vide* Appendix VI.

[2] A marked exception to the aerial conditions noted in General Graham's despatch of May 30th to Lord Wolseley:—"Unfortunately the prevalent high winds generally made it impossible to employ the balloon."

for an occasion, regarding which the *Diary of the Expedition* states :[1] "The enemy was *not seen,* and the balloon was used for *the first time with success;*" and of its second and last appearance on April 2nd, General Graham tells us : " Endeavours were made to reconnoitre from the balloon at the head of the column, and it was reported that parties of the enemy were descried some miles in front. The wind, however, increased so much as to render the balloon unserviceable, and at 11 o'clock it had to be packed up,"[2] *i.e.* after being in use *less than an hour.* After all the labour, expectancy, and expense, such were the only two occasions on which the Balloon did duty in the Eastern Sûdan. The " success " claimed was limited, of course, to the Balloon's own flotation and management; a success with which, on the 2nd of April, the elements rudely interfered. In both cases the enemy was invisible except from the car, and had evidently no intentions of attacking. Well might the *Daily Telegraph* state : " Thus far, it cannot be said that balloons have been of much practical use in the conduct of military operations."[3] What the record would have been had the balloon been sent out on the 22nd instead of being delayed till the 25th, it is impossible to tell, but it is certain the events not only of that day, but of the 23rd and 24th, would have been very different. In its issue for the 23rd the *Times* states :

"A *ballon captif,* sent up at a spot two or three miles from Suakin, would have probably rendered the surprise impossible."

From the details of the actual ascent we learn that, while the practical outcome " in presence of the enemy," meant very little, the panoramic view obtained gives a good idea of the loss necessarily entailed by the absence of the Balloon on the 22nd. In the issue for the 28th the *Times* correspondent writes as follows :—

"SUAKIN, March 27th.

" I have had a conversation with Major Templar and Lieutenant Mackenzie, of the Balloon Corps, regarding the ascent on Wednesday last, thinking that

[1] P. 25.   [2] Despatch, 8th April 1885. *Parl. Papers,* Egypt, No. 13 (1885), p. 27.
[3] *Vide* p. 253 *postea.*

an authentic account of the *first ascent ever made on active service in the English army in presence of the enemy* might be interesting.   I send a brief *résumé* of what they were kind enough to tell me :—

"The balloon was taken to the right Water Fort on Tuesday, and filled from the compressed reservoirs during the night.   At daylight, when the convoy was ready to start for the zariba, Lieutenant Mackenzie ascended 200 feet, and was then towed by a rope, attached to a wagon, in the centre of the square. Major Templar was in charge below—a post requiring much care and attention, in order to keep the wagon steady, if possible, so as to avoid breaking the rope.

"Lieutenant Mackenzie says that the bush, which *seen from the ground is dense, and obscures the view, seems quite open from a height.*   He saw the enemy's camel posts out a mile on the road towards Hasheen.   Another body was retiring towards Tamai, and a third, near the sea-shore, was engaged in capturing or destroying the stampeded camels.   The enemy were also seen at some 400 hundred yards distance from the convoy, and they came out into the open space left in front to examine the balloon.

"Messages passed between Lieutenant Mackenzie and Major Templar, written on small pieces of paper attached by a loop to a rope.   On the arrival of the convoy in the zariba the balloon was hauled down, packed, and brought back to Suakin.   It is made of goldbeater's skin, contains 7000 cubic feet of gas, is 23 feet in diameter, and its total weight is 90 lbs.

"I asked Lieutenant Mackenzie what he would do in the event of a disaster below.   He replied that he had thought of that point while in the air, and had decided to come down and anchor 50 feet from the ground, and defend the anchor from the balloon until rescued.

"Major Templar is much pleased with the result of the ascent, as proving that a war balloon can render good service far from home, and remain up for nine hours with gas made in Chatham.   Besides the balloon, he has a portable lime search light, which is constantly used in the camp and zariba, with success."

Thus further commented on in the issue for the 30th :—

"Our Correspondent's account on Saturday of *the first ascent of a British balloon in warfare* is of great interest.   It will be observed on reference to his telegram that the balloon is light—only 90 lbs.—and that, inflated with gas made at Chatham, it remained up nine hours.   The great difficulty to be overcome has hitherto been the operation of filling the balloon when at a distance from gasworks.   That difficulty has now been overcome, and a wide field for the use of this adjunct to war is at length, after upwards of 90 years of intermittent experiment, opened. The balloon was without difficulty towed by a rope attached to a cart, Major Templar being in charge of the latter and Lieutenant Mackenzie making the ascent. Constant communication took place between the two by means of slips of paper attached by a loop to a rope. Lieutenant Mackenzie said that, looking down, the bush, so dense on the ground, seemed quite open. He distinctly saw several bodies of Arabs who were quite invisible to our scouts. As we have always maintained, the *ballon captif*, now that the practical difficulties in the way of inflating it in the field have been vanquished, is calculated to render most valuable services, especially in a country like the Soudan. Of course there is the risk of the balloon being riddled by bullets, but every operation in war is attended with more or less danger, and the Arabs are bad shots."

On an unreconnoitred route such an outlook, soaring 200 feet in vertical height, would have been invaluable, and would undoubtedly have modified the whole conditions of the march out, while the entire movements of the enemy within a circuit of many miles would have been as distinctly visible as those of bees in a glass hive.

The reader may easily judge what the result would have been, and also how imperative it was that a Force, with outposts invisible to each other, or to the main body, should be safeguarded by whatever exceptional methods the skill and labour of many years had succeeded in bringing to some degree of perfection. What were the actual facts? The entire apparatus, conveyed four thousand miles, floated ten hours [1] on active service; the "success" achieved being experimental only, and such as might have been equally well attained, with less expense and trouble, on a Review day at Aldershot or Brighton, while at the same time there was allowed to slip one of the grandest opportunities the ever-changing exigencies of War could possibly have presented.

To a very modified extent the same remarks apply to the Crow's Nest, the materials for which were only sent out with the Convoy on the 23rd. Although not to be compared with an altitude of 200 feet, a platform 30 feet high proved extremely useful. This top platform had a slight railing round it, and was capable of accommo-

---

[1] Nine hours on March 25th, one hour on April 2nd.

dating five people. There was also a small platform half-way up.
From this elevated perch a constant look-out was kept, and communication maintained with Suâkin, by heliograph during the day
and lime-light at night. A constant stream of messages came from
the Base—orders about next day's Convoys, counter-orders,
questions, etc. Amid the wide sea of thorn-bush, stationed at
intervals on the landward side, were seen the enemy's look-outs.
They, too, had their crow's nests, each formed of nothing more
artificial than the flat top of a mimosa bush, with a hide spread
over it, on which, like so many vultures, dark forms were squatted,
also maintaining a constant watch. Between these posts and
Tamai or Hashin, constant communication was kept up by means
of camel-men, who could be seen going their rounds and collecting
all the latest intelligence. During the night the lime-light became
the favourite target of the Arab marksmen, but, in spite of constant practice, they never managed to hit it, and aimed with so
high a range the bullets flew harmlessly over the zeriba.

Such was the extremely serviceable apparatus which, owing to
the telegraph wire having been cut on the evening of the 22nd,
during the occupancy of the zeriba, formed an ever-ready means of
communication with the external world. The only pity is it was
not at once available on the 22nd. The information thereby
obtained might not have arrested the attack, but it would have
certainly forewarned the Force of approaching danger, and also,
when the fight was over, gone far to obviate the harassing
uncertainty, compelling the troops to be always on the alert for a
renewal of the attack which might occur at any moment. Towards
the close of the day, by means of a cart, some makeshift was rigged
up, so as to communicate by heliograph—at least with Hashin;
but it was a poor substitute for the Crow's nest or the Balloon.

The hostile look-outs thus stationed *vis-à-vis*, recall another
omission which, had the relations between the combatants been
more of a civilised and less of a savage character, might have been
extremely embarrassing, viz., the want of an Interpreter. Contrary

to the usual practice in such circumstances, during the entire occupancy of the zeriba, no provision was made for a contingency which might easily have arisen, and made it very desirable that communication with the natives should take place through some more refined medium than that of bullets and cold steel.

The important omissions just referred to, and totally inadequate means provided for exploring the surrounding district, or acquiring information as to the immediate presence and movements of the enemy, combined with the composition of the Force sent out on the 22nd, as a semi-combatant one, intended for fatigue-duty and convoy-work rather than fighting, at once raises the question of what has been rather confidently, not to say unscrupulously, termed "a surprise." Taken in its military sense this is a very ugly and uncompromising but, at the same time, very easily abused term; it is a term, moreover, which cuts many ways, has many bearings, and used unjustifiably is very apt to recoil with no small amount of interest on those so employing it. Ere the Pen with its quirks, its verbal traps and logomachies, be allowed to ride rough-shod over the Sword in this jaunty style, it will be desirable to ascertain more accurately what the term so used really amounts to. If, unlike human affairs in general, it is assumed that in War the "unexpected" ought never to happen, then the sooner the practice of War, and with it the criticism of military operations, is abandoned the better. War, however, will go on, and, in the future as in the past, will continue to maintain its character as pre-eminently a game of chance, of cross purpose, and of effort by every means possible, *per fas, aut nefas*, to take advantage of and circumvent an enemy. So much is this the case, that one of the most interesting and instructive of modern military works is entirely devoted to this aspect of the question. I refer to the volume on *Ambushes and Surprises,* by Colonel G. B. Malleson, C.S.I. Before going further, it may be useful to note in what the distinction between an Ambush and a Surprise really consists. In an Ambush the one belligerent having laid his plans and made his preparations with all skill and secrecy, awaits the approach of his antagonist in some selected position, through which he must necessarily pass. In a Surprise, on the contrary, the plotter generally assumes the aggressive, and by manœuvres executed with skill and rapidity, as well as secrecy, strives to take his adversary at a disadvantage; but these two phases of warlike action often glide into each other insensibly, and it is not always easy to draw a very close or accurate distinction between them.

From the reports afterwards brought in by the spies, there can be no doubt that, acting on information only too faithfully placed at their disposal, the Arab intentions were, in the first instance, to prepare an Ambush at the eight-mile distance for the Force sent out on the 22nd, the unexpected arrest of the march at the six-mile distance, after the lapse of time requisite to traverse the intervening ground, necessarily converting it into an *attempted* Surprise. To the Imperial Force at Tofrek this was undoubtedly the "unexpected." With no means provided for independently ascertaining the movements of the enemy, and no information conveyed as to the Arab concentration, of which the Authorities at Suâkin must have been fully cognisant, it could not be otherwise. But, on General Graham's own showing, the "unexpected" had happened in both the critical battles of the previous campaign, and in either case had told disastrously, and left its indelible impress on the British plans. In his despatch of March 15th, relative to the battle of El Teb, General Graham states very clearly what, from the British point of view, the *beau ideal* of an Arab attack should be, at the same time expressing his expectation that such would have been the tactics actually employed:

"We did not anticipate having to attack the enemy in an entrenched position, but thought he would come out and attack my square in large numbers, be repulsed, and then be cut up by the cavalry.

"The charges actually made were upon masses of the enemy not yet engaged with my infantry, and although most gallantly and skilfully executed, *the loss of officers and men is deeply to be regretted.*"[1]

[1] Supp. to *London Gazette*, March 27th, 1884.

Founded as it was on known Arab characteristics, in the very reasonable expectation mentioned, General Graham did not stand alone. With reference to this point, in its tactical bearings, an anonymous writer states :—

"Among the many lessons learnt, not only in the late European campaigns, but in our own savage campaigns, is the almost unconquerable defensive power of the modern rifle when in the hands of well posted troops, not yet demoralised, especially when open ground had to be crossed by the assailant. This fact is of vast importance in warfare, and points out that *the keynote of our tactics should be to persuade the enemy to assault over the open ; to halt, and meet this assault by fire, and only to deliver the counter assault when the enemy's power is broken.*" [1]

While such advantages accrue to the civilised Force, the motives impelling the savage antagonist so to attack are thus stated :—

"In all our savage wars our troops are invariably greatly outnumbered, and hence invariably outflanked. *The mere smallness of our numbers, the fanaticism with which they are possessed against us, will nearly always induce them to attack us voluntarily ;* or if not, then such foes as the Zulus and Soudanese can be made to do so by an advance close up to their position, followed by a halt, and, if necessary, a simulated retreat, *when down they will pour over the open, offering the most perfect mark for rifle fire.*" [2]

At El Teb, however, the "unexpected" happened, and the enemy taking the full benefit of local circumstances, clung to the entrenchments with desperate tenacity, and, when driven from these, sullenly drew off towards Tokar in large masses, without affording the desired opportunities for punishment and decimation. Thus, escaping the Infantry, the Cavalry Brigade forming up in three lines, charged gallantly, but, being greatly outnumbered, the Arabs attacked the flanks of the lines with such vigour and success, as not only entailed serious loss but, before the pertinacious enemy could be got rid of, necessitated a complete change of front. The tables were thus completely turned, and, as admitted by General

---

[1] *The Late Battles in the Soudan and Modern Tactics.* London, 1884. P. 37.
[2] *Ibid.* p. 38.

Graham, "The Cavalry charges were made with masses of the enemy *never yet engaged with my infantry.*" Or, as more minutely described by an eye-witness :—

"During this halt the cavalry have moved round behind us, and we can now see them advancing towards a large mass of the enemy, who are making off in the distance. They are manifestly quickening their pace. Faster and faster they go. Their sabres are flashing in the sunlight, and they dash into the mass of the enemy. Right through them they cut their way, and then turn sharp back again. The Arabs do not fly, but stand and fight stubbornly and gallantly, displaying as much courage as against the infantry. Again and again they are dispersed, but each time they gather together as the horsemen come on, and the cavalry, although cutting down many, go by no means scatheless through them. Major Slade, of the 10th Hussars; Lieutenant Probyn, of the 9th Bengal Cavalry; and Lieutenant-Colonel Barrow, and Lieutenant Freeman, of the 19th Hussars, were all speared, and upwards of twenty of their men."[1]

And again, as illustrating the regular and unbroken formation of the enemy so attacked :—

"Among the feats of Friday's battle none was more brilliant than those of the 19th and 10th Hussars. In the charge the 19th found themselves confronted by a large body of rebels, mounted on camels and horses, the former masking the latter, behind which again were considerable numbers of spearmen on foot. The rebel horsemen, armed with two-edged swords, made for the 19th, producing, however, little or no effect. The real opposition was from the spearmen, who, lying down as the cavalry galloped on, started up and attempted to hamstring our horses. Lieutenant-Colonel Barrow, leading the charge, received a spear wound, but rode until his horse fell. The colonel's trumpeter coming to the rescue was severely mauled. Lieutenant Probyn, attached to the 10th, was the first to fall in this charge. Major Slade, of the same regiment was not missed until the cavalry had for some time been returning to the square. Major Slade is supposed to have been killed in an attempt to help Lieutenant Probyn. Twelve spear wounds were found on his body. Sergeants Phipps and Conolly deserve something more than verbal recognition of their brave rescue of one of their comrades. In this attempt Phipps was twice wounded."[2]

[1] *Standard*, March 3rd, 1884.   [2] *Daily News*, March 3rd, 1884.

2 E

It was to explain how this state of matters arose, that General Graham wrote the apologetic extract already given from his despatch. Under the same expectation, at the succeeding battle of Tamai, every preparation was made for effectively dealing with the enemy on the lines laid down. The Infantry were drawn up in Brigade Squares, ranged in *échelon*, and the Cavalry, kept well in the rear, were ready to sweep down upon the demoralised and defeated foe. Again, however, the "unexpected" happened, and, as at El Teb, the Arabs took advantage of the entrenchments, so at Tamai, taking advantage of the khor, they prepared an ambush, entailing most serious losses and temporary disorganisation to part of the British Force. This took place in the teeth of information, expressly conveyed by Admiral Hewett, whose unavailing care and promptitude in this matter, contrast most favourably with the apathetic indifference or unaccountable neglect, shown with regard to the Arab concentration a year afterwards.

As in 1884, to the "unexpected" discomfiture and "surprise" of the tacticians, the Arabs took advantage of the entrenchments at El Teb and the khor at Tamai, so in 1885 they took advantage of the thick Tofrek jungle, and that under circumstances in every way exceptionally favourable, yet, as we have already seen,[1] resulting in a much greater "surprise" to themselves than to their antagonists. To inflict such a punishment and effectually secure results so enduring, it was indeed worth while being the object of an attempted surprise. Had the trap been laid strategically for the Arab, instead of *vice versâ*, it could not have been better planned. I do not know whether, in the next edition of his book on *Ambushes and Surprises*, Colonel Malleson will include the battle of Tofrek as the most recent addition to the number. If the question be determined by the intentions of the enemy and the voice of the critics, he will no doubt do so. At the same time only one place can be accorded to it, and that is alongside the brilliant exploit of Lord Mark Kerr at Azamgarh. In a survey of military history extending from

---

[1] Preface, p. xvi.

the days of Hannibal down to the Indian Mutiny, of this event Colonel Malleson tells us :—

"The battle of Azamgarh stands out as the only instance in history in which an army, surprised by an enemy lying in ambush for it, *succeeded in defeating the surprisers* ... The case of the battle of Azamgarh is, then, unique in history. It is in very deed, I repeat, the only instance on record in which an army, surprised by an enemy in ambush, *succeeded in inflicting a crushing defeat upon its enemy.*" [1]

As a well-deserved tribute for a service so distinguished, Colonel Malleson dedicates his work to Lord Mark Kerr, at the same time stating, in terms equally applicable to the action at Tofrek, that the surprise and ambush of Azamgarh—

"Was disastrous to the surprisers because the commander of the surprised *was a real soldier, a man who thoroughly understood his craft, whose mental energies were never better directed than when he was in the presence of danger.*" [2]

It is true the proportion in point of numbers was very different. Lord Mark Kerr having under him only 22 officers, 444 men, two six-pounder guns, and two mortars, while Kunwár Singh is said to have had 12,000 men at disposal. At the same time the British Force was manœuvring in comparatively open ground, was engaged not with the main body, but with the rear-guard, and subject to no sudden and terrific assault like that at Trofek, while in resolute determination, the character of the enemy seems to have been very different.

As already stated,[3] the nature of the assault delivered on the 22nd was that known in military language as "shock tactics," and that in their most determined and dangerous form. A favourite mode of attack with savage races, like the Zulus and the Sûdanese, "shock tactics" have acquired historic fame through the use made of them by Napoleon in the French wars, and notably at the battle of Waterloo. The recent proposal for their resuscitation has also been referred to,[4] and whether capable or not of being realised in

---

[1] *Ambushes and Surprises,* p. 403.
[2] *Ibid.* p. 394.
[3] Preface, p. xv.
[4] *Ibid.* p. xvi.

French practice, in the *beau ideal* of this mode of fighting presented by General Boulanger in a letter written in 1884, as exactly suited to the temperament of these races, the true character of a Zulu or a Sûdanese attack, could not be more graphically described :—

"Tout le mal vient de ce fait, qu'on a cru devoir calquer nos procédés tactiques sur les règlements allemands, sans tenir compte des différences de caractère. *Le Français n'est lui-même que lorsqu'il se porte en avant, lorsque de toute l'impulsion de sa nature ardente, il se précipite tête baissée sur l'adversaire.* Rien de plus difficile (je l'ai vu en 1870), rien de plus contraire au tempérament de nos soldats que l'attente sur place. Avec les qualités natives de notre race, l'offensive s'impose, et c'est à elle qu'on reviendra fatalement, soit dans nos règlements, si on veut bien les reviser, soit dans la pratique le jour où de nouveau nous nous retrouverons sur les champs de bataille de 1870. Trop de troupes furent, dans cette guerre insensée, immobilisées l'arme au pied, lorsque de leur choc le succès pouvait dépendre, et c'est là le plus grand enseignement que nous devions tirer de cette campagne où dans plusieurs circonstances graves l'initiative des chefs ne répondit pas à l'ardeur des troupes.

"Mon plus vif désir serait donc, en dépit des calculs de nos théoriciens en chambre, de voir reprendre dans l'armée les traditions d'autrefois.

" Qui empêche d'ailleurs de concilier cet esprit d'offensive avec les dispositifs q'exigent le nouvel armement et la puissance actuelle du feu : je ne demande pas d'exposer de gaieté de cœur au tir de l'ennemi des masses profondes pendant cette période de préparation qui consiste à gagner du terrain à l'abri d'une chaîne de tirailleurs ; *mais je voudrais qu'au moment de l'assaut, au moment décisif, une poussée formidable, irrésistible, surhumaine, se produisît à l'aide de réserves massées de colonnes d'attaque puissantes,* se substituant à ces cordons fragiles e désunis sur lesquels nous comptons trop actuellement. On verrait alors si non bataillons français, musique en tête, officiers en avant, et le feu au cœur, ne passeraient pas partout, comme ces grenadiers de la Grande Armée qui arrivaient sur l'ennemi sans avoir brûlé une amorce.

"Vous m'objecterez peut-être ces exemples terribles depertes subies, par le feu rapide ; encore tout récemment ce régiment russe, le régiment de Kiew je crois, qui perdit en quelques minutes tous ses officiers et les trois quarts de ses hommes devant Plewna : je vous répondrai qu'après la défaite il en meurt bien plus encore sur les chemins et dans les prisons de l'ennemi. Et puis, la guerre d'aujourd'hui c'est la guerre sans merci ! ce doit être au besoin la moitié du pays qui se fasse tuer pour sauver l'autre, et il ne doit plus y avoir dans les bouches qu'un seul cri : *En avant !*"[1]

How truly dangerous, such "*une poussée formidable, irresistible, surhumaine*," delivered by a horde of savages really is, has been very well expressed by General Viscount Wolseley in his closing remarks on the Lecture, already referred to, on "Infantry Fire Tactics : Attack Formations and Squares," delivered by Lieutenant-General Sir Gerald Graham, V.C., K.C.B., G.C.M.G., at the Royal United Service Institution :—

"The vital thing you have to think of and to prepare for is, that determined charge of a body of fanatics who come upon you, determined if they cannot win, at least to die. Such a charge is nothing like a charge of cavalry that can be well met now by determined infantry in line. Anyone who has ever seen a charge of cavalry knows very well that after all the man who rides the horse has nerves and heart, and that if he is met by stubborn resistance nine times out of ten he will sheer off before he reaches the square ; he won't go straight in on the square, and his horse very likely won't face the bayonets. But these Arabs who charged our squares were determined to get at the squares. It is all very fine to say you ought to have received them in line, and if you had they never could have reached that line ; but all I can say is that they actually did charge, and were fired upon, and did reach our squares ; and if they reached a square I imagine they could have reached a line."[2]

As mentioned by the anonymous writer previously quoted, the war with the Zulus supplied striking evidence to the same purport :—

"An officer who served in the Zulu campaign has stated that he considered that the effect of a charge of the best cavalry could not be compared with that of a rush of an apparently endless cloud of savages, rising suddenly out of the ground at close quarters, and probably, such is really the case, as the moral effect of an immense number of howling, fantastically-dressed savages,

[1] *La première bataille Franco-Allemande, le 18 Aout 18—* ; pp. 67-69.—Paris, Dentu et Cie, 1887.

[2] *Journal of the Royal United Service Institution*, 1886, vol. xxx. p. 273.

bounding forward to the attack, must be greater than that of cavalry, which has some distance to come before it can strike, and from the feeling that the men have that the horses themselves will try to avoid them." [1]

As further illustrating this mode of attack, and its most striking analogue in European warfare, the same writer states :—

"The Zulus invariably attack with a main central column, which is always the first to show, to draw the attention of the enemy, and with two enveloping wings or horns ; they never in the Zulu war acted on the defensive. When they begin their attack the main body delays awhile to allow the wings to envelop the enemy, and then, at a given signal,[2] dash forward in a dense deep mass, without wavering or stopping. *Their very depth is their main element of strength ; it is a revival of the old French deep columns of attack, but moving forward with far greater impetus and speed.* The sight of such an attack is very imposing, and tends to demoralise the enemy, for there seemed to be no stopping the black advancing stream, for, as the leading Zulus were shot down, others from behind poured on." [3]

To be the object of such " shock tactics " in the open, surrounded on every side with an ample " zone of fire," and thoroughly prepared with all the varied resources the Expedition had at command, was indeed the great desire and strategic aim of the British General. In his own way the Arab fully reciprocated these ideas. To " shock tactics " he was most anxious to resort, if they could only be carried into effect, despite that engirdling " zone of fire," with its storm of leaden hail, baffling revenge, and sweeping the fierce and swarthy levies by hundreds to the ground. So the plotting goes on round the obverse and reverse of the one idea. " Shock tactics," a bait to lure the Arab to his punishment and doom. " Shock tactics," an instrument to drive the hated *Kaffir* from the Red Sea wastes. The too well-informed and watchful Arab must have had good warning of the anticipated Movement, and judged that for him the one great opportunity of the Campaign had come. If Head-Quarters knew little of the unreconnoitred route the

---

[1] *The Late Battles in the Soudan and Modern Tactics,* p. 43.   [3] *Ibid.* p. 44.
[2] Usually the smoke of burning grass.

enemy knew it well, and laid his plans accordingly, and as the antagonist against whom it was directed, he was best qualified to rate at its true value a strategy whose earliest development he circumvented with the utmost ease.

It has already been stated [1] that of this strategy the action at Tofrek formed no part. Its ultimate aim was to coax or coerce the Arab into a great battle at Tamai, and perhaps another at Tamanieb. In the exercise of his belligerent rights the Arab chose to try conclusions much sooner; and heavily reinforced by a Dervish Contingent from Khartûm, in one of the most skilfully-contrived, and most dangerous and determined onslaughts of modern times, fought out the death-struggle of Madhist supremacy in the Eastern Sûdan. If the presence of this new element on the Red Sea Littoral was not recognised at Suâkin it was known in London at least a week prior to the action at Tofrek, as we find it stated:

"It has been reported, and is likely, that a brigade of dervishes has been sent to reinforce the levies assembled in front of General Graham; and we may assume that more, if they can be spared, are already on the road eastward." [2]

With Mahomet Achmet then, rather than with Osman Digna, as the presiding genius of the fight, the small Imperial Force, firmly knit together, faced their antagonists in this the crowning battle of the two Campaigns. Under heavy disadvantages, and against superior numbers, they fought it with the failed and miscalculating strategy, *tumbling about their ears*, of which the day's Movement, with its zeriba-building and storing, its inordinate Transport convoy, and equally inordinate want of Cavalry, formed a part.

It was only the complete ignorance, prevalent at the time, as to the temper and disposition of the Arabs, which prevented the completeness of the Victory being fully recognised, while the stubborn Convoy fights of the next two or three days kept up the illusion that they were still unbeaten, and the advance upon Tamai still a necessity.

[1] Preface, p. vi.   [2] *Daily Telegraph*, March 16th, 1885.

In terms, considered at the time apologetic rather than literally true, in his telegraphic despatch to Lord Hartington of March 23rd, General Graham stated that he was " of opinion that M'Neill did everything possible UNDER THE CIRCUMSTANCES." Yes; with their scope extended a little beyond Sir Gerald Graham's intentions at the moment, these words *"under the circumstances"* form the key to all the difficulties which cluster around the events of the 22nd.

Determining, as it did, every material question as to strength and composition of Force, distance and direction of march, duties for the day, and whole purpose and character of the Movement, —of these circumstances the first, and incomparably the most important, was the general strategy of which it formed but a subordinate and fractional part. The first developments of this strategy on the 19th and 20th were intended to pave the way for that of the 22nd. The result of the two days' work was the establishment of a strongly-fortified post, supposed to mask the favourite haunting-place of the Arabs at Hashin, and command the defiles issuing therefrom.

For this procedure three reasons are given by General Graham, and they are important as exemplifying a strategic scheme which it was hoped, by a decisive battle at Tamai, would terminate in the destruction of Osman Digna's power. The first step toward this achievement was the formation of the post mentioned, and the reasons given for it are these—

First, It was *required* in order to protect the British right flank in the impending advance on Tamai.

Second, To obtain a post of observation near to the mountains.

Third, To assist in overawing the tribes.[1]

Now, if the British *right flank* has a meaning at all, it refers to

[1] *Parliamentary Papers*, Egypt, No. 13 (1885), p. 19.

the Movement of the 22nd, and the Secondary Base of operations it was thereby intended to establish. Beyond the storing of this Advanced Depot, and the daily use of the Line of Communications between it and Suâkin, no other movements of any consequence were anticipated or necessary until the time arrived when, in gathered strength and resources, independent of all subsidiary aids, ready for any foe, and determined to achieve Victory, the Imperial Forces moved on to Tamai for the final struggle.

To this extent, then, the protective necessity for the fortifications at Hashin was strictly limited; and if they failed to be of use on this the nearest section of the route to the Arab stronghold, the first reason given for their existence, and to it we may add the third, falls completely to the ground.

We know that such was indeed the case, and no blame to the gallant defenders, who could but shell a distant enemy, and make him keep beyond their own range: for all the protection afforded to the British right flank, either on the 22nd or any other day, the fortifications at Hashin might as well have been fifty miles off as six. The truth is that, depending only on British vigilance and the constant use of the heliograph, if the game were worth the candle, while the second reason for erecting these fortifications was valid enough, the expectations raised by the first and third proved to be hopeless fallacies.

Based on, and for its due appreciation requiring the exercise of, reason and judgment, the Arabs understood and cared no more for the nice manœuvring of the civilised and highly-educated strategist than would a herd of wild animals. Confronted with a ferocious and fanatical barbarism, akin to that which centuries before had threatened to engulf Christendom, except as instrumental in effecting direct destruction, the skilled resources of modern warfare were deemed of no account.

Movements which, to a civilised army, would have appeared of considerable import, being thus utterly meaningless, it is clear, that from tactics *quâ* tactics a great deal more was expected than

2 F

the savage foe was at all willing to concede. Regarded no doubt as a mere freak of the invader, the occupancy of a particular position could not terrorise him. The only warfare he understood was to kill or be killed. His daylight strategy differed but little from that of his midnight assault; and, to use General Graham's own words, in both cases the great aim was, with all the "stealthy cunning and ferocity of wild beasts,"[1] getting to close quarters with the enemy as quickly as possible, to spear him, stab him, cut his throat, and, in the spirit of the old war-cry, "the Koran or the sword," with passions unrestrained, in hacking, hewing, and merciless slaughter, revel in outrage both on the living and the dead.

With a race like this, of whose bigoted and ferocious creed, with its evil and demoniac inspirations, the only logical result was, a human shambles and universal destruction, what power had the strategical measures adopted by Head-Quarters at Suâkin either to protect or overawe?

"Protect the right flank." Well, the Army of Occupation at Cairo lay on the right flank, so also did the garrison at Malta, and they were just as efficacious in securing either one or other of the objects mentioned in the despatch of March 23rd, as the Regiment shut up six miles off, with two Krupps for offence, two Gardners for defence, and no option but to remain "disgustingly safe" within its prison-post. To get a Force entrapped in the centre of the jungle, over-weighted with a most tempting amount of Transport, and shorn of all the important adjuncts playing so prominent a part on all previous occasions, either in 1884 or 1885, was for the Arab the one glorious chance of the Campaign; and so, without let or hindrance, without one warning whisper, either from Suâkin or Hashin, with all the steady, stealthy circumspection of the tiger, taking full advantage of the unwonted opportunity, he prepared unawares to spring upon his prey.

Although, powerless to exercise on the Arab the influence

[1] Despatch of June 15th.—*London Gazette*, August 25th, 1885.

anticipated, the reasons for establishing the fortified post at Hashin proved to be utter fallacies, their effect upon Head-Quarters itself was none the less pernicious and detrimental. The only reason that can be given for the most peculiar composition of the Force sent out on the 22nd is, that the strategy then in vogue was expected to be thoroughly successful,[1] Only in this way can we account for the Mounted Accompaniment being reduced down even below that given in the written Instructions. On this assumption only, is it credible that every item of Transport then available in Suâkin should be gathered into one great mass, and sent out with a Force overweighted with guard and with fatigue duties, and from which every means of independent patrol, or even of adequate outpost duty, beyond its own immediate surroundings, had been summarily struck out.

True, the price of these tactical misfortunes had to be paid. The casualties were heavier than under more favouring circumstances they would have been. In war such incidents are inevitable. It reminds us of what befell at the battle of Bannockburn, when King Robert the Bruce, on his little palfrey, encountered Sir Henry de Bohun on his charger. The Southron was cleft through helm and skull, but with the victor remained the regret, " I am sorry for my good battle-axe." So was it at El Teb in the losses sustained by the 19th Hussars and other Cavalry; at Tamai, 1884, by the Black Watch; and at Hashin by the 9th Bengal Cavalry; proving that, with all his love for "rushes" and " shock tactics," the Arab knew well how to take advantage of the smallest slip,

[1] As the keynote to all that followed, the opening sentence of General Graham's telegraphic despatch to Lord Wolseley, written on the spur of the moment just after the return of the troops from Hashin, ought never to be forgotten :—

" *Suakin, March* 20, 1885, 9.35 P.M.

" The result of to-day's operations has been to establish a strong position commanding the Hashin Valley, protecting my right flank and line of communications in the ensuing operations against Tamai."—*Parliamentary Papers*, Egypt, No. 9 (1885).

In this spirit of unbroken and assured confidence the Instructions for the 22nd were drawn up and preparations made, and it is evident, from the subsequent alterations, that as time went on this confidence in the precautions adopted on the 20th increased rather than diminished.

accidental or otherwise, and emphasising the advice given by General Gordon, that with such a foe war ought to be waged only " WITH THE GREATEST PRECAUTION "! [1]

There is yet another point claiming a few words, and that is, the relation borne by the General in Command to the action, and to the soldiery.   Save for the attitude assumed by a goodly portion of the Press, I venture to say on a point like this no question could possibly have arisen.   Based as it was on the most serious mis-conception as to the true character and bearing of the events at Tofrek, to this attitude attention will be more particularly directed in the succeeding Chapter.

At the very outset of our remarks, it ought to be distinctly understood that amongst all civilised nations, in War as in Industry, work must ultimately fall back on the many, while all that gives that work value, all that leads it to a successful or a determinate issue, must ever depend entirely upon the few.   To say then of Tofrek that it was "a soldiers' battle," is to say nothing more than has been truly said of many great and important conflicts both in ancient and in modern times.   Many battles wherein large armies were engaged, have been so fought, that it could not be otherwise.   Even under two such leaders as Napoleon and Koutousoff, with 140,000 French pitted against a proportionate number of Russians, the battle of Borodino was pre-eminently of this character.   As Sir Robert Ker Porter tells us, " The plans of attack and defence were simple ; and it was soon seen that the day was to be won more by undaunted courage than skilful manœuvre.   Where the powers of the head are equal in contest, the victory must depend on the superiority of heart." [2]   So was it at Waterloo ; so was it at Inkerman ; and many other instances which might be cited.   Wherever the brunt of a battle turns round the attack and defence of a position, or series of positions, the contest must necessarily fall back for its decision upon the ranks.   In this no supersession of the General's functions is

[1] *Vide* quotation prefixed to Chap. I., and pp. 156-7.
[2] *Narrative of the Campaign in Russia in* 1812, p. 146.

inferred. It lies with him not only to conduct all the operations, often requiring great tact and judgment, leading up to a battle, but also to arrange the various dispositions under which it is actually fought. No matter how much of a hand-to-hand encounter it may be, how much of a mere physical struggle between masses of men, rare indeed is the occasion when the General is not from first to last the inspiring and controlling power. If the character of the leaders be considered, and the tremendous issues at stake, perhaps in modern times Borodino may be cited as a contest of the first magnitude, in which strategy was reduced to an absolute minimum. The numbers engaged were such as might have covered square leagues of territory with their manœuvres. Yet, from early morning till latest evening the day was spent in the terrific and determined assault and defence of the most concentrated positions. So encumbered was the field with dead, that, as Napoleon drew off his baffled legions, he was compelled to exclaim, "*jamais on n'a vu pareil champ de battaille.*" Over more extended ground, for most part of the day, Waterloo, and to it we may add Inkerman, presented pretty much the same features. These are all notable instances of "soldiers' battles," where strategy and manœuvre were comparatively in abeyance.

On all the occasions mentioned, while, in the repulse of the assailants and a successful defence, the ranks fought with desperate valour; whether in the open field or within defensive positions, the firm hand of military discipline and of pre-determined formation was clearly seen. It was this which conferred value on the gallant deeds of the individual soldiery, and crowned their combined efforts with success. The same principle holds good in all military operations without exception, no difference being implied save that of numerical variation. Between two conflicts like those of Borodino and Tofrek, the distinction is in degree only, not in kind. In the one case the assailants were fourteen to twenty times more numerous, and the defence proportionately strong, but the essential principles on which the operations were conducted are exactly the same.

We have seen what the defensive arrangements at Tofrek really were, and that, apart from accidental circumstances, over which there was no control, they were pre-eminently successful. To meet the enemy in the formation selected for them in the earlier part of the day, and in that formation do their duty, was for the troops the one guarantee of safety for themselves and for all it was their business to defend. These are matters we need not here recount, but we cannot overlook that absolute ignorance of all such formation, for months characterising almost every reference to this action. To debit the General in Command with the results of that ignorance, and by way of compensation place it to the credit of the soldiery, was robbery of the very basest character. As, I trust, the course of this narrative has shown, I have not the slightest desire to detract from the well-earned meed of praise due to any one ; but it is no gain, nay, rather an irreparable loss to the private soldier, by unjust depreciation, under any pretext, to filch from their rightful owner the hard-won laurels of victory. Giving just praise to all engaged in a struggle like that at Tofrek, be it ours rather to recognise in the success achieved that "three-fold cord not easily broken," as woven by the old Greek poet in immortal verse :—

"Skill, Bravery, Strength, the strife maintain." [1]

The General is, however, expected not merely to think, to devise, and plan, but to exemplify in himself all those martial qualities it is the soldier's duty more particularly to display. In a sudden exigence like that at Tofrek this was a point of vital moment, the coolness and self-possession of the General, his prompt action and ready resource, exercising a magnetic influence on those around him. Qualities like these are pre-eminently exemplified by Sir John M'Neill. In the words of his gallant coadjutor Sir John Hudson, "He is one of those men whose *bearing* and *example* in the field are so valuable in an Army—men who exemplify the saying that 'whatsoever men dare, they can do,' and who 'fear no foe.'" [2]

In thus recording his opinion, General Hudson writes from

[1] Pindar, Ode V. Strophe I.   [2] Letter *penes me.*

practical experience, acquired under the most trying circumstances, well fitted to revive old memories of Lucknow and the Indian Mutiny. Not less emphatic is the testimony of General Lord Wolseley, who, in his speech at the Mansion House, July 29th, 1885, thus expressed his views not only of the criticisms then so freely indulged in, but of Sir John M'Neill's well-tried abilities in the field, and so conveying *his verdict* regarding the action at Tofrek :—

" Of the gallant conduct of the men in the face of the enemy, an instance was seen in the repulse of the attack upon the Zariba of General Sir John M'Neill. Their conduct in that repulse was especially admirable. There had been severe criticisms upon that action and upon the General ; but he had no hesitation in declaring that if he should be sent into the field to-morrow, there was no Officer whom he would sooner have with him than General M'Neill ; and that was not only his own opinion, but the opinion of ninety-nine out of every hundred who knew the circumstances."

This tribute, so generously rendered to the Officer who was his Chief of the Staff, and Second in Command in the Ashanti War, vividly recalls his Lordship's words as to the uselessness even of the very best Army without a good Staff, and the remarks are equally applicable to the functions discharged by a good General :—

" It is not possible for the most transcendent genius to command an army successfully without able assistance from others in matters of detail. Armies are held together by discipline, and discipline is essentially a matter of detail and attention to small things.

" The best example of how helpless an army must be without an efficient staff is that afforded by the army organised at Washington by M'Clellan, and, in a lesser degree, by his successors. Hundreds of thousands of men were enrolled, splendidly equipped, abundantly fed, provided with all sorts of artillery and engineer material of the most approved patterns and upon the most lavish scale ; yet, as a distinguished officer said, it was a huge giant lying prostrate on the ground, who, though powerful in outward appearance, was destitute of bones and muscle, and consequently helpless for action. The bone and muscle required was a good staff to put it properly in motion. In the Southern Army affairs were never so badly conducted as in the North, which, in a great measure, is to be accounted for by the fact of its having received into its ranks the large proportion of regular officers who had been educated at West Point." [1]

Such, then, is a very masterly and vivid description of a Military Force either without a leader, or the means of conveying a leader's instructions to the troops. It was indeed a most extraordinary parody on the action at Tofrek, to place it in this category, and depict it as a scratch arrangement of men, caught in a sudden emergency, throwing themselves into any formation accident favoured, or their wits suggested. The truth is *exactly the reverse.* Just in proportion as the troops retained the formation originally intended for them, or recovered it, was their safety secured, and their efforts crowned with success. Their strength lay in its retention, and their weakness in its loss. To maintain this formation by the 17th N.I. Major Beverhoudt unavailingly sacrificed his life, and Sir John M'Neill and other Officers strained every effort.

Lord Wolseley has well said, "A battle cannot be won every day"; [2] and with the disgraceful story of Britain's late Egyptian policy ever before the world, we cannot afford to have an action giving to the Eastern Sûdan a permanent and settled peace, so seriously misrepresented. Compared with the blundering of the diplomat and the politician, the brave deeds of the Army in Egypt, from those of General Gordon downwards, SHINE OUT LIKE STARS AGAINST THE BLACKEST NIGHT. In the eyes of Europe its toils and privations, its courage and endurance, have redeemed the British name from ineffable disgrace. The sands of the desert have been watered with its bravest and its richest blood, and the graves of its heroes lie unseen by any eye, unvisited by any foot, save that of the wandering Arab. In an action, then, whose name is inscribed on the colours or enrolled in the honours of every Regiment engaged in it, thus to malign a General Officer who was gallantly serving his country in one of her darkest hours of need, when the privileges so abused were still in their earliest infancy, was—we again repeat it—*a robbery of the very basest character.*

[1] *The Soldiers' Pocket-Book for Field Service,* p. 127.   [2] *Ibid.* p. 352.

"WHAT IS NEWS?"

"Any statement that is new, unexpected, and calculated to satisfy curic
News need not be true in order to be news. In fact, for newspaper
poses, it would seem to be better that it should not be true. For insta
a newspaper states to-day that the Russian Government have occu
Sarakhs. That is to-day's news. To-morrow the same newspaper con
its previous news, and states that the Russian Government have not occu
Sarakhs; and perhaps on the third day the same newspaper will state
the place called Sarakhs does not now exist. Thus we see that one si
fact, or *absence of fact*, may furnish endless news paragraphs, only on
which, or no one of which, is true, but each of which is news at the tin
is given. Let us not immediately despise all news, for 'Rumour, with
hundred tongues,' often tells truth with one, though she may lie with
ninety-nine others; and we must, perforce, listen to all the hundred,
we miss that one which does tell the truth."—*Fortnightly Review*, vol. xx
N. S., p. 17.

"As with news, so is it with opinions for the purpose of a daily ne
paper. The opinion expressed need not be true; it is enough if it be
and plausible. Nay, for it to be true is a fatal defect; for in that cas
can only be asserted once as a new thing, and must henceforth be me
repeated as an old and stale thing; whereas if it be false, any number of
changes may be rung upon it. Truth is one, but falsehoods are many. W
an editor declares that two and two make four, there is an end of his lea
on that subject; but if he points out that many thoughtful persons have l
that under certain circumstances they make seventeen, and that in cer
places the sound good sense of the majority has accepted them as mal
fifty-two, then an interminable vista of leaders is opened up on practica
opposed to theoretical arithmetic, on circumstances, places, conditions,
nesses, experiences, and what not. Thus, indeed, it is alone that the po
bility has been realised of many daily newspapers publishing three or :
leaders each every morning, and no two of them saying the same thing al
the same facts."—*Ibid.* p. 27.

CHAPTER VIII.

THE PRESS AND THE BATTLE.

"There were no correspondents with them, and—happy thought!—suppose a battle, or, better still, a *catastrophe!* Why, we should have it—the news—all to ourselves. The fancy of such a thing happening lured us on."—*Desert Warfare, being a Journal of the Eastern Soudan Campaign.* By Bennet Burleigh, 1884. P. 73.[1]

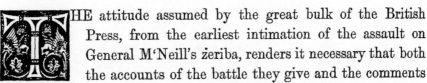THE attitude assumed by the great bulk of the British Press, from the earliest intimation of the assault on General M'Neill's żeriba, renders it necessary that both the accounts of the battle they give and the comments thereon should be subjected to a closer scrutiny than the ephemeral nature of such productions might otherwise justify. This becomes all the more necessary when we remember that, whether to use or to abuse, whether to do good or to effect mischief, the position of the Press at the scene of hostilities was one of special and exclusive privilege, and that the enjoyment of this privilege was conferred by the Authorities at the War Office only.

It is not too much to say that, as between the Public and the Press, the relation is in the main a commercial one, and in the principles by which it is regulated, exclusively so. The proprietors of the Public Journals are vendors, and their ware is news. Hence "supply and demand" forms the keystone of all their procedure. To whatever object the public attention may be

[1] The italics and notes of exclamation are given *literatim.*

directed, wherever its interest happens to be keenest, there does the Public Journal find its most effective field of operations. It matters not whether it be at home or abroad, a *cause célèbre*, or a terrible disaster, the execution of a criminal, or an important battle, all alike are fish to its net, if only its *clientèle* be adequately interested. And, according to the ever-varying degree and intensity of that interest, must be the more or less elaborate nature of the means adopted to meet the demand for prompt and reliable information. On no subject that can agitate the public mind is there keener avidity for intelligence displayed than when the British Army is engaged in active operations at some important seat of war. To gratify this thirst for knowledge as promptly and completely as possible, no expense is spared; by means of the telegraph time and distance are all but annihilated, while to act as feeders for the messages flashed homewards at lightning speed special correspondents are sent out, whose business it is, according to their enterprise and ability, or the want of it, to collect what is certain in any case to be accepted as authentic and reliable information. Content with acquiring such "information" at second-hand one man may shirk his work as much as possible, while another may accompany the Army in the most dangerous operations, and keep a cool head even in the roar of battle. So far as the Authorities at the War Office take cognisance, it is "Every man in his humour." As a question concerning only themselves and their employers, the qualifications and special aptitude of the correspondents for the position they occupy is left to chance and the newspaper proprietors. It is their business; and beyond the pass given on credentials duly presented, and a certain measure of surveillance and censorship, the Authorities, through whom alone the privilege can be acquired, give themselves no more trouble in the matter.

How thoroughly mercantile in character is the basis upon which Public Journalism rests, is very well stated in an article in the *Fortnightly Review*, one or two extracts from which are prefixed to this chapter, the interior economy of the newsvending art being thus vigorously vivisected.

"A newspaper lives not upon its circulation but upon its advertisements. In fact, it buys publicity for its news by selling publicity for its advertisements; it gives away for nothing the news which it professes to sell, on condition of being paid for the advertisements which accompany it. Its real customers are not its readers but its advertisers; the commodity it deals in is not news but attention. It buys the attention of its readers by its news, and sells that attention to its advertisers for their money. Thus, it will be seen that newspapers are in reality somewhat in a false position. They profess to sell news and to give advertisements to boot. What they really do is to sell publicity for advertisements and to give news to boot."[1]

The dissemination of intelligence, the vending of "News," as the only stock in trade the Press *per se* really has at its disposal, is thus quite subordinate to the requirements of the yet larger commercial world from which in all monetary matters it derives its true patronage and support—a patronage and a support directly purchased by the Press through the intelligence it diffuses and the attention it is thereby able to command. A public print devoted to news only would not pay; devoted only to advertisements, except to a very limited extent, would not be read; and the objects both of the Press and the advertising world would thus be completely baffled. The leading aim and vocation of the Press then, is to act as an intermediary between two great sections of the community—those who buy and those who sell; the one section requiring the widest possible publicity, the other the maintenance of unflagging interest, and curiosity incessantly purveyed for and gratified. In newspaper economy, "News" takes the place of the comparatively small portion of goods tastefully arranged by a merchant in his window, in order to attract the public and call attention to the much larger stock within; and, in plain terms, rank also with flaring posters, sandwich men, and other means innumerable, by which those to whom publicity means fortune and success, ever seek to keep themselves before " the

---

[1] *Fortnightly Review*, vol. xxxvi. p. 25.

eye of the world." Sales limited to goods displayed would soon read bankruptcy; it is the stock stored and warehoused, and for the most part withdrawn from public view, which forms the real basis of commerce. As a not less effective illustration, "News" may be compared to bait or the gaudy fly with which the angler charges his hook, hoping thereby to obtain not merely "nibbles" but heavy captures. So prosecuting its vocation in public waters, practically it is the commercial world and not the "silly fish" which pays for bait, hooks, and all angling requisites, the bait acting merely as a blind for anticipated "takes"! An attractive display of "News" awakening curiosity, whetting appetite, and calling attention to a matter of fact and forbidding mass of advertisements, is thus the real basis of that daily-issued "gospel of print," constituting so important an element in the formation of public opinion, be that opinion on any given point right or wrong. It is well that these analytic results should be carefully kept in remembrance; they are conditions essential to its existence which the Press could not alter even if it would, and we do not suppose it has any wish to do so, its interest rather being to strengthen and fortify its position in every possible way on the lines laid down. To us the interest of the inquiry lies in the manner in which the character and quality of "News" are thereby affected. That they occupy quite a subordinate position to the advertising necessities of the commercial world is evident, and must take their colour and bias accordingly. The writer in the *Fortnightly*, already referred to, has clearly indicated the manner in which this subordination operates. "News" and Truth are not only dissevered but become antagonistic. "Rumour with her hundred tongues" sits enthroned as mistress of the situation; every twist and turn of these waspish and lying organs being deemed of equal importance, and acquiring equal currency and value. Add to this the subtle influence of these old friends the "three crows" acting persistently on all who serve the Press; as the author remarks:

"Not only leader writers but foreign correspondents, reporters, and penny-a-liners have an enormous power of subsequent exaggeration of that matter

[News], and this has sufficed to make of the modern newspaper one of the most potent of all possible agencies for good or for evil." [1]

A close analogy is thus observable in the place held by Intelligence in the Public Press and on the Stock Exchange. In both instances it is introduced for ulterior and commercial ends. In the Press it attracts attention to a large body of otherwise uninteresting and unreadable matter, for which publicity is a prime requisite; in the other, exercising a barometric influence on the rise and fall of stocks, it is an essential factor in speculation, with all those gambling transactions inseparably connected with it.

Apart altogether from the influences thus necessarily tending to deteriorate an agency like the Press, which can only maintain its position by subserving diverse and often contradictory requirements, it must at the same time be admitted that a rigid and disinterested adherence to truth ought clearly to be the *beau ideal* of every instrumentality whose professed or principal aim is to instruct and enlighten the public mind. It is to the lasting honour of the British Press that, to an extent unequalled perhaps in any other country, this ideal is to a very large extent successfully attained. Let it not be for one moment supposed that in anything that has been or may still further be said, it is our intention to undervalue the services either of the Press or of its correspondents. The latter, especially, are, in the great majority of cases, selected for their ability and enterprise, and for their experience in arduous and troublesome undertakings. These devoted men are not seldom to be found enduring privation and facing danger and difficulty in their endeavour to perform their duties to their employers and the public. It is, however, often next to impossible that in the uncertain and ever-changing eventualities of War, the precise condition of affairs at some critical moment can be ascertained by them in time to telegraph the necessary intelligence with that fulness of information which is indispensable. The special correspondent is unfortunately compelled to reverse the dictum well known in

[1] *Fortnightly Review*, vol. xxxvi. p. 28.

literary matters, that it "takes time to be brief." He is brief, because time and telegraphy are against him; and as the requirements of the public demand immediate news of an event, it is inevitable that during occurrences of a hurried and sudden description, correspondents should frequently transmit intelligence necessarily incomplete and not unfrequently inaccurate.

In a case like the present, where unsparing criticism promptly followed in the track of very partial and imperfect information, the evils referred to are very forcibly illustrated. It may indeed be affirmed that such criticism was by no means universal,—true, but at the same time it must be admitted that had even one special on the spot, or one journal of authority in Britain, reported the facts of that 22nd of March, as they were to be seen, not in the first turmoil and confusion of an Arab "rush," but as they were during the preceding uneventful hours of steady labour from 10.30 A.M. to 2.30 P.M., diatribes and misrepresentation would have been alike nipped in the bud. "It is the unexpected that happens," and it is clear that no one was more taken by surprise than the special. One of the number states that "no fighting was anticipated," and in this impression all appear to have participated. The zeriba and its labours, the troops and their dispositions, seem to have been regarded with all the indifference of an ordinary military bivouac, uninteresting to every one save those whose business it was, under a torrid and blazing sun, to obey the imperative behest of duty. So far as the Press then is concerned, the major portion of the day intervening between the march out and the attack is a total blank, the curtain being suddenly raised on a scene of unexpected panic and confusion, against which no precautions had been taken, and in which soldier and civilian were alike caught and all but swept away as by the sudden outburst of some resistless torrent.

As befits its position at the head of the British Press, our first reference is to the *Times*. Its facts, so far as stated, in the main correct; its criticisms guarded and impartial, the leading journal presents a marked contrast to some of its contemporaries. Still, in conveying to the British Public some approximately trustworthy idea of a conflict like that of Tofrek, from its columns, we shall be able to judge how far, in such qualities as sound judgment, accuracy, and completeness, a special, or an editor even at the best, may fall short of a very modest ideal.

In the issue of the 23rd, the leading military intelligence of course relates to the fight of the previous day. After describing the hubbub, under any circumstances inseparable from a sudden attack, the editor proceeds to sketch for the benefit of his readers the leading features of the event :

"The enemy were, however, checked by the fire of two companies of Marines—probably either a covering party or off work for the time and close to their arms—who poured in a steady fire. The rest of the force, though taken by surprise, and, so to speak, *en déshabillé*, rallied at once in small parties at the angles of the zariba—we imagine outside it—and, regiment mixed up with regiment, fought back to back, and shoulder to shoulder, with a vigour and tenacity which no troops in the world could have displayed in greater profusion ; the Sepoys, as they have often done before, rivalling their British comrades in valour and discipline. It was, indeed, a struggle not merely for honour and victory but for dear life. During half an hour the fire, the din, and confusion were terrific ; and, to quote the exact words of our Correspondent, ' None but steady troops could have stood the fearful tension of the moment.' "

If the reader believes our previous statements to be fact, not fiction, we ask if the above narrative can be accepted otherwise than as a very partial description of that " hard-fought action of the 22nd of March which crushed the power of Osman Digna." Only think of it. That morning there marched out from Suâkin a fighting Force of between three and four thousand men, comprising five Regiments, British and Indian, divided into say from thirty to forty Companies. At the close of the march, presumably in good order, by 2.45 P.M. they have become so disorganised that only two Companies of Marines are in fighting trim, and even their preparedness is attributable to the accidental fact that they were " either a covering party or off work for the time and close to their arms " ! The remainder of this large Force, even abstracting the two Companies, still numbering over three thousand men, were so much of a half-armed rabble, so lost to all discipline and regular formation, that albeit "with a vigour and tenacity which no troops in the world could have displayed in greater profusion," they were reduced to fight, "regiment mixed up with regiment, back to back, and shoulder to shoulder," under all the disadvantages of a most desperate scrimmage.

So far the editor. Turning to the report of the correspondent, we see at once that the few paragraphs so deftly transformed into a complete account of the contest convey nothing more than a personal experience during a very brief period of time and within a very limited area—a mere episode in a struggle spreading over half a square mile of ground, and of which, involved as it was in clouds of smoke and dust, it was impossible for an individual observer to see more than the fractional portion forming his own immediate surroundings. Add to this the demand on every faculty for prompt attention to personal safety, and to the various incidents of the *melée*, and it is clear no time could be spared, even had opportunity been favourable, for a wider observation. As has been well remarked—

"It is of the nature of things that a man in the heat of action, in which all the faculties of body and mind are absorbed in immediate attention to his own fighting business, should [only] see what is near at hand once he gets into the thick of it, and therefore no two men will give the same account of an episode of battle at close quarters."[1]

If this be true of a military man, how much more of a civilian? if it characterise the variant accounts of a single episode, how much more is it true of a complicated struggle, the major portion of which was as much out of view as if it had taken place miles off, and of which it could only be said, "The fire, the din, and the confusion were terrific." Happily, we have now the parallel, but much fuller and detailed narrative, of Major de Cosson,[2] who was caught in

[1] *Army and Navy Gazette,* March 21st, 1885.
[2] *Days and Nights of Service,* chap. vi.—The Fight.

the same camel-stampede with the *Times* special, and, with some difficulty, also found shelter in the redoubt occupied by the Royal Marines. While thus corroborated, the report of the *Times* special is strictly limited to a purview of what took place at one particular corner of the field of battle, cut off from the rest by mimosa fencing, and once caged within it, escape was impossible while the fight raged. We are thus able accurately to analyse all the elements of alarm and panic, of severe reflections upon "the arrangements of gallant officers in the field"; of shame and annoyance incurred in the face of Europe at their supposed short-comings and delinquencies, as these were all unwittingly, we admit, yet inevitably promulgated by the leading journalistic authority in Great Britain. The momentary collapse of the 17th Bengal Native Infantry led to the camel-stampede. Caught in the fierce rush the *Times* special got into the Marines' redoubt, through which charged a large portion of the frightened animals, with men and Arabs intermingled, so leading to partial disorganisation. All this, how-ever, was a mere episode, affecting only one angle of the defences. Wired home, it is at once adopted as an authentic account of the entire operations. Always excepting that lucky "two companies of Marines" accidentally ready for the foe, "the rest of the force," three thousand odd men, "taken by surprise," "*en déshabillé*," rally at the exterior angles of the zeriba. A few stray individuals of the 17th Bengal Native Infantry, perhaps a few Berkshires, Marines, and Blue Jackets certainly, are magnified into Regiments mixed up with Regiments, fighting "back to back, and shoulder to shoulder," with vigour and tenacity. Could anything be more preposterous or misleading! A part put instead of the whole; an angle-work seriously affected by the camel-stampede, made to do duty for the much larger portion of the defences over which it had no influence. A few picturesque incidents in the way of mingled arms magnified into "*the rest of the force.*" The Berkshire half battalions in rallying square and redoubt, the 15th Sikhs, and 28th Bombay Native Infantry, whose formations were always intact, all are

2 H

" taken by surprise, and, so to speak, *en déshabillé!* " the Indian lines and British concentration a mere rally " in small parties at the angles of the zariba." How necessarily inadequate and illusive were the ideas thus conveyed as to the true character of this important conflict, and especially the dispositions on which it was based ! These remarks are more or less applicable, not to one newspaper report only, but to all. Like the seven sleepers, the gentlemen of the Press seem to have been simultaneously awakened at the moment when the Arab, in the shape not of a *deus* but of a *diabolus ex machinâ,* suddenly appeared. The interest of the day and with it " News " then begin. No inquiry seems to have been made into, or the slightest note taken of, the most patent dispositions—not one idea acquired which might enable the civilian to give an intelligent or even a common-sense and approximately accurate account of the deadly struggle. Not a special present seemed to realise the fact that, to have given a correct idea of the precautionary arrangements and the manner in which they bore the stress of the Arab attack, would have been much more important than to describe accidents inseparable from a battlefield, its flurry and excitement, its " fire and smoke and hellish clangour." In this respect we may well quote the remarks of a writer already mentioned :—

" To find out and to bring together news is not by any means so simple a matter as might be supposed. Most men do not know news when they see it; that is to say, that they learn a fact or see an event pass before their own eyes without it ever occurring to them that for the rest of mankind that fact or that event is new and unexpected, and its publication calculated to satisfy their curiosity—that, in fact, it is news." [1]

These remarks are specially applicable to the events of the 22nd of March. Even from the public intelligence point of view, second only in interest to the attack itself, were the arrangements made to meet that contingency. Without some adequate knowledge of these it was morally impossible for any one, especially a civilian, to understand, much less describe, either the main features or the

---

[1] *Fortnightly Review,* vol. xxxvi. p. 24.

various phases of the conflict.   That the most carefully-devised and ultimately successful arrangements were made we know on unexceptionable authority.   That these arrangements received not the very slightest attention is evident from every line written by the Press, both at the time and for long afterwards.   Yet this was precisely the "News," the "missing link," the counter-evidence against the various mis-statements indulged in, which were most urgently in request for months thereafter; and the Press did not know it.   Entirely dependent for their interest on that most uncertain eventuality, an Arab attack, by the civilians present, the preparations of the British received just as little attention as the approach of the enemy.   It was the old question over again of Mrs. Barbauld's, "eyes and no eyes."   The eye only sees what the mind has been trained to recognise; and, after a long hot ride through a troublesome country, arriving at an open space without the slightest shelter from the vertical rays of a tropic noon, military dispositions seem to have been viewed with as much indifference as the mirage of the desert or the heat-haze obscuring the distant view.

Such being the case with regard to the precautionary measures actually adopted by the Generals in Command at Tofrek, it occasions no surprise to find that the most pessimist views were entertained as to the fate which for the time being hung over the Imperial troops.   Indulging in severe reflections on Head-Quarters at Suâkin for the assumed absence of connecting links and supports, the editor remarks :—

"The first thing that must strike any person with the slightest knowledge of military matters is that, considering the march was not to exceed five miles, it would have been a prudent precaution, and one involving very little fatigue, had connection between Sir John M'Neill and Suakin been kept up by parties of Mounted Infantry and Cavalry, echeloned along the road and supported by the brigade of Guards at a spot, say a mile beyond our most advanced batteries.   *It is evident that the force was within a hair's-breadth of destruction, and had it been destroyed thoughts would have gone back to Isandlana, where the troops in camp were annihilated within sight of Lord Chelmsford's army."* [1]

[1] *Times*, March 23rd, 1885.

And again, on the 24th it is stated—

"Evidently there was a neglect of ordinary precaution, and the result was a heavy loss and *a narrow escape from destruction*."

Now, the editor was just as unwitting of the precautions adopted at Suâkin as the special was of those in force at Tofrek, with this difference—the one man was on the spot while the other was in London. There had been a squadron of Cavalry patrolling the Line of Communications from 10 A.M., and, although confined to camp, the Guards had orders to be in readiness to march at a moment's notice at a still earlier hour.

As it actually befell, owing to the effective character of the dispositions made at Tofrek, which the Press failed to recognise, it was found unnecessary to bring those adopted at Suâkin into play, and the Guards were recalled on receipt of a telegram from Sir John M'Neill. So far as these special precautions went, matters were all right then both at Suâkin and Tofrek, yet in both instances, and especially the latter, condemnation was dealt out by the Press, and that without any real foundation.

As an apt illustration of the curious discrepancies by which the public mind was then distracted, it may be remarked that on so simple a point as the despatch of the Guards, the *Times* and *Daily Telegraph*, in their issues of March 23rd, take up directly opposite positions. The *Times* rates General Graham for not sending reinforcements at all, while the *Daily Telegraph* avers that the Guards went right out to the zeriba, and remained there ! As a curious example of contradictory statements on the part of two papers regarding an important movement, whose correspondents were both on the scene of action but on opposite sides of the zeriba, we place the two statements in juxtaposition :—

Times, March 23rd.

We gather from our Correspondent's telegram that the attack was made between 2 and 3 P.M., and had lasted at least an hour, yet at that time there was no sign of the arrival of reinforcements. Apparently the messenger sent by Sir John M'Neill took a long time reaching Suakin, for our Correspondent's telegram, which must have been carried by that messenger, was not sent off from Suakin till 9.30 P.M. Still at 5.20 [1] Sir Gerald Graham had heard from the field of action. But we should have thought that the smoke of the action would have been seen from the tops of the men-of-war. Had it been seen, a force of Cavalry and Mounted Infantry could have reached the zariba before our Correspondent's message left. We cannot help thinking that an impression prevailed that the enemy, disheartened by the heavy loss which they suffered on Friday, would not dare to attack so formidable a force as five battalions of infantry, besides detachments of cavalry, sailors, and Engineers. Even, therefore, if Sir Gerald Graham knew that a fight was going on, *he probably deemed it superfluous to send out reinforcements*, especially as he must be anxious to husband the strength of his troops.[2] A *ballon captif*, sent up at a spot two or three miles from Suakin, would have probably rendered the surprise impossible, and we are rather surprised to hear that no chain of signallers along, at all events part of the road, was established.—*Editorial*.

[1] Time at which the first telegram from General Graham to Lord Hartington was despatched.

[2] These comments, so wide of the mark, so diametrically opposed to all the facts, and based not on information, but on its entire, though it may be accidental, absence, *i.e.* on mere conjecture, are really amusing. Much more significant than "smoke" seen from the crows' nests, was the heavy rattle of the musketry, distinctly heard at Suâkin, and in consequence of which the Guards who had received orders at 9 A.M. to hold themselves in readiness to turn out at short notice, were at once despatched.

Daily Telegraph, March 23rd.

It was determined to send reinforcements from Suakin, although General M'Neill declared they were not needed, and a body of the Guards, with some horse artillery guns, carrying a hundred rounds of ammunition, was despatched. The Bengal Cavalry under Peyton also started.—*Special Correspondent*.

How seriously the incident was regarded at headquarters may be inferred from the fact that the Guards, who had remained in camp, were at once sent forward to reinforce the brigades at the zereba, and that they were accompanied by artillery. The step was amply justified, if not imperatively called for, by the discovery that the Arabs, in large numbers, were so near the position, and that they had acted with more than usual audacity. It is, indeed, a rare occurrence, this charge upon even an imperfectly fortified post. As a rule, the Arab shows an undue respect for the slightest artificial obstacles. No zereba was assaulted during last year's campaign. The fort at Abu Kru was never attempted. It seems probable that the levies who followed Sir Redvers Buller did intend to rush his camp; but the first show of resistance turned the charge into a species of imperfect investment, and no formed body endeavoured to approach the line of redoubts. Tokar was a heap of mud ridges over which a horseman could ride, yet the Hadendowahs did not betray the faintest inclination to storm the paltry defences. Yesterday, however, they came on at a zereba, probably for the first time.

With the exception of one battalion, retained for garrison duty at Suakin, *the whole available force commanded by Sir Gerald Graham is now at the front, and in contact with the enemy*. The unexpected vigour of the Arabs produced this result, *by bringing the Guards upon the scene of combat*.—*Editorial*.

The same position is held with regard to the means of communication between the zeriba and Suâkin. The correspondent of the *Daily Telegraph* remarking :—

"General M'Neill drew in his forces, and all stood to their arms, while the telegraph wire laid down during the march, yard by yard, of the advance, kept him in direct communication with headquarters at Suakin." [1]

In addition to the statement in the above extract from the *Times* as to the tedious delay of Sir John M'Neill's messenger! and General Graham's supposed tardiness, in the same paragraph the editor expresses surprise "That no chain of signallers along, at all events part, of the road was established"! unwitting all the while that the best of all signallers was in constant operation throughout the entire route.

Here we have an instance of serious insinuations being made against a General Commanding-in-Chief, through one correspondent failing to mention what the other fully details. It should at the same time be noted that the *Times* special, remaining all night at the zeriba, did not know, or at all events fails to mention, anything about the Guards, while the *Daily Telegraph* special, who rode into Suâkin, though fully aware of reinforcements having been sent out, seems to have been quite unaware of their recall. General Graham is thus in the one case blamed for keeping all his troops to himself; while, in the other, with the exception of a Battalion left behind to defend the camp, he sends them all to the front, and "in contact with the enemy"! and this through the quite unimportant and accidental fact of two specials, who happened to be at opposite sides of the zeriba during the action, being at opposite extremities of the Line of Communications after it.

By the next morning a complete change has come over the spirit of the scene, and, without any attempt to explain the contradiction, we are told on the 24th by that cool and ever-confident censor the *Daily Telegraph*, that

---

[1] *Daily Telegraph*, March 23rd, 1885.

"Sir Gerald Graham, with the Guards, started yesterday (23rd) for the front, towards Tamai, in order to look into the state of affairs on that side, and repair, as far as possible, the mischief which had been done."[1]

And so rattles on, from one blunder into another, this amusing but originally most mischievous category of contradictions.

Pessimist misconceptions were by no means confined to the brief period during which the Damocles' sword of the Arab was supposed to quiver through the sultry air. How completely the Press was at fault not only with regard to all the main facts, but still more as to the real character and ultimate issues of the conflict at Tofrek, is testified by the forecasts persistently indulged in regarding the future of the campaign, until the force of events proved to demonstration that its further prosecution was utterly superfluous. As the Press sowed so did it reap. It knew of nothing save a brainless and invertebrate scrimmage, in which by the exercise of sheer pluck and vim, the troops saved their lives "by the skin of their teeth." Such a struggle, by exhibiting the desperate courage of the enemy, could only aggravate instead of lessen the anticipated difficulties yet to be overcome. Hence, before the Expedition, there is spread out a lengthened vista full of hazard, hard fighting, and arduous toil. It is not at the close, but only at the commencement, of its work, and Osman Digna is still a power to fear and a name to conjure with. Nor is there any exception to this combined chorus of the misinformed and the miscalculating. One and all fail utterly to grasp the situation, placing amongst the eventualities of an uncertain future that which was already *un fait accompli.*

As may easily be imagined from the very imperfect account of the fight published in the *Times,* and the singular fact that, notwithstanding there had been ample time and opportunity to supplement the extremely partial and scrappy notes telegraphed on the 22nd, it could only affirm on the 24th—

[1] *Daily Telegraph,* March 24th, 1885.

"More light has during the last 24 hours been thrown on the fight which took place on Sunday. As to the main features, though, there is little to add to the information *first sent home by our correspondent!*"

Jupiter tonans has little comfort to give. "The day of the decisive battle" still awaits the British march on Tamai; but even this prospect is dashed by the following pleasant reflections :—

"Will, however, Osman Digma accept a decisive battle? That remains to be seen. It will be very unfortunate if he does not, for in such a case Sir Gerald Graham will either have to carry on approaches as at a siege, by establishing himself in successive positions, thus frittering away much of his force in garrisons, or he will be compelled to adopt the hazardous tactics involved in making a forced march and trying to surprise his foe. This is no easy task, but exploits as difficult have been accomplished against Arabs in Algeria, especially by Marshal Bugeaud and his lieutenants. When Sir Gerald Graham does succeed in bringing the Arabs to action, it is to be hoped that he will endeavour, by combining the operations of two or three columns, to make defeat equivalent to destruction, for it is evident that Osman Digma is becoming cautious, and will not, if he can help it, continue to occupy a position when he sees himself threatened with defeat, and to catch flying Arabs in such country is not easy. We fear that even when the principal army shall have been broken up, a good deal of hard work will remain to be accomplished. Probably we shall have to deal with the Arabs as we have dealt with the Caffres—viz., send out flying columns to seize their cattle, seize or destroy their grain, and in this instance hold their wells; but the campaign will not enter on this phase till the main bodies of the enemy shall have been disintegrated. *It looks as if the campaign will be longer and more arduous than people have imagined!*"

General Graham's visit to the zeriba with the Guards on the morning after the battle has in no way improved the position, and the pleasant reflections *ut supra* are still continued.

"Sir Gerald Graham returned to Suakin from the scene of action in the afternoon, and we shall probably within the next 24 hours discover some indications of his plans. It is impossible that he can remain passive. He must either advance on Tamai or withdraw to Suakin, and there can be no doubt as to which will be his decision. The original scheme will, we suppose, be carried out and another zariba be constructed some five or six miles nearer

[1] *Times*, March 23rd.

Tamai. He will fill the zaribas with stores and try to bring Osman Digma to action with the least possible delay. That leader is said to have 25,000 men under his command. This is probably an exaggeration, but he has shown himself so good a strategist lately that we may count on his assembling all the force available at the right time. It does not however follow that the whole of his force will directly oppose our advance. On the contrary, we believe that a portion of the Arabs will fall on our rear while we are engaged in attacking the works in front. It will, however, be a great point in our favour if we can persuade the enemy—whatever their devices—to fight a pitched battle. What we fear is that Osman Digma is too wary to do so. He will probably repeat the tactics of last Friday, giving way in front only to fall upon our flanks, and carefully retaining the means of retreat. The ground is of such a nature that Sir Gerald Graham could not, by dividing his force into, say, three columns, enclose the Arabs in a circle of fire and thus in a military sense destroy the enemy's army. We have the precedents of Algeria for surprising the Arab camp, but Osman Digma is so much better served by scouts and spies than we are that such an enterprise seems almost hopeless. Still every opportunity should be sought to fall on him suddenly and disintegrate his force. *If we cannot with all our efforts decide the campaign in one or more general actions, it is evident that the war will be indefinitely prolonged*, and that we shall, as we remarked yesterday, have to repeat the method adopted against the Caffres by seizing stores of food, holding wells, and capturing cattle. In short, we shall have to render it impossible for the Arabs to exist in our vicinity, securing our lines of communication with the base by constructing fortified forts at frequent intervals." [1]

One short sentence in the issue for the 25th shows still further that, on the question at stake, the leading organ of public opinion in England had reached the climax of misconception and misrepresentation. With reference to the list of casualties then officially announced, all unwitting that Sir John M'Neill had already destroyed Osman Digna's power, it is remarked—

"And, we would ask, what have we gained to compensate for our heavy loss? *Absolutely nothing but a negative victory;* that is to say, we prevented the Arabs from destroying Sir John M'Neill's column!"

And, equally unwitting that all "strategical results" had been

[1] *Times*, March 24th.

effectually forestalled, in the issue for the 26th occurs this sapient supplement :—

"Our fights on Friday and Sunday have been *absolutely barren of strategical results,* for the bush between Suakin and Sir John M'Neill's zariba continues to swarm with Arabs."

While the reflections still run on :—

"The headquarter camp at Suakin was yesterday shifted to a spot two miles nearer to Tamai. We presume that the bulk of the troops have moved with it. This is an indication of an advance, and it has been rumoured that the force is to commence its march to Tamai to-day and attack Osman Digma —who is said to have 25,000 men with him—on Friday. The telegram which we publish to-day from our Correspondent shows that, considering the scarcity of transport and the distance, the attack must still be postponed for a few days. That it will be an obstinate engagement there can be little doubt, but what will follow? Evidently, it is not sufficient to beat the Arabs —they must be disintegrated, slain, or starved before we can make any progress towards Berber. To disintegrate a host of this sort in a difficult country familiar to the Arabs, and where we cannot follow up a success, is almost impossible, for the nature of the enemy's position at Tamai is such that a little Sedan is not to be accomplished. To slay even half of the enemy is a task beyond our power, and slaughter only seems to inspire the survivors with fresh fighting fury. *A decided and real victory over Osman Digma* would, however, clear the way for the most effectual measure, that of rendering it difficult for a large body to remain collected in one spot, by depriving them of the means of subsistence. At Tokar, some 40 miles from Suakin, is a vast store of grain and other food, and that place ought to be our objective after we have delivered one strong blow at Osman Digma. That place would, however, not be reached without much desultory fighting and without great precautions against surprise."

In precisely the same tenor are the forecasts indulged in by the *Daily Telegraph.* The only deductions it can draw from the purview of the conflict telegraphed from Suâkin, tell the old story of hard fighting, toil, and difficulty still to be encountered. In the issue for the 23rd it comments as follows :—

"It is now plain enough that the troops will have plenty of hard fighting, and that the General [Sir Gerald Graham] will enjoy ample opportunities of displaying his skill as a captain. The enemy may not relish close quarters, but he has already exhibited afresh those formidable qualities which were so conspicuous twelve months ago. Whether Osman himself engages in battle, or, like the famous Tantia Topee in Central India, merely directs the movements, his levies and their leaders have proved that their pugnacity and desert craft have suffered little or no diminution. They are checked, thwarted, beaten, but they still come on, and the British troops will have to win by toil and endurance, as well as by cool valour."

Quitting such generalities the *Daily Telegraph* concentrates all its hopes and its prognostications on that great event, the impending advance on Tamai. So much does it stake upon, so keenly is it interested in, this grand contingency, that, alone of all its compeers, it introduces a map of the ground " THE BRITISH ADVANCE " must cover. As an example of the curious topographical *misin*-formation, provided by a leading Daily for the enlightenment of the British Public, we give the explanatory note appended to this sketch :—

" In view of the probability that, before the end of the week, an important and perhaps decisive action will be fought by the British and Indian forces under Sir Gerald Graham's command at or near Tamai, where Osman Digma's followers are posted in numbers *variously estimated at from* 15,000 *to* 25,000 *men,* we reproduce a sketch-map of the ground upon which our troops will be called upon to operate. The map in question, copied from a sketch by Lieutenant-Colonel H. E. Colvile, of the Grenadier Guards, was originally published in Mr. Bennet Burleigh's ' *Desert Warfare,' in which that gentleman described the tract of country intervening between ' Baker's Zereba ' (the scene of last Sunday's severe fighting)* and Tamai, a village captured and burnt by the British on March 13, 1884. Tamai is situate in a rocky ravine *about four miles from the above-mentioned zereba,*[1] the intervening plain gently sloping upwards to the base of the foothills, in a vale or nullah of which the village lies. The slopes are covered with high grass, scrub, and underbrush, dotted with clumps of mimosa and cactus 7 ft. high in some places, and interspersed with dry watercourses. They terminate abruptly, about half a mile from Tamai,

---

[1] By Intelligence Department Map, and other authorities, over seven miles.

where a strip of broken rocky ground occurs, traversed by nullahs 60 ft. deep and from 200 ft. to 300 ft. wide, with steep sides, almost impassable for cavalry. This difficult terrain is backed by a ridge of red granite and gneiss hills, amongst which Osman Digma has taken up the formidable position from which General Graham's force is advancing to expel him." [1]

Passing over the exaggerated numbers of the enemy as a mere *on dit,* we find here the identification of "Baker's zereba" with General M'Neill's zeriba carried to its extreme limits. Baker's zeriba is not only "the scene of last Sunday's severe fighting," but the British force that marched out from Suâkin on the 22nd of March 1885, with all the convoys following it, and ultimately the Expeditionary promenade to Tamai under General Graham, traversed exactly the same route described by the *Daily Telegraph's* special correspondent, Mr. Bennet Burleigh, when he accompanied General Graham's previous advance on the 11th and 12th March 1884. The map is to the unusually large scale of "3 inches to one mile," and on the right hand top corner "Baker's zereba" is duly set down at a distance of just $2\frac{1}{4}$ miles from Tamai, against 7 miles on the Intelligence Department map. Assuming this minutely-detailed and elaborately-stated identification to have been correct, having previously traversed the ground over which the two Brigades were sent on the 22nd to Tofrek, it was a public loss that Mr. Bennet Burleigh was not at Suâkin on that occasion, in order to act as guide instead of Colonel Elliot Wood. It must however be admitted that both in his letters to the *Daily Telegraph* in 1884, and their republication in *Desert Warfare,* whatever information may have been conveyed as to the "four miles" between Baker's zeriba and Tamai, he gives wonderfully little about "the tract of country intervening between" Suâkin and Baker's zeriba to the extent of six or nine miles, which form the actual distance from Suâkin to the zeribas respectively named after General M'Neill and Baker Pasha. As to jungle or dense bush, or Tofrek the "thick place," on this the first and longest stage of

[1] *Daily Telegraph,* March 25th.

the journey, he is utterly silent—a bad omen either for Mr. Bennet Burleigh as an informant, or for those who, with a well-traversed and unimpeded route before them, sent a British Force into a tract of country like that almost daily traversed by large bodies of troops and heavy convoys from the 22nd of March to the 6th of April inclusive.

On the principle that "no news is good news," we adduce this silence not only of Mr. Bennet Burleigh and other correspondents but of the official despatches, as to any special difficulties having been encountered between Suâkin and Baker's zeriba as enforcing our whole argument not only that the route followed in 1884 was entirely distinct from that followed in 1885, but that between these two routes there was no comparison in point of eligibility as Lines of Communication between a Primary and a Secondary Base from which subsequent operations might be carried on.

That the critical battle of the campaign fought on the 22nd was an "absolutely barren" and "negative victory," as asserted by the *Times*, is fully endorsed by its contemporary, skilled only in the art of drawing large deductions from slender premises.

"The attention of the country is naturally concentrated, day after day, upon those burning plains of the Soudan, where the disciplined and dutiful valour of our British troops encounters, and with difficulty overcomes, the fanatical courage of the desert tribes. Englishmen are generous enemies, and a sincere regret is felt that events have obliged us to destroy so many of these really heroic barbarians, who know as little of fear, apparently, as their conquerors. Meanwhile any signs of giving way are not as yet visible among our brave opponents in the Eastern Soudan. They are neither dismayed nor even apparently discouraged by the havoc wrought in their loose formations whenever they have come within short range of the deadly infantry rifle. We could not encounter in any quarter of the world an enemy more disdainful of death and regardless of wounds. Not for one moment have the Arabs retired from the thickets and hollows near the line of zerebas where so many hundreds fell on Sunday. After that horrible combat they did not, indeed, renew the attack; but symptoms of their presence in greater or smaller numbers were perceptible, and practically they have remained as close as the foreposts of a besieging army would hold themselves to the outworks of a fortress. Dark, dense, thorny coverts and broken ground conceal them, but ever and anon our troops have noisy and stinging evidences of their neighbourhood. Measures have been taken to scout through the rude country and prevent a second surprise similar to the first ; still, as we understand the reports from the scene of action, by night, if not by day, the persevering warriors of the desert move up towards the enclosures, sharply spying out what chances there may be 'for them. On Monday night they advanced so far forward as to be able to pour in heavy volleys, like those which were showered into the redoubts at Abu Klea ; and when the dawn lighted up the dreadful plain, they actually delivered a desultory attack, which does not seem to have been pressed—an incident affording the only present indication that the strength of the zeribas, the vigilant guard, and the fatal firearms, have produced greater caution." [1]

All is to go well, however, "as soon as Sir Gerald Graham *has thoroughly defeated* Osman Digma"!!! [2] This crowning achievement is close at hand.

"Our Special Correspondent reports that the forward move to Tamai will probably be made on Thursday. That is to-morrow. If so, then or on Friday the principal effort will be made to crush the enemy, who, a prisoner asserts, are sending the women and children to the hills, *and intend themselves to fight a desperate battle.* Before the end of the week, therefore, we shall have some plainer indications bearing on Osman's future prospects, and the *length of this second Red Sea campaign.*"

Some toilsome convoys, the military promenade to Tamai, a few "flying columns," protecting twenty miles of railway from "nowhere to nowhere," summed up the labours of the Expedition of 1885. As to real fighting "the *length* of this second Red Sea campaign" had already been measured and, at a considerable saving both of money and men, the "scuttle out" policy of 1884 might just as easily have been repeated on the *first of April* as six weeks later.

Yet another choice *morceau* from this editorial of the 25th:—

"It is painful to know that our noble soldiers are obliged to live, even for

[1] *Daily Telegraph*, March 25th.   [2] *Ibid.*

a brief space, in an atmosphere like that which is polluted by the decaying masses of men and animals strewn over the desert area by the recent slaughter. The troops have been occupied in assiduously burying the dead, and thus improving the unsanitary condition of the camp. It may be questioned, however, whether sickness would not have been lessened by choosing another site, especially if it be true that hard by there are bare open hills. Had the camp been originally pitched in such a situation, Sunday's calamity would have been averted, and invaluable transport, so difficult to renew, even in the adjacent lands of the camel, would not have fallen a sacrifice to want of business-like foresight."

We have already seen that the gentlemen of the Press were entirely at sea as to the exact *locale* where the battle of Tofrek took place. It would, then, serve no useful purpose to enquire whether the "bare open hills" referred to are "hard by" Baker's or M'Neill's zeriba, or whether they exist at all. The reference is clearly inapplicable to the latter position, which was determined by an ideal line initiated by General Graham, pursued by his deputy, and the distance fixed by the inability of the Transport Train to struggle any farther.

As in a lady's postscript, the point of the quotation, however, lies in the last sentence, which we are free heartily to endorse, and would only enquire, "To whom does this smart writer mean these remarks to apply?" They are no doubt applicable somewhere; and, interpreted by the general tenor and bias of the article, there can be no doubt they are intended for the General in Command on the 22nd, who, by selecting a site inviting disaster instead of one "hard by," where it could so easily have been "averted," to this extent utterly failed in his duty, and thereby exhibited a most glaring "want of business-like foresight." The cool assumption, of course, is, that this General had the option of going where he pleased, and had "bare open hills" at his disposal, as well as "dark, dense, thorny coverts." From the facts already stated it will be seen that nothing can be further from the mark than this assumption and the implication it conveys. The truth is, that acting under Orders strictly laid down, and with an Officer of the Royal Engineers deputed from Head-Quarters to see that these Orders were not deviated from, and to point out the spot where the Secondary Base was to be fixed, there was no option in the matter. The only option was that open to Head-Quarters itself at morning parade, when instead of wheeling the Squares round an eighth part of the compass so as to march directly towards the thick Tofrek jungle, they might have let well alone, and permitted the Brigade arrangements for marching by the Kassala route to Baker's zeriba to remain unaltered.

As the best commentary on the quotation just referred to, we ask the reader to turn to that already given at p. 163, from the *Daily Telegraph* of March 10th, 1884, where it is stated that, in addition to other advantages possessed by the zeriba in question, "The low mound of earth all round affords perfect security against rifle fire, *as the country is quite flat there,*" and inferentially free from vantage points and cover for an enemy. Under such circumstances it is extremely probable that the editorial prognostication would have been fully realised :—

"Sunday's calamity would have been averted, and invaluable transport, so difficult to renew, even in the adjacent lands of the camel, would not have fallen a sacrifice to want of business-like foresight."

Like an Arab sword, double-edged, the sentence cuts both ways, and we leave the reader to apply the simile.

The same principle applies exactly to an equally illogical and spiteful attack on General M'Neill in the issue for the 26th. Commenting on the statement of the previous day that "The Guards and Sikhs in the advanced positions are cutting and burning a wide road through the bush," the editor remarks :—

"Sir John M'Neill's advance was preceded by an operation which might with profit have been undertaken at an earlier stage. He bethought him that it would be well to employ part of the force in cutting and burning a wide pathway through the bush; and the useful work was allotted to the Guards and the Sikhs. The Duke of Wellington many years ago laid it down that the best way of working through a jungle—and the desert is a thorn jungle—was to open a broad road by destroying the trees and undergrowth. His remarks, if we remember rightly, referred to military operations in the Wynaad; they were, at any rate, the fruit of an Indian experience. Much is taught and much is forgotten; yet the recollection of Wellington's shrewd observations and their prompt application would have saved the transport-cattle and more than three hundred brave men from death or wounds. As, however, the line lengthens, and as the Arabs are still alert and vivacious, it will require more men to guard the track, although so short. The favourite stretch of the line upon which the enemy assemble to deliver attacks is that nearest the seashore base, showing a correct appreciation of vital points on the part of the Arabs."

The natural, the implied, the designed inference, from a statement like this is, that not until the 24th did Sir John M'Neill commence the *ex post facto* performance of a duty which ought to have been thought of and discharged either prior to or current with the march on the 22nd, and which, duly attended to, "would have saved the transport-cattle and more than three hundred brave men from death or wounds"!

The writer does not condescend to tell us how even "cutting and burning a wide road through the bush" would have materially altered the circumstances, unless indeed, over several square miles the plain had been so far devastated with fire that "Tofrek, the thick place," reduced to ashes would have ceased to exist. That, however, is a trifle; to be taken into account only by those who look to *facts* instead of *phrases*.

In illustrating his dictum, "Much is taught, and much is forgotten," this writer might have gone beyond the days of Wellington, and adduced the invariable practice of the Romans in cutting military ways, "Lines of Communication," through the dense and trackless forests then covering large parts of Britain and Northern Europe. In so doing it is certain, however, that neither Wellington nor any Roman general would have acted in the absurd and preposterous manner suggested at the bidding of a petty spleen. Ascertaining by trustworthy information or careful reconnaissance

2 K

that a tract of country so encumbered had to be traversed, prior to any movement of the main body, a corps of pioneers suitably provided would have been sent on, "to open a broad road by destroying the trees and undergrowth." Under any well organised and preconcerted plan of action, such operations would have been anticipated either by Head-Quarters or by a General of Communications, instead of being flung at the head of a marching Force, as one of the unpremeditated duties of a day already surcharged with occupation. With duties commencing only at parade, and, until the moment when the Squares were wheeled in the direction of Tofrek, a route unknown and unreconnoitred, encumbered with a jungle that would not burn until the sap had dried out of it, and, unless dragged out of the way, just as troublesome felled as standing; we ask what possible justification there was for a charge like that commented on? Such being the complete divorce between the actual facts at Suâkin, and the phrases so cleverly penned in London, it is clear that if to save "three hundred brave men from death or wounds," it was necessary that the Tofrek jungle, or a passage through it, should be burned, the responsibility lay at other doors than that of General M'Neill. Even after considerable labour, the combined effort, both from the zeriba and from Suâkin, to clear a road, was never fully completed, and the fact stamps with idiocy the idea of such a road being cut and the Transport sent over the smouldering ashes of a bush fire, *pari passu* with the march out on the 22nd. We have dwelt at length on this episode because it exemplifies in a marked manner the utterly irrational character of the criticism to which the events connected with the action at Tofrek were subjected.

With just as much reason might General M'Neill have been blamed for not carrying out, on the morning of the 22nd, another suggestion, to which the subsequent convoy-troubles gave rise, and, in recounting the miseries of the daily march, thus referred to by the *Daily Telegraph* :—

"This morning (March 28th) a convoy started to the zereba, escorted by our whole infantry force, including the Guards. The strain on the troops was very severe. They had to face clouds of smothering dust, to march under the glare of a fierce sun and over heavy sand. The consequence was that the pace was less than a mile an hour, frequent halts having to be made to beat off the enemy and clear the bush.

"Operations of this kind repeated day after day are literally killing work.

"It is universally regarded as a great misfortune that a light railway line was not laid down from Suakin in the direction of Tamai. This would have obviated the hateful and injurious necessity of dragging a host of camels backwards and forwards day by day, and, while it would have spared the men, would have been a great economy. If this step had been taken the advance would have been rendered comparatively easy, the troops would have been saved a succession of useless engagements, and a vast amount of unnecessary toil scarcely less disastrous." [1]

"The transport cattle and more than three hundred brave men saved from death or wounds." "The troops . . . saved a succession of uselesss engagements, and a vast amount of unnecessary toil scarcely less disastrous," and all because some one, in Head-Quarters secrets, did not beforehand burn the bush or lay down "a light railway line" over the route to Tofrek. What a condemnation of the some one, whoever he may have been ; and, compared with the experience, already noted, of 1884, what a condemnation of the route so deliberately selected !

Few words are needed to bring the vainglorious vapourings of the *Daily Telegraph* to their natural *terminus ad quem*. The "British advance on Tamai," heralded in such magniloquent terms, proved a complete fiasco ; enemy, worthy of the name, there was none, while "Tamai and its welcome pools of water" proved an *ignis fatuus*, entailing immediate retreat. Previously there was a battle, and no success, "absolutely nothing but a negative victory," "barren of strategical results," now, as "an abrupt and illogical ending ;" to so many anticipations on paper in London, to so

[1] *Daily Telegraph*, March 30th, 1885.

much wearisome toil at Suâkin, there is no battle, and yet success is by no means awanting !

"Yesterday passed over without a battle, though *not without success*, in the barren wastes on the Red Sea coast. OSMAN DIGMA, for reasons best known to himself, preferred the counsels of discretion to those of valour; and Tamai, after a weak resistance, *which can scarcely be dignified by the name of a skirmish*, was occupied, burnt, and abandoned." [1]

Veni, vidi, vici! the "decided and real victory over Osman Digma" had been at last achieved, with wonderfully little to show as the result. "The work performed during the last two days was principally a test of endurance, *since the element of danger was absent*" ![2] and so with a report befitting an Easter Monday Review, combined with much gratulation and effusive thanks for small mercies, the boasted "Advance" drops out of sight, presenting an exact parallel to another curious feature in the Tamai-mania, of which the *Daily Telegraph* made itself the leading exponent, viz., the patronage bestowed on the balloon. In noticing the immunity from attack of the convoy on the 25th, when the aeronauts first made their *début*, the fact is thus expatiated upon :—

"Perhaps the captive balloon, a novel sight in the Eastern Soudan—a mysterious figure in the sky—played some part in keeping back the superstitious Arabs." [3]

And still further to the same purpose in the issue of April 2nd:—

"Probably the astonishing portent provided by Major Templer in the shape of a balloon has played its part by acting on native superstitions. Death and wounds from the hands of men the Arabs understand, but anything like magic is more than they can quietly endure. It would not be surprising were we to learn that the æronaut in his weird machine was regarded as a powerful 'djin,' held captive by the General to work discomfiture among the Mahdi's faithful followers. At any rate, the vedette aloft should be able to perform useful services in the coming operations."

Like "The bright little cherub that sits up aloft, keeping watch o'er the life of poor Jack," the happy omen which had safe-guarded

---

[1] *Daily Telegraph*, April 4th, 1885.   [2] *Ibid.*   [3] *Ibid.*, March 26th.

the convoys for the last few days is still to hang an ærial providence over the promenade to Tamai.

"We have already spoken of the services which Major Templer's balloon might render; but we are glad to have, from our Special Correspondent, the assurance that this novel war machine will be *with the army*. At two or three miles from Tamai the watcher in the ærial car should be able to see and report on the numbers and stations of the enemy; while they will assuredly fight none the better when the mysterious object rises into the sunny air." [1]

The next day the telegrams announcing the bloodless and unopposed advance on Tamai also record this most amusing finale :—

"At ten o'clock the balloon was inflated, but owing to the high wind it burst an hour later." [2]

On the 4th, in a column intended apparently to be an In Memoriam of this special "gas-bag," the editor indites its obit, at the same time, like our first parents when driven out of Paradise, dropping over so untimely a fate "some natural tears," shed in sympathy no doubt with the tears, equally natural, inflicted by the mimosa bushes on the unfortunate defunct :—

"It was to be hoped that the captive balloon which floated above the zerebas formed in the neighbourhood of Suâkin would be of great and unusual advantage in pointing out the direction from which a sudden rush of the wily enemy was likely to come, had not the novel weapon of war unfortunately collapsed when it was most needed."

So ends this brilliant episode, so disappears this powerful "djin" of the editorial fancy: "Gone up like a rocket, and come down like a stick," the only result being that, with fresh emphasis and a new illustration, the verdict pronounced in the above obit on all previous military ærostation may safely be repeated. "It can hardly be pretended that, *thus far*, balloons have been of much practical use in the conduct of military operations." A thought nevertheless is thereby suggested. The *Daily Telegraph*, and with it the entire

---

[1] *Daily Telegraph*, April 2nd.   [2] *Ibid.*, April 3rd.

London press, lost a great opportunity. As a "foeman worthy of his steel," it is but too evident that the Arab deemed the British soldier of small account. Personally he was only a *corpus vile*, whereon with greatest gusto all lethal arts might be freely practised. For any dread they created his arms might be toy-weapons "spitting water," and breaking and bending like so many withes at the first contact with the foe. Inspired with the same temper as the wildest of the *feræ*, for the Arabs the Briton was but a *Kaffir*, a natural enemy, and a prey. Hence the bright suggestion that success, so difficult to wring from their courage, might be more easily extorted from their fears. The idea is by no means original, and had been suggested in various ways in connection with the Abyssinian war. The literary *quidnuncs* of London should have known this, and, formulating proposals, have acted upon them accordingly, ere the country was committed to the costly and troublesome *arbitrement* of the sword. Private enterprise might thus have effected what a well-known author thus vainly hopes for from the obtuse official mind :

"As the natives are impressed by enchantment, and are not all impressed by our soldiers, I should propose that in any future war of the same kind there should be an officer appointed under the title of magician to the forces, and that he should have sub-officers as assistant magicians and deputy-assistant magicians. The duty of these officers should be to exhibit signs and wonders. Mr. Anderson might perhaps be induced to undertake the control of the machine tricks and general magic ; Mr. Home would do the spiritual business, and could astonish the native mind with the sight of elephants floating in the air, or could terrify a negro potentate by tweaking his nose at a durbar by invisible fingers. One of the deputy-assistant magicians should be a pyro-technist, whose duty would be to light up the camp with unearthly fire, and to place strange portents in the midnight sky. Certainly, had this depart-ment been organised before the Expedition began, and had a few of its officers been present, we might have dispensed with several regiments, and the cost of the Expedition would have been greatly lessened, however munificent the remuneration of the chiefs of the department might have been. Should

Government adopt this suggestion, and I have no doubt they will do so, I shall expect a valuable appointment in the corps."[1]

This lively writer is, of course, only poking fun. Not so a worthy and enterprising mariner, Capt. W. P. Snow, of Patagonian Mission fame, who offered to secure the release of King Theodore's captives, if not without fee or reward, at least without any material aid except his own. The amusing but quite serious correspondence lies entombed in the blue-books; but the following extract will give some idea of the Captain's methods :—

"You are aware, my Lord, that all medicine-men, wizards, demented persons, cunning men, skilful craftsmen, etc., are in a measure held sacred in the East. I have found it so among all the many wild tribes visited by me in various parts of the globe; and a reference to any of my works, or to official reports, will show that I have invariably succeeded among even the most savage races of mankind. I simply study them, and then adapt myself to their ways (without entirely losing my own self-respect), until I win their goodwill and carry my point.

"It may appear absurd to relate how, sometimes as an acrobat, then a medicine-man, next a grave reader of the stars, a laughing merry-Andrew, but always kind and gentle as well as firm, I have got on. Playing with the children, admiring the women, no matter how ugly, and humouring the men (who are often but big babies), I have passed scatheless through wild people who, before and afterwards (most remarkably in two cases, Australia and Tierra del Fuego), murdered the white men visiting them. A bold, fierce dash, with no shadow of timidity, is however necessary, and they respect it.

"But to sum up all on this point, let me simply say that a man must be a student of human nature in all its variety, and, with a shrewd penetrating mind, work upon it as he finds best at the time. To this there must be an eye which never quails; and though I profess no adherence to any particular dogma of spiritualism or mesmerism, yet I add that magnetic power can be tried, and, as I well know, tried successfully.

"To you, my Lord, and to thinking minds of experience, these remarks will not on consideration appear rhapsodical or visionary. I have no visionary ideas at all in me. Real matter of fact is ever before my eyes. But I do

[1] *The March to Magdala,* by G. A. Henty, p. 268.

believe that in a good and righteous cause (and what can be more good and righteous than the trying to save others, especially in connection with the honour of our beloved flag?) God designs [deigns?] to manifest His countenance and support to whomsoever may have faith in Him, not omitting manly self-reliance and courageous trust in a strong mind with a supple arm."[1]

Addressed to the same statesman who fled from office at the apparition of an Indian Contingent appearing in the Mediterranean, and ingeniously contrived to halve Papua with Prince Bismarck, the proposals were of course snuffed out, with a costly expedition as the inevitable alternative. "Much is taught and much is forgotten"; under happier auspices why did not the *Daily Telegraph* revive Capt. Snow's panacea and earn the lasting gratitude of the British tax-payer?

To revert, however, to the Press and the action at Tofrek; although moderation itself compared with the *Daily Telegraph*, the *Standard* is not less decided than the *Times*, as to the outlook for the future. So little had its special contributed to the true reading of this event, so unwitting its editor that the "grand attack," the fortunes cast "on one throw," the "clear issue fought out," which he desiderates had already taken place, that on the 23rd the toilsome work yet to be undertaken is thus recounted :—

"From step to step fortified posts must be constructed to guard the line of communications, and facilitate the advance of the railway. When those first placed are firmly built, and stored with supplies, especially water, the Force can have its base at Suakim, but for some time to come the process must necessarily be slow. *Unless the Arabs combine for a grand attack or defence, and cast all their fortunes on one throw*, there must be a contest which may last a considerable time, though it can only end in one way. Driven step by step from their villages and wells, our foes must yield by degrees. But for every reason—for our sakes, for the sake of the gallant enemy, and, we may add, the future of the Soudan—it is sincerely to be hoped that, whether at Tamai or elsewhere, there may be *a clear issue fought out between* OSMAN DIGNA *and the English.*"

[1] *Parliamentary Papers,* "Abyssinia," vol. lxxii. No. 774.

And on the 25th the special thus records his conviction :—

" It is evident that we must prepare for stubborn and desperate fighting, for the heavy losses that they have already suffered appear to enrage rather than to intimidate the enemy."

Although deprecating rather than indulging in criticism, the *Standard,* unfortunately, in no way falls behind its contemporaries in the absurd inaccuracy of its reports, and in the failure to comprehend what really constituted the vital points in the action. Thus, in the issue for 4th April, we find the editor remarking :

" If home criticisms on Generals *who are not careful enough* are to lead to other officers being so careful as to lose time, perhaps the criticisms had better have been left unwritten or unspoken."

We find it also stated—

" Our men have, as usual, displayed a great deal of courage and many soldierlike qualities ; they have shown that even *when surprised in no formation at all* they could more than hold their own against the Arabs."

Again, referring to the large Force called out, and elaborate precautions adopted, when General Graham was personally in Command, it is remarked—

" There are two exaggerations equally to be avoided—*the exaggeration of carelessness* and that of over-care, which leads to unnecessary use of large bodies where small ones would perform the work as well, or better. Certain military precautions are as well known by all instructed officers as the sword exercise, *and should never be neglected ;* but we are quite at a loss to know why the whole Division must invariably march to meet the enemy in such a massive formation as that described by our Correspondent."

The words italicised in each of the quotations just given infer a state of matters at Tofrek directly the reverse of what was actually the case, the expression *" when surprised in no formation at all "* supplying the key to all the others. We acquit the editor of any *intention* to disseminate a statement in itself most erroneous and misleading ; but the *fact* nevertheless remains unaltered. Why this contradiction between an honourable intention and the *ipsissima*

2 L

verba set before the public? The editor most assuredly did not know how matters really stood. The reports received erred not only in positive statement, they erred still further in what was entirely omitted. Nor, by subsequent inquiry, was the defect ever remedied, the quotations occurring in an editorial, written a fortnight after the action. One thing is clear, the reports are due to hearsay, and not to personal observation. That for the 22nd confessedly details the events of the day as seen from, or known at Suâkin, and errs even in that. From first to last no mention is made of the Lancer squadron, its place being taken by the 20th Hussars. "The force paraded at five o'clock, and moved off at once," its destination being "*the site occupied by General Graham's force on the occasion of their advance against Tamai last year, and known as Baker's Zareba;*" and it is expressly stated that "no fighting was anticipated"! Diligent inquiry being substituted for a visit to the scene of operations, the next day a report is sent with a still further increase in the list of errors. The start is shifted from five o'clock to daybreak; but in spite of the day's experience, the destination remains unaltered. Italicising the errors, we will let the report speak for itself, as with the utmost confidence the writer trips from one blunder into another :—

'SUAKIM, *Monday.*

"I am now able to furnish you with *full details* of the desperate fight of yesterday on the road to Tamai.

"The Marines, Berkshire Regiment (49th), Naval Brigade, and Indian Infantry, *marched out at daybreak on the Tamai road to the point where Baker's Zareba formerly stood, about six miles*[1] *from the water-fort of the Suakim lines.* . . .

"The Column reached its destination *without seeing anything of the enemy,* and then proceeded to build three lozenge-shaped zarebas. . . .

"The central zareba *was fully three times as large as the others. It was to be occupied by the Indian Infantry, and here the camels and mules of the Transport Corps were all to be placed in shelter.*"[2]

---

[1] In 1884 General Graham gave the distance to Baker's Zeriba as 8½ miles.   Now, in accommodation to the new movement, it is "six."

[2] *The Standard*, March 24th, 1885.

The glaring errors as to plain matters of fact studding almost every paragraph of these reports,—always excepting the change in the locality,—do not after all materially affect the fortunes of the day, their significance lying rather in the way they tell on the credibility of the writer. It matters little at what precise hour the Force started in the morning, be it five, daybreak, or seven; whether its scouts were 20th Hussars or 5th Lancers; whether Arabs were seen on the march out or not. Details such as these, might have been according to the report, and not according to fact, and no harm done. The case is very different with regard to the defensive formation of the day, and the manner in which the troops were disposed, in order to guard against, and repel any possible assault. Yet, on vital points such as these, there is complete silence, the errors of omission thus outweighing those of commission a thousandfold. "A heavy musketry fire" six miles off, first wakes up the special to a sense of duty, while a few facts patent to everyone at Suâkin, and some scraps of information *"gathered from the fugitives who have come in,"* [1] complete it. Need we wonder that the editor introduces the subject to the British public in the following terms :—

"Yesterday's fight near Suakim was not altogether satisfactory. *We should be loth to form a hurried judgment on insufficient knowledge;* but certainly the news, *as we have it,* seems to point to more valour than discretion among the troops. There is an old English habit which seems to cling to us still, and display itself at intervals in a very inconvenient manner. That habit is carelessness in presence of an enemy. Like most vices, it is the exaggeration of a virtue, but it is a fault which modern conditions render every day less permissible in warfare."

"Loth to form a hurried judgment on insufficient knowledge"! It would have been much more correct to have said "upon *no knowledge at all.*" "A fight there has been, but as to its real character information we have none." That would have been honest and truthful; but the editor must assume that the special

---

[1] *Standard,* March 23rd, 1885.

had done his duty; and so, making the best he can out of what is said, and still more, *what is not said,* by the next morning a version, it may be as wide asunder as the poles from truth, is served up to the British public along with its coffee and rolls.

Not merely does the special fail to give the remotest idea of a defensive formation, of which he himself knew nothing, and had taken no trouble to inquire into, by implication the defence is completely paralysed.   On the 24th it is stated—

> "The Indian Infantry in the large zareba fought at a great disadvantage. Not only were the lines of fencing unfinished, but the baggage animals were at first between them and the enemy, and so hindered the fire of the defenders; and as the Arabs charged down, many of the panic-stricken camels, horses, and mules, rushed through the gaps into the zareba, creating the utmost confusion, and carrying the soldiers before them." [1]

The truth is that "The Indian Infantry in the large zareba," are entirely a fiction.   Not an Indian was posted, or would have been there, were it not that it became a refuge for the derelict 17th, whose business it was to have covered the Transport instead of being charged by it.   The six Companies whose formation was thus disorganised were but *one fourth* of the "Indian Infantry," the remaining three-fourths being entirely unaffected by the stampede, and from first to last doing their duty gallantly, save the enemy there being not a man or an animal in front of, or masking their fire, at any time.   Statements similar to these just made will be found subsequently repeated in more permanent form, and the same answer may suffice. [2]

We cannot close these remarks on the Press animadversions without more particularly directing the reader's attention to an error, vital in its bearing on the fortunes of the day, and based on complete ignorance as to the local topography at Suâkin.

It is a curious fact, but by no means an unimportant one, that, with very few exceptions, the Press insisted that the scene of conflict on the 22nd was "Baker's Zariba," and it is on the basis of

[1] *Standard,* March 24th, 1885.   [2] *Vide* pp. 194-197.

a catastrophe supposed to have happened at this locality that all their criticisms are levelled. Amongst the exceptions may be enumerated the *Times*, an editorial in the issue of the 24th, remarking of the zeriba: "The ground was surrounded by thick bush, whereas, not far off, near Baker's Zariba,[1] there are cleared mounds which would have afforded a much better position." At the same time, in a Reuter's telegram it is stated that "Neither the Hasheen nor Baker's Zariba, *the one formed yesterday!* were attacked by the enemy last night." The usual designation, however, in the *Times*, is "M'Neill's Zariba," and its *locale* "in the direction of" or "towards Tamai." Although the fiction of "the Tamai road," or "road to Tamai," is by no means infrequent.[2]

The *Standard*, however, is impervious to the distinction. In its first references on the 23rd, the object of the "second move of the campaign," is stated most circumstantially, by its special correspondent at Suâkin, to be "to form a zareba eight miles out, on the site of that occupied by General Graham's force on the occasion of their advance against Tamai last year, and known as Baker's Zareba," glossed in the editorial as the reconstruction of "the old and well known 'BAKER'S Zareba,' about six miles out on the road to Tamai."

In the case of the *Daily Telegraph* we have already seen[3] that in the complete identification of the two localities, "the force of folly could no further go." So also in the issue of March 26th, the same special apparently who had been out at the zeriba on the 22nd telegraphs on the 25th: "A convoy will go to Baker's Zereba to-morrow. If sufficient stores be then collected there the advance will take place on Friday." While further down the column there is given a list of "The Casualties at Baker's Zereba."[4]

---

[1] We have seen, at pp. 31-2, that, according to the map of the district around Suâkin, published by the Intelligence Department, the distance between Tofrek and Baker's zeriba in a direct line is about three miles, and that it is approached by an entirely different route.

[2] With that strict adherence to actual fact characterising its special reports, the *Morning Post* also entirely escapes this egregious blunder.

[3] *Vide* the singular remarks in an editorial of the 25th, commented on at p. 243 *antea.*

[4] As may be seen from the despatch pub-

So unacquainted then was this correspondent, with the localities situated within a few miles of Suâkin, that he imagined he had ridden out on the 22nd to a historic site, lying in an entirely different direction, and where, in all probability, the unexpected apparition of the *diabolus ex machinâ*, which occasioned such a stir, could not possibly have taken place.

As the following quotations will show, the *Daily News* is still more emphatic in the identification of Tofrek with Baker's zeriba :—

"SOUAKIM, *Sunday*, 9.30 P.M.

"General M'Neill's brigade was attacked to-day when at luncheon by about three thousand Arabs *at Baker's zereba*, six miles from Souakim. . . ."

"General Graham was repeating the operations with which last year he gathered his little army together, sixteen miles from his base on the sea-coast, for the final struggle at Tamai. *In fact, yesterday morning the English and Indian troops passed over the same track which was followed by the gallant little force in the last campaign.* We gather that the Arab rush upon General M'Neill's troops yesterday morning must have taken place *at or near Baker's zereba, which was one of three which our troops occupied last year. It can hardly be on the exact site, however, because Baker's zereba is a first-rate work of the kind, situated on rather elevated ground, commanding a good view all round, especially on the sides facing the hills, the ground to which slopes gradually.*

"Immediately after the rainy season, and when the bush has grown up and is in full leaf, even then comparatively elevated ground might easily be approached by an enemy unseen. But at this season the bush is pretty well shrivelled by the heat. If General M'Neill's force halted on the lower portion of the plain—say between Baker's zereba and the hills—a surprise might have been much more easily effected, for in some of these lower portions the mimosa trees are high and the scrub very thick. Moreover, the ground there is in many places scarred with water-courses, which of course are now dry, and [in] which an enemy may conceal himself. But then this too probable fact would naturally render a commanding officer all the more cautious—all the more careful to get his scouts well out.

"Even Baker's poor Egyptians raised their zereba there, and marched to and from Souakim in perfect security against a too sudden surprise. They

lished in the same issue, General Graham as persistently calls it "M'Neill's Zereba," a fact which at last compels a tardy attention even from the editor. (*Vide* p. 266 *postea.*)

probably would have bolted had they seen the Arabs coming, *but still they would have seen them in good time."* [1]

Damaging admissions these, either for a denunciatory and hyper-critical Press or a blundering Head-Quarters. Every sentence is double-edged, and enforces our main contention that, in 1885 as in 1884, Tamai ought to have been approached by, and with the aid of Baker's zeriba. By the 24th the guess of the previous day, as to the proximity of the old and new zeribas, has become a certainty, and we are confidently informed that the Guards' convoy of the 23rd

"Started at half-past six for the zareba, *which is close to Baker's old zareba of last year.* The progress was slow owing to the numbers of camels in the square *and the mimosa bushes."*

And again, among the first of the forecasts of hardships and hard fighting yet to come—

"We don't believe that Osman Digna's people have been cowed by their repulse *near the site of Baker Pacha's old zereba,* any more than they have been cowed by their punishment at the Hasheen Wells on the preceding Friday. *A stubborn battle is imminent on, or close to, the site of the fierce fight of March* 1884. The positions are shown on the above map. The zereba where General M'Neill was surprised last Sunday is about six miles from Souakim, *almost close to the site of Baker's old position."* [2]

The localities are thus not only identified, but the topographical features of the one are, with the greatest coolness, transferred to the other, and all the advantages of the position, carefully selected by Baker Pasha, credited to that so roughly guessed at by General Graham, as lying eight miles ahead on a due south-west line !

"At the point marked in our map as the second zereba—that is, the zereba on the Souakim-Tamai route, the ground is *comparatively high, flat, and free from scrub, therefore commanding a far view of the plain onwards to Hasheen Wells on the right flank, and Tamai in front."*

With such an outlook all round them, an astonishing position indeed for a British Force to be surprised in ! Unfortunately, as its

[1] *Daily News,* March 23rd, 1885. [2] *Ibid.,* March 24th, 1885.

very name implies, all these advantages, instead of being applicable to Tofrek, are to be credited only to the writer's ignorance. "Tofrek, the thick place," lying in the heart of the district so graphically described in the succeeding sentence :—

"The whole country round, from Hasheen to Tamai, in a semicircular direction, is thickly covered with scrub, and plentifully indented with khors (dry water courses), in which an enemy may find first-rate ambuscade."[1]

Yet, almost in the same breath, certainly in the same editorial, we are told—

"The triangular tract of land between Hasheen, Tamai, and Suakim is comparatively level; and it is there that an English General would choose his ground for a decisive battle with Osman Digna. But Osman Digna's tactics are to inveigle the English General into the hilly tracts westward of the line which is shown in the accompanying map, as extending from Suakim to Tamai."[2]

Thanks to the most inadvertent choice of the "English General," the "decisive battle with Osman Digna" was fought on the ground indicated, but under circumstances reflecting little credit on the accuracy of the information possessed either at Suâkin or London.

After this topographical *tour de force*, with equal perspicuity the writer goes on to prognosticate that

"Within twenty-four hours an *obstinate engagement* may be fought on the scene of last year's brilliant victory."[3]

This feat performed, as also predicted by the *Daily Telegraph*, General Graham is to carry his triumphant arms to Tamanieb, and thence to Sinkat, "if we may use the simile, the Simla of the Eastern Soudan," and where the army is at last to find "pleasant summer quarters."

"'What's in a name,' the name cannot alter the facts, and on these we take a bull-dog grip." So we fancy might argue the specials' "Abbot of Unreason." Unfortunately, in the present

---

[1] *Daily News*, March 24th, 1885.   [2] *Ibid.*   [3] *Ibid.*

instance, so far as the question of responsibility is concerned, the
name is everything. In the previous chapter we have seen what
Baker's zeriba really was—the great halting-place and *point d'appui*
of every preceding military advance on Tamai; than which no other
had ever been dreamt of. In 1884 the first point seized by the
Black Watch; and, except the zeriba improvised close to Tamai,
owing to its being too late in the afternoon to fight, none other
being required. What Tofrek was, the Press itself has fully
witnessed, and ought to be best able to estimate the enormity of
its own blunder. All the vials of its wrath are poured on a General
who allowed himself to be surprised in a locality where misadventure
had previously been conspicuous by its absence, and where all the
known features seemed to forbid such an occurrence. Nothing can
be more circumstantial than the way in which this utter fiction is
insisted upon, and if this *consensus* of belief and of expectation
proves one thing more than another, it is, that such ought to have
been the route selected. This insistance on the identity of two
localities, in direction, and in their surroundings, so essentially
distinct as Baker's zeriba and Tofrek, both falling within a few
miles radius from Suâkin, is at the same time an extraordinary
instance of inaccurate information on the part of those whose chief
business it was to instruct the public.

Another most singular error, which found currency in most of the
papers, relates to a second zeriba said to have been constructed by
the Guards two miles nearer Tamai than that around which the
action of the 22nd was fought.

As reported in the papers, two distinct moves took place on the
25th. The *Times* of the 26th gives a telegram of the previous day
from its correspondent at Suâkin, wherein, with reference to the
anticipated attack on Tamai, it is stated—

"Almost the whole of the camp is now struck and withdrawn inside the
inner lines, preparatory to the general advance, which is expected within a
few days."

And in a Reuter's telegram of same date it is stated "The Head-

2 M

quarters' camp moved to-day to a point two miles nearer to Tamai." A later telegram from the same source also states with reference to the zeriba, "This afternoon the Guards moved to fresh camping ground nearer Tamai," regarding which the editor makes the following comments :—

"The stench at the zariba from the number of unburied men and animals is described as most offensive. We are glad, therefore, to hear that yesterday afternoon the Scots Guards and Coldstreams moved to fresh camping-ground nearer Tamai. We presume that the Berkshire and Marines remain for the present in the old zariba."

The above Reuter's telegrams were repeated in all the papers; and in the *Daily Telegraph* for the 26th the editor thus delightfully blends the two announcements into one :—

"Yesterday the Head-quarters camp was moved forward about two miles on the road to Tamai, and therefore stood between five and six miles from that rocky stronghold(!). Consequently there are now three stations in the desert, the first a short distance outside Suakin; the second what Sir Gerald Graham calls M'Neill's zereba—if this be still tenable; and the third that in which the officer who gave his name to an enclosure, the scene of Sunday's combat, has now established himself."

What a delicious medley does this paragraph exhibit! In the first place, it is impossible to tell whether, by the "Head-quarters' camp," the editor means that of Lieut.-General Graham or Major-General M'Neill. If the former, he must have been a bold man to move himself and his belongings from the Base to within five or six miles from the "rocky stronghold" of Tamai, and so anticipate on the 25th of March the movements of the 2nd of April; if the latter, then the *Daily Telegraph* editor is the only man who affirmed that General M'Neill's Head-Quarters did so move. The error becomes all the more conspicuous if we interpret, as we are evidently expected to do, the first statement in the paragraph by the last. The first statement is little more than a verbal repetition of the telegraphic announcement as to the Head-Quarters at Suâkin, the last is an equally unequivocal reference, to a proposed alteration which never took place. It was easy to talk of shifting the camp, but to remove the massive water-tanks, with their store of costly fluid, was a different question, and so, perforce, the garrison was tied down to abide by its water-supply, and on the 30th, through the agency of Colonel Leach and the Royal Engineers, the defences, "still tenable," were modified into the form shown on plate II.[1] The change in Head-Quarters' camp was merely part of the general concentration of the troops at Suâkin, preparatory to partaking in all "the dangers and glories of the grand advance."[2] While the various regiments gathered themselves together, as intimated by the *Times*, General Graham moved up to the Water Forts, as we find correctly stated by the *Morning Post* :—

"To day (25th March) the head-quarters camp was moved to the extreme southern end of the camp, where now all the troops at Suakim are concentrated."[3]

In Reuter's telegram, the "point two miles nearer to Tamai," is reckoned from the town of Suâkin as distinct from the various camping lines and defensive works, while, in addition to confounding two independent reports, the one true, and the other fallacious, the *Daily Telegraph* assumes the reckoning to have been from General M'Neill's zeriba.

Such are only a few of the many erroneous and contradictory statements made by the Press regarding the events in question. Attention has been chiefly confined to those of vital importance from a military point of view; but, by widening the range, the catalogue might have been indefinitely extended. Under the circumstances, errors in one form or other were no doubt inevitable, but a consciousness of the fact, and of the really slender information at command, might well have induced a more modest and guarded expression of opinion on all points affecting personal character or responsibility.

[1] *Vide* p. 63, *antea.*   [2] *Daily Telegraph*, March 27th, 1885.
[3] *Morning Post*, March 26th, 1885.

"SUAKIN, 1885."

BEING A SKETCH OF THE CAMPAIGN OF THIS YEAR.

BY AN OFFICER WHO WAS THERE.[1]

"Quidquid agunt homines, votum, timor, ira, voluptas,
Gaudia, discursus, nostri est farrago libelli."

"Men's hopes, men's fear—their fond, their fretful dream,
Their joys, their fuss—that medley is my theme."
                                    Juvenal, Satire I., 85, 86.

In rushing into print and making capital out of the public interest, so long as it lasted, as well as in its mischievous misrepresentations, second only to "our own correspondents," was the compiler of a book published anonymously under the above title. In the preface the author modestly assures the reader that "Every statement may be taken as fact, and the experiences are those of one who took part in the campaign—the author." How far these confident assertions are borne out in the work itself remains to be seen. Even in a Field Force, of course, there are Officers and Officers; some "serve tables," others devote their attention to more warlike work, as may well be supposed, the "experiences" in either case being very different. A string of first impressions, run off the reel in a light, chatty, gossipy style, readily written by anyone adequately endowed with the *cacoethes scribendi*, the quality of the book is easily gauged, only the most cursory perusal being required to show that the author's place was anywhere rather than in the "fighting line," and that his duties lay much more about the quays and the depôts at Suâkin, or in the rear of the camel-columns, than "at the front."

Identifying himself in every respect with the Land Transport Corps, he makes it clear that all his avocations, interests, and

---

[1] London, Kegan Paul, Trench, and Co., 1 Paternoster Square, 1885; and 2nd Edition, 1886.

sympathies lie with that branch of the Service. Whether to belaud efforts or air grievances, for it he holds an ever-ready brief. So much is this the case, to such an extent does the book reflect the minor personalities, individual or collective, incident to a campaign, that no words could more fitly characterise its general tenor, its undercurrent of thought and feeling, than the lines above quoted from the great Roman satirist. We are thus able to estimate at their true value the very confident assurances with which the volume is prefaced. In so far as personal, "the experiences," especially in warlike operations, must necessarily be extremely limited, and the guarantee given that "Every statement made may be taken as fact," becomes qualifiable at once *cum grano salis.*

The part of the book we have chiefly to do with is "Chapter VIII. The Zariba." Notwithstanding the averments in title-page and preface, and the simulation of an original narrative by the skilful use of personal pronouns, on the authority of his superiors, we have every reason to believe the author was not present at the Battle of Tofrek on the 22nd.[1] In spite of the most carefully conserved anonymity, to those familiar with the *personelle* of the Land Transport Corps, aided by the author's own statements, there could be no difficulty in establishing identity. The identity was so established, and its accuracy confirmed, when with the second edition the mask was thrown off. The whole tenor of the chapter in question, its numerous and glaring errors, the entire absence of personal incident and observations, especially such as might naturally have occurred to a Land Transport Officer, the generalised character of the information, easily acquired at second hand, all carry convincing evidence as to the truth of the surmise just made. Let us glance at a few of these discrepancies, always remembering the author's assurance that on the word of "An Officer who was there," as "a simple record of events," "every statement made may be *taken as fact.*"

The first error, p. 169, relates to the Mounted Accompaniment,

---

[1] In charge at the Base, of No. 12 Company, Commissariat and Transport Corps.

where, enumerating the Force despatched to Tofrek, in addition to a squadron of the 5th Lancers, there is added the "9th Bengal Cavalry." We have seen [1] that no such movement took place until late in the afternoon, when Major Frank Graves returning to Suâkin met a squadron of the 9th Bengal Cavalry under Lieut. Peyton coming out to relieve him.

A second error, on the same page, relates to the hour of starting. "We were *all on the move* by half-past four o'clock," *i.e.* the combined Force assembled at the rendezvous in front of the Water Forts, and not individual Regiments from their camps at Suâkin, it having been previously mentioned that "by four o'clock we were marching off to join the remainder of the Transport up at the Right Water Fort, where also the whole of the troops were paraded before starting." Now, as we have seen,[2] parade was not ordered until daybreak, or *circa* 6 a.m., while according to General Graham's despatch the troops did not start until *circa* 7 a.m.

On the same page occurs yet another error, where the author informs us "The orders were that this force was to advance *about five or six miles* in the direction of Tamai . . . and there halt and build a zariba, in which the stores and water were to be left," etc. The Order, as we have seen,[3] was most distinctly *eight miles*, and included the formation of two zeribas.

At p. 170, in amusing contradiction to the authoritative statements, we are informed that "The advance was undisturbed by the enemy, *who indeed showed no signs of being anywhere in the neighbourhood.*" The Cavalry reported the Arabs as appearing in small parties, who retired before the British advance, and were seen in large bodies from the ships at Suâkin and the redoubts at Hashin.

For a personal observer connected with the Land Transport Corps, on the same page occurs one of the most singular statements in the Chapter :—"The first part of the march was through country covered with small isolated patches of bush, but nothing to impede the advance of the troops. Farther on, the bush became much

---

[1] Page 79.   [2] Pages 20, 30, 34.   [3] Page 20, *seq.*

thicker and closer, *and the Cavalry had some difficulty in forcing their way through it, being thus prevented from obtaining a thorough view of the surrounding ground.*" Now, this is the only instance we are aware of in which the Cavalry were commiserated on the bad character of the bush they had to traverse. According to all other accounts they saw quite enough to do their turn, and to enable them to report the enemy in small parties retiring as they approached. But the most unaccountable thing for a Transport Corps Officer who professes to have been on duty on the march out is the entire absence of any reference to the most outstanding feature of that march—the difficulties encountered by the Land Transport Train and the Indian Contingent as its guard. The density of the bush is fully recognised as an impediment to the Cavalry, which no one else troubles about, but the incomparably greater impediment of that bush to the Transport Train, which disorganised and altered all the plans for the day, has inferentially no existence. It is never once alluded to or recognised, and when, "Having arrived at length at a point about six miles out, the whole force was halted and three zaribas marked out," etc., Head-Quarter intentions were fully complied with, and there had been no break-down of the Transport, and no compulsory stoppage and arrest. Is this at all compatible with the personal observations, the "simple record of events," unavoidably made by *any* Land Transport "Officer who was there?" We suspect not, and why it should be entirely omitted from the narrative of one who, possessed of "sound judgment," and "an observant eye," "writes boldly and criticises scathingly," and is careful to air much smaller grievances, to bestow unmeasured condemnation on much more doubtful occasions, is a mystery to be solved only on one assumption. Why, the Transport Train was the Hamlet of the march, and here it is entirely omitted by a Transport "Officer who was there!" How carefully he mentions the inconvenience incurred by a single squadron of Lancers, riding light, unencumbered, in open scouting order, and in which he had no interest. How completely silent as to these 1500 to 1600 animals, camels, mules, and horses, all heavily laden as beasts of burden or draught, jammed together in broiling heat and clouds of dust, subject to every annoyance and delay a dense mimosa jungle could possibly occasion, until at last matters reached such a pitch that Head-Quarter arrangements had to be flung overboard and a stop made two miles short of the distance designated! In all this the "Officer who was there" must have been not a mere spectator but an active and very much interested agent; yet the whole matter is passed *sub silentio.* Is this credible of any man possessed of a "sound judgment" and "observant eye"? Is it at all likely of one who "writes boldly and criticises scathingly," that he shall keep silence as to the powers that be who, right or wrong, he holds responsible for placing his branch of the Service at such disadvantage?

At p. 171 we are informed that the central zeriba "was occupied by the Indian Brigade;" and again, at the moment of attack, "the Indian Infantry were hard at work on their zariba." Now, the truth is, the Indian Contingent had no zeriba, express orders having been given that it was to return to Suâkin with the empty Transport, the zeriba at the five-mile distance which it was to construct and occupy having been countermanded.

On the same page the author states: "After a short interval for rest, a part of the force was ordered to pile their arms and set to work," etc. The operations commenced as soon as the troops were on the ground. In the same loose style it is also stated, "Later on the men were allowed to sit down and have their dinners," etc. Men must dine sometime, of course; but what "men"? The whole Force sitting down and having their dinners, such is the natural inference, while the facts really were—Marines dined, 12.30; Berks, by half-battalions, *circa* 2 P.M.; Indians never, eating chuppaties from their haversacks as they felt inclined. On p. 171, also, is given the only attempt in the Chapter to describe the disposition of the troops, inaccuracy marking almost every statement. It is brought in as a sequel to the dining and the resting, the result being that "The men were immediately before the attack thus for the most part *much scattered about;*" while two-thirds of the Force had been from the first under arms, and in concentrated formation, a fact which the writer never once alludes to.   The next sentence is still more erroneous and absurd.   "Two companies of the 49th were out some forty yards away from their zariba, their arms lying down on the ground, while they hacked and hewed at the tough growth of the bush."   A few of the Berks were so engaged to the west of their zeriba, where their arms had been previously piled inside, but they promptly ran in at the first alarm, the Arab attempt to play at "devil take the hindmost" being gallantly checked by Subadar Goordit Singh.   We are then told, "The Marines were similarly engaged, and the Indian Infantry were hard at work on their zariba as well;" but the Marines' zeriba or redoubt, the shelter trench excepted, was finished, and they had been moved into it about two o'clock.   The Indians, as we have seen, had no zeriba, and were for the most part drawn up in line with fixed bayonets.   On page 172 we are told that "The camels were drawn up in a body on one side of, and *about seventy yards from,* the zaribas of the Marines and the Indian Brigade."   Now the empty Transport was drawn up immediately in rear of the 17th Bengal N.I., and close to the south-east angle of the centre zeriba, from which the camel column was massed diagonally, in the direction of Suâkin, so as to march clear of the Royal Marines' redoubt, this fact rendering the stampede very handy for the Arab and dangerous for the Force.   The closing sentence of this brief paragraph, sixteen lines in all, out of thirty-six pages, relates to the Cavalry vedettes, of which more anon.

At p. 172 it is stated that on the first Cavalry alarm, "*The General was asking the man in what force he thought the enemy were,* when a second vedette came in telling the same story," etc. On the testimony of Sir John M'Neill, and of those immediately around him, no such words were uttered, the orders immediately given to Lieut.-Colonel Kelly being to call in the working-parties, and for the whole Force to stand to their arms.

At p. 173 a statement occurs showing complete ignorance as to the dispositions of the Force. We are informed that "the 17th Native Infantry had possession of *this side of the centre zariba*, the Marines being on their left. It was on this point that the confused mass of men and animals fell. The 17th were for the moment completely scattered, but groups of men stood fast here and there, and poured in their fire, in the general confusion, right into the men and animals in front of them." This statement is based on a complete inversion of the facts. The context gives no clue as to whether by "*this side* of the centre zariba," is meant the south or the east side, the Marines being on the left would naturally infer the latter. The entire statement, however, proves ignorance as to the disposition of the 17th Bengal N.I., who were drawn up in line outside the zeriba, and covering the empty Transport, and only lined the centre zeriba after their collapse and rally. There were no troops originally posted *within* the central zeriba, nor did it require any, being quite sufficiently defended by the Indian lines and the flanking fire from the redoubts and Rallying Square. It was the wild firing of the 17th Native Infantry lining its eastern face which placed the Rallying Square in jeopardy. The 17th Native Infantry broke before the stampede took place, not *vice versâ*.

At p. 175 it is stated that the enemy outnumbered the Imperial troops by "ten to one." Various calculations were made as to the probable numbers of the enemy, but over 30,000 Arabs is greatly in excess of all other estimates. So, also, on the same page, the number of Arabs who entered the Berks redoubt is given "about a hundred and fifty," one hundred and twelve being the usual number; and again, at this point, occurs one of those curious medleys, stamping the information as a mere second-hand acquisition. The author has mixed up the doings of the half-battalion of the Berkshires in the redoubt, and that in the Rallying Square in the most wonderful manner. Two Companies of the Berkshires again crop up. Instead, however, of being "some forty yards away from their zariba," with "their arms lying on the ground," they are attacked by the hundred and

fifty Arabs, who, " as most of the men were . . . outside cutting
down the bush," had managed to enter the redoubt.   " Getting their
arms as quickly as possible," the small body of men "formed rallying squares,"—plural mark it, inside the enclosure, and got out of
two Companies,—" and in this formation none of the Arabs could
touch them," and this though " they did their best with shot and
spear alike, led on, as in other parts of the field, by sheikhs carrying
banners, on one of which was inscribed the words in Arabic ' Whoso-
ever fights under this banner shall have victory.' "   This gallant
repulse of one hundred and fifty Arabs by say one hundred and
sixty or seventy Berks in " rallying squares," takes place ostensibly
within the redoubt ; yet in the next sentence, and with reference to
the same event, we are informed that " So crafty were the enemy in
the way they attacked these detached portions of our force *that
they got round between them and the zaribas, as they saw that our
men would not be able to fire in this direction for fear of injuring
their friends.*   But cold steel did what the bullet was unable to do."
Commencing with a fight inside the redoubt, and ending with its
transference to the exterior, Arabs entering, Berks rallying, by a
melodramatic shifting of the scene, same Arabs craftily getting round
between said " detached portions " and the zeriba, so that the Berks,
afraid to use the bullet, have to polish off their enemy with the
bayonet.   Was a more ridiculous medley ever penned ?   Were two
entirely distinct episodes, one half battalion of the Berks fighting
inside their redoubt, and the other half battalion fighting on the
original site of the Rallying Square, ever more inextricably confounded ?   The Arabs, by all reliable accounts, one hundred and
twelve, not *fifty*, entered by the as yet unfinished salient, and over
the mimosa fence on the south, from which the 17th Bengal N.I.
had recoiled.   The Berks were lining the western face, when, by
orders of Sir John M'Neill their rear rank faced about, met the Arabs
half-way, and left not one of them alive.

At p. 176 it is stated that " Nothing could have exceeded the
coolness and signal bravery of the 49th [Berks] as they fought their

zariba against overwhelming numbers, *who never faltered for a moment in delivering charge upon charge.*" With exception of their first temporary success, there was no further serious assault made by the Arabs upon the redoubt occupied by the Berks, who, lining the exterior faces of the work, played their part in gallantly repelling the general attack. On the same page the sensational fiction set a-going by the Press is diligently re-echoed. " Had it not been for the sterling quality of the English troops, another catastrophe *more awful than that of Isandlanha, another massacre more fearful than that of Maiwand, must have occurred that Sunday afternoon.*" But for the "sterling quality" not a doubt of it; but in stating such a truism, neither the Press nor the author of " *Suakin*, 1885," need have gone so far a-field. They might have said if the British had been Egyptians, and hares instead of lions, as Shakespeare would say,[1] Tofrek would have been El Teb over again. Of course it would, but it was not; and save as a bit of sensational writing it is impossible to understand what advantage accrues from the dissemination of such screaming fictions.[2]

At p. 177 the author harks back upon the 49th, with a second version of the story already mangled at p. 175. The number of Arabs killed in the Berks redoubt is now given as one hundred and twenty-two, the odd twenty-eight of the one hundred and fifty who entered,[3] we may presume, escaped. According to more reliable authority it is averred that all the Arabs who entered were killed, and

---

[1] *Coriolanus*, Act I., Scene I.

[2] In the same spirit of extravagant exaggeration the following reflections occur at p. 189 : " And thus the Force was delivered that day from a slaughter almost unparalleled in the annals of war, from a catastrophe which would have carried weeping and mourning into a thousand households, and make our country shake to her foundations, while people mute with horror looked each other in the face and realised, as one realises the meaning of some faint far-off sound, what war really is."

[3] When " Englishmen and Indians stood back to back fighting for life against an overwhelming force" (p. 173), it would be interesting to ascertain who had leisure to pay such close attention to statistics and act as timekeeper to the enemy. To say of a body of Arabs entering a redoubt that none fled, and that 112 dead bodies were found afterwards is one thing ; to say that 150 entered, and that 122 being killed, inferentially 28 escaped, is quite another.

after the fight was over one hundred and twelve dead bodies were dragged out by the heels. Next follows an equally lucid account of the Gardner guns episode. If there is one thing clearer than another it is that the guns in the Berkshire redoubt were never in position—never opened fire ; and that it was at the uncompleted salient the Arabs rushed in, killing Lieutenant Seymour and several sailors. Here the catastrophe is attributed to the jamming of the guns, which had previously " opened on the enemy and swept the ground in front, carrying death and destruction wherever they were pointed," the Arabs who had escaped being blown to bits by the dreadful fusillade being " among the sailors *in a second!*" Smart work that for the bullet-dodging Arabs.

At p. 179 dispositions never otherwise alluded to are inadvertently recognised. At p. 171 it is stated that at the moment of attack " The men were thus for the most part much scattered about," and the whole tone of the chapter is disorder and unpreparedness. Without the slightest intimation as to the formation in which they fought we are now told that " the Sikhs and 28th had a hot time of it. The Sikhs especially behaved most gallantly, magnificent fellows that they are. They were perfectly in hand the whole time, and stood as firm as rocks, carrying out the orders of their officers and plying their bayonets with the utmost effect." ·It is a pity the " Officer who was there " did not open his eyes a little further, and let us see the complete anticipative order for whatever might befall during the day, the result of which we have here a very partial glimpse.

At p. 191 it is incidentally mentioned that " It was not until after ten o'clock that the moon rose and threw her white light over the field." Now, according to the Almanac for the Sûdan, prepared by the Intelligence Department, on the 22nd of March the moon set at 11.46 P.M., and must have been high in the heavens at sundown, and at ten o'clock within an hour and three-quarters of her setting. On the evening of the 22nd the sky was completely veiled with clouds. This fact is borne out by the *Times'* correspondent, who passed the night at the zeriba. Writing at

7.30 P.M., he states, "the sky is entirely overclouded, and no moonlight can reach us."[1] This expression shows that even at this early hour the correspondent understood that the moon was well up in the sky, and at 10 P.M. he writes "the moon has just come out and is now shining brightly,"[2] and then proceeds to describe the battlefield as so illuminated. There is a marked distinction, difficult for a personal observer to overlook, between the moon visible at once above the horizon in a presumably cloudless sky, and the same moon unveiling herself from a mass of clouds nearly two hours prior to her setting, and this in a climate where moonlight remarkable for its brilliance is second only to day. Slight as this incident may appear, it has by no means an unimportant bearing on the question whether the author was present on the scene or not. Were it not for the constant and skilful use of personal pronouns, the natural inference would be that the writer is dealing with things he had never seen, and even as narrated by others, did not understand. As we have seen, even the most striking incidents are hopelessly confused, the statements throughout are loose and disjointed, and save for the reflections thrown in, differ in no respect from the ordinary run of the newspaper reports. The chapter is certainly not written from a military point of view, and in its entire absence of accurate and circumstantial detail compares most unfavourably with the narrative of Major de Cosson,[3] stamped as it is with the unmistakable *imprimatur* of immediate observation. There are indeed two pages, in their straightforward and circumstantial character, presenting a marked contrast to the rest of the chapter. These are pp. 192, 193, and describe the events of the day as seen from or known at Suâkin, with the measures thereupon adopted. If the reader will only compare these two pages with the preceding part of the chapter, mark the minuteness and fulness of detail of the one as compared with the

[1] *Times,* March 24th, 1885.
[2] *Ibid.*
[3] *Days and Nights of Service with Sir* *Gerald Graham's Field Force at Suakin.* By Major E. A. de Cosson, F.R.G.S. Chapter V. "Tofrek."

looseness, inaccuracy, and generality of the other, little doubt will remain as to whether on the 22nd of March 1885 the author was at Suâkin or Tofrek.

The mischief a book of this sort can do is simply incalculable, and places it exactly on a level with the current newspaper reports, to which in all that is omitted or stated in its "Zariba" chapter so close an analogy is presented.   As an illustration of this mischievous influence, we may mention that in the leading organ of public opinion in Britain, the *Times* of August 18th, 1885, considerably more than a column was devoted to the review of this book. Relying on the statements in the title-page and preface, it was very naturally accepted by the reviewer as a narrative of personally-observed and reliable facts.   With special reference to the action at Tofrek, he thereupon proceeded to make some very stringent remarks on the conduct of the General in Command, who felt himself compelled to adopt such measures as at once brought the matters in dispute to a decisive issue.

The reviewer begins by bestowing high laudation on the anonymity of the author, a breach of which, if not dangerous to others might very likely be so to himself, "for he writes boldly and criticises scathingly."   He is not only laudatory, he is tender, and in this vein remarks—

" *We shall not seek to raise the veil with which he has prudently enveloped his identity,* but it is clear not only that he possesses sound judgment, an observant eye, and a knowledge of his profession, but also, from his position —which was that apparently of transport officer—enjoyed good opportunities for becoming acquainted with the incidents of the campaign.   He asserts in his preface that *his statements are facts* [*sic ! ! !*], the result of *personal knowledge* [question]; and it must be admitted that the facts in question are not such as to cause much admiration for the commander of the expedition and his chief lieutenants; while, on the other hand, they are highly creditable to the corps employed."

With this brave opening the reviewer runs over various items,— night attacks, camp arrangements, unfriendly "friendlies," railway, soldiers *versus* navvies, purchase of water-skins, Hashin, etc., etc., all samples of adverse criticism, until he gets down to Tofrek, of which he writes—

"The part of the book relating to the unfortunate affair of the 22nd of March is of great interest, but for what the author narrates we must refer to the author himself, and confine ourselves to his brief criticism. There is no doubt that the tactics of the Arabs were admirable and that the surprise was complete. Now, we have authority for saying that, though it may not be discreditable to a general to be beaten, it is eminently so to be surprised. Our author thus sums up the case : [1]

"One word before dismissing this tragic incident. A measure of the precautions taken is afforded by the fact that few of the Cavalry vedettes were more than 30 yards from the working-parties.

"To sum up, our regiments seem to have distinguished themselves by the courage, discipline, and endurance they displayed, and the various departmental corps worked well and efficiently. When, however, we come to the arrangements and generalship of the higher authorities, all that we can say is that this campaign is highly instructive, being full of lessons as to what should be avoided in future."

The whole tenor of the above article, and especially the statement that "few of the Cavalry vedettes were more than 30 yards from the working-parties," being deemed actionable, Messrs. Tods, Murray, and Jamieson, W.S., of 66 Queen Street, Edinburgh, agents for Sir John M'Neill, wrote to the publishers of the work in question, requesting to be favoured with the author's name; on their declining to give it up, a letter was forwarded to him under their charge, stating that unless a public retractation and apology were forthcoming legal proceedings would be instituted. The result was that in the issue of November 3rd, 1885, a notice to the following effect appeared in the *Times :*—

"M'Neill's Zariba.—We are asked by Messrs. Tods, Murray, and Jamieson, of Queen Street, Edinburgh, acting on behalf of Sir John M'Neill, to state that the author of the book entitled 'Suakin, 1885,' reviewed some time ago in our columns, an officer who has not disclosed his name, has

---

[1] The quotation is given at p. 283, 1885 edition, p. 201.

written a letter to the publishers, Messrs. Kegan Paul, Trench, and Co., in which he says, with reference to his account of the attack on M'Neill's zariba :—' 1. That he learns, after careful inquiry, that he was mistaken in stating that the nearest Cavalry were only 30 yards from the working-parties. 2. As regards the precautions taken, that at least two-thirds of the force were standing to their arms during the whole time the ground was occupied, this being proved by General Hudson's report. 3. It therefore appears obvious that Sir John M'Neill used his best endeavours to protect the force.' "

In a brief paragraph appearing in an obscure corner of the *Times*, such was the first check on the bold writing and scathing criticism which, with perfect immunity, had for several months freely abused the public mind. The admissions relate only to two points, the posting of the Cavalry and the formation of the Infantry. Under the novel doctrine that statements—"every statement" "may be taken as fact," fact and statement being equivalent, or rather statement making the fact, the reviewer had adopted the "fact" of the vedettes being only 30 yards—90 feet, the breadth of a good street—in front of the working-parties as a test, "a measure of the precautions taken," for the safety of the Force. Under the pressure of legal proceedings, *ex post facto* "careful inquiry" had exploded this fiction, hence *peccavi*. Pity the "careful inquiry" had not taken place a little earlier and stultification been avoided. "An Officer who was there" might be excused for not seeing Cavalry in a dense bush, as, under the same circumstances, the Cavalry must be excused for not seeing the enemy, but how about the "fact" that not in the bush but in the open "at least two-thirds of the force were standing to their arms during the whole time the ground was occupied," fencing in and guarding the Transport it had previously convoyed? This admission is made on the strength of General Hudson's report, a document with which, very much to its own loss, the public has never been favoured. But General Hudson could only report facts, open to every one on the spot who was adequately inquisitive. Before an " Officer who was there," who " writes boldly and criticises

2 o

scathingly," and whose "every statement may be taken as fact," presumed to address the public, is it not reasonable to expect that by personal observation he ought first of all to have made sure of his facts, instead of having to re-learn his lesson and make a humiliating confession by reference to a document locked up in the archives of the War Office, and to which the public have not access? A curious light is thereby thrown on the art of getting up for the market books with catching names, further illustrated in the modifications made on the second edition, and which, as a direct result of the steps taken by Sir John M'Neill, are herewith appended :—

First Edition, 1885.   Page 169. Second or Expurgated Edition, 1886.[1]

The force which marched out this Sunday morning, the 22nd of March, was composed as follows : The 49th, the Royal Marines, the Indian Brigade, a battery of four Gardner guns, a detachment of the Royal Engineers, and a squadron of the 5th Lancers, *and 9th Bengal Cavalry.*

The force which marched out this Sunday morning, the 22nd of March, was composed as follows : The 49th, the Royal Marines, the Indian Brigade, a battery of four Gardner guns, *manned by the sailors,* a detachment of the Royal Engineers, and a squadron of the 5th Lancers.

Page 170.

The whole of the force was under command of General MacNeill, and the advance was undisturbed by the enemy, who indeed showed no signs of being *anywhere* in the neighbourhood.

The whole of the force was under command of General MacNeill, and the advance was undisturbed by the enemy, who indeed showed no signs of being *in force* in the neighbourhood.

Page 171.

The men were thus for the most part much scattered about. Two companies of the 49th were out some forty yards away from their zariba, their arms lying down on the ground, while they hacked and hewed at the tough growth of the bush. The Marines were similarly engaged, and the Indian Infantry were hard at work on their zariba as well. The greater part of the transport animals had been unladen, and the stores placed in the centre of the large square. The camels were drawn up in a body on one side of, and about seventy yards from, the zaribas

A considerable portion of the force were standing to their arms, while the remainder worked at the zaribas. Small pickets consisting of from four to five men each, drawn from the Indian Brigade, were thrown forward into the bush, which was especially thick on the side where the 28th Bombay Infantry were stationed. Beyond these infantry pickets were the cavalry pickets and vedettes. The greater part of the transport animals had been unladen, and the stores placed in the centre of the large square. The camels were drawn up in a body on one side of, and about

---

[1] In these extracts the portions of the first or 1885 edition, given in italics, are excised in the second or 1886 edition ; while those given in italics in the latter are superadded to, or substituted for, the statements made in the first edition.

of the Marines and the Indian Brigade. *A few cavalry vedettes were out in the bush, but few of these were more than thirty yards away from the working parties.*

seventy yards from, the zaribas of the Marines and the Indian Brigade, *and those that had been unladen were waiting for orders to start on their return march to Suakin, according to the pre-arranged plan.*

Page 177.

The Gardner guns had opened on the enemy and swept the ground in front, carrying death and destruction wherever they were pointed, but *they became jammed almost immediately, and then* the enemy were among the sailors in a second ; a few only escaped being wounded, while many, alas ! were killed.

The Gardner guns had opened on the enemy and swept the ground in front, carrying death and destruction wherever they were pointed, but *heedless of danger and with surprising agility* the enemy were among the sailors in a second ; a few only escaped being wounded, while many, alas ! were killed.

Page 201.

It remains a fact that cannot be contradicted *or gainsaid,* that this terrible loss of life was *occasioned by neglect in taking proper precautions, and a foolhardy carelessness combined with a total disregard of the most ordinary military principles. The force was halted in the wrong place to begin with, and* had the line of country more towards the sea been adopted, the enemy, if they had attacked *us* at all, would have done so at *great* disadvantage, *as* there is *there* much less bush, and we should have been apprised of their approach. We should have been also in an equally good position as a halting-place on the road to Tamai, and more protected from *any* attacks while the depôt was forming. Instead of this, *we were* marched into a *thick impenetrable* jungle, *thereby* giving all the advantage to the enemy and putting a surprise at a premium. *Sufficient precautions were not taken to protect the force while working at the zaribas—why, nobody knows. The result was what ? A surprise.*

It remains a fact that cannot be contradicted that this terrible loss of life was *due to the fact that the force was surprised. There is no doubt too, that one squadron of cavalry was wholly inadequate either to form an efficient protection, or, in a country such as that surrounding the zaribas, to give timely notice of the approach of the enemy. The place selected for the halt might have been better chosen by Head Quarters.* Had the line of country more towards the sea been adopted, the enemy, if they had attacked at all, would have done so at *a* disadvantage, *for in this part* there is much less bush, and we should *therefore* have been apprised of their approach. We should have been also in an equally good position as a halting-place on the road to Tamai, and more protected from attack while the depôt was forming. Instead of this, *the force was marched* into a *dense* jungle, *thus* giving all the advantage to the enemy and putting a surprise at a premium.

Page 202.

I have no wish to be critical. I confine myself to facts in telling this story, and I leave others to comment and to make further inquiries. There were grave mistakes committed that day, but why those mistakes were committed there are others better able to judge than I am. It is their duty to inquire.

This paragraph omitted.

The elimination of this latter paragraph is, however, more than counterbalanced by the retention of another at the close of the preceding chapter, where, referring to the unguarded state of the Transport at Hashin, and expressing surprise that " the enemy did not take advantage of this, as he might so easily have done by one of his rapidly executed movements," the author states :—

" Many hours were not, however, destined to pass before a fearful fate was to overtake this same transport, *through the laxity and carelessness on the part of those responsible for its protection, and through an overweening confidence in their own strength.*"

What is to be said of a writer whose diatribes bear no logical relation to the events so freely criticised, and than whom in the use of their rifles on the 22nd, the 17th Native Infantry were not more reckless?   Let us note a few facts.   We have seen at pp. 11, 12 that the combined British and Indian Force which marched out to Hashin on the 20th was over 8000 strong, and the formation that of a single Square, marching with an open rear.   It is evident, then, that the miscellaneous contents of the Square, Transport, Artillery, Engineers, Sappers, Medical department, etc., had, or were intended to have, the entire strength of the Expedition for the day, available for their defence, *i.e.* their guard, and at p. 11 *antea*, it has been calculated that the ratio of Transport to fighting men was as 1 to $5\frac{2}{3}$.   After giving the composition of the Square, at p. 140 of *Suakin,* 1885, it is stated, "The troops *inside the square, besides the Commissariat and Transport Corps,* were," etc. ; and at p. 141, *seq.,* the march out and arrival of the Convoy at its destination is narrated as being consentaneous with that of the Imperial Forces, subject only to this drawback—

" The square moved *a little too fast* for the baggage animals, and there being no rear face to it, there was a good deal of straggling in spite of all endeavours to push the camels along.   It was a perpetual drive, drive, drive ; but very few loads were displaced, and none of the water was lost except through the leaking of the barrels and the skins."

Again, at p. 163, after a good grumble at the inadequate guard placed over the Transport in its position for the day between the two conical hills referred to, in apparent oblivion of what he had previously written the author proceeds :

"There was another thing at which we were somewhat astonished, and that was that the Transport, comprising in all, that day, somewhere about twelve hundred camels, *was suffered to march the whole way out from Suakin* to where the force made their first halt, a mile from the conical hills, *without any guard whatsoever.* We have often wondered *since* how it was the enemy did not take advantage of this, as he might so easily have done by one of his rapidly executed movements."

I ask the reader whether the statements just quoted are at all consistent ? Those taken from the earlier part of the chapter clearly infer that the great bulk of the Transport, all of it, indeed, except a certain amount of "straggling," due to the want of a rear face, was, as evidently intended by the authorities, *within the Square,* which, up to the full fighting strength out on the 20th, formed, or was intended to form, its guard ; and at p. 139, in a passage too long for quotation, describing the parade and start, the idea of a simultaneous advance of Transport and fighting Force is still more emphatically conveyed. The statement at p. 163, however, contradicts those made at p. 139, 140, 141, *seq.*, on every point. It is not now "a good deal of straggling," but the entire body of Transport, to a most exaggerated number of camels,[1] which was "*suffered*," mark it, some one clearly responsible for that, "to march the *whole way* out" to the first halting-place, "*without any guard whatsoever.*"

Statements like these require no comment, they speak for them-

---

[1] The *Diary of the Expedition* states that 739 camels accompanied the Force on the 20th ; and Major de Cosson, in his *Days and Nights of Service*, p. 91, gives 500 as the number employed in water transport. Hence, it is clear that the remarks on the unforeseen absence of a guard is applicable to the latter section only. In order to make the assumed neglect appear in the worst light, "Suakin, 1885," however, throws the two sections together, making the Commissariat and general Transport share the same risk with that conveying the water. At pp. 133, 137, he makes the water-camels 700, and at p. 139 reckons these "but a quarter" of the Transport gathering.

selves, and not less effectively in this, that the author *post dates* his feelings of alarm, and has "often wondered *since*." Aye, "since" Tofrek and its subsequent Convoys. So the absence of a special guard for the belated Transport to Hashin is made the basis of a criticism deriving its sting from the experiences at Tofrek, while Tofrek in its turn gets the benefit of a most unjust and reckless criticism, tagged on to the self-contradictory statements regarding the Transport on the 20th.

If we turn to the narrative of Major de Cosson, who was in command of the Water Transport on the 20th, matters assume a very different aspect. He states—

"*March 20th.*—By the first streak of dawn we were in the saddle, and had the *large convoy of* 500 *camels* laden with water fairly under way, marching in a compact column of companies of fifty camels abreast, towards the western mountains.

"It was two miles from the seashore to the point of rendezvous South of West Redoubt, and, by the time we reached it, *the troops had already gone forward,* and were only visible as a cloud of dust advancing slowly across the plain *some miles before us,* with the sun playing brightly on the glancing bayonets which flashed through it here and there." [1]

So the Transport moved on in the loveliest of mornings, with a cool northerly breeze making the air delicious, while the Officers "laughed and chatted gaily together," their very horses seeming to share in the general animation. The Arabs and danger were alike undreamt of, no more warlike associations attracting attention than that of the ring doves flitting about, or the larks singing, not "from Heaven's gate," but on the ground, which find for themselves a habitat even amid these arid wastes.

"We were now marching due west, across a broad sandy plain dotted with mimosa trees, *without guard or escort of any kind,* except the few men of the Commissariat and Transport Corps who accompanied the camels." [2]

This most uneventful and pleasant morning march was continued until

[1] *Days and Nights of Service,* p. 91.   [2] *Ibid.,* p. 92.

"At 7.45, when nearing the lowest spurs of the mountains, the whole force halted for twenty minutes, to allow our convoy to overtake it, and the column of water-camels entered the square, and closed up in rear of the front line."[1]

The *Diary of the Expedition* states that on the morning of the 20th "The Force advanced in a westerly direction at 6.20 A.M.," and in his despatch of the 21st General Graham states: "The cavalry moved off at about 6.10 A.M., the infantry following at 6.25 A.M.," when the sun must have been only a few minutes above the horizon, in lat. 19° 2' north, "the first streak of dawn" cannot have been much earlier, so that Water Transport and troops must have started with two miles in favour of the latter, but with slight difference in point of time. Under these circumstances one thing is clear, Head-Quarters, not anticipating a belated Transport,[2] did not see any necessity for two corks to the bottle, hence the *de post facto* alarm and criticism. On the previous evening the moon had set at 8.49 P.M., leaving the earth shrouded in the intense darkness of a tropical night. The water depôt, from whence the camels had to load up and start, allowing for winding through the camp, was quite two miles in rear of the rendezvous, and as they could not move until there was at least a little light, and even then at a comparatively slow pace, with the troops also taking advantage of the earliest daybreak, there was bound to be a hitch; but it happened only once; on all succeeding occasions, by utilising the electric light from the ships, the Water Transport parading at the same time with the rest of the Force. If the statements quoted be a fair sample of that bold writing forming the necessary foundation for the scathing criticism eulogised by the *Times*, the reader will agree that the less of it there occurs in military annals the better.

Such is only one out of the many contradictions *Suakin*, 1885,

---

[1] *Days and Nights of Service*, p. 93.

[2] In the despatch just quoted General Graham states that "The water camels and transport animals followed *in rear of the* 2nd Brigade," forming as it did the front face of the Square, with the Guards on the right flank and the Indian contingent on the left.

presents. Of these, save on one assumption, and scarcely even on that, none is more unaccountable, none more damaging to the pretensions of the author, as a Land Transport Corps narrator and critic, "*there*" or "*not there*," than the complete silence as to the difficulties experienced on the 22nd, by the "huge number of transport animals carrying supplies for four thousand men for three days,"[1] in relation to which in the earlier part of the chapter the personal pronoun is invariably used.[2] To any compact body of men, with whom the maintenance of a regular formation was a vital necessity, the obstacles presented by the mimosa bush on the way to Tofrek must have been very serious. To a mass of heavily-laden Transport, with its ill-adjusted and easily-displaced loads, just at the level where the horizontally-spread and thorn-armed branches were most dangerous, these obstacles were still more annoying, and, as we know, ultimately insuperable. Of these facts the best proof is to be found in the Report of General Hudson, cited by the writer in correction of his errors, and, if not from personal experience at least from its perusal, several effective paragraphs might have been gleaned. Facts omitted tell a tale just as effectively as facts misrepresented; and "conspicuous by its absence," as if expressly to contradict all asseverations as to the trustworthiness of the narrative, for the story of this Convoy, with its difficulties and its breakdown forming the real keynote of the day, we have an utter blank, with a Cavalry reference thrown in to make the writer's silence more emphatic.

[1] *Suakin*, 1885, p. 169.

[2] After the attack and stampede this peculiarity is transferred to the main body (p. 184 *seq.*); and, instead of having "to turn before the storm and fly with the rest in the direction of Suakin" (p. 180), with it the writer represents himself as virtuously sharing all the toils and dangers of the succeeding night, and then returning with the Transport on the morrow.

"THE EGYPTIAN CAMPAIGNS, 1882 TO 1885, AND THE EVENTS WHICH LED
TO THEM." BY CHARLES ROYLE, BARRISTER-AT-LAW. [1]

In the earlier part of this Chapter our chief business has been
with the Press itself in some of its more typical representatives,
and we have seen that in giving any accurate or trustworthy idea of
what, as "tested by results," has ever since proven itself to be by
far the most important action of the campaign, the Press was utterly
at fault. In "*Suakin*, 1885," we had to deal with the work of "An
Officer who was there," *i.e.*, at the actual scene of operations; but
whose account of the action referred to, very far from bearing any
stamp of originality, derived no doubt from kindred sources, runs
on all fours with the ordinary newspaper narratives. In the present
instance we have to do with the work of a commentator who confessedly was *not there*, nor any closer to the scene of conflict than
Alexandria, or perhaps Cairo.

Mr. Royle opens his preface with the statement :—

"In offering the present work to the Public the author does not claim for
himself any special qualification for the work he has undertaken.

"He has, however, had the advantage, if such it can be called, of residing
in Egypt during the last ten years, and has enjoyed, so far as the expression
is applicable, opportunities for personally observing many of the events
referred to.

"He has also been brought in contact with several of the principal actors
in the drama, or rather series of dramas, played in the 'Land of the Nile.'

"Whatever pretensions to merit may be found in this work are based on
its being, so far as the author has been able to make it, a fair and impartial
narrative of the circumstances recorded."

The disclaimer conveyed in the opening sentence is, of course,
quite relative in its terms, and is susceptible of being greatly
modified by the various circumstances mentioned in the two
succeeding paragraphs.

The work under consideration is pretty equally divided between
the political aspects of the Egyptian question and the armed inter-

[1] In two volumes. London, Hurst and Blackett, 1886.

2 P

vention to which it ultimately led. Now, if there is one subject more than another which the training and preliminary studies of an English barrister should qualify him to understand it is Politics ; whereas, between forensic learning and War, either as a science or an art, there is no practical relation.

It will also be noticed that the advantages cited as tending to modify the confessed absence of "any special qualification," bear exclusively on the political question. Ten years' residence in Lower Egypt could give no experience as to the Red Sea Littoral, bring events therein transpiring under the author's observation, or even place him, except by accident,[1] in contact with any of the "principal actors" in that special "drama." We accordingly find that in Chapter xxx., vol. ii. pp. 347-358, "Attack on M'Neill's Zeriba," Mr. Royle has no new information to convey. On the contrary, if we except Sir Gerald Graham's despatch of March 28th, which is the only official document quoted,[2] his sources are of the most ordinary and defective character, Press narratives, such as those discussed in the earlier part of this chapter, being introduced as "unofficial reports"! For once, indeed, the best and most useful traditions of the Law, its careful sifting of evidence, its rigorous search into, and nice discrimination of, the ever-varying value of testimony, and not less the well-recognised desirability of reserving judgment, until all the circumstances of any particular case have been fully understood, seem to have been entirely thrown aside.

[1] Mr. Royle will no doubt remember, with reference to the special contents of this chapter, that such accidental opportunity did occur one day in May 1885, at his brother's house in Port Said. On that occasion, *if at all aware of Mr. Royle's intentions,* a "principal actor" would have given correct information on the subject freely and without reserve, but during an interview, lasting at least a couple of hours, not the slightest allusion was made by Mr. Royle to his intended publication.

[2] Following his usual custom, the author abridges even this admittedly meagre despatch (given in full in Appendix I. pp. 317-20), so that it can only be accepted as a version "according to Royle." Not only is the diagram omitted, but with it all those portions of the text connected with it, giving accurate and precise ideas as to the disposition of the troops, especially the Indian Contingent.

The result, beyond all question, is the least satisfactory of the various chapters in the work, directly dealing with the operations of War. The opening sentence, indeed, not only places the subsequent criticism entirely at a discount, but at once raises the question, "What, then, is Mr. Royle writing about?" Without further preface, we are categorically informed that, "By the establishment of the fortifications at Hasheen, General Graham *was able to protect his right flank and line of communications in the ensuing operations towards Tamaai!*"[1] the author then proceeding to state the composition of the Force which began these operations. If, then, the British right flank and Line of Communications were so protected, what is the meaning of this action at Tofrek, and especially of that vituperative criticism with which Mr. Royle in so far identifies himself? The Force going out on the 22nd did not invade or even approach any of the enemy's haunts, and was evidently designed to act entirely on the defensive. If the "fortifications at Hasheen" were of any service at all, they ought to have protected a site on the proposed "Line of Communications," and less than their own distance out from Suâkin. This they did not do, nor did they exercise the very slightest influence on the fortunes of the 22nd. From first to last the post at Hashin, in its formation covered by the whole strength of the Expedition, was "able to protect" nothing except itself, and to act as a signalling station. It may be that the view entertained at Head-Quarters was exactly the same as that stated by Mr. Royle; and if this be the case it will explain many things not otherwise easy to understand. One thing is clear, had the initial statement we have quoted been even approximately true, there ought to have been no occasion for this chapter being written; and so far as General M'Neill and those under him are concerned, the criticisms it contains stand condemned from the very outset.

After the glaring contradiction presented by the prefatory paragraph to the rest of the chapter, it is but a slight error in detail to

[1] Vol. ii. p. 347.

find "one squadron of the 20th Hussars" enumerated with the troops, which "moved out from the camp" on the 22nd. When the Cavalry strength, or *weakness* rather, forms so important an item in the day's proceedings, it is necessary to be particular, even to the movements of a squadron, and Mr. Royle ought to have known that the primary relation the 20th Hussars held to the Tofrek Force was that of a visiting patrol sent out towards noon, with a view probably to the returning Transport Train and the Line of Communications,[1] although events enabled them to render essential service to the main body. In the way of reinforcements it is still more curious and amusing to be informed that the Imperial Forces, comprising, of course, "a company of Madras Sappers, the 15th Sikhs, the 17th Bengal, and 28th Native Infantry," left the camp, "*supported by the Indian Brigade under General Hudson!*" Where Mr. Royle gets this second Indian Brigade it is impossible to say, and its existence seems just as apocryphal as the protection accorded to the "right flank and Line of Communications." After embodying an abstract of General Graham's despatch of March 28th, 1885, the sources upon which Mr. Royle has elected to base his criticisms lead him to make the following remarks:—

"The attack on the zeriba and the successful repulse of the enemy on the 22nd constitute another of the events of the war which were more creditable to the individual officers and men engaged than to those who held the command.

"It has been said that General M'Neill has denied that what occurred was a surprise. This, however, hardly makes the matter better, so far as regards those who are responsible for what occurred. It was probably not a surprise in the sense that is understood of a night attack, or an assault by an enemy whose presence was neither known nor suspected; but that the attack, when it came, found the British force in a state of unpreparedness is a proposition which can scarcely be contested.

"The place selected for the zeriba, situated as it was in the midst of thick bush and brushwood, was such as to suggest the necessity for taking

---

[1] This becomes apparent from the yet stronger squadron of the 9th Bengal Cavalry, 120 all ranks, sent out in the afternoon to relieve Major Graves. *Vide* p. 79 *antea*.

the utmost precautions. The enemy were known, or might have been known, to have been in the neighbourhood. As a fact, large bodies of them had been observed from Souakim at 7 A.M. that morning crossing from the direction of Hasheen. This being so, it seems hard to believe that, even allowing for the difficult nature of the ground, a proper system of scouting and outposts would not have revealed their approach and given time to prepare for their reception.

"Instead of this, what was done was to employ a portion of the squadron of Lancers in forming a chain of posts at a distance of 1000 yards, or a little over half a mile, from the zeriba; to form the remainder on open ground 500 yards nearer still, and to keep a squadron of Hussars patrolling between the zeriba and Souakim, the side the least likely to be attacked. Of the outposts thrown out from 80 to 120 yards in advance of the Indian Regiments it is unnecessary to say anything. The inadequacy of these precautions was shown by the result."[1]

Mr. Royle is extremely fond of discussing the technicalities of a surprise, and seems to imagine that if it be only possible to connect this term in any way with some particular episode in War, a feat has been achieved equivalent to that of attaching a tin kettle to the tail of a dog. Failing this device, there remains in reserve yet a second, "a state of unpreparedness;" in its duality this clever combination constituting "the horns of a dilemma," from which, he avers, there is no escape.

The Egyptian campaigns supply our author with three notable opportunities of exercising on this point his dialectic skill—Tel-el-Kebir, El Teb, and Tofrek. With regard to the first, in his despatch of 16th September 1882, Lord Wolseley claims that "The enemy were completely surprised;"[2] and that in a position, where for 13,000 men to attack over 38,000, effectively armed with breechloaders, would, under ordinary circumstances, have entailed

---

[1] Vol. ii. p. 350.

[2] Nothing can be more clear and incisive than Lord Wolseley's remarks on the attitude of the Egyptians at their sudden awakening to the imminence of the attack :

"The enemy were completely surprised, and it was not until one or two of their advanced sentries fired their rifles that they realised our close proximity to their works. These were, however, very quickly lined with their Infantry, who opened a deafening musketry fire, and their guns came into action immediately."

extreme peril and severe loss, they were very cleverly and very effectively surprised, few, except the captious or the quibbling, will be inclined to deny. If he does not exactly go this length, Mr. Royle makes the scale tip heavily in favour of the foe, and will only admit that "it is much the fashion" so to describe that silent night march, that sudden assault before the dawn, of the far-ranging and massive entrenchments at Tel-el-Kebir. True, ere they crossed the ditch and rushed the glacis, the British Force had to sustain a combined artillery and musketry fire, seriously increasing the list of casualties. But in storming a position occupied by an army of from 30,000 to 40,000 men, to have crowned the ramparts with a second line of defence in rear without alarming the enemy, would have been a feat all but impossible. Mr. Royle wishes to convince us that for Arabi's army the horns of his favourite dilemma had no existence. Lord Wolseley claims a surprise, and the wind is at once taken out of his sails by the assertion that the Egyptians, in a great measure prepared for an assault, took heavy toll ere they turned and fled. How does Mr. Royle know that the preparations on the night of attack were in any degree exceptional? If, instead of being surprised, the Egyptians were really apprised of the British advance, it is clear that, behind formidable entrenchments, lined with guns and rifles *ad libitum*, in failing to deal with their enemy from the moment he came fairly within range, they lost the one great opportunity of the campaign; and despite the darkness, or rather aided by it, the best proof that with them lay no surprise, would have been the preparation of an easily-contrived surprise for the foe. On the other hand, to capture a strong position and disperse an army thrice their own numbers, with only a *nominal* loss, was more than the British had any reason to expect. The real question was how to *minimise* a loss, certain under ordinary conditions to be most serious, amounting to decimation or perhaps worse. That the ratio did fall to 3·4 per cent of the attacking force is the best proof that can be given of the success of Lord Wolseley's tactics.

From Tel-el-Kebir to El Teb is a long step, and from a military point of view the actions are mutual antipodes. To our critic, however, their chief interest lies in the relation borne to the dialectic dilemma. If its horns are dropped before the levies of Arabi it is only that they may be more vigorously reasserted before those of Baker Pasha. Even as stated by Mr. Royle, the circumstances at El Teb were such as to render surprise impossible to any body of well-disciplined and courageous men. The country was open, the enemy known to be at hand, and to a Force like that which landed about three weeks afterwards, every circumstance was favourable. The best commentary, or criticism if you will, on the first battle of El Teb, was the second. In his eagerness to secure some game for his verbal trap, Mr. Royle avers that if General Baker was not surprised "his army undoubtedly was," and if not surprised they were unprepared, and "the battle lost before the men had time to defend themselves."[1] "Defend themselves!" and against a foe like the Sûdanese Arabs; under almost any circumstances this was what the Egyptian levies could not do, and the battle of El Teb was lost *ab initio,* months before the motley gathering set foot on the shores of Trinkitat. The truth is that, sent on a forlorn hope, and that hope confined to their own breasts, there was not a European there who was not in a false and an unfortunate position; a position which it took the apathy and the imbecility of two Governments to create. Months had been spent in an effort as hopeless as that of transmuting sun-dried bricks into genuine granite, or some base alloy into tempered steel. With fellaheen facing the desert tribes the result was a foregone conclusion; and, as we have seen at p. 166, prompted as they were by a strategy of despair, the only pity is that, in the disasters at this fatal spot of 6th November 1883 and 4th February 1884, credit should have been imperilled, or valuable lives thrown away on such wretched experiments.

These notable examples of dialectic acumen brought to bear on military events, may well prepare us for the presentation of the

[1] Vol. ii. p. 118.

alternative horns of the dilemma to the action at Tofrek. There could be little objection to as many horns as the author pleases, if the rules of equity and fairplay be only observed. We do not say wittingly, yet none the less inevitably, it is unfortunate that in the present instance the reverse is the case. It is easy to represent a Force as being unprepared, if all its defensive preparations be suppressed, and surprised, if the special avocations and duties of the day be entirely forgotten. In General Graham's despatch, as prefixed by Mr. Royle to his criticism, the disposition of the Indian troops, whose duty it was to keep unbroken watch and ward throughout the day is so far clearly indicated. This fact, however, Mr. Royle entirely ignores. Save the "trouble" with the 17th Native Infantry, and the erroneous statement as to the "transport charge," to be noticed presently, the only remark he condescends to make is to the following effect :—"*As to the Indians, a correspondent says they were just 'falling in to start;' which would imply that they were not formed up in readiness to repel an attack.*"[1] I venture to say that no combination of words could be used more directly at variance with the actual facts of the case than those just quoted. The authority cited, the "unofficial report" of "a correspondent," is directly contradicted by the statements of the General Officers in Command and by well-authenticated facts. There had been no alteration in that defensive formation of the previous four hours, never once alluded to by Mr. Royle. The Orders given[2] affected only the Transport; and not until the Indian Brigadier had returned to Sir John M'Neill, *circa* 3 P.M., could instructions be issued for the troops to form "column of route." Correspondents saw many things on the 22nd which never existed except in their own fancy; and the question is not so much what the correspondent saw, as the use the critic makes of an entirely unsupported statement. Drawing a sweeping generalisation from an apocryphal premiss, with one stroke of the pen Mr. Royle annihilates the carefully-planned defensive dispositions of the day. Seen "falling in"! The direct

[1] Vol. ii. p. 352.   [2] *Vide* p. 66 *antea*.

inference is "they were not formed up," nor in any degree of "readiness to repel an attack," and this although there is no evidence to show that, except the "trouble" with the 17th, there was any material change from the dispositions selected *antea* 11 A.M. Mr. Royle has made up his mind to a foregone conclusion, and with all the skill of a special pleader makes everything work toward that end.   Having got rid of the treble line of Indians, the two-thirds of the Force, a Brigade of men, always under arms, he next attacks the British, and draws a picture of "confusion worse confounded." Strong in inuendo, if what "a correspondent says" in his "unofficial report" be serviceable, not less so is that which in his official despatch General Graham *fails to say.*   It is evident, to use Mr. Royle's own words, that the despatch on Tofrek, like that on Tamai in 1884, "scarcely does justice to the events of the day,"[1] a fact of which full advantage is taken.   Among many other omissions, while stating that "the Marines were inside the north zeriba, having *just finished* cutting brushwood,"[2] General Graham, probably not knowing, does not mention "what they were actually doing at *the precise moment of the attack.*"   Fatal flaw!   Our author who, like the correspondents, seems to have been afflicted with "lunch" or "dinner" on the brain, at once turns "*brush*wood"[3] into "*fire*wood,"—firewood naturally suggests fire, and on a broiling day like the 22nd, of what use could a fire be save for culinary operations, *ergo* the Marines, "possibly, like the half of the Berkshire Regiment, *were also having their dinners!*"   Luckily, by Brigade Order, the Marines had got over this troublesome operation two hours previously, leaving the critic with his guesses and his inuendoes still in the lurch.   Not to be beaten, if information fails for some particular moment, Mr. Royle knows exactly what ought to have been done, and supplements the defect accordingly. To have "been standing at their arms ready for any eventuality"

[1] Vol. ii. p. 168.
[2] *Vide* Appendix I. p. 318.
[3] This brushwood was not cut for cooking purposes, but for defence, and in order to fill up the interstices left by the larger mimosa bushes in the thorn fence.

was the right thing for the Marines to do, and if so engaged in doing their duty, according to Royle, "the fact would probably have been mentioned" in the despatch. It is not mentioned; and, on the Royle principle, so much the worse for the Royal Marines. The despatch "official," found wanting and dismissed, in the next paragraph the report "unofficial" is cited with the usual point blank discrepancy. The Royal Marines, who "had just finished cutting firewood," and at the precise moment of attack were supposed to be dining, having piled arms, are now represented as just "commencing to dig their trench!"[1] We are next informed that "dinner and water had been served out to the men."[2] What men is not stated, but from the context the unavoidable inference is "the whole force." The only colour for this misleading statement is the fact already noted by the author in the preceding paragraph as to the half battalion of the Berkshire Regiment, who added to the enormity of dining by doing so, "250 yards from the zeriba,"[3] that is to say, on the site of the original Rallying Square! Now, where, pray, could brave men, who had not broken their fast for eleven hours, dine better than just at the post of duty, where their arms were piled, and themselves in readiness instantly to form square, and without the loss of a man repel the enemy with a loss of two hundred killed, and doubtless many more wounded? Never does this persistent misrepresentation and worrying on trifles look worse than when confronted with the actual facts of a case, hard and stern in its realities, where long hours of constant toil under a torrid sun, meant also lengthened periods of abstention from food and water.

Criticism conducted on such principles can be only mischievous and misleading; to be of the slightest service, to be even moderately accurate, it must rest on a broad and definite comprehension of *all essential facts.* How completely Mr. Royle's narrative fails in this respect the reader may judge from previous remarks. In the opening of the chapter we found the Indian contingent doubled and moving out of camp *supported by itself.* This was, of course, a

[1] Vol. ii. p. 352. [2] *Ibid.* [3] Vol. ii. p. 351.

clerical error, but not so its subsequent treatment, which is still more unreasonable and absurd. In all its real duties for the day, its formation and its functions, the Indian Contingent receives not the slightest attention: practically it is blotted out of existence. That the three Regiments were drawn up so as to cover the entire operations; that they were standing at their arms with bayonets fixed and cartridges ready from before 11 A.M. ; that this was the formation they occupied at the moment of attack, and, with exception of the 17th, that in which they fought, and retained, until withdrawn within the zeriba; that their great function was, to the extent of two-thirds of the entire fighting Force, not for half an hour, but for *all the working hours of that day,* to act as guard, ever keeping armed watch and ward, while the remaining third carried on their varied and laborious duties; for these facts Mr. Royle has not the slightest recognition; finding no place in the "unofficial reports," he accords them none. True, the Indians are mentioned, but after what fashion we have already seen. With faith unhesitating in scraps and "oddments" of information, Mr. Royle draws his deduction from Indians seen "falling in" to Indians, *all the Indians,* not ready. Whatever grounds there may be for what was seen or *mis*seen, knowing as we do from unquestionable authority that the reverse was the case, without further explanation we decline to accept this statement. Yet another rebuff is given to the Indians, in the reference to their pickets, about which the author considers it "unnecessary to say anything," the "inadequacy of these precautions" being "shown by the result."[1] What result? It so happens that this question of pickets is specially mentioned by General Hudson in his Report, their distribution in small groups instead of one large picket being considered by him to be, under the circumstances, a much better arrangement, as the men could thus run more quickly upon the flanks of the Companies from which they were drawn, and the front being thus clear fire could be opened at once. Now, always excepting the *six* Companies of the

[1] P. 293 *antea.*

17th, can Mr. Royle or any other man say this was not done, and done instantly and effectively on the Orders being issued? It is so embodied in General Hudson's Report, and with that dissentients must reckon.

The sable warriors being thus consigned to oblivion and summarily dismissed, Mr. Royle proceeds to criticise the arrangements of the British, as if the weight of guard duty lay exclusively with them. Careful to remind us that the Berks and Royal Marines "formed the only two English battalions on the field,"[1] on the principle *divide et impera* the Berks are first taken, then the Royal Marines. Of the first, half are cutting brushwood—why not *fire*-wood? and the other half dining. It is then averred of the Marines that they also may have been following the bad example of the diners; and so the entire effective strength, both British and Indian, as being "found in a state of unreadiness" is summarily swept off the board. The climax of such folly is attained when, at page 353, we find the editorial expansion of the *Times* correspondent's notes, already commented on,[2] adopted word for word, as a veritable description of the action at Tofrek. On such points as the Cavalry dispositions, the possible knowledge of the enemy's presence, the site of zeriba, etc., I must refer to the discussion on such matters in Chap. VII. *in loco.*

As we found the Indians doubled at the opening of the chapter, so is a similar process carried on throughout the narrative, several of the incidents doing duty twice over. Due to the want of a clear and comprehensive view of the military dispositions for the day, and dragged in as illustrating a disorganised state of defence! the result is most unfair. The simple and natural incident of the half battalion of the Berks occupying the original site of the Rallying Square occurs first at p. 351, where they are represented as "having their dinners 250 yards from the zeriba," being, of course, a double misdemeanour; then at p. 355 they reappear in a still more distorted form, as caught on fatigue duty and "cut off

[1] Vol. ii. p. 351.   [2] *Vide* p. 231, *seq.*

from the main body," a square being " quickly improvised" round the Regimental Officers ! What else would they have done? Is it not the business of a square to act independently, and with safety to itself to be so " cut off " ! By some freak or other the Native Infantry, whose "trouble" had been dealt with at page 353, reappear at this point. "*Here*," *i.e.* at the Rallying Square, "the 17th Bengal Infantry were sadly unsteady," etc., whereas their wild firing took place *from* the zeriba, where they were lining the hedges. By a confusion as to the nomenclature, the same episode is given twice over, as if it affected different parts of the defences. Technically, there was a central zeriba and two redoubts, disposed at opposite angles in echelon, but in ordinary parlance they were all zeribas. At p. 353 we are told—

" The scene inside the zeriba is described as terrible, a hand-to-hand fight raged there. The Arab swordsmen were cutting and slashing at soldiers, camels, and horses alike. The Native Infantry were inextricably mixed up with baggage, camels, and mules in the wildest disorder.[1] The number of the enemy who got into the zeriba was just over 100. These were all killed, and 105 bodies were counted there when the fight was over." [2]

Then follows the *canard* about General M'Neill's personal danger, and his rescue by Lieutenant Charteris, clearly indicating that the scene of this dreadful conflict was not the central zeriba, as the author seems to infer, but the Berkshire redoubt; and the Arabs entering, with a praiseworthy effort at accuracy given as "*just* over 100," in numbers as variable as those of Falstaff's "rogues in buckram,"[3] the same given by "*Suakin,* 1885," at "about a hundred and fifty," and of dead bodies counted " one hundred and twenty-two." [4]

A little further down the same page, as if commencing an entirely new narrative, the author informs us that,

" The redoubt towards Tamai was the scene of a desperate struggle. There

---

[1] This reference is evidently to the Regimental and Staff equipage, and animals conveying it, and not to the ordinary Transport.

[2] Vol. ii. p. 353.

[3] *Henry IV.*, Act 2, Scene iv.

[4] *Vide* pp. 274-76 *antea.*

were killed, Lieutenant Seymour of the *Dolphin*, and five men of the Naval Brigade, all being stabbed with spears."

Then follows the well-known incident as to the attack on Lieut.-Colonel Kelly, and Captain Domville's prompt use of his revolver, the killing of their horses, etc.; clearly showing that the scene is again laid in the Berkshire redoubt, and at the first brunt of the attack. By the simple process of inverting the order of events, putting the cart before the horse, and calling the same work in the one instance a zeriba and in the other a redoubt, not only are two distinct conflicts thus got out of one, but the impression given to every one, except the instructed reader, is, that the Arabs in their assault had got free access to the entire works, more especially invading the central zeriba,—impressions totally at variance with the facts. Owing to the guns not being in position the Arabs got access to the Berkshire redoubt by the uncompleted salient, and, although brief in its duration, it was at this point the fiercest internal conflict took place. A few Arabs also followed the camel-stampede into the redoubt occupied by the Royal Marines, but were very soon disposed of.

Another most misleading statement occurs at p. 354, where the author writes: "*Having shaken off the incubus of the Transport charge*, the bulk of the Indian infantry held their own in gallant style." Now, the bulk of the Indian Infantry never were affected by the camel-stampede at all, but from the very first note of warning, the moment their fronts were clear of the pickets Mr. Royle so much disparages, were fully occupied in delivering that "furious rifle fire" to which he elsewhere refers. The only Indian Infantry who were incommoded by the Transport were the 17th Bengal Native Infantry, whose duty it was to have defended it. Mr. Royle thus not only fails to instruct his reader, but exhibits his own ignorance as to the dispositions of the Indian troops, upon whom chiefly fell the duty of keeping fully-armed watch and ward throughout the entire day, a fact which takes the sting out of all his remarks as to the British unpreparedness.

As Mr. Royle opened this chapter with the fortifications at

Hashin, so does he also end it. There is, however, no question now of their power to protect, but a notice only of their destruction, after having existed five days! Although the author apparently does not see it, embodying in his narrative facts so antithetical, as it were mechanically, and without evincing any intelligent appreciation of their significance, between these two notices, so contradictory in their terms, there lies the record of a failed and miscalculating strategy, the *point d'appui* of which had been found by stern experience, as already stated, powerless "to protect" anything except itself, and to act as a signalling station. From first to last this chapter is a proof that General Graham did not succeed in doing that which in his opening sentence Mr. Royle affirms that he did, and the statement at the close proves that of this fact Head-Quarters itself had become convinced, and this a week prior to the advance upon Tamai, which, on General Graham's own showing, the "fortifications," if at all serviceable, ought effectually to have covered. I have stated that Mr. Royle's opening sentence is at direct variance with the entire subject of his criticism. In the special Field Force Order issued by General Graham, May 16th 1885, this contradiction is brought out in still more striking relief:—

"5. In the action at Hasheen *the enemy was dislodged from his position on the flank of the line of advance,* and in the subsequent fight at the zeriba *his sudden and desperate onslaught, made with fanatical determination, was repulsed with heavy loss, by the coolness and discipline of British and Indian troops.*"

Can Mr. Royle, who is so clever in getting up dialectic dilemmas, tell us the exact meaning of the passage just quoted; and, more especially, how an enemy can be dislodged from a position and yet remain there, and concentrate in many thousands two days afterwards? Or how the right flank of a line of advance and communications can be protected in terms of one statement, and then furiously attacked by overwhelming numbers in terms of a second? If Mr. Royle can harmonise these two contradictions he will achieve a feat more wonderful than the discovery of many surprises, only to be consigned eventually to Colonel Malleson's waste-basket.

"HISTORY OF THE WAR IN THE SOUDAN," BY JAMES GRANT.
CASSELL & CO. LIMITED, LONDON, 1886.

This chapter cannot be closed without reference to a still later account of these Egyptian Campaigns, written by a recently-deceased fire-eating romancist. Were it not that the work in question was issued by a leading publishing firm in London, in so far as the action at Tofrek is concerned it would have been in every respect undeserving of attention. Its errors would have been inexcusable even if written in March 1885, instead of a year afterwards. The merit of a historian is usually estimated by the originality and accuracy of his information, and the care and discrimination shown in the selection of his sources. No such criterion is applicable to the brief narrative in question. To repeat the worst that could be, or was said, seems to have been the writer's only guide, and for him careful inquiry, official statements, and trustworthy documents, have no existence. Comment, under such circumstances being useless, as the most effective refutation a few quotations must suffice. In keeping with the reckless and foolhardy spirit, which the author would fain have us believe characterised the proceedings of the 22nd, we are told that General M'Neill—

" Marched his force towards Tamai in two squares, *and in full sight of the enemy, mustered in force on the Hasheen hill, from whence they attempted to check his advance,* but were checked in turn by the shell fire from the works manned by the Surrey regiment . . . while the two squares disappeared in the dust and obscurity of the desert." [1]

Being thus foiled in stopping the march of the two Brigades, the Arabs, under the belief that Suâkin was denuded of troops, menaced it, but finding themselves mistaken, again direct their attention to General M'Neill :—

" Who of course knew nothing of their whereabouts, but had by this time

---

[1] *History of the War in the Soudan,* by James Grant, vol. iv. p. 134.

partially constructed one zeriba *about five miles from the coast* (!), and had begun the formation of another . . . when a terrible surprise ensued, one that might have proved another Isandhlwana—a surprise caused by the neglect, apparently, *of all the precautions usually taken in war*, especially one with stealthy savages." [1]

The inspiring genius here seems to be "*Suakin, 1885*," whose statements are not only adopted, but, after the manner of the "three crows," very much improved upon by this romancing *redacteur*, who most assuredly was "not there."

"Of the cavalry vedettes thrown out, *none were more than thirty yards in advance of the working-parties*, who had piled their arms, and were hewing down the tough thorn bushes; *and we hear of no outpickets being distinctly posted, or of sentries*."

Not content with the "thirty yards" distance for the vedettes, the statement already given [2] from the *Daily Chronicle* is quoted in proof of the fact that there were only eighteen Lancers, although, had such been the case, the fault would certainly not have lain with General M'Neill. The performances of the *Standard's* special "Umpire-in-Chief" are also highly applauded; but the climax of all this absurdity is reserved for the close, when, referring to the precautions adopted for the night, and assumed absence of pickets and sentries during the day, it is stated—

"That was done now which should have been done before the working-parties began to break ground,—*patrols were thrown out* (!), *and outposts were strengthened* (!), and all other requisite precautions taken." [3]

Outposts and sentry work an afterthought due to the bitter experience of the day! This fairly beats the "cutting and burning a wide pathway through the bush," or even the "light railway!" [4] In this case, however, the jibe was based on a road actually being formed, the averment being that it ought to "have been undertaken at an earlier stage," *i.e.* the march out. Our romancer goes

[1] *History of the War in the Soudan*, by James Grant, vol. iv. p. 134.
[2] *Vide* p. 192 *antea*.
[3] *History of the War in the Soudan*, vol. iv. p. 147.
[4] *Vide* pp. 248-254, *antea*.

beyond this, and after denying the existence of suitable guards during the day, avers that they encircled the zeriba during the night; the fact being that not a man was permitted to go outside the fence, while the entire Force was under arms and practically on guard, sleeping and watching by alternate ranks.

On a narrative like this serious criticism would be thrown away; and were it not for the wide circulation any publication issued by the Messrs. Cassell must necessarily have, might well be treated with the contempt it so richly deserves. Enjoying, however, a publicity far beyond its deserts, so flagrant an instance of malicious misrepresentation could not be overlooked, and the same measures were accordingly adopted as those already mentioned with regard to "*Suakin*, 1885."[1] In the present case, the author having been called to his account before another tribunal, the attention of the Messrs. Cassell was drawn to the matter, when they at once, on evidence submitted, in the most honourable way fully admitted and recognised the reprehensible character of the statements so made, and, at the instance of Messrs. Tods, Murray, and Jamieson, W.S., 66 Queen Street, Edinburgh, inserted an apology in the *Times* for 9th July 1887 to the following effect :—

MESSRS. CASSELL AND COMPANY, Limited, have ascertained that the STATEMENTS reflecting on MAJOR-GENERAL SIR JOHN M'NEILL, K.C.B., in the account of the action at Tofrek, given in the late Mr. Grant's *History of the War in the Soudan*, published by them, are INCORRECT, and they REGRET that they were published upon information which they are satisfied was inaccurate. The account of the action has been revised, and the corrected version will appear in all future reprints of the work.—La Belle Sauvage, Ludgate-hill, London, July 8, 1887."

[1] *Vide* p. 280.

APPENDICES.

APPENDIX I.

EXTRACTS FROM

PARLIAMENTARY PAPERS, RELATIVE TO THE CAMPAIGNS IN THE EASTERN SÛDAN, 1884-85.

1. ADVANCE ON TAMAI BY BAKER'S ZERIBA, March 1884.

Parliamentary Paper, Egypt, No. 12 (1884).

No. 233.

Telegrams communicated to the Foreign Office by the War Office, March 11.

(1.)

MAJOR-GENERAL SIR G. GRAHAM TO THE MARQUIS OF HARTINGTON.

Suakin, March 9, 1884, 5.50 P.M.

Went with squadron to Baker's zeriba, eight miles in front, this morning. Will occupy it with infantry to-morrow, and store water on Tuesday. All infantry bivouac at zeriba. On Wednesday cavalry joins infantry, and all force moves to Osman's camp, where water is plentiful, and entrench.

(3.)

MAJOR-GENERAL SIR G. GRAHAM TO THE MARQUIS OF HARTINGTON.

Suakin, March 10, 1884, 7.55 P.M.

Royal Highlanders marched out to zeriba, nine miles in advance, this morning. Owing to sudden heat some slight cases of sunstroke occurred, which are doing well. Disembarkation must continue to-night, so will delay advance till Wednesday. All precautions against sunstroke will be taken. Men's health excellent.

No. 239.

MAJOR-GENERAL SIR G. GRAHAM TO THE MARQUIS OF HARTINGTON.
(Received at the Foreign Office, March 12.)

(*Telegraphic.*) *Suakin, March* 12, 1884, 9.40 P.M.

Marched whole force out to zeriba last night. Reconnoitred enemy this morning.

Moved to within two or three miles of Osman's camp this afternoon. Too late to attack. Formed zeriba. Will attack to-morrow. Troops all well.

2. INSTRUCTIONS, ETC., RELATIVE TO CAMPAIGN OF 1885.

Parliamentary Paper, Egypt, No. 9 (1885).

No. 9.

THE MARQUIS OF HARTINGTON TO GENERAL LORD WOLSELEY.

(*Telegraphic.*) *War Office, February* 17, 1885, 3·25 P.M.

Following is force which will concentrate at Suakin between 6th and 10th March :—

Cavalry, four squadrons Lancers and Hussars ; artillery, two-thirds horse, and one screw battery, and one garrison battery to man defences of Suakin on marines going to front ; Engineers, one Field and one Railway Company and Telegraph and Balloon Sections ; Guards, three battalions ; infantry, three battalions ; Departmental Corps. Total British troops, about 7,250 all ranks. A battalion of marines will be made up to take part in operations.

Indian Contingent consists of—cavalry, one regiment ; infantry, three battalions ; sappers, one company. Total Indian contingent, about 2,800 men.

New South Wales contingent—artillery, one battery 16-pounders ; infantry, one battalion of 500 men. Total about 620. This contingent will reach Suakin about 3rd April.

Force at Suakin now consists of—cavalry detachments ; artillery, two guns Horse Artillery ; Engineers, one company ; infantry, one battalion ; marines, one battalion. Total, about 1,650 all ranks. Grand total of above 12,320.

Graham commands, with Greaves Chief of Staff ; Fremantle commands Guards Brigade ; M'Neill, other brigade ; Ewart, cavalry.

No. 16.

THE MARQUIS OF HARTINGTON TO LIEUTENANT-GENERAL SIR G. GRAHAM.

(Extract.)   *War Office, February 20*, 1885.

On arrival at Suakin to take command of the force, which will shortly be assembled there, you will make the best arrangements—which the shortness of the time at your disposal, before the hot weather commences, admits of—to organise a field force, and to make such transport arrangements as are possible to enable it to secure the first and most pressing object of the campaign on which you are about to enter—viz., the destruction of the power of Osman Digna.

Owing to the short time which has been available for the collection of transport, it may probably happen that your troops may arrive before your transport is ready for them. In such case you are authorised to detain the whole or any part of them at Suez until you are ready to receive them at Suakin, or whatever other point on the coast you may decide upon for the commencement of your operations.

You are aware that an agreement has been made with an eminent firm of contractors (Messrs. Lucas and Aird) to construct a railway from Suakin to Berber, and on this you must greatly rely for your means of transporting supplies.

It will therefore be of the first importance that every possible facility should be given to Messrs. Lucas and Aird in the conduct of their operations.

Your first object, as I have stated, is the destruction of Osman Digna's power, and to effect this you will, as early as possible, proceed to attack all the positions which he occupies, and to disperse the troops defending them.

It is to be hoped that good healthy positions in the mountains may be found there for British troops.

The pushing on of the railway from Suakin towards Berber is the next point to which you will direct the greatest attention; but until the districts above mentioned have been entirely pacified it will probably not be possible to push the line beyond Tambuk Wells.

To cover the advance along the Berber line the sooner Ariab can be occupied and held the better. Every effort should be made to clear out the wells, and increase the water supply there.

If Berber is not taken this summer by Lord Wolseley, the railway cannot be pushed much beyond Ariab, and there all the railway plant and material necessary for the 100 miles between it and Berber should be collected as soon as possible, so that the advance, when the cool weather begins, and Berber is taken, may be made at once.

You will consider yourself under the orders of General Lord Wolseley, commanding in Egypt, and you will place yourself in direct telegraphic communication with him.

You will report all operations to Lord Wolseley, transmitting copies by post and telegraph direct to the Secretary of State for War.

Within the limits of the above instructions you have perfect discretionary powers to conduct operations in any manner which you deem best.

No. 20.

GENERAL LORD WOLSELEY TO THE MARQUIS OF HARTINGTON.

(Received February 22, 1885, 12.30 P.M.)

(*Telegraphic.*)   *Korti, February* 22, 1885, 12.10 P.M.

Yours of 21st.

When I have concentrated my force on this part Nile, I have no fear for my communications, so I do not want any more troops here now. It is important to thoroughly crush Osman Digna, and restore peace to country now under influence, in order to push forward railway, and, by a brilliant success near Suakin, make Soudanese realise what they must expect when we move forward in autumn.

No. 29.

THE MARQUIS OF HARTINGTON TO LIEUTENANT-GENERAL SIR G. GRAHAM.

SIR,   *War Office, February* 27, 1885.

With reference to, and in continuation of, my letter of the 20th instant,[1] I desire to draw your attention again to the necessity for rapidly constructing the railway from Suakin to Berber, and to the extreme importance of the services it will be required to perform, not only in connection with the advance of your force, but also in connection with the troops under Lord Wolseley's command when concentrated at Berber.

By this route alone, when the railway shall have been completed, can that force be supplied, re-equipped, and reinforced with that precision and certainty so essential to the future operations on the Nile.

[1] No. 16.

When the first and essential operation of crushing Osman Digna and clearing the country sufficiently to make it safe for the constructors of the railway is accomplished, the next most important duty will be the pushing on of the railway, and I request that you will facilitate and aid this object by every means in your power. You will, of course, decide what military posts you will occupy, and when their occupation should be effected, but in deciding on such matters it will be desirable to bear in mind that the interval between the advanced troops and the advancing railway should be as short as is compatible with military necessities, in order that the weight of transport arrangements may not hamper or delay the construction of the railway.

Though the direction of the works will be entirely under your orders and control, their detail execution will be in the hands of the constructors, and in order not to weaken their authority or delay their action, it is essential that this division of duty should be observed.

As the immediate military control of the works will, in accordance with the practice of the Service, be in the hands of the officer commanding the lines of communications, Brigadier-General Ewart, C.B., an officer of experience in works, has been selected for this appointment, and has been ordered to join your command at once. The preliminary survey and location of the line will be carried out by him under your orders. Any deviation by the constructors from the line indicated to them which structural necessities may dictate must be submitted for your approval.

You will be so good as to transmit weekly reports of the progress of the line.—I am, etc.   HARTINGTON.

3. TELEGRAPHIC AND OTHER DESPATCHES RELATIVE TO THE BATTLE OF TOFREK.

No. 59.

LIEUTENANT-GENERAL SIR G. GRAHAM TO GENERAL LORD WOLSELEY.

(Received March 22.)

(*Telegraphic.*)   *Suakin, March* 22, 1885, 5.20 P.M.

Moved out 2nd Brigade, under General Sir John M‘Neill, supported by Indian Brigade under General Hudson, with four Gardner guns, this morning at 7. A number of camels and transport animals were inside Indian Brigade square; six miles from camp a zeriba was commenced. At 2.45 a heavy and sudden attack was made by enemy, but repulsed with heavy loss to them. M‘Neill reports our loss not very severe, but camels and transport animals suffered much, as enemy came between them and zeriba. Charteris wounded in hand.

No. 60.

LIEUTENANT-GENERAL SIR G. GRAHAM TO GENERAL LORD WOLSELEY.

(Received March 22.)

(*Telegraphic.*) *Suakin, March* 22, 1885, 7.24 P.M.

Losses at present ascertained :—

Naval Brigade, Lieutenant Seymour and six men killed, four wounded. Berkshire, Lieutenant Swinton and ten men killed, seventeen wounded. Marines, eight killed, twelve wounded. Royal Engineers, Transport Corps, and Indian Brigade not yet reported.

Parliamentary Paper, Egypt, No. 13 (1885).

No. 1.

LIEUTENANT-GENERAL SIR G. GRAHAM TO THE MARQUIS OF HARTINGTON.

(Received March 23.)

(*Telegraphic.*) *Suakin, March* 23, 1885.

Following to Wolseley, March 22nd :—

" Following just received from M'Neill, 9 P.M. :—

"' Berkshire—Killed, Lieutenant Swinton and 12 men. Marines—8 men killed, 12 wounded. Navy—Killed, Lieutenant Seymour, 6 men. Royal Engineers—Captain Romilly and Lieutenant Newman killed. Indian Contingent—about 25 killed, including Major von Beverhoudt, and 70 wounded.

"' It is impossible at present to get further information. Enemy broke into square of zeriba, which was imperfectly formed. Attack lasted about 20 minutes. Enemy lost near 1000. Very great loss in transport camels, horses, and mules ; and no firing from enemy at present.' "

On first hearing firing, at 2.45 P.M., I ordered out Guards, except one battalion previously dispatched to Hasheen with convoy. Remaining battalions, with Horse Artillery, advanced 2 miles towards zeriba, and were retired on receipt of telegram from M'Neill. Two battalions go out tomorrow with further supplies. I shall accompany Guards, and will send further details.

No. 2.

LIEUTENANT-GENERAL SIR G. GRAHAM TO THE MARQUIS OF HARTINGTON.

(Received March 23.)

(*Telegraphic.*)   *Suakin, March* 23, 1885.

Following to Wolseley :—

"Advanced zeriba, 12 noon.   Arrived here with Guards and large convoy. Am sending in wounded and baggage animals, with Indian Brigade and Grenadier Guards, under Fremantle, leaving two battalions of Guards here with M'Neill's Brigade.

"A strong zeriba has been constructed, and I consider position secure against any number of enemy.   The attack yesterday was very sudden and determined, and came unfortunately on our weakest point held by 17th Native Infantry, who were driven back.   The other Indian battalions behaved well, the Sikhs charging the enemy with bayonet ; the Berkshire behaved splendidly, clearing out the zeriba where entered, and capturing three standards ; Marines also behaved well.   Naval Brigade was exposed by retreat of 17th Native Infantry, and suffered severely.   Engineers also suffered heavily, being out working when attacked.

"The enemy suffered very severely, more than 1,000 bodies being counted ; many Chiefs of note are believed to have fallen.

"I deeply regret our serious losses, but am of opinion that M'Neill did everything possible under the circumstances.   The cavalry, 5th Lancers, did their best to give information, but the ground being covered with bush it was impossible to see any distance.   All the Staff and Regimental Officers did their utmost.

"Enemy charged with reckless courage, leaping over the low zeriba to certain death, and although they gained a temporary success by surprise they have received a severe lesson, and up to present time have not attempted again to molest zeriba."

No. 4.

LIEUTENANT-GENERAL SIR G. GRAHAM TO THE MARQUIS OF HARTINGTON.

(Received March 25.)

(*Telegraphic.*)   *Suakin, March* 25, 1885.

Following to Wolseley :—

"This morning sent out convoy to M'Neill's zeriba, with escort 15th

Sikhs, 28th Bombay, and Madras Sappers. At 3 miles distant convoy halted as ordered; commenced cutting road and formed zeriba. A battalion of Guards and Marines from M'Neill's marched towards them, and were attacked on the way by long-range fire, Lieutenant Marchant, Marines, and one private being wounded.

"About 2 P.M. the escorts met, when Guards and Marines took over convoy, giving over two wounded to return to Suakin. Returning to zeriba Guards and Marines were attacked twice. No complete Report yet received from M'Neill. Cavalry escort accompanied convoy, consisting of one squadron Bengal Lancers, one squadron 20th Hussars. Cavalry behaved very well when square was attacked, keeping clear of infantry fire, and checking enemy's advance by volleys from dismounted men. Guards and Marines showed great steadiness under fire. Cavalry escort and Native Infantry returned to Suakin.

"Casualties, as reported, were: Killed, Coldstreams, 1 private. Wounded, Captain Dalrymple, 8 men; Marines, 5 men. Nominal rolls to-morrow."

No. 5.

LIEUTENANT-GENERAL SIR G. GRAHAM TO THE MARQUIS OF HARTINGTON.

(Received March 26.)

(Telegraphic.)   *Suakin, March* 26, 1885.

Just arrived with large convoy. Attacked by enemy about 2 miles from here. Enemy charged head of square, and were repulsed with considerable loss. Our casualties, three wounded. I have not lost a single camel load. Several slight cases of sunstroke; men otherwise healthy. Marines suffer most. Am bringing in Scots Guards.

No. 17.

LIEUTENANT-GENERAL SIR G. GRAHAM TO THE MARQUIS OF HARTINGTON.

(Received April 6.)

(Telegraphic.)   *Suakin, April* 6, 1885.

A large convoy of over 2,000 camels and 1,500 mules, escorted by four battalions under Sir John M'Neill, marched at 5 A.M. to clear out No. 1 zeriba, bringing in garrison 28th Bombay Infantry, and will arrive about 5 o'clock.

     *   *   *   *   *   *   *

Last night enemy fired into M'Neill's zeriba for three hours, wounding one man and two mules; replied to by Gatlings and rifles.

No. 28.

General Graham's Despatch relative to Battle of Tofrek.

LIEUTENANT-GENERAL SIR G. GRAHAM TO THE MARQUIS OF HARTINGTON.

(Received April 14.)

My Lord,   *Head-quarters, Suakin, March* 28, 1885.

In continuation of my despatch of the 21st instant, I have the honour to report that on the 22nd instant I ordered the force, as per margin,[1] under Major-General Sir J. M'Neill, V.C., K.C.B., to march from Suakin taking a line leading directly to Tamai.

My intention was to form a zeriba about 8 miles from Suakin, to act as an intermediate depôt for the supplies and water required for an advance in force on Tamai. I further intended that the Indian Brigade on returning should leave one battalion in an intermediate zeriba, about 4 miles from camp.

The force advanced in echelon of brigade squares, the 2nd Brigade leading; the Indian Brigade, under Brigadier Hudson, following on the right rear. I myself proceeded with the force for about 2½ miles, then returning to camp.

At about 2.45 P.M., heavy firing was heard in the direction taken by Sir J. M'Neill's force, and I immediately ordered out the Guards Brigade and the Horse Artillery battery, and proceeded about 3 miles, following the line to Tamai. Receiving a message from Sir J. M'Neill that he was in no need of assistance, I returned to camp with the Guards.

Sir J. M'Neill's convoy, on its march through the dense scrub which lies between Suakin and the hills, experienced much difficulty. The great mass of camels inclosed in the Indian Brigade square was continually getting into disorder, owing to the high prickly bushes through which it was obliged to force its way.

Thus frequent halts were necessary in order to get the camels back into position, and restore the chain of defence with which it is necessary in such a country to surround the transport animals and non-combatants.

It was soon apparent that the original plan could not be carried out in its entirety; since, if the force advanced 8 miles, there would not remain

[1] One squadron 5th Lancers, Naval Brigade with four Gardner guns, detachment Royal Engineers, Berkshire Regiment, Royal Marines, company Madras Sappers, 15th Sikhs, 17th Bengal N.I., 28th Bombay N.I., one squadron 20th Hussars patrolling rear between force and Suakin.

2 T

sufficient daylight to allow a zeriba to be formed, and then for the Indian Brigade to return and form an intermediate zeriba.

Sir J. M'Neill, therefore, determined to halt and form his zeriba at about 6 miles only from the camp at Suakin.

The force was formed up as follows : the Indian Brigade took up three sides of a square fronting nearly east,[1] south, and west; the transport animals were in the centre. The Berkshire Regiment, Marines, and the Royal Engineers and Madras Sappers, began at once to cut brushwood.

The zeriba was traced out as shown in the sketch plan X, attached.[2]

The work proceeded steadily, and the south zeriba, ABCD, was told off to the Berkshire Regiment, with two Naval Gardners ; the north zeriba, EFGH, to the Marines, also with two naval Gardners. The central zeriba, PCFO, was intended to contain the stores.

At about 2.30 P.M., the disposition of the force appears to have been as follows (see sketch plan X, attached).[2]

Half the Berkshire Regiment were south of the zeriba ABCD, cutting brushwood; their arms were piled inside. The line AL was held by six companies 17th Native Infantry, their left being somewhat *en l'air* ; the line DK by the 15th Sikhs ; KN by the 28th Bombay Native Infantry ; NG by two companies of the 17th Native Infantry. Outposts *a, a, . . .* , consisting of groups of four men each, were thrown out from 80 to 120 yards to the front of the three Indian regiments. These three regiments themselves were formed in two-deep line. The other half-battalion of the Berkshire Regiment were having their dinners at about the point R, 250 yards to the east of the zeriba. The Marines were inside the north zeriba EFGH, having just finished cutting brushwood. The camels had been unloaded in the central zeriba and had begun to file out, in order to be formed up outside ready for the return march. The squadron 5th Lancers formed a chain of Cossack posts (each four men), at a distance of about 1,000 yards from the force, the rest of the squadron being held in support on some open ground about 500 yards to the south-west of the zeriba. A squadron of the 20th Hussars was patrolling the ground between the zeriba and Suakin.

Shortly after 2.30 P.M. three messages were sent in from the 5th Lancers outposts, announcing first the presence of the enemy on their front, and immediately afterwards his advance. Very soon after this the cavalry galloped in, closely followed by the Arabs.

The 15th Sikhs and 28th Bombay Native Infantry stood firm and main-

---

[1] So in original, but ought to be north.   [2] *Vide* Plate II., p. 63 *antea.*

tained an intact line, receiving and repulsing successive attacks with a heavy fire.

The attack was delivered mainly in the direction shown by the arrows. A large number of the enemy entered the south zeriba at the salient B, where there was no brushwood and merely an unfinished sandbag parapet. The Gardner guns were being placed in position at the time and could not be got into action so that their detachments, who stood their ground gallantly, suffered severely.

Other parties of the enemy, following the retreat of the 17th Native Infantry, dashed into the central zeriba PCOF, and caused a stampede among the animals and panic among the native drivers. A general rush of the latter took place both to the open side PF and also through the north zeriba, where a portion of the Marines were for the moment carried away by it.

In a short time the whole of the Arabs in the south zeriba were killed or driven out by the half-battalion of the Berkshire Regiment, who captured a flag, which the enemy had planted on the sandbag parapet at B.

The Marines cleared the north zeriba, and assisted by the Berkshire, the central zeriba also.

Meanwhile, the half-battalion of the Berkshire Regiment, which was dining near R when the alarm was given, formed rallying square, and succeeded in repelling two successive attacks without loss, afterwards fighting their way back to the zeriba.

Other small bodies of men, who were outside the zeriba at the moment of the attack, were similarly collected by the exertions of the officers, and succeeded in making their way back to the zeriba.

A large number of camels which were outside of the zeriba before the attack took place, or had stampeded on its occurrence, were unavoidably shot, as the enemy rushed in among them, cutting and ham-stringing them in all directions.

The whole affair appears to have lasted about twenty minutes, and the attack seems to have been delivered in two main rushes. The enemy's force was not less than 2,000 strong ; but, under the circumstances, it was impossible to form an accurate estimate. The attack was delivered with extreme determination, the Arabs charging at full speed, and in some cases even leaping over the low bushes forming the unfinished zeriba.

The great loss of transport animals was due to the rush of the enemy through the south and central zeriba. The animals stampeded, became mixed up with those already formed up outside the zeriba, and the enemy being among them in all directions, they were shot in large numbers by our own men.

The detachment of the Naval Brigade in the south zeriba gallantly stood to their guns, and suffered very severely. The Marines, also, behaved very well; and though their zeriba was broken through by the rush of transport animals they reformed at once, and contributed effectively to the repulse of the enemy.

The 15th Sikhs had to sustain several rushes of the enemy, and, together with the 28th Bombay Regiment, maintained an unbroken front.

The loss in officers was severe, and was due to the fact that, in the confusion arising from the sudden attack, individual attempts were gallantly made to collect isolated bodies of men to stem the determined rush of the enemy.

I may mention Major von Beverhoudt, of the 17th Native Infantry, Captain Romilly and Lieutenant Newman, of the Royal Engineers, as instances of officers who lost their lives in the brave effort to check the enemy's fierce onslaught; while Lieutenant Seymour, R.N., with his gun detachment, also met death at the post of duty.

Although our sacrifice has been severe, I am convinced that the complete repulse and heavy loss which the enemy has sustained, involving (as it has done) the destruction of more than 1,000 fighting men, will prove to have produced an impression which will definitely facilitate my future operations.

The zeriba has since been strengthened considerably, and no attempt has been made to attack it. I am now storing water and provisions there, with a view to a further advance as soon as possible.—I have, &c.

(Signed) GERALD GRAHAM.

4. Correspondence as to Nile and Eastern Sûdan Expeditions.

No. 26.

THE MARQUIS OF HARTINGTON TO GENERAL LORD WOLSELEY.

(*Telegraphic.*) *War Office, April* 13, 1885.

In the condition of Imperial affairs it is probable that the expedition to Khartoum may have to be abandoned, and the troops brought back as soon as possible to Egypt. Consider at once what measures should, in that case, be promptly taken for safe withdrawal of troops.

This would involve stopping advance from Suakin, but not hurried withdrawal.

No. 32.

GENERAL LORD WOLSELEY TO THE MARQUIS OF HARTINGTON.

(Received April 15.)

(*Telegraphic*.) *Cairo, April* 15, 1885.

Mine yesterday dealt exclusively with military matters, unconnected with policy of retreat indicated in yours of 13th instant.

I venture to express following opinion on that policy:—

At, and south of Assouan, I have about 7,500 British fighting soldiers. Retreat policy will require at least 2,500 on the frontier, leaving 5,000 available. For the sake of this handful, is it advisable to reverse Soudan policy? Retreat from Dongola hands that province over to the Mahdi, and renders loyalty of Ababdehs and other frontier tribes very doubtful. On them we rely very much for peace in Egypt. Troops now in Province of Dongola seriously threaten Mahdi, block his advance northward, and encourage his enemies. He might now, at any moment, be joined by his regular troops, the backbone of his military strength. Many circumstances may lead to his sudden disappearance; time is a great element in our favour if we rest on our arms where we are.

This policy entails no risk, for we could concentrate near Dongola or Hannek whenever we wished, and I would strongly recommend its adoption, as most befitting our national dignity, and most likely to secure eventually the objects we have in Egypt.

Withdraw Graham's force if necessary; this will not seriously disturb Egypt; but hold on to Dongola province. As long as you do this you prevent Mahdi-ism spreading to Egypt, secure allegiance of frontier tribes, and save henceforth trouble, disturbances, and possibly local risings, which policy of retreat will probably entail, and which will necessitate increased garrisons in Egypt and military occupation of large towns.

I send a copy of this to Sir E. Baring.

No. 36.

GENERAL LORD WOLSELEY TO THE MARQUIS OF HARTINGTON.

(Received April 17.)

(Telegraphic.) *Cairo, April* 17, 1885.

News have been received from Intelligence Department that a letter has been received by Mohammed El-Kheir, the Emir of Berber, to the effect that he should cease fighting, as the English are coming by way of Suakin to Berber, and that it is impossible to fight them again after the fights that have taken place lately ; and that the Arabs have left him and dispersed.

APPENDIX II.

INFORMATION REGARDING OSMAN DIGNA AND HIS FAMILY.

Parliamentary Paper, Egypt, No. 5 (1884).

No. 16.

THE SECRETARY TO THE ADMIRALTY TO SIR J. PAUNCEFOTE.
(Received January 11.)

SIR,   *Admiralty, January* 10, 1884.

I am commanded by my Lords Commissioners of the Admiralty to transmit to you, for the perusal of Earl Granville, copy of a Report addressed to Rear-Admiral Sir William Hewett, respecting the state of affairs in the Soudan.
—I am, etc.   G. TRYON.

Inclosure in No. 16.   *Report.*

I have the honour to bring before your notice the following information respecting Osman Digna, the rebel Chief of this district, in accordance with your desire. The Digna family were previously rich and influential, but on the abolition of the Slave Trade they suffered some severe losses, and some of them were imprisoned for being implicated in dealing in slaves, and the family gradually became poor and in debt. Ali Digna, one of the brothers, was caught by Her Majesty's ship "Wild Swan," with ninety-six slaves, off Sheek Beragoot, a small harbour about 30 miles north of Suakin; this was a loss of at least 1,000*l.* to the family. The capture took place, I think, 1877.

Osman Digna, the head of the family, then became a broker in the town of Berber, a town on the Nile 280 miles from Suakin, and occasionally came here to sell merchandise of various kinds. Last year he brought some ostrich feathers and shipped them to Jeddah, remaining here himself, and staying about six months, and then left for Khartoum, afterwards going to Kordofan, where he remained some months, and then returned to Erkowit about the 23rd Ramadan, or the 28th July 1883, bringing letters from the Mahdi to Tewfik Bey, the Governor of Suakin, the Prefect of Sinkat and Tokar, Mohamed-el-Amien, Sheikh of the Erkowit tribes, and Said Ahmed-el-Shingety, the Mufti of the Council at Suakin "Megliss."

The Government received news of his being at Erkowit on the 2nd August at about 7 P.M., and the Governor left for Sinkat the same night with the intention of taking the rebel.

On the 5th August we received news to the effect that the rebels were collecting in force near Sinkat, and on the 6th we heard that they had attacked and were repulsed with a loss of about eighty men, including Ahmed Digna and his son, the brother and nephew of Osman Digna, who was himself wounded in two places.

After this defeat most of the tribes left him, and he could only muster about 150 men in all.

The Governor then offered pardon to all who came in, and many of the Sheikhs did so, and took the oath of loyalty to His Highness the Khedive; and his Excellency Soliman Pasha, who joined the Governor about this time on his way down from Khartoum, gave them presents of clothing. A few days after this, Soliman Pasha left Sinkat and came to Suakin, and called the Sheikhs to him and spoke with them, and all declared their loyalty. He remained here a few days and then went to Tokar, where he also called in the Sheikhs, and made them take the oath, and gave them some more presents of clothing, and on his return to Suakin he informed the merchants and employés that everything was quiet and there was nothing to fear.

On the 10th September Tewfik Bey, with a force of 250 men, left Sinkat and attacked the rebels at Ghabbat, where he gained another success, killing about fifty of the rebels, and, after confiscating about 5 cwt. of ivory, he burned about seventy araibs of sourah (native grain), and ten or fifteen huts. He then returned to Sinkat, where he was met by Soliman Pasha, who considered it better to deal with the question in a diplomatic manner, and not by force of arms as Tewfik Bey wished to do. Osman Digna at this time had only about seventy-five followers, and was going from place to place trying to gather the confidence of the tribes a second time, and no attempt was made to catch him, as his Excellency Soliman Pasha believed that the loyal (?) tribes would bring him in.

On the 16th October, Major Mohammed Khilil, in command of two companies of infantry, each man having 100 rounds of ball-cartridges with him, and having a reserve of 24 cases of 1,100 each case, and accompanied by about 100 women and children, left for Sinkat to strengthen the garrison there. On the 18th news was received that they had been attacked in a mountain-pass on the Abeint road to Sinkat, about 30 miles from here, and only twenty-five men had escaped.

From this date Osman Digna gained strength, and the tribes commenced to return to him, and he made his head-quarters at Temanieh, where he remained until after the fight took place at Teeb, on the road to Tokar, when he came still nearer to Suakin.

Towards the end of October Mahmoud Tahar Pasha was appointed in command of the troops in the Eastern Soudan, and arrived here from Cairo on the 23rd, and took charge of the military arrangements, and was preparing a force to go to Sinkat, when news was received from Tokar saying that Feggi Khedre, Feggi Mahmoud, and Feggi Mousa, Sheikh of the Artagah tribe, and Hassan, Sheikh of the Kamilah tribe, had revolted in consequence of a letter which they had received from Osman Digna, and that the town was in danger. Mahmoud Tahar Pasha then decided that it would be better to relieve that place first, and on the 3rd November an expedition of about 500 men of all arms and one gun, accompanied by Consul Moncrieff and four Greeks, under the command of Mahmoud Pasha, left in the steamships "Gafarieh" and "Tor" for Trinkatat, the sea-port of Tokar. On the 4th the troops were landed at daybreak, and started in the form of a square at 8 A.M. to march on Tokar. The "Gafarieh" returned on the same day and brought me a letter from Captain Moncrieff, forwarding another for Sir E. Baring, and saying that they were just off, and that the Arabs were reported to be in the road.

On the 5th, at 5 P.M., the steamship "Tor" returned, bringing Mahmoud Pasha and the remainder of the troops, and I was informed that there had been a fight, and that the square was broken by about eight rebels, and the whole of the officers and men took flight to the shore, and Captain Moncrieff and four Greeks were seen surrounded by rebels fighting hard.

This second heavy loss on the part of the Government caused the whole of the tribes to go to Osman Digna, as he had such numbers now that many who, I believe, would have remained loyal were forced to join him, as the Government was not strong enough to protect them.

On the 26th November the steamship "Gafarieh" arrived from Massowah with one regiment of black troops, under the command of Major Khasim,

2 U

having been brought with the intention of making another attempt to relieve Tokar, but on the 2nd December Mahmoud Pasha sent them out with about 225 Egyptians and Bashi-Bazouks to make a reconnaissance in the direction of Tamanieh, but being badly officered, and having no advance-guard or scouts, were led into an ambush, and after some severe fighting all were lost with the exception of the two staff-officers, thirty-two cavalry (irregular), and fifteen infantry, ten being black, eight of which were wounded.

Since this time I hear that the whole of the Hadendowar tribes from near Kassala up to beyond Rahwayyeh have joined the rebels, with the exception of the Fadbab tribe, under Sheikh Mahmoud Ali Bey, who had assisted the Government almost alone from the commencement of these troubles.

Suakin, December 19, 1883.

2. Memorandum by Brewster Bey, addressed to Brigadier-General Sir John Hudson, K.C.B., Commanding the Indian Contingent at Suakin.

The following Memorandum, kindly communicated by Brigadier-General Sir John Hudson, K.C.B., was drawn up at his request by Brewster Bey, who, from the important position he occupied at Suâkin, and lengthened residence there, had exceptional opportunities for ascertaining the facts. The *canard* prevalent at one time as to the French descent of the rebel leader may thus be safely dismissed.

MEMORANDUM, respecting the Birth, Parentage, and Antecedents of Osman Digna.

The founder of the Digna family was a bastard—half Turk, half native of this coast. His name was Ali Digna, and he became in some manner attached to the Turynai tribe of the Erkowit Mountains. He had two sons, named Feggi Ali Digna and Abou Bakre Ali Digna.

Feggi Ali Digna had five sons, named Moussa Feggi, Mahomed Felik, Ali Feggi, Ahmed Feggi, and Feggi Feggi.

Moussa Feggi Digna had five sons, of whom only Mahomed Moussa Digna and one small child remain alive.

Ali Feggi Digna had four sons, Mahomed Fir, Moussa Ali, Mahomed Noor, and one small child; Mahomed Noor is dead.

Ahmed Feggi Digna had three sons, Mahomed, Ahmed, Hamed Ahmed and a small child; Hamed Ahmed is dead.

Feggi Feggi Digna had no children.

Mahomed Felik Digna had three sons, viz. Ahmed Gadi, Osnuk, and Ahmed; the two latter are dead.

Abou Bakre Digna had, Omur [Abou] Bakre Digna, Ali Abou Bakre, and Osman Abou Bakre Digna, the notorious rebel.

Omur Abou Bakre Digna had no children.

Osman Abou Bakre Digna had one son, Ali Osman (killed at the zareebah on 22nd March 1885).

Abou Bakre Digna was a notable and a merchant of Suakin, and married two wives; one of them (Osman's mother) belonged to the Bishareen Gual-i-ab (Hadendowa) tribe, the other to the Tinker-ab (also Hadendowa) tribe.

Osman Abou Bakre Digna, the rebel leader of the Eastern Soudan, was the youngest son of Abou Bakre Digna. He was a slave merchant and produce broker, living principally at Borkh, but travelling all over the Soudan, and at times visiting Egypt, Jeddah, and Hodeidah. It is not known if he ever went to Turkey, but it is thought he probably did.

Of Osman Digna's relations, the following have been killed during the rebellion :—

Omar Abou Bakre Digna, killed in Kordofan, fighting for the Mahdi.
Ahmed Ali Digna, killed by Friendlies at Sheik Beragoot.
Medany Ali Digna, killed at Baker Pasha's Teb.
Ahmed Feggi and Feggi Feggi Digna were both killed at Sinkat.[1]

(Signed) A. BREWSTER BEY.

Suakin, 8th Sept. 1885.

3. EXTRACT FROM PAPER READ BY CONSUL CAMERON BEFORE THE ANTHROPOLOGICAL INSTITUTE OF GREAT BRITAIN AND IRELAND.

In a most interesting Paper, read before the Anthropological Institute of Great Britain and Ireland, Nov. 23, 1886,[2] by Consul Cameron, the

---

[1] To these must be added Ali Osman, son of Osman Digna, killed, as mentioned above, at Tofrek, March 22nd, 1885.

[2] "On the Tribes of the Eastern Soudan.

By Donald A. Cameron, Esq., H.B.M. Consul for the Eastern Soudan."—*Journal of the Anthropological Institute*, vol. xvi. p. 293.

following remarks on Osman Digna occur. Mr. Cameron also calculates that the Northern Hadéndoas immediately under his influence in 1884-85, "must have numbered at least 15,000 desperate fighting men."[1]

"Digna himself is a Hadéndoa, and for the last three years he has succeeded in collecting at Tamai a large number of the Northern Hadéndoas, Artégas, and some Amárrars. Thus the word Hadéndoa is now almost synonymous for the rebels. The natives whom I have consulted all insist that the Hadéndoas are not of Arabian origin, and that they are an early emigration from the centre of Africa, west of the Nile. The Amárrars look upon them as a wild inferior race, who somehow have learned the Tobedawiet language, but who are quite distinct from the Amárrars, Ashrafs, Beni Amers, and Bishareen. They say that the Hadéndoas freely intermarry with other tribes, that their sheikhs have not much influence over them, and that they easily shift their allegiance and follow any leader of their fancy, like bands of brigands rather than tribes under a sheikhdom or patriarchal government."

[1] " On the Tribes of the Eastern Soudan. By Donald A. Cameron, Esq., H.B.M. Consul for the Eastern Soudan."—*Journal of the Anthropological Institute*, vol. xvi. p. 293.

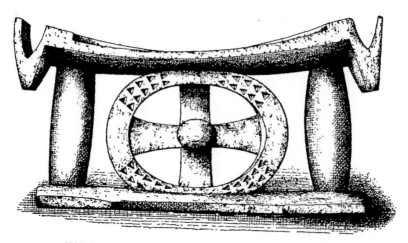

WOODEN PILLOW FOUND IN OSMAN DIGNA'S HUT AT TAMAI.

APPENDIX III.

"DIARY OF THE SUAKIN EXPEDITION, 1885,"

RELATIVE TO GENERAL M'NEILL'S ZERIBA.

THE *Diary of the Expedition*, from which these extracts are taken, is a blue book of 84 pp., issued from the Quarter-Master-General's Department of the Suâkin Field Force, the information, as far as possible, being given in a tabulated or statistical form.

The period embraced ranges from the landing of Head-Quarters at Suâkin on March 5th, to May 16th, 1885. It is signed by the Assistant Quarter-Master-General, and under date May 20th is endorsed by Sir George Greaves as Chief of the Staff. Under such auspices, it might reasonably be expected to be, not only authentic, but reasonably accurate and complete, and to contain a fair and impartial statement of the various transactions recorded.

The autobiographic Diary of an Expedition, following *de die in diem*, the fortunes of its various component Corps, might be indeed replete with living interest. To the reader, however, who may have supped on horrors, as these are usually served up, well spiced, by fire-eating specials, editors, and *redacteurs* of all kinds, we commend a perusal of the following pages as an effectual antidote to any unwholesome food of which he may have partaken. In the original, from the first page to the last, no touch of pathos, no gleam of sentiment, disturbs the "cold dry light" of the official narrative. As things go, perhaps, this is not a disadvantage; but compared with the information, with reasonable care and industry so easily and authoritatively obtainable, and the valuable purposes such a Diary, fully and faithfully kept, might have subserved, it must be admitted that it is an extremely meagre, inaccurate, and most disappointing production, in real interest contrasting greatly with Colonel Robertson's able Report on a more limited and unpromising field—the Commissariat.

Confining attention to matters bearing on the present subject, it may be remarked that the list of errors commences with the first extract made. Sir John M'Neill landed on the 8th, not the 7th of March. He made the passage from Bombay with the Head-Quarters of the 9th Bengal Cavalry,—of whom by the way, no mention is made,—in the British India s.s. "Bancorra," correctly noted in the Diary amongst the arrivals on the 8th.

The "Bancorra" left Bombay Feb. 25th, and approaching by the mid-channel, arrived off Suâkin on the afternoon of the 7th. The westering sunlight, however, making it extremely difficult even for an experienced pilot to distinguish the edges of the coral reefs by which the immediate entry to the harbour is beset, she was ordered to the south anchorage, two or three miles below the town, and lay there until the morning of the 8th, when she got into the harbour. General M'Neill then landed, went to Head-Quarter Camp, and being the Senior Officer present took the Command. These facts are impressed on General M'Neill's memory by the circumstance that the first report made to him related to the attack made during the previous night on the Head-Quarter Camp, when a charger belonging to Colonel Gordon of the 93rd, Camp Commandant, and afterwards Provost-Marshal, the last scenes of whose life have been so touchingly narrated by Major de Cosson,[1] was stolen, and the groom severely wounded.

Merely mentioning that the returns of casualties for the 20th are *entirely omitted*, we reach the 22nd. In the enumeration of the Force sent out four errors occur, one of them clerical, and three serious. In the Cavalry moving out "at 7.5 A.M.," are included one squadron of the 20th Hussars and one squadron of the 9th Bengal Cavalry, who, sent out from Suâkin during the day, were only intended to act as patrol and relief on the Line of Communications. The Cavalry accompaniment is thus made to appear much more imposing than it really was, the patrol, however useful its duties ultimately became, being of no service in scouting or outpost work.

As if to counterbalance this excess in one arm, the Royal Marine Light Infantry are entirely omitted! while the 17th Native Infantry are reckoned as belonging not to the Bengal but to the Bombay Army! an error repeated in the Table of casualties, and in the list of troops returning to Suâkin on the 23rd, notwithstanding their being correctly designated in the notice of attack.

In the account given of the Movement, the reason given for the halt at the

[1] *Days and Nights of Service*, pp. 314-316.

6-mile distance is, "the lateness of the hour"! the real reason being the impossibility of carrying the Transport any farther, owing to the density of the jungle. That the time, *in any case*, would have been all too short to carry out Head-Quarter plans in their entirety is evident, but, most emphatically, that was not the reason why a stoppage short of the distance designated was made.

Unless an error in the reckoning be assumed, whencesoever the information as to the triple events represented as occurring at 1.55, 2 o'clock, and 2.10, was derived, certainly no such intimations reached Sir John M'Neill, on this point his own testimony, and that of General Hudson, being clear and emphatic.[1] Yet another clerical error occurs, where the squadron of the 20th Hussars is placed under the Command of Major Greaves. The withdrawal of the enemy is much too early timed at 3.30, and the numbers of those in attack, and of those who fell, is egregiously understated.

In this narrative, if such it may be called, of what was admittedly the most important action of the campaign, we see the art of military chronicling reduced to zero, and almost cease to wonder at the blank ignorance of the specials. Except as represented by a few scratches on the plan, the leading dispositions of the day are entirely *non est*. The enemy we are told "made no impression on the North and West faces," but to whom this was due, or why it should be so, we are not informed. Neither Indian Lines, nor British Rallying Square, receive the slightest recognition. Equal silence is observed as to all precautionary measures ; not a picquet or an outpost being mentioned. We are left to surmise that, with all the materials at command, the eye and the appreciations of the soldier are sadly missed, all the tactical arrangements of the day, whether good or bad, having practically no existence.

These are not the only important points upon which a curious and most unaccountable silence is observed. The "Hamlet of the March out," is not more completely omitted by "Suâkin, 1885" than it is by the official Diary. As will be noted from the entries in all subsequent movements, such as those of the 23rd, 24th, 25th, 26th, 28th, and 30th March, of which Convoy was the object, the extent and composition not only of the escort but also of the Convoy, down even to the gallons of water carried, is carefully enumerated, generally in tabular form. In the present case it is escort only that is given, and that exaggerated in the very element in which it was specially weak. The first notice that there was Convoy at all occurs in the casual statement that after the zeriba was completed the Convoy was to be sent back the same day, but of its extent and composition, its difficulties, and break down, there is not the very slightest mention.

[1] *Vide* p. 68.

The sketch plan annexed also claims a word or two. The Rallying Square, *circa* 2.30, reduced to a half battalion of the Berks, and so given in the plan accompanying General Graham's despatch,[1] is here broken up into two small squares, placed widely apart, and each designated "1 Co. Berks." There is also an *N.B.*, stating that "At 2.40 P.M., dotted lines presented no obstacle to attack." These dotted lines delimit one half of the redoubt occupied by the Royal Marines and of the centre zeriba, with exception of the Berks redoubt, which is shown complete—one half of the defences. As the Diary is the only authority for the triple events said to have befallen *circa* 2 P.M., and also for the severation of the half battalion of the Berks, so also is it the only authority for this denudation of the defences. (*Vide* description of Plate.)

In the Diary for the 23rd, we are informed that while the Coldstream and Scots Guards remained at the zeriba, the 15th Sikhs and 17th *Bombay* Native Infantry returned to Suâkin, leaving presumably the 28th Bombay Infantry behind. Notwithstanding this, on the 24th, we find the latter Regiment forming part of the escort sent out from Suâkin to the zeriba. So far as Tofrek is concerned we will close this comedy of errors with the statement made under date March 30th, viz., that the zeriba as altered on that day was intended to hold "15,000 camels! or 600 Cavalry."

This gigantic array of the *Camelus dromedarius* naturally invites further statistical inquiry. We find that, to begin with, there were 339 camels at Suâkin, by means, unnoted, raised by the 5th March to 351; notwithstanding two arrivals on the 6th—by clerical error, evidently—the number is *reduced* to 253, corrected on the 7th-9th to 353. One arrival gives 354 for the 10th-12th; when an increment of 207 gives 561 for the 13th-16th inclusive. 248 arrive with Indian troops on the 17th, raising the number for the 17th and 18th to 809. On the 19th 423 arrivals with the Bombay Staff Corps, gives for the 19th and 20th 1,232 camels, raised on the 21st by more Indian arrivals to 1,443, on the supposition that all were effective, this being the number available for the Transport on the 22nd, arrivals the same day raising it to 1,542. Further Indian arrivals give 2,094 for the 23rd-25th, while an almost daily increment brings the number up on the 31st of March to 3,203 camels. On the first April 300 camels arrive, yet, apparently by a clerical error akin to that of the 6th March, the number from the 1st to the 4th, covering the period of the Tamai advance, stands at 2,460. The arrival of 198 riding-camels on the 5th, left out of account, a correction in the leading numeral gives for the 5th-15th 3,459, which seems an admission of one camel lost in the advance,

---

[1] *Vide* Plate II., p. 63 *antea*.

although Colonel Robertson in his Report (p. 4) states there were three (one killed, two died on road). The latest-arrival noted is 290 camels on the 16th, although from that date to the close of the Diary—a month—the number is placed only at 3,488, instead of 3,749, as would naturally be expected. It will be observed that in the above reckoning no notice is taken of the losses on the 22nd, set down in the Commissariat Report (p. 4) at 723. The Diary, in fact, seems to go on the principle that a camel, like a king, never dies, and, if such indeed be the explanation, save the variation above noted, casualties are left entirely out of account.

Reference to Colonel Robertson's Report, and especially to the Tables given in this Appendix, at pp. 349, 350, make the matter still more inexplicable, the camels found on the spot being *nil*, and the total rising to 8,227; a number still far short of 15,000.

(Extracts.)

Saturday, 7th March.

Major-General Sir John M'Neill, V.C., K.C.B., K.C.M.G., disembarked, and assumed command of the forces and of Suakin.

Sunday, 22nd March.

MOVEMENTS.

A force composed of—

1 Squadron, 5th Lancers	
1 „ 20th Hussars	
1 Section Gardners (4), R.N.	British.
Berkshire Regiment	
Detachment Royal Engineers	
1 Squadron, 9th Bengal Cavalry	
15th Sikhs	
17th Bombay Native Infantry	Indian Contingent.
28th „ „	
Madras Sappers and Miners	

under command of Major-General Sir J. M'Neill, V.C., K.C.B., advanced in a south-westerly direction from Right Water Fort at 7.5 A.M., with orders to march to a point eight miles distant, form a zeriba, and send back the convoy the same day.

The force marched in two squares, 2nd Brigade leading; the Indian Contingent following at interval of half a mile on right rear. At 11.10 a point 6 miles distant was reached, and owing to the lateness of the hour, halted

2 x

and proceeded to form zeriba. (*Vide* sketch.)[1] During the march, the presence of the enemy in the neighbourhood was reported by the Cavalry. At 1.55 the 5th Lancers reported the enemy to be advancing from south-west. At 2 o'clock a party of fifty men were reported advancing on the zeriba from west-south-west, and at 2.10 two of the Cavalry Cossack posts had to retire before the advancing Arabs. At 2.40 the order was given to form up return convoy on south-east side of the zeriba. The position of the troops was as indicated in sketch. The Berkshire and Marines were out cutting wood, having left their arms in their respective zeribas. They were assisted by the Royal Engineers and the Madras Sappers and Miners.

At this moment shouts were heard. The Berkshire came running in from south-west, followed by the 5th Lancers, these by the Arabs. The Berkshire got possession of their arms and broke the enemy's onslaught, who swept round by both flanks. They made no impression on the north and west faces, but broke through the south face, which was held by the 17th Bengal Native Infantry, who turned and fell back into the zeriba in confusion. Many of the Arabs forced their way into the zeriba, driving baggage mules before them. The camels rushed past the sea face of the zeriba into the bush, affording shelter to the advancing Arabs. The attack lasted 20 minutes.

The enemy remained in the bush skirting the clear ground, bodies of them making several determined rushes at the several faces of the square, while others were occupied in maiming the baggage animals and pursuing the followers, who were fleeing towards Suakin. The pursuit was checked by a squadron of 20th Hussars, under Major Greaves, and another of the 9th Bengal Cavalry.

The enemy finally withdrew at 3.30. The troops formed upon various faces of the work, and the zeriba was completed by small working parties, covered by armed parties in advance. The zeriba was completed by sunset. As many stray animals as possible were brought in, and the troops bivouacked under arms.

The enemy was estimated at 2,000, of which 1,000 fell.

Telegraph.

A ground line was laid down by the Royal Engineer Telegraph Section, under Major Turner, and communication was established with Quarantine Island, to which place, when the immediate danger was over, an account of the affair was telegraphed, whereby a panic was avoided. The line remained

---

[1] This is merely a rough outline of the plan given with more detail in Plate II. p. 63.

open until 6.40 P.M., when it was cut, and never again available for use. Captain Cardew's vibrating sounder was the instrument used, and with excellent results.

The casualties were :—

Corps.	Killed.			Names of Officers.	Wounded.			Names of Officers.	Missing.			Names of Officers.
	Officers.	N.-C.O.'s and Men.	Followers.		Officers.	N.-C.O.'s and Men.	Followers.		Officers.	N.-C.O.'s and Men.	Followers.	
;h Lancers	...	1	...		...	...	...		1	4	...	Lieut. Richardson
)th Hussars	...	...	...		...	1	...		...	...	...	
oyal Artillery	...	...	...		1	3	...	Lieut. Benson	...	2	...	
oyal Engineers	2	6	...	{ Capt. Romilly Lieut. Newman	1	3	...	Capt. Wilkinson	...	7	...	
oldstream Guards	...	...	...		1	...	...	Lieut. Charteris	...	...	...	
erkshire Regiment ...	1	16	...	Lieut. Swinton	...	31	...		...	9	...	
oyal Marines	...	7	...		...	16	...		...	1	...	
;th Sikhs	...	9	...		...	11	...		...	...	...	
'th Bombay Native Inf.	1	20	...	Major Von Beverhoudt	2	32	...	{ Lieut. Drury Jemadar Luckman Pandy	...	...	...	
;th Bombay Native Inf.	...	1	...		2	9	...	Lieuts. Edwards and Thompson	...	6	...	
adras Sappers & Miners	...	6	...		1	19	...	Jemadar Venaigmoorthy	...	6	...	
)llowers, etc.	...	...	34		...	...	18		...	...	122	
Total	4	66	34		8	125	18		1	35	122	

MOVEMENTS.

Monday, 23rd March.

A convoy of 1,200 camels escorted by the following force :—

Corps.	Officers.	N.-C.O.'s and Men.	Horses.	Mules.	Followers.
Grenadier Guards ... ... Coldstream ,, ... Scots ,, ... Mounted Infantry ... 9th Bengal Cavalry ... 1 Bearer Company ...	105	2,454	332	85	103

proceeded to M'Neill's zeriba to bring back empty water vessels. The square formation was maintained on the march. The force started from the Right Water Fort at 7.20 and reached the zeriba at 11.30 A.M. The Coldstream and Scots Guards remained at the zeriba, and the 17th Bombay Native Infantry with the 15th Sikhs returned to camp at Suakin. The wounded of the previous day were brought in. No opposition was encountered.

Tuesday, 24th March.

MOVEMENTS.

A convoy of 425 camels, 18 carts, 8,000 gallons of water, with escort as follows :—

Corps.	Officers.	N.-C.O.'s and Men.	Horses.
15th Sikhs ... ... 28th Bombay Native Infantry ... 9th Bengal Cavalry	4	1,424	78

proceeded to M'Neill's zeriba. At a distance of three miles from the zeriba halted, and commenced clearing the bush. The Coldstream Guards and Royal Marine Light Infantry marched from the zeriba to meet them. At about 2 o'clock P.M. the forces met, and the zeriba escort took over the convoy. On their way back, the Guards and Marines were attacked by the enemy in considerable force, and in closing up the square 117 camels were left outside, and either killed or lost.

Casualties.	Officers.	N.-C.O.	Men.	Followers.
Killed	...	...	1	...
Wounded ...	3*	1	19	5

* Captain Dalrymple, Scots Guards ; Lieutenant Maclurcan, Royal Marine Light Infantry ; Lieutenant Marchant, Royal Marine Light Infantry.

The Shropshire Regiment conducted a convoy of unloaded camels to Hasheen, leaving camp immediately after the men's dinners, and returned with stores prior to abandoning the zeriba to-morrow.

Wednesday, 25th March.

MOVEMENTS.

A convoy composed of 500 camels, 7 carts, 3,480 gallons of water proceeded to and returned from M'Neill's zeriba. The enemy was not seen, and the balloon was used for the first time with success.

		Officers.	N.-C.O.'s and Men.	Horses.	Camels.	Mules.	Followers.
Escort	Cavalry Brigade ...	3	85	...	...	...	...
	Guards	28	597	8	139	28	153
	Indian Contingent...	17	1,546	...	...	...	...

The East Surrey and details garrisoning the zeribas (3) near Hasheen returned to camp. The zeribas were dismantled and abandoned.

The Head-Quarter Camp was moved to ground close to and north of Right Water Fort.

Thursday, 26th March.

MOVEMENTS.

A convoy of 580 camels, 480 carrying water (9,000 gallons), escorted by the following force, assembled at the Right Water Fort at 6 o'clock A.M. The Cavalry advanced at 6.25, 20th Hussars in front, 5th Lancers on left flank, and 9th Bengal Cavalry on right flank.

Corps.	Officers.	N.-C.O.'s and Men.	Horses.	Mules.
Cavalry Brigade ...	12	265	277	...
Grenadier Guards ...	27	677	34	...
East Surrey	15	580	7	7
Shropshire	25	502	5	...
Indian Contingent	18	1,556	18	...
Total ...	97	3,580	341	7

The Infantry formed square with a front of two companies, enclosing the convoy, and advanced thus at 7.35, under command of Lieut.-General Sir Gerald Graham, V.C., K.C.B.

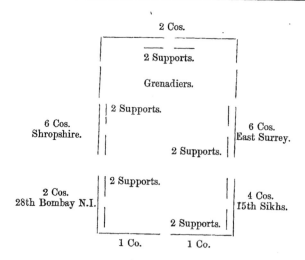

The rate of march was about 1¼ miles an hour. At 8.15 the Cavalry exchanged shots with the enemy. At 9.10 the scrub got thicker on front and flanks, and the enemy was seen swarming in it close by. The Staff got inside the square, which halted to enable the Sappers to cut down scrub inside and to allow right face to clear the bush with volleys. At 9.40 A.M. about 30 Arabs rush on our right front corner, but are shot down. The remainder keep off. 10.50. Two Royal Horse Artillery guns open fire from right rear, sweeping the bush in front, and the square advances slowly. 11.25. The ground becomes more open and the front face of square is increased by one company.

12 noon. Sir J. M'Neill with the Coldstream Guards meet the convoy about 1 mile from the zeriba. The Grenadiers are halted, and the remainder move on and deliver loads without loss.

1.30. The square starts back. The convoy laden with empties, etc., arrives at the Right Water Fort at 6 P.M.

The enemy's loss could not be correctly ascertained, but it is reported to have been large. Our single casualty was a slight spear wound. The heat was great and the dust very trying. Two cases of sunstroke.

Intrenching, Cutting Tools, etc.

100 long-handled (3 ft.) bill-hooks were supplied to battalions to-day, besides the regular number of intrenching tools. It was thought that they would prove invaluable for clearing the bush. The following report, however,

has been made on these tools :—"They are next to useless, defective in following respects—

"1. Weak in the handle, break off near the head.
"2. Metal generally bad, points bend, edges break."

Experience shows that the only useful implements for clearing the mimosa bush in the neighbourhood are—1st, felling axe; 2nd, cross-cut saw; and 3rd, rope to lay bare the roots. The service bill-hook and hand axe are perfectly useless for this work. Wire (14 B. W. G.) most useful for securing butt ends of bushes for forming "zeriba."

Saturday, 28th March.

WEATHER.

Heavy mist cleared by cool north-west breeze at 7.30, followed by dust storm, wind shifting to north-east.

MOVEMENTS.

A convoy composed of—

Camels.	Carts.	Water Supply.
800	33	Gallons. 16,000

and escorted by—

Corps.	Officers.	N.-C.O.'s and Men.	Guns.
Scots Guards ... ... Grenadier Guards ... ... East Surrey Regiment ... ... Shropshire Regiment ... ... 2 guns, Royal Horse Artillery ... 5th Lancers (1 squadron) ... ... 9th Bengal Cavalry (1 squadron) ... 15th Sikhs ... ... 28th Bombay Native Infantry ...	121	4,209	2

started from the Left Water Fort for M'Neill's zeriba at 7.15. It arrived without opposition at 11.20 A.M. After delivering stores and water, the convoy commenced return journey at 1.30 P.M., arriving at 4.30. All empties were brought back.

The Marine Light Infantry returned with the convoy, being relieved by the Grenadiers.

WATER ARRANGEMENTS ON THE MARCH.

To facilitate the distribution of water to the men on the march, each battalion was supplied with eight mules (one per company), carrying two eight-gallon tins and water buckets, besides a water cart. This was found to provide an ample supply of water, and to work very satisfactorily.

Monday, 30th March.

MOVEMENTS.

A convoy, strength and escort as follows, under command of Brigadier-General Hudson, started for M'Neill's zeriba at 6.35 A.M., and returned without loss or opposition by the enemy :—

	Corps.	Officers.	N.-C.O.'s and Men.	Horses.	Guns.
Escort	Royal Horse Artillery ...	1	25	30	2
	Mounted Infantry ...	3	75	78	...
	Guards Brigade	51	1,287	12	...
	Second ,, ...	58	1,456	19	...
	Indian Contingent ...	17	1,581	...	...

	Camels.	Carts.	Water.
Convoy	900	23	Gallons. 18,000

OPERATIONS.

M'Neill's zeriba was altered in form, so as to admit of its being held by a garrison of one regiment only. Water depôt protected by impregnable work, furnishing flank defence to zeriba, which is to hold 15,000 camels or 600 Cavalry.

Wednesday, 1st April.

MOVEMENTS.

The Officer Commanding M'Neill's zeriba reported this morning that " Mounted Infantry report Tamai held by large force and is returning." Orders for an advance on Tamai were in consequence issued. The force as under to start at 3 A.M. The camps were struck at 4 P.M., and the tents put away in accordance with orders.

Thursday, 2nd April.

MOVEMENTS.

Number for Tamai :—

Corps.	Officers.	N.-C.O.'s and Men.	Horses.	Mules.	Camels.	Followers.
Head-Quarter Staff ...	40	50	52	...	...	...
Guards Brigade ...	79	1,945	26	...	...	...
Second ,, ...	66	1,715	23	...	...	...
Royal Engineers ...	5	143	11	...	...	...
Royal Artillery and Royal Horse Artillery	24	324	154	...	...	...
Cavalry Brigade ...	31	743	773	171	1,639	...
Indian Contingent ...	25	1,585	24	...	...	...
Medical Staff Corps...	16	164	22	...	...	...
Balloon Detachment	2	15	10	...	...	...
Commissariat and Transport	16	200	16	...	...	...
Total	304	6,884	1,111	171	1,639	...

The force did not move off until 4.30 A.M., the Guards Brigade and a portion of the Commissariat and Transport having assembled in front of the Right Water Tower instead of the Left as ordered. The night had been dark and cloudy, but cleared up before the appointed time. The force was formed up in one large oblong figure, with a front face of three companies, about 70 yards long and 750 yards deep. The convoy—628 camels, 115 mules, 33 carts, and 22,000 gallons of water—was placed inside. M'Neill's zeriba was reached at 8.25 A.M. (5¾ miles). A halt was made for breakfast. At 10.10 the force again formed up in square with the G Battery B Brigade, Royal Horse Artillery, inside square in rear of the front face. A captive balloon was sent up for observation, but the wind soon sprang up, and after a little while it fell to the ground torn in two parts. The Cavalry was scouting to the front

2 Y

and flanks. After an uneventful march of an hour, following a bearing of 158 degrees, the direction of the march was altered to south-west on Teselah Hill, thereby avoiding the thick bush. Teselah Hill (7 miles) was reached at 4.50 by the square, and the ground was occupied as shown in accompanying sketch.[1] The enemy opened musketry fire at long range at about 12.50 P.M., but was silenced by one round from one of the guns on the hill occupied by the Shropshire, at 1.10. The casualties were—killed, 1 private, East Surrey Regiment; wounded, 2 privates, Berkshire Regiment.

Friday, 3rd April.

MOVEMENTS.

The force was ordered to form up as follows at 7 A.M., to be ready to move off on the arrival of the Cavalry, which had been sent back the previous evening to M'Neill's zeriba for watering purposes:—Two lines of quarter-columns by brigades; 2nd Brigade in front facing south-west; the Guards Brigade in rear. To remain in camp—the East Surrey and Shropshire. The Transport not to be loaded up, but ready packed for an immediate start. At 8.15 A.M. the force moved off thus:—

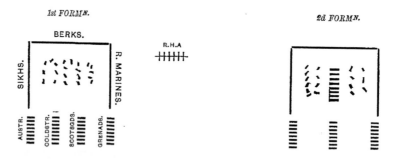

At 8.45 the Mounted Infantry exchanged shots with the enemy's scouts on right front. At 9 o'clock very undulating broken ground was reached. The hollows were occupied by numerous huts which showed signs of recent occupation. These are said to be Tamai. At 9.20 the front face of the square reached the edge of the Khor, the firing in the meantime being kept up between the Mounted Infantry and the enemy's scouts. At 10.10 the front and side faces of the square had advanced across the Khor and occupied the far edge, opening a brisk fire on parties of the enemy. A party of Sappers

[1] The Mounted Infantry were pushed on to the Khor, but the enemy did not permit them to reach it.

proceeded to search for water in the bottom of the Khor on the near side. The wells had been filled up. They did not find any. At 10.30 the Infantry was withdrawn in successive lines, covered by guns in position and Cavalry on flanks. At 11 the Infantry formed up on commanding ridge with Royal Horse Artillery on right flank. The guns opened fire, and the huts were all set fire to. Large quantities of rifle ammunition which was concealed in the huts was destroyed. At 12.30 the force reached the Teselah zeriba. After short rest and " dinners," the force reformed and marched off at 2.20 in square, reaching M‘Neill's zeriba at 5.40 P.M.

The enemy kept concealed, and therefore no correct estimate of his strength could be made, which was supposed to be about 200, with reserves in the hills. His losses are also unknown. Our losses amounted to 1 man killed ; 1 officer, 14 men, and 1 follower wounded.

Saturday, 4th April.

MOVEMENTS.

The force, returning from Tamai, left M‘Neill's zeriba at 9 A.M. under command of Major-General Fremantle, and arrived at Suakin at 12.20. No casualties.

The 28th Bombay Native Infantry and a detachment Royal Navy, with two Gardner guns, were left at the zeriba as a guard.

Monday, 6th April.

MOVEMENTS.

A convoy under Major-General Sir J. M‘Neill composed of—

Corps.	Officers.	N.-C.O.'s and Men.	Horses.	Mules.	Camels.	Followers.
2nd Bn. East Surrey 1st Bn. Shropshire ... 1st Bn. Berkshire ... 15th Sikhs, etc. ...	82	2,545	183	1,269	2,165	1,665

proceeded to M‘Neill's zeriba at 5.30 A.M. to carry away all stores, etc., previous to its evacuation, and arrived at 8.30 A.M. Owing to systematic arrangements the work was promptly and thoroughly effected. Nothing was left on the ground. The force started on return journey at 1 o'clock, arriving at the Right Water Fort at 4.30.

The escort was too small to form a continuous square round the convoy. On going out, half company intervals were adopted with connecting files. On returning, full company intervals with two connecting files and sharpshooters on the flanks. This eased the march of the convoy very considerably. The fast going animals, etc., moving with the head of the square, the slower ones being brought up by the rear face as a rear guard. Sir George Greaves accompanied this convoy and introduced the above modified order of march.

Friday, 1st May.

RECONNAISSANCES.

A force consisting of—

Corps.	Officers.	N.-C.O.'s and Men.	Horses.
Mounted Infantry ...	10	94	104
9th Bengal Cavalry ...	1	73	74
Total ...	11	167	178

reconnoitred towards Tamai. The M'Neill zeriba was burnt. No traces of the enemy having been there recently were discovered.

APPENDIX IV.

EXTRACTS FROM

REPORT BY THE SENIOR COMMISSARIAT OFFICER, SUAKIN EXPEDITIONARY FORCE 1885.[1]

1. COMMISSARIAT ARRANGEMENTS in connection with GENERAL M'NEILL'S ZERIBA.

On the 21st March orders were issued to prepare for an advance towards Tamai on the following day. Again [2] an all-night working was necessary.

On the morning of the 22nd, the Infantry Brigade, with some Cavalry and Artillery under the command of Major-General Sir John M'Neill, marched to a spot, afterwards known as Tofrik, with a convoy of 1,080 camels carrying water and supplies. An action, the most decisive of the campaign, resulting in a crushing defeat of the enemy, took place after the convoy had formed up to return to Suakin. All the supplies and water had already been secured, but the transport suffered very severely, many men and 723 camels having been killed.

On the 23rd 40,000 rations and 3,000 gallons of water were successfully thrown into the zeriba at Tofrik.

On the 24th a convoy of 225 camels was sent to Tofrik with forage and tanks for the storage of water. It reached half way in safety, and was taken over by an escort from Tofrik, under command of Colonel Lambton, Coldstream Guards. The escort was attacked, and 117 camels with their loads were lost.

On the same day 70 camels were sent to Hasheen for water tins, and on the following day that post was abandoned.

---

[1] London : Printed for Her Majesty's Stationery Office, by Harrison and Sons, Printers in Ordinary to Her Majesty.

[2] The reference here is to a previous statement as to the arrangements for 20th March :—
" The Commissariat and Transport arrangements were efficiently carried out. They involved much labour, particularly the filling and loading on camels of the water tins, which occupied the whole night."—(*Report*, p. 3.

On the 25th and 26th large convoys of supplies went to Tofrik Zeriba.

On the 28th about 1,000 camels and 29 water carts went there also carrying supplies, forage, and 7,500 gallons of water.

On the 29th another convoy went to Tofrik, carrying 19,500 gallons of water, and four days' supply for the full force intended to advance on Tamai, consisting of—

> 650 camels, and 32 carts with water.
> 450 camels with supplies.

This completed provisions and water for 7 days.

On the 2nd April the advance on Tamai took place. The Commissariat and Transport Corps carried supplies and water for two days, and the force was thus rendered, to that extent, independent of the seven days' reserve already stored at Tofrik.

The troops marched at daybreak on Thursday, and returned to Suakin on the Saturday evening following, the camels having been without water from Wednesday evening until Saturday evening.

The following are the transport beasts that went out and returned :—

	Horses.	Mules.	Camels.
Went out	65	171	1,639
Returned	65	168	1,636
Killed in Action ...	...	1	1
Died on the road ...	...	2	2

This result is satisfactory evidence of the efficiency of the Transport.

The troops and Medical Services were well supplied, ample water was carried, and there was no complaint or failure of any kind.

On the 6th April Tofrik was abandoned, and the stores and supplies were withdrawn by about 2,000 camels, 500 mules, and 25 horse carts.—(*Report*, p. 4.)

2. THE LABOUR QUESTION.

In all active service an ample supply of labour is necessary, not only at the base, but at all depôts along the Line of Communications.

The Commissary-General had foreseen this, and, at his instance, a corps of 500 labourers, entirely for Commissariat purposes, was sanctioned to be raised in India. Unfortunately, through some misapprehension, these men were engaged not for Commissariat services, but to work on the Suakin and Berber Railway, and thus the foresight of the Commissary-General was of no avail, owing to the mistakes of others. The labour at Suakin was very heavy. The wharves had to be cleared of vast and ever-recurring accumulations of stores and supplies, which could be discharged from ships with much greater rapidity than they could be afterwards removed. Then these stores had to be piled on Quarantine Island, and afterwards loaded up on camels. At H Redoubt these camels had to be unloaded, and the stores rearranged. And with every convoy another laying out of loads and loading up of camels was involved. As the convoys had to start at daybreak, the loading had to be done in the night. The water convoys also involved much labour, cleaning the tins, filling them with water, screwing the stoppers, laying them out at the proper distances of camel loads, and the loading. This also had to be done almost entirely at night.

At first an immense amount of work at the wharves was done by fatigue parties of British troops, but this had soon to be stopped, as the weather became too hot for Europeans to work.

Local labour was largely availed of. This was obtained through an influential friendly Sheikh, who found men at 2s. each per diem. But there was much trouble with them, and frequent strikes took place.

On the 22nd March about 300 Bhistis arrived from India in the "Rosina," and on the 28th March 200 Kahars arrived in the "Kildare." These men, the former on water-filling duties and the latter (when not required as dhooli bearers) as labourers, were utilized to the fullest extent. Large fatigue parties were also obtained from the Indian Contingent.

But, as the advance with the railway progressed, the labour question became more serious, and Cairo was communicated with by telegraph, to arrange for Egyptian labourers.

A contract was made at Cairo, with a Mr. Hassan Rifky, to furnish Egyptian labourers, at the rate of 2s. 5d. per man per diem, with free rations.

This turned out a failure.

The first detachment of the men arrived on the 20th April in the "Geelong." Within eight days the balance arrived as under:—

Per "John Redhead"	...	...	36
"Australia"	...	...	48
"Imoin"	...	...	17
"Deccan"	...	...	70

By the 9th May these men were found so useless, even though they had been stimulated (their privilege as Egyptian citizens), by corporal punishment, administered by the Egyptian authorities at Suakin, that I recommended the General Officer Commanding to cancel the contract, and passage was provided for them, on the 15th May, to Egypt in the "John Redhead."

By this date the operations were over, and the troops were embarking every day, so that the labour question was practically at an end.

These Egyptians had been engaged for the base only ; but I would strongly recommend that all future arrangements for Corps of Labourers should be irrespective of place and for general service.—(*Report*, pp. 6, 7.)

3. EXTRACTS bearing on the INDIAN TRANSPORT.

Four companies of the Commissariat and Transport Corps were sent out from England as a nucleus for expansion.

Camels were ordered to be purchased and forwarded to Suakin with the utmost possible despatch. Mules were ordered from Gibraltar, Malta, and Cyprus.

Drivers were also procured from the same sources as the beasts.

It was understood at first that the organization of the whole transport was to be by expansion of the companies of the Commissariat and Transport Corps, and this principle was acted upon till the 20th March, when it was intimated that the Camel Transport from India would be organized there, and would land at Suakin in an efficient condition.

Before this was known, the first instalments of the transports from India were detailed in expansion of the companies, but, with those exceptions, the Indian Transport was kept separate.

The whole transport was under my charge as Senior Commissariat Officer, and the Director of Transport, immediately responsible to me, and through whom all orders and instructions were issued, was Lieut.-Colonel Walton, Assistant Commissary-General. The Indian Transport was under the immediate charge of Lieut.-Colonel Beckett, Bengal Staff Corps, but he was entirely under my orders, which he received through Lieut.-Colonel Walton. Thus the whole of the transport was under the control of the Senior Commissariat Officer.—(*Report*, p. 9.)

Having heard it openly stated that the Transport Department from India did most of the carriage that had to be done, I would here, in justice to the Officers and men of the Commissariat and Transport Corps, point out the incorrectness of that statement. I do so without desiring for a moment to discredit the Indian Transport.

Its work was done thoroughly and well, and it did its proper share of the work, but no more.

I have in my reports to the Chief of the Staff, dated 11th May 1885, fully acknowledged the valuable services of the Indian Transport.

The greatest strain on the Transport was between the 6th and 22nd of March.

Camels were then arriving and had to be organized and detailed for immediate work.

Up to the 21st March, inclusive, 1,550 camels of the Indian Transport, with five Officers, were at work, while the animals up to the same date, working with the Commissariat and Transport Corps, and not obtained from India, were 2,493 camels, 66 draught horses, and 678 mules.

Lieut.-Colonel Beckett, the Director of the Indian Transport, only arrived on the 23rd March, after the Hasheen expedition, and the day after the battle of Tofrik (McNeill's Zeriba).

I enclose a statement showing the dates of arrival of the transport.— (*Report*, p. 10.)

STATEMENT SHOWING ARRIVALS OF INDIAN TRANSPORT.

Date.	From whence received.		Horses.	Mules.	Camels.	Donkeys.	Remarks.
1885.							
March 13th	From India		...	...	327	...	*Ex* " Winchester."
,, 16th	,,	,,	...	...	207	...	,, " Nyanza."
,, ,,	,,	,,	...	...	346	...	,, " Clan St. Clare."
,, 17th	,,	,,	..	...	247	...	,, " Colaba."
,, 19th	,,	,,	...	...	423	...	,, " Sirdhana."
,, 20th	,,	,,	...	...	320	...	,, " Nows hera."
,, 23rd	,,	,,	...	...	252	...	,, " Roma."
,, ,,	,,	,,	...	...	194	} ...	,, " Chupra."
,, 24th	,,	,,	...	...	144		
,, 28th	,,	,,	...	...	380	...	,, " Nuddea."
,, ,,	,,	,,	...	...	244	...	,, " Elliott."
,, ,,	,,	,,	...	...	377	...	,, " County Kinross."
,, 31st	,,	,,	...	...	238	...	,, " Kangra."
April 1st .	,,	,,	...	...	370	...	,, " Clan McKay."
,, 7th .	,,	,,	1	...	197	...	,, " Bhandana."
	Total .		1	...	4,266	...	

(*Report*, p. 25.)

[COMPARATIVE TABLE OF TRANSPORT.]

From whence received.	Horses.	Mules.	Camels.	Donkeys.
Found on spot	58	114	...	...
Aden	...	...	697	...
Berbera	...	...	1,000	...
Cyprus	25	299	...	...
Malta	...	65	...	...
Gibraltar	...	100	...	...
Suez	39	476	2,264	155
India	1	...	4,266*	...
Total	123	1,054	8,227	155

* Of these 487 were riding camels and were handed over for a Riding Camel Corps apart from transport purposes.

(*Report*, p. 25.)

(*Extract.*)

REPORT OF LIEUTENANT-COLONEL PARKYN, A.C.G., COMMANDING COMPANIES, COMMISSARIAT AND TRANSPORT CORPS.

Camels.

The camels were obtained from India, Lower Egypt, Aden, and Berbera. Those from India came in charge of the Indio-British Transport Contingent, and were in all respects the best; those from Lower Egypt were, I believe, obtained there through the Commissariat, were heavy, strong, good weight carriers, but slow; the Aden and Berbera were of a much lighter breed, the former the better of the two, both fast, but not up to much weight.

(*Report*, p. 38.)

4. PERSONNEL.

The personnel consisted of :—

      Commissariat and Transport Corps.

      European Muleteers, from Gibraltar, Malta, and Cyprus.

      Egyptians.

      Aden men.

      Men from India attached to the Transport raised there.

The Commissariat and Transport Corps were employed chiefly in the expansion of the companies, and considering the circumstances, viz., want of knowledge of the dialects of the camel men, and the habits and management of camels, they worked well.

They evinced a disposition to learn, and soon became acquainted with the manner of loading camels, &c., &c.

The Spanish muleteers from Gibraltar were good. The Maltese were bad, arrant cowards; and the Officer of the Royal Malta Fencible Artillery, who came with them, had little or no control over them.

The Cyprus men, mostly Greeks, worked well.

The Aden men were good hard-working fellows, and, when properly understood, are manageable.

The Indian Transport having been organized in India, and its Officers, Warrant Officers, &c., being acquainted with the language and customs of the men, had that superiority which all organized bodies possess over what might be termed "Scratch" arrangements. They did excellent work, and, had the main body arrived earlier in the campaign, would have been kept entirely separate from the Companies, Commissariat and Transport Corps.

The roughest work was at the commencement, when the camels from Egypt, Aden and Berbera had to be marked and classified, and hired drivers collected and detailed to look after them. But all worked well and did their best.

(*Report*, pp. 10, 11.)

(*Extract.*)

REPORT OF LIEUTENANT-COLONEL PARKYN, A.C.G., COMMANDING COMPANIES, COMMISSARIAT AND TRANSPORT CORPS.

The Maltese proved a worthless lot, utter cowards, refusing to go to the front, stating they had engaged to work at the base only, and persuasion of any sort was thrown away upon them. I should never recommend their being engaged on future occasions, as the advantage gained by their knowledge of mules is lost by their uselessness. These men came under charge of a Lieutenant Vella and two serjeants of the Royal Malta Fencibles, all of whom knew nothing of mules, and had not the least control or influence over the men. With the last batch of men from Gibraltar came a foreman named "Ryan," a most excellent and useful man, thoroughly acquainted with both the management of the animals and his men, both of which consequently were well looked after. He was attached to the Small-Arm Ammunition Column, Royal Artillery.

The Cyprus men were composed chiefly of Greeks, who worked well, although at times inclined to be insubordinate. This was, however, soon obviated ; they had also an excellent hard-working foreman, called Ceklein, a German by birth.

The Aden and Somali "boys" had a good many very old cripples and mere lads amongst them, and were a little difficult to manage at first, but after a time this was got over, and they did well when understood, tact and management being required.—(*Report,* pp. 39, 40.)

5. ORGANISATION and WORKING.

As regards general transport work it is, I think beyond doubt that, when possible, the various kinds of transport should be kept distinct, and as little mixed up as possible, and that with Eastern races, only one race, sect, or caste, should be in one section.

When the square formation is necessary, the camels should be first formed up, and the square formed round them. At the beginning of the campaign, although most of the camels then available had but little training, the opposite plan was adopted.

The camel should never be hurried or hustled, and the pace of the column always regulated by that of the slowest camel.

Too much should not be expected of the drivers on the march. A man in charge of two camels has quite sufficient to do to look after his beasts, and when loads fall off they should be picked up and loaded by the troops. Captain Francis, D.A.C.G., Indian Transport says :—"If loads fall off, the Transport Officer, his Serjeant and drivers have to put them up again, while as often as not the whole rear face of a square stands looking on."

Diversity of opinion exists as to the usefulness of transport soldiers in the expansion of auxiliary transport.

Personally, I consider that if it were possible to give them some instruction at home in camel loading and equipment, even if a "dummy" camel had to be used, they would be of service. Of course ignorance of language is always a drawback, but men soon pick up a few necessary phrases, and sufficient interpreters should be provided. Instruction in loading should be given generally throughout the service. The want of this knowledge was much felt at Suakin. In the Afghan war loading was taught to all the regiments at Cabul and Candahar.

I enclose extracts from a report of Lieut.-Colonel Walton, Assistant Commissary-General, who was Director of Transport with the expedition.

I would suggest that he be selected to compile regulations for auxiliary transport.

I would specially invite attention to the following points in Lieut.-Colonel Walton's report :—

1. The importance of having a company of the Commissariat and Transport Corps sent from England to act as a Depôt at the Base.

2. When a campaign is conducted in a climate adapted to Eastern races, that auxiliary transport should always be provided from India fully organized.

(*Report*, p. 12.)

(*Extracts*.)

REPORT OF LIEUT.-COLONEL WALTON, A.C.G., DIRECTOR OF TRANSPORT.

IV.—ORGANIZATION.

There is one misconception into which it is very possible for any General to fall, upon finding himself landed with a fully complete transport organization on paper. There would be a natural inclination to be in a hurry to move, and to forget that, although the whole of the troops may have arrived at the seat of war, their primary (and, for the time, most important) duty is the protection of the landing of the stores, and of the organization of transport. No time is saved by this oversight; on the contrary, operations undertaken from hand to mouth, before plenty of transport has arrived and has been properly organized, are bound to fail (and possibly disastrously) should they meet with an early check, or should an unexpected loss of transport occur. There is no necessity for dilatory wasting of time; indeed, a good Director of Transport will probably organize almost as fast as his transport comes under his hand; but an unreasonable hurrying of transport into the field without organization and without adequate reserve, may not only prove immediately detrimental, but might hamper a General up to the very end of the campaign.—(*Report*, p. 34.)

*　　　　*　　　　*　　　　*　　　　*

IV*b*.—NECESSITY FOR SUFFICIENT SPACE AND FOR PROTECTION.

One essential accessary to a rapid organization is sufficient space, and, of course, under proper protection; and this should be considered in planning the first encampment of the troops. The absence of such consideration on this occasion cruelly hampered the transport. There were some 10,000 troops covering Suakin in front, the sea on the rear, and ships of war on the flanks, and there was ample space between the walls and the troops for a vast body of transport, while the concensus of military opinion as to the facility of so encamping the troops as to ensure perfect safety for this space was over-whelming. Nevertheless, the Board of Officers which (as I understood) had laid out the camp prior to the arrival of the Head-Quarter Staff, had so planned it as to afford no safety to the parking of transport; it was feared to bring an animal outside the town; and the multifold operations of reception and organization and equipment of such an army in itself as 7,000 men and 10,000 animals had to be carried on in a confined, undrainable, and filthy space within the walls, and whose only egress and ingress to water, to supplies and forage, to draw equipment, or to duty, was by two narrow gates, where only one animal could pass at a time, and that only when the gates were clear of other traffic. A simple arithmetical calculation of the time necessary for passage at camel pace will at once show how serious an obstacle was thus raised by so unaccountable an oversight in planning an encampment for a rendezvous in the presence of an enemy.—(*Report*, p. 35.)

USE OF WHEELED VEHICLES.

I would strongly recommend the dispatch of plenty of wheeled vehicles with mules or horses—and harness complete—to any seat of war for the first landing operations, no matter what kind of transport may be eventually necessitated by the nature of the country. Wheeled transport is so much more rapid in loading and unloading and in movement than any pack trans-port, and rapidity of clearance of the landing places, and of even the first mile or half-mile may very materially influence the result of a campaign. It would be seldom that a landing would be undertaken upon so precipitous a coast that wheeled transport could not be also largely utilized for several miles inland. At Suakin such transport might have been utilized, so far as safety could be ensured, for return of the animals (to water), within 12 or 16 hours.

*   *   *   * (Report, p. 36.)

6. WATER TRANSPORT.

A principal peculiarity of the Eastern Soudan campaign was the necessity for water-transport, *i.e.*, the conveyance of water for use of the troops by means of transport.

As this may be regarded as the crowning success of the transport in this campaign, it may be worth while to briefly describe the simple but complete system by which a constant readiness and an extreme promptitude were secured.

The water (which in this instance was condensed on board ship and run off ashore by hose) was run into large iron tanks, themselves rigged with moveable emptying pumps. Application was made to the Royal Engineer to lay common wooden troughing from these tanks along an open and convenient space. The troughs were fitted with cocks at intervals of every four or five feet.

The transport vessels (galvanised iron "tins," or camel-tanks and wooden kegs) were always stacked, on coming in, at a very short distance from the troughs.

A large, perfectly free space was selected for loading up, at such a distance from the troughs as in nowise to interfere with the work of filling.

The fatigue party (reliefs of 100 were found sufficient generally) was divided into four portions—one (a small section) to pump from the tanks into the troughs; one to convey empties from the stack to the troughs, and to convey full vessels thence to the vehicles (carts or trucks) held in readiness to carry the vessels to the loading-up ground; one (a small one) to run off the water from the trough-cocks into the vessels; and one to receive the vessels at the loading-up ground, off load them from the trucks, and lay them out in readiness for loading up. This last party has the hardest work.

Every vessel was made to pass to the trucks by one lane, where non-commissioned officers were placed, furnished with keys, to inspect each one to see that there was no leakage, and to tighten the bung-screw with the key.

The laying out at the loading-up place was conducted by carefully placing vessels of *equal weights* in long ranks at intervals, so as to allow of a camel coming in and lying down betwixt each two vessels or sets of vessels (one on either side of him), space being left between the ranks for the camel's length, and for the drivers to bivouac in rear of their camels. The camels were not marched to the spot until all was ready, and usually just before sunset. Responsible Officers and Warrant Officers were charged with the direction of each several operation.

This laying out of loads in anticipation of convoys might be extended with the greatest advantage to commissariat supplies and other stores.

At the arrival end a Transport Officer was held ready to receive the convoy, to see that the vessels were emptied in due time into the storage-vessels, and to ensure the timely return of the vessels for fresh convoys.

As it is seldom possible for the vessels to be emptied in time to return immediately by the same convoy, sufficient stock is needed to enable their detention for two or three days to be reckoned upon.

The vessels were galvanised "iron tins"—(the use of the word "tank" was found to be confusing)—of 12½, 10, and 8 gallons, besides kegs or barrels of various capacities. The "tins" were found infinitely preferable to the kegs. The latter did not keep the water sweet for nearly as long, and in the cases of some woods imparted a bad colour and smell to the water almost immediately. They are also not adapted for use in a hot country, because they cannot lie empty without detriment.

The use of several capacities was found to be confusing and troublesome. The vessels should be all of one capacity. For a camel-load or for loading in carts 15-gallon tins may be recommended as the most serviceable size, being equivalent to about 150 lb. of water, and 25 lb. or 30 lb. for the vessel, thus making in all for a camel-load about 360 lb., leaving a margin of about 40 lb. for forage, saddle, and driver's kit. The vessels should be so made that they may pack well in a forage cart, and should be rather long than broad, so as to occupy less side room in a camel-convoy. The edges should, if possible, be rounded off so as not to cut the loading-nets or ropes. It is not worth while to consider the weights adapted for pack-mules, as camels alone could be used in a waterless country. Pair-horse carts could be utilised for short convoys on flat ground, because it would repay to carry water for the horses as part of the loads.

The "tins" supplied from England were good, but those purchased by the Ordnance Store Department in Cairo were useless, being leaky, with badly-fitting bung-screws, with keys that did not fit, and many being also foul with some pitchy substance inside.

The country "mussocks," or goat skins, purchased by the Ordnance Store Department at Suakin were also found for the most part useless, and could not have been tested prior to purchase. Mussocks were also found to be unremunerative for carriage, because of the evaporation.

The galvanised rubber mussocks sent from England, although good, are not to be recommended. They also are liable to evaporation, and they are too tender for the somewhat rough usage to which they are necessarily exposed in a campaign in fitting, screwing, roping, and carriage.—(*Report*, pp. 36, 37.)

(*Extracts.*)

REPORT ON WATER DUTIES BY CAPTAIN DE COSSON, ACTING
DEPUTY-ASSISTANT COMMISSARY-GENERAL.

My orders were to "superintend the supply transport and distribution of water to troops in the field," and I accordingly established a depôt at No. 5 Pier, where the water was pumped from the condensing ships into iron reservoirs, in front of which wooden troughs were erected fitted with six taps each, so that a large number of vessels could be filled at the same time, a continuous supply of water being furnished to the troughs by tripod pumps fixed on the reservoirs. These appliances answered admirably, and it was found that a fatigue party of 100 men could fill camel tins to carry 16,000 gallons of water in about eight hours.

The camel tins, when filled, were placed in rows on an adjacent piece of ground, each row consisting of 100 tins arranged in groups of two at intervals of 8 feet apart, so that the camels could be made to kneel down between them at sunset, and the tins at once lifted into the "suleetahs," when the order to load was given in the early morning. By following this method 500 camels, picqueted in 10 rows of 50, and carrying 12,500 gallons, could be loaded simultaneously and marched off in column without delay or confusion.

The system of working the supply was as follows :—

The number of troops proceeding to the front, and the amount of water they were to be provided with, having been ascertained, a proportional number of water tins were filled. The camels were furnished to me at sunset each day in as nearly as possible entire sections from the different transport companies, with their own officers, non-commissioned officers, and drivers complete. The camels were then picqueted between their loads ready to start at the first streak of dawn. The convoy was always accompanied by myself or one of my Officers in administrative charge of it, the duty of this Officer being to keep the water convoy together and close to the front, to superintend the stacking, guarding, storage, and issue of water to troops in the field, and to send back all empty tins by the first return convoy to the depôt, where the work of filling and laying out the vessels continued without intermission, a reserve of 6,000 gallons being always kept on hand for any emergency. If a very heavy demand was made on the water supply at short notice, the work was continued during the night by means of the electric light, and it was found advantageous to keep a special corps [1] of men for fatigue duty on the water, as to fill tins rapidly without waste, screw them up securely and lay them out at proper intervals for camel loads, requires a certain amount of practice.

The organization, though frequently strained by large demands at short notice, and changes in the movements of troops, was thoroughly successful in its working, and in no case did the supply of water ever break down.

This was mainly due to the great support and help I received from the Senior Commissariat Officer and the Director of Transports, and the zeal and

---

[1] Bhisti Corps.

3 A

energy of the Officers detailed to assist me, who never flagged in their endeavours to forward the work, which at times was exceedingly heavy, as it had to
be carried on both by night and by day, and they were frequently compelled
to be for many hours together under the full heat of the sun.

I will now briefly submit a few observations, the result of my experience
on this duty :—

I.—VESSELS.

The 12½-gallon iron "camel tin" of English manufacture appears to be the
best for ordinary purposes of transport, and I would strongly recommend that
in future these water tins should be all of the same capacity, as the three sizes
in which they are now made—8, 10, and 12½ gallons—lead to confusion and
loss of carrying power. It was originally intended that the strongest camels
should carry four 12½-gallon tins; those of medium strength, four 10-gallon
tins; and the weakest, four 8-gallon tins;[1] but I found practically that it was
unsafe to load a Berbera camel with even as much as four 8-gallon tins on a
long march, and that the system of trying to proportion the loads to the wants
of each individual camel was productive of great delay, when the loading had
to be got through rapidly and in semi-darkness ; moreover, it made it practically impossible to lay out the loads beforehand, as it does not answer to
separate camels from their companions or sections in order to classify them as
strong, medium, and weakly. I would, therefore, suggest that for water convoys, which must necessarily keep well to the front, the heaviest load the
weakest camel can carry should be the average taken for the whole.

Two 12½-gallon tins when full weigh about 316½ lbs., to which must be
added the weight of the camel saddle and the forage, which, in a water convoy, each camel should carry for its own consumption, as, if placed over the
tins, it keeps them cool and renders each camel of the convoy self-supporting
on the march. I am of opinion that if the capacity of the camel tins were
increased to 15 gallons each, two of them would make a fair load for an ordinary camel, and they would still be not too heavy for a couple of men to lift.

I found that two 15-gallon barrels made a fair load, but in the Soudan
barrels are so apt to shrink the moment they are empty that they are practically useless as a means of water transport, besides which it was found that
when made of new wood they gave a very unpleasant taste to the water, and
the tan in the wood combining with the rust from the iron reservoirs often
turned it to the colour of ink.

[1] Board on Water Transport, Supply, and Storage, Cairo, 24. 4. 84.

The indiarubber bags supplied for this expedition were the cause of great complaints, owing to the strong taste of indiarubber which they imparted to the water. They also proved to be scarcely strong enough for the rough usage they got on the march, as the pressure of the ropes and the jolting of the camels often caused them to give way at the seams, besides which it was found very difficult to get natives to fill and lace them up properly.

Skin mussocks were also tried, but they gave so strong a taste to the water, that they had to be discontinued.

Eight-gallon tins on mules answered fairly well, but of course they are not an economical means of carrying water on a long march, as the mules themselves require at least two gallons of water per day each.

The last, and, in my opinion, the best means of transport for water in a country like the Eastern Soudan, where the plains as a rule are hard and level, is the ordinary regimental water-cart, holding 108 gallons, and drawn by two mules. I noticed some of these carts belonging to regiments on the marches to Hasheen, Sir J. M'Neill's Zeriba, Tamai, Handoub, &c., and in every case they appeared to answer admirably. It will be seen that 100 of these carts would carry 10,800 gallons for the troops, and two days' supply for the mules; they would keep the water in better condition than the small camel tins, which soon get heated right through, and they would afford every facility for the distribution of water without waste or loss of time, as they could quickly be removed to any point where they were required; the escort necessary to protect them would be much smaller than that required for a camel convoy, as in cases of danger the carts could be formed into a laager offering easy means of defence, while the pace at which they would march would be nearly double that of a camel. They would only require 100 drivers, who might be armed, instead of the 200 helpless natives who, with a percentage of Officers and non-commissioned officers, would be necessary for a convoy of 400 camels, carrying 10,000 gallons of water. It is true that a few carts would have to accompany the mules with compressed forage, but a convoy of 400 camels would require to be provided with at least 40 spare animals, and would take up a much larger space inside a square, besides constantly delaying the march to rectify the shifting of loads, which, when camels are crowded together, can never be entirely avoided, even with the greatest care.

For these reasons I would strongly urge that in any future operations in the Soudan, a train of 100 water carts should be provided to accompany the Field Force on rapid marches, and I would suggest that the carts should be of a pattern where the centre of gravity is sufficiently low, and that the upper portion of the water barrel should be covered with thick felt to protect it from the action of the sun.

II.—Storage.

The waterproof stuff storage tanks provided for the expedition proved very valuable, both from their lightness when empty, and the facility with which they could be erected at each zeriba. There was of course a slight loss of water by filtration, but this was of very little consequence in proportion to the advantages they afforded in enabling the camel tins to be emptied and returned at once, and as a rule the water remained remarkably sweet in them.

The 400-gallon iron storage tanks proved, of course, the most useful reservoirs for permanent purposes, but they have one great defect, viz., the difficulty there is in cleaning them thoroughly. I would submit that this might be obviated if they were all fitted with a large vent hole at the bottom, closed by a screw plug, so that they could be thoroughly washed out when necessary.

(Report, pp. 41-43.)

APPENDIX V.

BRITISH GENERALS, AND WAR CORRESPONDENTS AS UMPIRES-IN-CHIEF.

DURING the past month it has been known in certain quarters that several British Generals, as experienced as they are distinguished, have quite made up their minds that they will never accept the command of a body of troops in warlike operations while their military reputation is to be placed at the mercy of war correspondents who may think fit to cast strictures upon their actions against the enemy.

In having come to this decision, these British Generals have shown sound judgment, and have arrived at a wise conclusion in reference to the probable result by which their whole life may be wrecked through the assumption of improper positions by inexperienced persons. These British Generals will in future decline to accept any position of responsibility in the face of this country's enemies, unless the authorities are able to make arrangements which will prevent war correspondents from taking upon themselves the position of umpires, either when present with our troops in the field or as soon as they arrive at home after the operations are over. The Generals have made the sarcastic observation that the reputation which they have so far gained by hard service is safe, and that, if the assumption of an improper function by quasi-military umpires is allowed to continue, it would be as well to give these men the charge of warlike movements against the enemy whenever they become necessary, instead of to experienced British Officers. They assert that at no time will they object to allow their actions in the field to become the cause of proper investigation by the superior military authorities, whenever such investigation is considered necessary. They declare they WILL NOT allow their military acts to be either considered or censured by a tribunal of war correspondents.

The pass to which matters have arrived concerning war correspondents' strictures upon the acts of Officers in the field is highly detrimental to the interests of the country. No commanding or other Officer's reputation is safe from the pen of these war correspondents, as soon as these men arrive at home and military operations are over for the time being. Our Generals are liable to be stabbed in the back directly any one or more of these war correspondents reach this country, and are safe from the effects of a most dangerous and misleading assumption of a position it was never intended they should occupy with our armies. The improper functions these correspondents take upon themselves are most unfortunately supported by a few men of weak judgment in the House of Commons, whether "put up" or not it is difficult to say. These weak-minded members rise in their places and ask all sorts of questions tending to destroy alike the reputations of British Generals and the confidence of our soldiers in the ability of their Commanders.

On the 8th ultimo two distinct questions were asked of the Secretary of State for War in the House of Commons. Here they are, and the answers given to them :—

"Mr. Gourley asked the Secretary of State for War when and what inquiry he intended instituting with regard to the loss of life caused by the surprise on the occasion of the attack on General M'Neill's zeriba, in the neighbourhood of Suakim ?"

"Sir G. Campbell asked the Secretary of State for War whether the promised inquiry into the conduct of operations in the Soudan by Generals Graham and M'Neill, and especially into the circumstances of the surprise of the 22nd of March, had been carried out and with what result ?"

The Marquis of Hartington. "As Lord Wolseley was about to proceed to Suakim, he was instructed to make personal inquiries on the spot, and to give his opinion upon the events referred to. In a despatch, in which he acknowledged the receipt of these instructions, Lord Wolseley strongly deprecated any further inquiry. I may perhaps be allowed to read a short extract from the despatch :—'But, at the same time, I would point out that I myself strongly deprecate (save in the most extreme cases) inquiring too rigorously into the conduct of Commanders after unsatisfactory engagements. It is hopeless to expect to find a General who does not make mistakes. The history of war shows that the greatest Generals have done so often. There may be cases in which these mistakes are of such a character as to call for the immediate removal of their author from his command. But, short of this, to examine minutely into any faulty dispositions that may have been made, and to publish to the world a condemnation of them, simply takes away from the General implicated all the confidence of his troops, without, as far as I can see, any compensating good result whatever.' Up to the present time Lord Wolseley has not sent any further report on this subject. Under these circumstances, H.R.H. the Field Marshal Commanding-in-Chief is of the opinion, in which I concur, that it would be advisable to await Lord Wolseley's return from Egypt before coming to any final decision on the whole question. This delay can have no unfavourable effect on the public service, as the Expeditionary Force is now to be broken up, and the Officers concerned are returning to this country."

It is very satisfactory to note the view General Lord Wolseley has taken, evidently upon the whole subject of destroying a General's reputation at one blow, because he happens to conduct an operation that does not turn out successful. Lord Wolseley feels a keen sense of his own position in reference to the matter. He has well read military history, and knows that such great Generals as Napoleon, Frederick the Great, Marlborough, Wellington, and others made mistakes—mistakes which, in comparison with those dealt with recently by war correspondents in the Soudan, entailed consequences of the gravest character to their soldiers and to their country. Lord Wolseley might have quoted the great Turenne's celebrated words, " The man who has not made mistakes in war has seldom made war."

War is a terrible game of chance, which the newspaper correspondent seems not to possess the faculty of perceiving or understanding. The soundest judgment, the best combinations, may fail at any moment through circumstances which are impossible for a General to foresee. Commanders of all ages have known this well; and it is not for a war correspondent to constitute himself the judge of a General's combinations, since he knows not the extent of his difficulties. In arriving at the view Lord Wolseley has expressed, he doubtless was guided by a consideration of the idea that it might be his turn to be attacked next, by any war correspondent who took upon himself to judge of his lordship's military capacity, and of movements which did not end so successfully as intended, and that his whole life's reputation would be swept away by a few scathing words written by some angry or indiscreet correspondent, *as soon as this man was safe at home* from the result of that which he dared not do when under military supervision. One portion of the question is—are these attacks upon the acts of British Generals in the field fair ? They are not. They are absolutely unfair. They are like shooting at men from a safe position, and one from which the persons who aim the shots cannot themselves be harmed. These shots are dastardly. Indictments of British Generals are not the acts for which war correspondents are granted permission to accompany armies in the field, and they would not dare to repeat them with Continental armies engaged in warlike operations. If they did, the newspaper they were engaged for would never again be allowed the presence of a representative.

The Press can exert itself for good or evil. At present the effects of recent strictures of British war correspondents are shaking the faith of able British Generals in any position of command in the field, as placing their reputations at the mercy of newspaper correspondents instead of the constituted military authorities under whom they conduct their operations of war.

Napoleon was fully alive to the demoralising effects of newspaper work amongst his officers and soldiers.

An able military historian makes the following remarks on this subject when alluding to the grand army of 400,000 men, which passed in review before the Emperor on the banks of the Niemen at the opening of the campaign of Russia :—

"When on the banks of the Niemen he saw 12,000 Cuirassiers, with armour flashing in the sun and cries of salutation pealing in unison with the thunder of the horses' feet, passing like a foaming torrent towards the river, he turned to Gouvion St. Cyr and thus addressed him :—

" ' No monarch ever had such an army.'

" ' No, sire.'

" ' The French are a fine people, they deserve more liberty, and they shall have it ; but, St. Cyr, no liberty of the press. That army, mighty as it is, could not resist the songs of Paris ! ' "

The Emperor was right. But times are changed, and in these days newspaper agents are allowed to be amongst our troops, even in the hour of battle. Let them work hard and honestly. Let them record all they see. But directly they are known to have assumed a position that is not theirs by right, and which has never yet been and never will be assigned to them, they should not again be allowed to accompany our soldiers in operations of war.

*   *   *   *   *

The military capacity of experienced Generals is generally measured by the ignorance of their detractors.

"Save us from our friends" is an ancient truism. The "oldest service journal," the *United Service Gazette*, appears to have strongly supported in two separate leading articles, the "slaughtering," to use a journalistic word, of British Generals by war correspondents. It its issue of the 13th ult. it says, in reference to its arguments for bringing one of the two Generals in command in the Soudan to a measurable punishment, "he may yet repair the omission, especially since the correspondent of the *Standard* has drawn up a formal and detailed indictment against him." So "the oldest naval and military service journal" supports an indictment of a British General's operations in the field by a newspaper war correspondent! Well—"save us from our friends?" If the gentleman who was responsible for the arguments in this service journal would be good enough to take the command of the next campaign, and have around him a small army of war correspondents whom he knew would have full liberty to indict him for every error of judgment and every shortcoming under every difficulty, he would soon find his position absolutely intolerable. Fatal hesitation would take the place of promptitude. Irresolution and fear of personal consequences would supplant that rapid decision which is necessary at critical periods. His army would be lost, and he would be indicted by his war correspondent umpires, eager to air their superior military knowledge. He would return home with a ruined reputation. *Then* what would this Editor have to say concerning the war correspondent umpires who had disgraced him in the eyes of all the world? We do indeed live in strange times of naval or military service, when we find "the oldest service journal" supporting a newspaper war correspondent's indictment against a British General. Once more—"save us from our friends!"

Soon after the above was in print, some facts came to my knowledge relating to the outrageous manner in which a number of war correspondents present in the late Egyptian operations openly called into question the acts of the Generals in command. These facts more than corroborate every word that has been here written on circumstances that have become scandalous in their results.—*The Illustrated Naval and Military Magazine,* July 1885.

APPENDIX VI.

A VOICE FROM AUSTRALIA ON MOUNTED RIFLES.

From *The Argus*, Melbourne, March 28th, 1885.

By Ivan.

For a community which wants to make the most of the men and money disposable, one of the first questions is—"What kind of drill, formation, and regimental organisation best suits the modern conditions of warfare?" Mounted infantry or mounted rifles are simply infantry men or riflemen who can get quickly from place to place. There might possibly be some prejudice against the mounted infantryman, as distantly suggesting the idea of a "horse marine," but it would not be shared by those who have looked into the matter. This kind of corps is being incorporated more and more into modern armies. Where the supply of men is not unlimited, training mounted infantry is more "thrifty" than training separate battalions of foot and regiments of cavalry; and it is a question for us colonists whether we ought not to choose the more workmanlike in preference to the showy system of organisation. True, that is not the sole consideration, because "looks" count for something—outward appearance and military display have a good deal of moral effect on parade, at a field day, or when soldiers march through the streets. A corps which has too rough-and-ready an appearance might make soldiering contemptible. It would have a depressing effect on the military ardour of our citizens to see 1000 men turn out for a review in Albert Park as gaunt, ragged, and kiln-dried as Wilson's men were when they marched fighting all the way from Metemneh to Goubat. If we could see the very men who made that march, we would forget what they looked like, thinking of what they had done; but soldiers who have still to earn their laurels must look as impressive as possible. A smart battalion of infantry, marching past in open column of companies, or wheeling and countermarching in close column, stepping well together and making the ground tremble as they go, is an imposing sight; and battalion movements have, of course, their place in warfare; but that is not the only point. After admiring our battalion we must remember that, in our case, they do not represent, as a Prussian battalion does, a fraction of an army corps, which is complete in every separate branch. We Victorians have rather to ask ourselves what use our 1000 men would be to the officer commanding a field force on an actual campaign—how would he be obliged to dispose of them so as to make the most of his resources?

If our infantry have to do any campaigning, it won't be like the "full-dress" performances which take place on the great battle-fields of Europe; it will, more probably, be like campaigning in South Africa, or in the United States during the "late unpleasantness" between North and South. The South African colonists have, unfortunately, had to dabble in warfare of one kind or another for the last 40 years, some "Caffre" or other war with hostile native tribes cropping up periodically. Hence they have plenty of experience of the best organisation for small bodies of men in a country where transport is always difficult and expensive. The latter conditions exist in Australia, and in other respects the problem is the same here as in the Cape. It is true that the Victorian defence force is recruited more from the class of men who are to be found in the German *landwehr*; but if we colonists ever took in hand to organise a special force, we could not take a better pattern than some of the Cape corps. Even if the infantry battalions of our defence force be intended mainly for garrison duty, training a portion of them to act as mounted infantry would in no way unfit them to serve behind works or defend forts.

The best known among the Cape corps was the old "Cape Mounted Riflemen." Originally the troopers were Hottentots and half-castes, but after a while it was composed entirely of white men, and became one of Her Majesty's regiments, although never serving out of Africa. The refusal of the Cape Government to contribute to the cost of keeping up this corps led to its disbandment a few years ago—the troopers being mostly transferred to serve out the remainder of their time in line regiments. The colonial authorities next made the experiment of a corps of mounted policemen, paid, armed, and equipped by the colony. This hybrid corps was anything but a success, and the disastrous result of an encounter with the insurgent Galekas at Guadana Hill, in 1877, showed that without a strictly military force operations of this kind ought not to be attempted. From the men and officers who had composed the Cape mounted police a corps of " Cape Mounted Rifles" was formed in 1877, and it owed the efficiency which it afterwards attained to the exertions of two of its commanders, Frederick Carrington, an ex-officer of the 24th, who was afterwards mortally wounded at Proleka Ridge, and Colonel James Baillie. The latter managed, with the Cape Mounted Riflemen alone, to capture Moirosi's Mountain in 1879, after several unsuccessful attempts to storm it had been made by other detachments. The fame of this corps has spread all over South Africa. It seems to be a model of what such a force ought to be.

The secret of its success as a fighting machine was the wonderful quickness of the men in advancing and retiring (mounted) in skirmishing order, and the perfect coolness with which, after a while, they would mount and dismount close to an enemy. The great point about a corps of this kind is that it can accustom itself to work as a rule without support or assistance from the other "arms," or from the transport service. The men themselves are always a pretty "mixed" lot. There were, of course, some Boers among them in the early days, and in addition, representatives of most known nationalities, colours, and classes, serve in its ranks.

It will be well to describe their clothing, arms, accoutrements, etc. The full dress uniform is a black " cord " patrol jacket and riding " breeches " (not trousers); this material can be dyed any colour required, and it is almost indestructible. Leather leggings—wide at the foot, and without straps or buckles—to be pulled on before the boots. The latter are regulation " ammunition boots;" the leggings are kept close down on the foot by the straps of the "hunting" spurs. White helmets.

The arms of this corps consist of (1) a Martini-Henry carbine, slung across the back. Some of the Cape mounted corps which have since been raised sling the carbine in a "bucket" attached to the saddle. There is a difference of opinion on this point, the Prussian authorities declaring that slinging the rifle across the back ultimately injures the lungs; on the other hand, it insures that if the man be thrown and his horse gets away he will have his weapon with him. The other weapons are (2) an "Adams" revolver; and (3) cavalry sabre. Whether this latter is or is not the proper arm for mounted infantry has, however, aroused plenty of controversy.

The ammunition is carried in a "bandolier," or cross belt, furnished with tubes to hold cartridges. The revolver holster is also worn at the right side of the body, not attached to the front of the saddle, as the fashion once was.

The saddles are comfortable and well padded, and have "Cape girths." A valise is carried in front; saddle bags behind. Military bridle (bit and burdoon); headstall and hide rope for picketing. Also a knee band, 18 in. long, which is buckled to the near foreleg above the knee and on to the headstall, when the horse is "hobbled" or turned loose to graze at night. "Patrol" mess tin and cup, fitting into each other, and done up in a leather case, constitute all the cooking apparatus required. Half a patrol tent and the telescopic poles for the same are carried on the valise in front of the saddle.

Whenever a troop or squadron becomes altogether independent of vehicular transport, many extras are carried by the men, such as a short axe in leather case, which can be stowed alongside the valise, entrenching picks, shovels, etc. A detached troop can easily carry six days' rations on their horses, quite independently of cattle, which, as a rule, are driven with the main column and slaughtered in camp.

When the men bivouack for the night, the horses are either "rung," *i.e.* fastened together—sometimes in a circle, sometimes in line—by the short hide ropes, from cheek to cheek; or, if there be plenty of grass, they are "hobbled" and turned out to graze all night, with a strong guard over them. On service, the "Cape Mounted Rifles" were accustomed to dismount so many men for infantry movements that six or eight horses generally had to be held by one man. Of course, rapidity in mounting and dismounting can only be attained by long practice, and the horses require a lot of training to get them used to so much knocking about.

The Cape Mounted Rifles were undoubtedly somewhat of a "crack" corps. During the Zulu war bodies of mounted infantry were organised by Lonsdale, Redvers Buller, Lumley, and others, on a more rough-and-ready footing. But the idea was always the same, that they should get about rapidly, carrying their own rations and equipment, and be able to throw themselves into a position where infantry movements were effective, holding it until the other arms and main body of the force could support them.

The experience gained from Caffre, Zulu, and other wars, has been utilised in organising the force now under Sir Charles Warren's command in South Africa. Colonel Methuen has two regiments of Mounted Rifles. The Royal Scots Regiment has a mounted company, and Knox's Regiment of "Pioneers," which has been raised in Cape Town, has one mounted also; the main point being to get hold of men who are good shots. Methuen constantly exercises his men while in camp at skirmishing on foot, firing at trees, rocks, etc.

It may be said here that even in the organisation of these South African corps,—which were never meant for show, but always for work—there has been some clinging to antiquated notions in the teeth of modern experience. There seems to be a rooted military prejudice in favour of arming mounted men with a sabre, in spite of the fact that the conditions of fighting on horseback have altogether changed in modern times. Prussian military authorities declare that wherever lancers were opposed to dragoons or hussars during the Franco-Prussian war, the lancers—no matter whether French or Prussian— had the best of it. The only French cavalry that the English soldiers in the Peninsula did not care to tackle were the Polish Lancers, and at Albuera these same lancers fell upon the flank of Colborne's Brigade, and nearly destroyed them. Hussars were able to do very little execution during the first operations under Graham near Suakin, and I see they have sent lancer regiments mostly this time. It is true that during the Tel-el-Kebir campaign the Household Cavalry managed to sabre a good many of the Egyptians; and Mr. Joseph Cowen, in the House of Commons, related the story of a Newcastle man belonging to the Life Guards, who, at Kassassin, cut off the head of an Egyptian artilleryman with one blow, and became a far greater hero in Newcastle than Mr. Cowen himself. But the Life Guards are the best swordsmen in the British army—perhaps the best in Europe now-a-days. They are constantly practising in London, for show and amusement, and carry off the prizes as a rule at the military tournaments. In ordinary hands the cavalry sabre will not do much execution, especially as nine men out of ten will use it to hack and not to thrust with. During the Franco-Prussian war, out of 60,000 killed and wounded on the Prussian side only six men were killed and 212 wounded by sabre cuts. It is obvious that the reach of a cavalry man's sword-arm is very limited, and when cavalry are going fast it is easy to "dodge" the blow. A lance seems to be a far more formidable weapon. It requires a lot of drill, however, to make men experts in lance exercise. Lord Chelmsford proposes to do away with the sabre for mounted infantry, and give them a long bayonet, which when fixed to the carbine could be used on horseback to thrust with, lance fashion. It is quite possible that a bad lancer would be really more effective than a good swordsman. The time when regiments of dragoons met for combat and conventional cut and thrust business on horseback is past and gone. The style in which the Prussian infantry at Reichshofen, although in no particular formation, let French cuirassiers pass through and through them, and then turned and shot them at leisure, shows that men armed with breechloaders have very little to fear from men armed with sabres. The Cape Mounted Rifles at close quarters generally trusted to their revolvers.

It is to be feared that the utility of our picturesque sword exercise is also vanishing. The Prussians, now-a-days, laugh at our right side and left side, and wrist and leg cuts, believing that a cut at the head is the only one worth thinking about.

It will, of course, be necessary to abandon old ruts and grooves, and to go to a great deal of extra trouble if we organise corps of mounted infantry, or a mounted company for each battalion of our defence force. There is nothing more comfortable than jogging along at company and battalion drill year after year. If there be no musketry instruction either, that state of things would constitute a sort of adjutant's paradise. But what would happen if our defence force ever had to take the field? The officer in command would simply be compelled to organise a force of mounted infantry on the spur of the moment. I repeat that if we had an efficient cavalry force here the case might be different. But we have not, and ought to remember that it takes an enormous amount of drill to make a smart cavalry soldier, and that he is a very costly individual. With infantry and artillery alone, a contingent would be helpless in the field.

As throwing light on this question, Colonel Malleson, in his *History of the Indian Mutiny*, vol. ii. p. 487, describes what a few mounted infantry men were able to effect. A field force without cavalry had been operating with little success against the Jaydispore mutineers in the autumn of 1858. At last it occurred to Sir Henry Havelock to get a few men from the 10th Foot and mount them for special service. The idea was very much opposed at first, but he ultimately was allowed his own way. Colonel Malleson says :—

"The staff officer, who was no other than Sir Henry Havelock,[1] deputy assistant adjutant-general of the force, had, in his experience of Frank's advance without cavalry from the southern frontier of Oude to Lucknow, noticed the enormous service which a few mounted soldiers of the 10th Foot, carrying rifles on horseback, had been able to render. Conceiving the idea . . . that the services of a few men might be advantageously utilised in a similar manner, he had caused 40 riflemen of the 10th Foot to be hastily trained by Captain Bartholomew, of that regiment. He now . . . received permission to employ the men so trained as mounted infantry—that is to say, who could pursue and overtake the enemy, then dismounting, hold them in check till the main body should arrive. He increased the 40 men to 60."

[1] Now Lieut.-General Sir Henry Marshman Havelock-Allan, Bart., V.C., C.B., eldest son of the celebrated General Havelock of Indian Mutiny renown, and author of the most valuable and instructive work entitled *The Three Main Military Questions of the Day :*—I. A Home Reserve Army. II. The more Economic Military Tenure of India. III. Cavalry as affected by Breechloading Arms.

Havelock then undertook the pursuit of the mutineers, and thanks to his mounted infantry alone, he succeeded in overtaking and destroying one body of them. "Without the presence of the mounted riflemen," says Malleson, "the enemy would, as on every previous occasion, have escaped unscathed." In pursuing the main body of the Shahabad rebels the infantry column, under Brigadier Douglas, was "guided by the reports from these same mounted riflemen," and Malleson sums up :—

"Thus 60 men, organised on a novel plan, and aided by a handful of cavalry, had effected, with almost nominal loss, in five days, what 3000 regular troops had for six months failed to accomplish, viz., the complete expulsion of 4500 rebels from the province, and the infliction on them of a punishment the effect of which has not been effaced to this day."

This is certainly a striking testimony to the utility of mounted infantry. It is well to recollect that mounted companies would cost us here a great deal less money than regular cavalry. There is another great advantage connected with them, which has already struck one of the officers connected with our defence force, that each troop, and even each squad, is a complete corps in itself, independent of army service corps, camp equipage, stores, etc. Every township that could muster a dozen young fellows willing to learn to mount and dismount quickly, stick on a horse some fashion or other, practise a few simple cavalry movements in single rank, look after their own horses, cook, and pitch tents, might thus have its own corps. They could be united at any time into a regiment, and would not have much that was novel to learn. Of course, it must always be kept in mind that shooting is the business of such a corps, not charging on horseback. A good shot, even though he be a bad rider, is worth three good riders who can't hit a target or a mark. I mentioned before the great stress that Methuen and such men in South Africa lay on accurate shooting. And they have good reason—as everyone knows. The Boers owed their success in the Transvaal business simply to their rifle-shooting. They had no artillery—and they had no bayonets! It was a miserable business altogether, but we ought to take a lesson from it. Fortunately for our people in the Soudan, the Mahdi's men do not know how to shoot; if they did, how many of Sir Charles Wilson's or Brackenbury's men would ever have got back to Korti? When there is time to think of such things, our defence force will doubtless get some kind of musketry instruction. I do not mean prize shooting at Williamstown, but "position drill," "aiming at the wall," judging distance drill, and occasionally firing at unknown distances. There must be many good shots in the ranks, but, on the other hand, hundreds of men who cannot shoot at all.

The expense of local squads of mounted infantry need not be very great. Possibly a small sum would induce farmers or selectors to hire out their horses once a fortnight for three or four hours' drill, with an understanding that they should be purchased at a fixed price by the Government whenever it was necessary to mobilise the whole force. With the local police stations, or even the local post-offices, as a place to assemble at, the whole of the detached squads could be mobilised in 24 hours. Meantime it might be worth trying the experiment of "mounting" one company from each of our infantry battalions, selecting the men who are the best shots, and practising them in mounting and dismounting, holding their comrades' horses, etc. The best among the Melbourne cab horses are about the kind of animals that would be required to carry them. Might not the volunteer cavalry corps which is now being enrolled in Melbourne do well to take Carrington's or Methuen's Mounted Rifles as their model? That would be better than any attempt to attain to 10th Hussars' "form" under the actual circumstances of the case.

EXTRACT ON MOUNTED RIFLES, from *The Operations of War.*
By Lieut.-General Sir E. B. Hamley, K.C.B., K.C.M.G.

"Some force which should combine the celerity of cavalry with the formidable fire of infantry would exactly suit the case; and such is to be found in a corps of *mounted riflemen.* Nor would the performance of such a duty by any means exhaust their functions. For seizing a post or a defile before infantry could arrive there, and which cavalry would be incompetent to hold—for rapidly turning a flank—for executing distant enterprises against communications,—mounted riflemen seem the inevitable solution of a problem, the conditions of which are speed of movement, with ability to contend with any kind of force. The Prussians propose to meet the case by arming their light cavalry with a better weapon. But this is only to create a more expensive and less efficient kind of mounted riflemen. Size and weight of man and horse are worse than superfluous where celerity, accuracy of aim, and readiness in obtaining cover, are the requisites. Light men on small horses, steed and rider active and enduring, with excellent weapons and careful training, will compose a description of force such as has not been seen on any modern European battle-field, but which will, at small cost, produce great results.

3 c

The nature of the service would render it especially popular with the active, the enterprising, and the ambitious; and (supposing we were desirous for once of devising something in war, instead of copying foreign examples in the way that Chinese artists copy Italian pictures), it would not be easy to lead the way more effectively than by organising a force of mounted riflemen. Its strength should be such as, after providing for the covering of the army on the march in its most extended order, should keep in hand for the day of battle a force which, joined to an equal force of cavalry, should raise the total of those two to the proportion hitherto considered necessary for the cavalry alone. But, indeed, mounted riflemen would be so generally effective, that the only limit to their numbers need be the means of maintaining them."—*The Operations of War,* ed. 1886, p. 439.

APPENDIX VII.

EARLIEST intelligence of the Battle of Tofrek, as published at London in a special edition of the *Daily Telegraph*, issued at 4.30 P.M., Sunday, March 22nd, 1885, or, allowing for the difference of time between the two localities, about four hours after the close of the action :—

SUNDAY AFTERNOON
SPECIAL EDITION.

THE DAILY TELEGRAPH OFFICE,
Sunday, 4.30 p.m.

SUAKIN CAMPAIGN
———◆———

SEVERE FIGHTING
TO-DAY NEAR TAMAI.
———◆———

AN ARAB SURPRISE.
———◆———

DESPERATE ONSLAUGHT
BY THE ENEMY.
———◆———

GALLANT BEHAVIOUR
OF THE TROOPS.
———◆———

[FROM OUR SPECIAL CORRESPONDENT.]

SUAKIN, MARCH 22 (4.10 P.M.)

Severe fighting took place to-day about seven miles from here, in the direction of Tamai.

A force of the enemy several thousands strong suddenly attacked a transport zereba in a most unexpected manner.

Most of the men were working fatigue duty at the time, when all at once an Arab was seen by one of our men to spear a comrade only four feet off.

Instantly a square was formed, as completely as the suddenness of the onslaught would allow, but the baggage animals were driven back in confusion upon the troops, camels, mules, horses, and men being carried away in the tumult and thrown into momentary wild disarray.

The Marines formed the east face of the square, and held the enemy at bay most gallantly.

On the west face the Berkshire also fired as steadily and coolly as if they had been engaged in a mere sham fight.

On the other two sides there was unfortunately some confusion, through the clouds of dust and smoke and the rout of animals and camp followers driven in by the overwhelming numbers of the enemy.

We await fuller details.

EXTRACTS FROM

THE GLASGOW NEWS, now *THE SCOTTISH NEWS,*
RELATIVE TO THE BATTLE OF TOFREK.

1. *The Glasgow News,* March 26th, 1885.

UNTHINKING CENSURE.

WE regret to see that a section of the people of this country has condemned a British General in his absence, and without any full knowledge of
facts. The letter signed " J. S.," which we publish to-day, is a remarkable
example of the unreasoning severity of judgment which is current in conversation, and which has even been exhibited by some journals of repute.
This correspondent, writing of Sunday's battle, asserts without qualification
that " General Graham's carelessness in neglecting to reconnoitre the ground
before commencing to build the zerebas deserves severe reprehension ; " and
he also asks in a sentence of censure, " What has become of the balloons
shipped at Woolwich ? " This style of criticism certainly does deserve
some reprehension. What right has any man sitting at home at ease to
assume that General Graham deserves condemnation for the surprise of an
advanced guard despatched under the command of an officer of high rank ?
Or, assuming for a moment that our correspondent means really to censure
Sir John M'Neill, how can he positively assert that that officer was careless,
and did not send out " a few scouts ? " It is quite possible that that is so.
The fact that a considerable British force was attacked without warning by
many thousand enemies is strange, and provokes comment ; but that comment
should be reasonable. The zereba was in the immediate neighbourhood of
scrub, which must be taken to be a tangled growth of what we would call

underwood. That scrub may have been searched thoroughly at an earlier hour. It may also have been pierced by a deep gully, along which the enemy might afterwards advance. It may also have been left unsearched. These are matters into which the Commander-in-Chief must inquire, and on which General Graham will report. Surely it is sufficient that the leaders of our armies are responsible to a chief who can remove them at will. If the conduct of our Generals is to be discussed in the same spirit as a statesman's speech or vote, but without the exact knowledge which renders possible a judgment on these, it will surely follow that our Generals will play to the gallery, and that, in place of considering how a certain movement will affect the enemy, they will rather consider how it will strike the distant public. A certain suspicion of this has already hovered over the Soudan War, and the sooner it is laid to rest the better for the nation. A grave responsibility in this matter rests upon those who conduct influential newspapers. These do good work in obtaining and publishing all facts regarding a campaign, and in criticising the political aspects of military movements. But clearly it is unjust and impolitic to assume that a General deserves censure for carelessness until he has had an opportunity of stating the many circumstances which may condition, control, explain, or excuse a doubtful action.

There are certain lessons to be drawn from Sunday's fighting, and these we offer, not to the military authorities, who can draw these lessons better than we can, but to the public, who are anxiously awaiting news of the expected attack on Tamai. The ground near Souakim is mountainous, and thickly covered with vegetation, and therefore favourable to the operations of an irregular force. Osman Digna, also, is pursuing tactics different from those of the Upper Nile tribes, and different from his own of a year ago. To overcome the difficulties of scouting in such a country, balloons are clearly most useful. One of these was used yesterday, and doubtless it would have been used sooner had it arrived. This at once demolishes the censure of one part of the letter we print, inasmuch as not even the most cantankerous critic would urge that the advance should not have been attempted without balloons. To meet Osman's changed tactics some change in ours is probably necessary. Advancing in hollow square, with herds of camels and camp-followers in the centre, is certainly too slow and cumbersome an operation. It is also useless for the purpose, and our Special Correspondent telegraphs us that a number of convoy camels were lost yesterday, with their loads. The experience of Sunday, when two companies of the Berkshire Regiment in rallying square defended themselves with ease and did fearful execution among the enemy, would go to show that a number of small squares, so disposed as to subject an over-adventurous enemy to a cross fire, could more easily defend the impedimenta in the centre, and destroy the foe. Another lesson of the fighting is that the Indian troops, while quite courageous and well disciplined, would be much the better of a larger number of European commissioned and non-commissioned officers. They have not the stolid coolness which prevents all fluster and flurry among our men, and probably also they have not the same assurance of success which prevents Britons from entertaining the least doubt of victory when facing Eastern troops, under any conditions or at any odds. The other, and perhaps the chief, lesson of the fighting is that in hand-to-hand conflict our soldiers have shown once more the vigour and success which has always distinguished the people of this island. A number of Arabs were able in the first surprise, and in shelter of the rush of camels, to enter various zerebas, but none came out again. The English bayonet soon overcame the ineffectual opposition of the Arab spear.

It may be argued, and it is said, that the functions of a General require him to consider the nature of the ground, the tactics of the enemy, and the formation of attack and defence, and that he should not need to be taught his work by a strategical reverse, which was only converted to a victory by the courage of our troops and the long-proven superiority of British stolidity over Eastern dash. That is begging the question in two ways. It first assumes that the General in command at Souakim did not consider these things, and it also ignores that he may have found serious objections to any other plan which may be suggested at home. It further assumes indirectly that the military authorities will neglect to consider these matters. Such assumptions are unfair and impolitic. They are the more dangerous because there underlies them the other assumption that we should make war without incurring the usual chances of war, and that unless uniformly successful we must have a scapegoat. This feeling is largely born of the fact that this generation has only seen little wars, all conducted, or easily capable of being conducted, to a more or less successful issue. If we intend to go to war with Russia, we had better get rid of such a feeling at once. We cannot expect to make war on a great scale without suffering many small reverses. Nor must we cry out when these come, and look around for some one to act as a scapegoat. All Generals make mistakes, like humbler men; but we must bear these in dignified moderation, unless or until we are convinced of our leaders' incompetence. That is a matter for the military authorities, and one in which any loud expression of public opinion is calculated to do harm. The function of public opinion, and of the journals which profess to lead or follow it, is to urge the Government to, or support it in, a line of policy. But the details of military administration in untried and puzzling circumstances are not fit matter for strong comment, the more especially when only one side of the case is presented to the public gaze. It may suit the excitable temperament of the French to recall their Generals after each reverse—Sunday's fighting was a strategical reverse—but we in Britain are accustomed to other methods, and it is in memory of these that we demand the suppression of any hasty censure of Generals in the field.

The letter referred to by the editor is as follows :—

MILITARY BALLOONING.

To the Editor of *The Glasgow News.*

Sir—What has become of the balloons which we were told some time ago were being shipped at Woolwich for Souakim? General Graham's carelessness in neglecting to reconnoitre the ground before commencing to build the zerebas deserves severe reprehension. A few scouts would have given him notice of the near approach of the enemy, but a balloon in the rear of his advance would most effectually have prevented surprise.—I am, etc.   J. S.

2. In the issue for April 8th, in the same tenor, the following remarks occur :—

The Souakim Expedition.

We are glad to see, from a telegram despatched yesterday by our Special Correspondent at Souakim, that the rash and unthinking criticism passed by many journals after the surprise at the zereba near Tamai is being estimated at its true value in the British camp at Souakim. As we pointed out at the time, such criticism was, under the circumstances, mischievous. It is impossible for anyone sitting at home to criticise judiciously the details of a military campaign from the information which may chance to reach him immediately after a battle. The general result may be well enough known, while the circumstances which led up to it are largely conjectural. In the particular instance commented upon we have already expressed the opinion that inquiry is called for, and it is certainly the interests both of the Commander-in-Chief and General Graham that the matter should be thoroughly investigated.   In the meantime, however, it is the duty of all to give General Graham and his subordinates all moral support in the arduous duties they have undertaken in fighting their country's battles, and upholding the honour of Britain in a distant land.   The British Army at Souakim has, as our Correspondent explains, the greatest possible difficulty in reconnoitring, owing to the scrubby nature of the country and the peculiar habits of the Arabs.   There is, therefore, some reason to believe that the surprise at the zereba was one of the unavoidable accidents of war, and, in any case, it would be wise to wait for the official report before forming a decided opinion on the matter.   The information which our Correspondent gives regarding the very brilliant manner in which the Indian cavalry are reconnoitring, and the way in which the British cavalry are following their example, are matters for sincere congratulation.

The telegram sent by Captain Norman, the Special Correspondent, on April 7th is as follows :—

SOUAKIM, Tuesday, Noon.

A general feeling prevails among all classes in the Camp, that the hasty criticisms which have been passed on our military operations in the neighbourhood of Souakim are not only most unjust, but they are without foundation.

These criticisms, passed by some writers at home, have been forwarded to us, and they are unsparingly condemned in the camp.

I have been through campaigns in several countries, and have consequently obtained a great deal of experience ; but never, till now, have I realised the existence of such immense difficulties as those against which our troops, and especially the cavalry, have to contend.

The Scouting operations of the cavalry have to be performed in a country where a high and almost impenetrable scrub obstructs the view beyond the first mimosa bushes.

When the reports of the experienced senior officers on the spot relative to the surprise of the zereba, on which so much comment has been made, are published, I think that my views will be confirmed, and that no blame can be thrown on the operations performed throughout the campaign by our cavalry scouts.

The Arabs move about in the brushwood like snakes, and their movements are not observable until they burst on our troops.

Day by day our young British Cavalry, who have never before been through a campaign, are becoming more and more perfect in their duties. They are learning to do all the work that can be expected of them, and they give promise of soon being as efficient as the Indian troopers, who have seen much active service.

The admirable work done yesterday by Jedamur Shere Sings, of General Hudson's Horse, in so effectively reconnoitring the country around Handoub (to which I called attention in my telegram last night), has excited the admiration of the authorities.

The surprise of Sunday the 22nd, when M'Neill's Zereba was temporarily broken, while no doubt unfortunate in the results which followed, is looked upon as one of those accidents of war which attend every campaign.

Whatever blame may be attached to the regiments composing the zereba garrison, there can be no doubt that the gallant behaviour all through the fighting of the Berkshire, the Marines, and the Sikhs, has wiped out any reflection which has been cast upon them by the critics at home.

A country that expects to be engaged in a war without suffering any casualties should remember that omelettes cannot be made without breaking eggs.

It is only fair to ask that officers and men who are performing arduous duties, under exceptional circumstances, should receive encouragement and support, and not have blame cast upon them when they are serving their country well and gallantly. These officers are certainly deserving well of their country.[1]

On the following day the same correspondent's letter ends with the clear recognition of the decisive character of the fight on the 22nd :—

"One or two scouts are visible at times, but the power of the enemy seems to have been entirely broken by the terrible punishment inflicted upon them by General M'Neill on the 22nd March."[2]   And with reference to the night attack on Adam Sardoun at Takdool, of Osman Digna it is stated: "All say that his power is broken and his career finished."

[1] *Glasgow News*, April 8th, 1885.   [2] *Glasgow News*, April 9th, 1885.

APPENDIX IX.

EXTRACTS FROM

THE INDIAN PRESS ON SÛDAN AFFAIRS.

1. THE SUAKIN-BERBER RAILWAY.

From *The Bombay Gazette*, March 2nd, 1885.

A CORRESPONDENT writes to the *Pioneer* : [1]—" The telegram announcing that it has been decided to make a line of railway from Suakim to Berber naturally suggests the thought, How is it to be done ? Is the Home Government going to do it unaided, or should the Indian Government be called to assist ? The question will be examined with a view to show who is in the best position to carry the work through rapidly and cheaply. How would the Home Government set about making the railway ? It has no organised railway staff of its own, and it would be compelled to fall back upon one of the large contractors. Any contractor who would undertake to complete the line in a certain time would be able to name his own terms. And even then there would still be no security that the work would be accomplished satisfactorily. An English contractor would have to send out a staff unaccustomed to the necessarily heavy exposure to the sun and weather, which all employed would have to undergo. To sum up, if the Home Government undertake this line, it will cost them an immense sum, and even then there would be no security of the work being completed in the time agreed on.

" On turning to the capabilities of the Indian Government the position is found to be totally different. This Government has a large and organised staff of experienced and acclimatised engineers and subordinates of all grades,

[1] Of Allahabad.

a portion of whom could be made immediately available, and most of whom have been engaged in the construction of railways in India for the last fifteen years.   To show in what high estimation Indian Government railway engineers are held in the open market, it may be mentioned that the private companies by whom railways have recently been constructed in India have universally borrowed Government engineers to make their lines in preference to obtaining men in the open market.   The Indian Government, therefore, if asked to assist in the construction of the Suakim line, is in a position to provide at once an experienced and well-seasoned. staff.   The Government has also a large fund to draw upon, belonging to its metre gauge State railways, for an immediate supply of rolling-stock and materials to make a commencement of the line during the time that further supplies are being sent from England.   Thus the Indian Government is in a position to send out from India at short notice a competent and acclimatised staff accustomed to railway construction, and also a supply of material sufficient to start the line at once, neither of which advantages would be within the reach of an English contractor.   The result of the above comparison suggests that, if the line is to be made at once, the Indian Government should at least largely assist in the undertaking.   With this view the following outline of the necessary arrangement is roughly sketched :—

"The arrangement will, it is assumed, be for the construction of a railway at the minimum rate of four miles a day, work to be commenced as soon as possible, the line to be also equipped with sufficient rolling-stock to enable it to carry supplies for the troops in addition to the material required for its own construction.   On this supposition, the first thing to do is to estimate at once the material and rolling-stock that would be required to complete the line, steel pot sleepers being used in preference to wood, which is easily destroyed by burning.   All the narrow gauge lines in the country and the State railway stores should be at once called upon to state what spare material and stock they could each supply ; the balance still short could be ordered from England by telegraph.   It would take at least a month to organise the staff required in India, and it would be another month before men and material could be landed, and before all could be in working order, at Suakim, so that there would be two months available in which to make the requisite material and send it from England.   A sufficient supply of engines and wagons of the metre gauge could certainly be supplied from India, and the only thing that might be short would be rails and sleepers, and these could be put in hand at once in England.   The staff should consist of one chief engineer, twelve assistants, and a locomotive superintendent, each assistant working direct under the chief, and each being in separate charge of a portion of the work of laying out, grading, plate-laying, maintaining stores in general. Each of the above works require to be in charge of two assistants who would relieve one another, and be in charge of separate gangs of men. Two separate gangs of men would be required for each of the above works, one gang putting in their two miles and then being relieved by another gang.

"The work would probably have to be done at night, as the rails and the sun would be too hot for work in the day. If the electric light be used there should be no difficulty : the chief of this line should not be selected on the grounds of departmental seniority : the man selected should be young and of sound health, and one who has been engaged in the construction of railways regularly, so that he could put his hand on a staff who knew him, and whom he knew were fit for the works. He would, of course, make his own selection of assistants. European drivers, firemen, platelayers, and artificers should be sent from India, as the men would be well seasoned to exposure. The chief difficulty would be in the collection of the native staff. To get the right men to go high wages would have to be offered, and it would require the personal influence of the members of the staff to induce the best men to join. On the supposition that no local labour would be procurable at Suakim, it would be necessary to send 1,500 picked labourers, with their head-men, and skilled mistrees, from India. These men could be recruited best in the Deccan and Kathiawar, and should contain a large contingent of lascars, who are the most handy of men, and accustomed to travel. Even if local labour is available, a nucleus of good head-men, jemadar or muccadums, recruited in India, would be necessary to teach the work. It should be remembered that high wages will have to be offered, and that it is not worth while, for the sake of a few rupees, to fail in collecting the men.

"The necessary phowras, picks, baskets, carpenters' and smiths' tools, trollies, platelaying tools, derricks, blocks, curbs, etc., for unloading the heavy stores, could all be obtained easily in India. It would also probably be necessary to make some arrangements for iron-plating the sides of the wagons as a protection, as the great difficulty of maintaining the road would commence and increase the farther and farther the force proceeded from Suakim. Each train would have to be provisioned and provided with spare ammunition for this purpose, and a guard of soldiers sent with it. The line would also have to be patrolled constantly by an armed train with a good supply of material to repair any damage that the enemy might do to the line. Steel plates attached to the sides of the wagons and loopholed would give a very good protection against any bullets that the Arabs fire. The above, of course, is merely a rough sketch of the general lines on which the expedition could be equipped. The first thing would be to select the staff, and then give to each man a separate work to do : some to collect the native staff, others stores and tools, others to go about to the different lines and push on the despatch of the stock, so that the expedition could start in as short time as possible. With the above arrangements, and if notice were given at once, the work might be started at Suakim by the end of April, and the line finished to Berber by the end of June."

2. Sir Gerald Graham's Operations at Suâkin.

From *The Bombay Gazette*, March 24th, 1885.

Sir Gerald Graham has adopted a plan of operations in the Soudan which merits attention. He is apparently feeling his way into the Hadendowah country, rather than advancing, and his method is to mark each stage to the front by there planting a zareeba and leaving a garrison to hold it. The first zareeba planted was that of Hasheen, the outcome of the fighting on Friday. On that occasion, it will be remembered, the beaten rebels retreated in the direction of Tamai, a place to the south-west of Suakim, and lying somewhat to the left of the main line of advance to Berber. General Graham, though he inflicted heavy loss upon the enemy, did not follow up his advantage, but returned to camp at once. On Sunday, precisely the same strategy appears to have been adopted. A mixed force under General McNeill set out for Tamai, the place towards which the enemy had retreated on Friday, advancing in two squares—a formation which, in spite of Sir Edward Hamley's accomplished criticism, is believed by those who are conversant with the scrubby nature of the ground, to be the safest order of advance in that country—their object being to construct a zareeba, and to leave there a garrison of the Berkshire Regiment. It is not easy to reconcile the accounts given in the two telegrams which we publish to-day, except on the incompletely warranted assumption that there were two attacks, one an attempt to intercept the force on its way to the ground chosen for the zareeba, the other upon the zareeba itself when formed. However this may be, the operation was successfully completed, and the rebels, who were exposed to a cannonade from the ships in Suakim harbour and from the six guns which had been left with the East Surrey men in the Hasheen zareeba, lost more than a thousand men. After this Sir John McNeill returned to camp. The result is a second defeat of Osman Digna, and the advance of our outposts to about six miles from Suakim. To accomplish this there had been an expenditure of fifty-six killed and a hundred and seventy wounded, in addition to twenty-two killed and forty-four wounded in the fighting at Hasheen two days before. Once more the question arises whether fine fighting, such as there has undoubtedly been at Hasheen and in the country beyond, leads to its legitimate results when it is repeatedly followed by a return to camp. We have got two zareebas, it is true, and the good work done by the East Surrey men and their guns in the Hasheen enclosure shows that these structures when well held are of substantial use; but there is no evidence as yet of any real impression having been made upon the rebels. Sunday's attack seemed to show that Friday's defeat had carried no lessons with it, and we are half inclined to ask whether Osman Digna's lieutenants have not been more impressed by the return of the British to camp than by the heavy punishment that has been given them. The Arabs in that part of the Soudan have seen too much of the "returns to camp" strategy to be as susceptible as they might be to the ordinary influences of defeat, and though it is gratifying to have to record warfare in which British and Indian troops fought side by side with such conspicuous gallantry, people will begin to hope either that there will soon be less fighting in that locality, or that there may be more to show for it. When we pay with nearly three hundred casualties for an advance of six miles, we pay rather dearly.

3. From *The Bombay Gazette,* March 26th, 1885.

The losses in Sunday's engagement near Tamai were more serious than the first accounts represented them to be. The killed numbered a hundred, and the wounded a hundred and thirty-six, while one officer and seventy men are missing. Besides these, a large number of camp followers were killed. It will probably be found that the casualties in the two days' fighting at Hasheen and near Tamai were not far short of five hundred, all told. This is a heavy expenditure—a too heavy expenditure, we fear, for the results obtained. These now appear to be very small. It is true that in Friday's fighting the enemy suffered heavy loss—no numerical estimate of the enemy's loss on that day, by the way, has been given—and that on Sunday about a thousand of them are reported to have been killed. But Friday's defeat did not deter them from renewing the attack on Sunday, and, as we learn to-day,

Sunday's greater defeat did not deter them from an extremely audacious attack upon one of our convoys on its way to the zareebas. It seems, therefore, that our successes in conflict have not yet had either the military or the moral results which were expected of them. They have not cowed the enemy, nor have they kept him outside the area which the zareebas, if they had fully answered the only obvious purpose which General Graham must have assigned to them, ought effectually to have commanded. For an attack upon a convoy on its way to the zareebas means that the enemy had succeeded in getting in the rear of these posts. General Graham doubtless intended, by thus advancing in zareeba stages, to make sure of his progress, or at any rate to keep the enemy at arm's length until he is prepared to make a final advance from Suakim. But this proves not to be the cautious strategy that its author must have meant it to be, and it is exceedingly wasteful. It would be difficult, indeed, to imagine smaller results derived from so large an outlay, and it will soon become a serious question whether General Graham ought not for the present either to adopt a more defensive attitude or to discover a more economical method. It from the first seemed a remarkable plan of operations which he had adopted; but unless there is a speedy change in the reports from Suakim it will soon be said that the most remarkable feature in it is the strange disproportion between the results achieved and the outlay incurred in achieving them. An advance of six miles into the interior is not enough to show for so large a sacrifice, especially since we have as yet no proof whatever that our successes have made any impression upon Osman Digna's followers.

APPENDIX X.

THE "WALLACE" ENTRENCHING TOOL AND PIONEER SPADE.

THE following description of the entrenching tools, used extensively on the 22nd of March in constructing the defences, may be of interest:—

"This tool, which weighs about 2 lbs. 5 ozs. and is 23 inches long, is patented in England and America and on the Continent, and has been adopted by the English and South Australian Governments. It is a small spade with a broad blade, and a crosspick for the handle. The pick consists of an armoured wooden crutch, the wood of which forms a strong backing to the steel point, and acts as a buffer against the jar caused by repeated blows. It is covered with steel sheathing, which is in two parts, fits closely to the wooden head, and is fastened on by rivets to the crutch, and by rivets and a band to the handle. Each point is composed of one-inch of solid steel, which, when blunted by use, can be sharpened. One end is a pick, the other a grubber. The metal used is very hard and well-tempered, while the tool is made so as to be easily repaired if damaged. To put it briefly, the chief virtues of the entrenching tool are the simple combination of pick and spade, which is obtained without any complicated arrangement; the shape of the blade; and the projection at the back, which guards the knuckles when digging, and also 'cants' the blade to clear the wrist when the pick is used.

"The British Government has just ordered 20,000 of these entrenching tools, having been previously supplied with 30,000. Foreign countries have ordered a supply for an exhaustive trial of their peculiar merits.

"The 'Pioneer' spade, is intended for clearing ground and for bushwork, where the combination of a serviceable billhook with a small pick and spade must often be very convenient. This tool is intended as a companion to the entrenching tool, and is the same length; it can, however, be made of any length for digging, sporting purposes, etc. It is also made portable for carriage on the saddle, etc., and fits into a case twelve inches long.

"Major Wallace's tools are not intended to take the place of the full-sized 'Pioneer' picks and shovels, which will still be necessary for all heavy digging and for rocky ground, though, on an emergency, the 'Wallace' spade may be found a fair substitute. It is claimed for these tools that they are of extraordinary strength for their size and weight, and that they may be relied on to stand very severe wear and tear, if fairly used, and even to do work of which, at first sight, they would hardly be thought capable. For instance, they will break down or loophole an ordinary stone or brick wall—though, perhaps, at the cost of some of the spades. Loopholing was successfully carried out with them in the first Egyptian campaign, when they were also found to be useful and efficient substitutes for small axes in cutting firewood, and invaluable in camp life. Numerous testimonials, from general and other officers, and also from civil engineers, are before the writer, in proof of the above. The spades are not offered as cheap tools. They are made of the very best materials—picked ashen shafts and steel of the first quality; and they have to be put together with great care. So long as this is the case the spades can never be cheaply turned out—though a large order can be executed at a considerable reduction in price. Their value depends so entirely upon their quality that the inventor declines to supply them except through his own manufacturer, as he can then guarantee the materials and the workmanship. Messrs. E. Lucas and Son, of Dronfield, are the manufacturers."—*The Illustrated Naval and Military Magazine*, July 1855.

APPENDIX XI.

EXTRACTS ON CAMEL DRILL AND TREATMENT.

In conducting Military operations in waterless and desert regions, indispensable as the camel may appear to be, its capacity for laborious exertion or rapid movement is severely limited. Between the treatment of this animal under ordinary conditions and its enforced usage in war there is the greatest contrast, and the waste is relatively enormous. The following extracts give a good idea of the camel, under comparatively favourable circumstances, both in ordinary use, during the piping times of peace, when it is the pet and companion of its master, and treated with the same care and consideration as the Arab treats his horse, and also as utilised in war, not as a beast of burden, but for riding purposes and as a mount, showing in this capacity much greater susceptibility to discipline and drill than might be expected. Our first quotation is from a well-known work—*The Geographical Distribution of Mammals*, by Andrew Murray. London, 1866. P. 138.

"The camel is a very ancient beast; one of the oldest, if not the oldest, species of mammal now living on the face of the earth, and it has apparently always been, as at present, a servant of man. Other domesticated animals—the dog, the elephant, the horse, the ox, and the sheep—have, with greater or less success, been referred by naturalists to their original wild types ; but all attempts to do so with the camel have stopped short at the threshold, from the simple fact that it is sole and singular, and has no allies in the hemisphere in which it is found, nor have any wild examples of its own genus ever been met with. The first accounts of it in perhaps the oldest book in the world (Job) speak of it as domesticated, and there are no records of its ever having been otherwise. But Sir Proby Cautley and Dr. Falconer discovered in the Sevalik formations in the Himmalayahs remains of it, or of species (they think there are two), so closely allied to it as to be scarcely distinguishable from it.

As the difference is so slight, it pleases us to think that we may have here, in this most ancient animal, a species which saw the miocene epoch, and which has survived all the chances and changes which have taken place since then."

Our second quotation, taken from a writer already referred to, gives a still more vivid description of the camel in its human relationships and environment :—

"The Arab, his country, and his camel, are in wonderful harmony with each other. Without the camel, the deserts which contain so many tribes of freemen would be uninhabitable, and one can imagine the camel without the Arab as little as the Arab without the camel. Its large soft eye looks from under its long eyelashes at its master, with an expression of recognition which one can hardly doubt is affection. He talks to it, and it seems to understand him ; he sings, and it quickens its steps, reviving from the fatigues of the way. The genuine Arab never beats his camel, he guides it with his voice, or with a light wand touching one ear or the other to make it turn to the right or the left, or gently tapping it on the crown of the head which it instantly lowers, and breaks into an amble ; or, if he wishes it to go still quicker, he presses its shoulder with his bare heel. When he stops, a touch on the knee accompanied by a gurgling sound makes it kneel down. This is a complicated movement, it sinks first on the fore-knees, then it bends its hind-legs, another movement doubles the fore-leg beneath the body, and finally it subsides with an undulatory motion till it rests with its legs doubled up, finding a fifth *point d'appui* in the prolongation of the breast bone, which, like the knees, is protected by a callosity. It is thus completely at rest. . . . The camel is eminently a domestic animal ; our dogs and horses can do very well without us, but it is doubtful if the camel could be *happy* without man, it so evidently sympathises with him. It has never been found in a wild state ; and the Arab tradition points to this, when it says that it was formed of the same clay as Adam, and that when turned out of Paradise he was permitted to take with him the camel and the date tree."—*Sinai, the Hedjaz, and Soudan,* by James Hamilton. London, 1857. P. 174.

The following extract from a letter by an Officer in the Grenadier Camel Corps, with the Nile Expedition, shows how very effectively the camel may be trained to the more delicate manœuvring, discipline, and drill, so essential in civilised warfare :—

CAMEL GRENADIER CAMP,

KORTI, *December* 27, 1884.

"The chief amusement since coming here has been perfecting our camel drill, which, being very simple, I will proceed to explain. The idea of our being on camels was, and is, to transport us quickly from place to place, and on no account to do any fighting on camel-back, but all on foot (except occasional scouting).

"The principle adopted is simply to form a square at one corner of the camels, or two squares at opposite corners. Suppose the commanding officer to give the word, 'Half-column on the left front,' when the battalion of four companies is moving (on camel-back) in column of companies.

"The command immediately follows, 'Close order.' The leading company halts at once, the rear rank jambs up close, and all the other companies trot up 'hard all.'

"When well jambed up against the company in front of them, the men dismount amidst a diabolical bellowing and grunting from their steeds, and double-knee-lash them with the head-rope. You then have all the camels in a square mass, unable to get up or move about. The right markers of companies, having handed over their camels to be lashed by one of the two men ordered to remain with the beasts of each company, dash out, and are covered at half-company distance from the rear, the men running out and forming up on them at once; they are then ready for forming square or other manœuvre.

"The same holds good for the other three corners, the directing flank always being nearest the camels.

"If the word is given, 'Square on left front,' the men run out to their places in square at once. For squares at opposite corners, four half-companies run to each place mentioned.

"When the battalion is required to manœuvre away from the camels, one company or less is left to defend them. In the case of two or more battalions the masses are formed in the same way in *échelon*, so as to cover each other. All this may sound rather difficult to do with unwieldy-looking beasts like camels, but it is extraordinary how quickly everybody, including the camel, has mastered the drill. The quickest time on record we have done it in as yet, from 'Close' to 'Prepare for Cavalry,' has been 2 mins. 20 secs. The other day, the whole of the 19th Hussars charged down on the mass of unprotected camels, cheering and yelling. Everybody expected to see the camels break their ropes and career wildly over the desert. The only result was that one solitary camel struggled to his feet, looked round, and knelt down again; the others never moved an eyelid. That was satisfactory; and as firing into them with blank cartridge and over them with ball has already been tried at Shabadud, with no visible results, the general opinion is that they will stand charging, niggers or anything else in creation, with equanimity."—*Army and Navy Gazette*, January 24, 1885.

Regarding a still earlier Camel Corps, under the command of Colonel Cavalier, the Records of the Expedition to Egypt in 1801 already quoted, furnish some interesting information. After narrating its capture by the British Army, Captain Walsh tells us :—

"The regiment of dromedaries had been a very useful corps to the French. It was composed of picked men chosen from the whole army, who, mounted upon these very swift animals, were employed in pursuing the Arabs through the desert, and overtaking them where it would have been impossible for any other troops. Tribes of Arabs retiring into the deepest parts of the desert, where they thought themselves secure, were soon dispersed by them, and their numerous flocks of sheep, sometimes as many as two or three thousand, became the property of the captors, among whom the value was afterward divided. By these means, several individuals of this corps had accumulated to the amount of 40,000 or 50,000 livres (sixteen or twenty hundred guineas), with which they were very glad to return to France. I have heard it constantly asserted that, when attacked by a very superior force of Arabs, the men dismounted from their dromedaries, and making them lie down, placed themselves behind them, the animal thus serving as a parapet to his rider."— *Journal of the late Campaign in Egypt.* London, 1803. P. 134.

In a note appended to his account of the same capture, Sir Robert Wilson also states :—

"It must not be supposed that this corps acts as cavalry. The dromedaries are only used for the speed of conveyance, and the men dismount when arrived at the scene of action. The idea did not originate with the French, but was the custom of the Mamelukes and all Africa. The French did not even improve the saddles, which are the most inconvenient and uncomfortable for a European tight dress imaginable."—*History of the British Expedition to Egypt.* P. 41.

APPENDIX XII.

EXTRACTS FROM

THE WRITINGS OF TRAVELLERS AND OTHERS ON THE THORNY ACACIA OF THE DESERT.

THE important *rôle* played by the Thorn bush or jungle during the entire course of the operations in the Eastern Sûdan, and especially those connected with the advance on Tamai in 1885, may excuse the citation of evidence as to its troublesome character. Wherever throughout the wide-ranging deserts of Africa or Asia this formidable plant occurs, there is directed against it on the part of travellers a chorus of united vituperation. If such be the experience of individuals, or even small caravans, how much more serious must the obstruction prove to large masses of men or of Transport, for their own convenience, and still more imperatively for safety, compelled, "in presence of the enemy," to maintain a close and regular formation.

With an occasional undergrowth of desert plants, the jungle in question is chiefly composed of the *Acacia Arabica*—the *Kittar* of the Arab, the *Kikar* of the Punjaubee, the *Babul* of the Hindu, the *Babla* of the Bengalee, and the *Soont* of Central Africa. Like all the Acacias it is a member of the *Leguminosœ*, or pod-bearing plants, one of the most widely-distributed and useful of all plant-families. In thoroughly serviceable qualities the Acacias yield to none, and of these the *A. Arabica* heads the list. In the Sûdan its range northward does not extend beyond 22 degrees of latitude, and so including all the district around Suâkin. South of this limit it occurs abundantly in the Southern Sûdan, Kordofan, Senaar, Central and tropical Africa, in Abyssinia; also, Colonel St. Clair Wilkins tells us that "The thorny acacia-tree occupies the passes as well as the plains, up to 5000 feet of elevation."—*Reconnoitring in Abyssinia*, p. 382.

Eastward, it is spread through all the coasts and islands of the Red Sea and the Arabian peninsula. As indicated by the native names already given, while believed to be indigenous in Scinde, Rajpootana, Guzerat, and the Northern Deccan, its distribution in India is most extensive, except in the more humid regions near the coast, being cultivated through most parts of that great Empire.

The best known product of this invaluable plant is the gum; it exudes in considerable quantities, chiefly in March and April, and is used not only in the arts, but occasionally as an article of food. There is, however, no part of its structure which cannot be turned to account. The wood is prized for all purposes where toughness and durability are specially required, as in the naves, felloes, and spokes of wheels; in sugar and oil presses, rice-pounders, agricultural implements, and tool handles; also for building purposes, and even railway sleepers. The bark, and even the seed-pods[1] and leaves, are used for tanning and dyeing. The green pods, shoots, and leaves form a valuable fodder for cattle, sheep, goats, and camels, and during the severe droughts in the North-West Provinces of India in 1876-77 preserved large numbers of these animals from starvation. So important a factor is this plant in the arts and commerce of India, that in Lower and Middle Scinde alone the Babul forests extend to over 27,000 acres, and in the Punjaub its cultivation is not less extensive. In Africa, also, the purposes to which it is applied are equally various and essential. On this point Sir Samuel Baker gives one or two interesting illustrations :—

" One of the mimosas yields an excellent fibre for rope-making, in which my people are busily engaged; the bark is as tough as leather, and forms an admirable material for the manufacture of sacks. This business is carried to a considerable extent by the Arabs, as there is a large demand for sacks of sufficient size to contain two hundred and fifty or three hundred pounds of gum arabic (half a camel load). Thus one sack slung upon each side can be packed easily to the animal. . . . One of the mimosas (*Acacia Arabica*) produces a fruit in appearance resembling a tamarind : this is a powerful astringent, and a valuable medicine in case of fever and diarrhœa; it is generally used by the Arabs for preparing hides; when dry and broken it is rich in a hard gum, which appears to be almost pure tannin."—*The Nile Tributaries of Abyssinia*, pp. 178-79.

[1] Sir Samuel Baker gives an interesting account of the process in which these seed-pods, or "*garra*," as the natives call them, are used in tanning.—*The Nile Tributaries of Abyssinia*, p. 180.

It is one of the advantages attending the cultivation of this tree that it naturally affects a sterile and desert soil.   Hence large districts can be turned to profitable account which might otherwise remain entirely waste.   How admirably adapted this plant is to the parched and rainless regions forming its most appropriate habitat, has been very well shown, in terms, fanciful perhaps rather than scientific, yet very expressive, and in the main true, by a traveller who describes from experience :—

"This tree, participating in the highest perfection of vegetable development, has the outlines which the lowest vegetable organisms assume : I mean those parasitic mushrooms which are still popularly known as the "fruit cups" of the stiff algæ, miscalled "lichens," and the analogy of grouping does not end with the outlines of the conical cups : for the tender and most active parts of both tree and mushroom are displayed and kept together, spread on the flat top.

"These skeleton funnel heads act up to their appearance.   Their tops are as sharp cut as if moulded by appointed gardeners into circular discs, flat and level.   It is easy to see how the maximum of the liquid Godsend is caught and conveyed to the eager sponges of the roots, which, you may be sure, retain it like the fifth spongy stomach of the camel, to keep the sleepless, leafless tree alive for ten or twenty months, when rain again is expected.   I believe the cut of the porphyry branches, tiny but firm and rigid, and very closely packed ; the arrangement of the thorns, and the shape of the leaflets, and even the blossoms, are calculated eminently to secure the greatest amount of water even from a fleeting sprinkle.   The leaves are cut into tiny spoons, and are capable of a nervous action.   The flowers are globular tassels perched on little stalks.   The branches are full of pointed cocoons, like grocers' coffins, or like pencil-point caps.   These cocoons open in due season, and the greater part of the tree is often found to be covered with a stout gossamer web. The whole is the perfection of a filter.   The smallest drops are absorbed at once.   The larger drops are caught, split up, and distributed by the thorns and the other organs ; they cannot rush through with a mere toll of a paltry kiss and then fall away.

"Having got all the moisture they can, they nourish a quantity of bloom and foliage proportionate to that moisture, and ripen quickly, shed their leaves, and work up and seal their juices in treasure-bags of gum, inside, and perhaps outside, the savoury glassy rind."—*Desert Life*, B. Falkonberg, C.E. London, 1880.   Pp. 63-64.

Attention has been hitherto exclusively directed to the more favourable aspects of this plant, and its undeniable utility in the industrial arts.   It is now necessary to consider it from a very different point of view, viz., in virtue of the formidable armature of thorns, often from two to three inches in length, by which it is chiefly characterised, as a very serious impediment to free locomotion, especially in those countries where it grows not in a cultivated but a wild state. We commence with quotations relating to the plant as found in the Eastern Sûdan; and first in its most favourable aspect as seen from the coast route pursued in 1884, where "distance lends enchantment to the view," we find its effect in the general landscape very graphically sketched by a participant in that campaign :—

"The rolling plain rises gently and evenly from the sea to the mountains, which close the background to the west, showing a well-marked line between them and the plain. The spurs ran towards us, and hence the plain, which appears as a sea of green prickly mimosa bushes, seems to invade the hills away from us in wide bays. The ground was firm for marching and for carriages."—"The Battle of Tamai. By a Soldier." *United Service Magazine,* 1884, p. 683.

Under more peaceful auspices Mr. Hamilton had found the scene not less agreeable and picturesque :—

"We only made two hours' march through the long plain which extends north and south as far as the eye could reach; this is covered with the thorny vegetation which affords so excellent a pasture for camels, and which the numerous flocks of goats scattered over it in all directions seemed to find equally to their taste. The setting sun cast a broad orange light over the plain, tinging the mountains which bounded it on the west with red and purple, while to the east the long line of sea seemed a stream of molten gold." —*Sinai, the Hedjaz, and Soudan,* p. 200.

This "sea of green prickly mimosa bushes" by no means improves upon closer acquaintance, as Mrs. Speedy very soon experienced.

"To my dismay we suddenly came upon a piece of land as full of mimosas as the other part had been bare. . . . I was often not aware of the bushes till I was upon them, and suddenly I felt a tremendous tug at my shoulder, and had a warm plaid shawl, which was wrapped round me, nearly torn off. A gigantic crooked thorn had buried its barbed point deep into it."—*My Wanderings in the Soudan,* by Mrs. Speedy. London 1884. P. 45.

A similar experience befell Dr. Josiah Williams, who informs us that after travelling through a forest of dhoum palms, "by way of variety, we pass through a mile or two of the horrid cruel thorns of the mimosa and kittar trees, which every now and then bury themselves in my flesh, and tear my

3 F

clothes and helmet as I duck my head to avoid having my face lacerated. The camel, of course, walks on in the most unconcerned manner, just as if he was on open ground, taking no notice whatever of these obstructions, but brushing past them as if they were twigs or straws. Everything, even the smallest of the mimosa tree, is armed with long, strong, very sharp thorns. Each thorn is as sharp as a needle and about an inch long; indeed, the native women use them as a cobbler does his awl, and I have often seen a woman using the thorn to pierce a girba and shreds of the palm leaf to sew it up with. The thorns of the kittar bushes are quite semicircular in shape, very near to each other, not long, but very strong, and each successive thorn crooks in a different direction to its predecessor—one crooks up and the other down. When they catch hold of any one they stick to him as close as a brother. If my clothes get entangled, I must stay and pick myself out, or if I elect to go on without doing so, I must submit to having my clothes, and perchance my flesh, effectually torn across."—*Life in the Soudan*, p. 161.

During the Expedition to Abyssinia the same difficulties were encountered.

"Where the green salt bushes, of two kinds, end, the thorny acacia or mimosa, called in India the *baubul*, commences, and with it the misery of mankind. Though food for the camel it is the enemy of man. These trees which, a few feet from the ground spread out like a teacup, are flat at the top, and growing close together, form a barrier to progress only to be removed with the axe. The tree is a terrible antagonist to the explorer and sportsman. Impenetrable excepting where the natives and their flocks have worn a path, to attempt to push through it only ends in failure, the loftier branches always having a few fish-hook-like thorns ready to uncover the rider's head the moment he thinks his way clear to pass on. In traversing this thorny jungle the most angelic temper soon gives way; but as hard words break no bones, neither do they cut down trees, so the traveller perforce relapses into a perfect state of resignation, and in time regards the destruction of his apparel and the scoring of his skin with indifference. The alluvial deposit of the plains, which gravitates towards the sea coast, leaves the plains at the base of the mountains rugged and rough with rocks and stones, and on this ground the baubul of Africa, which differs somewhat from that of India, flourishes."—*Reconnoitring in Abyssinia*, p. 364, by Col. St. Clair Wilkins, R.E.

All the characteristics just noted are very effectively summed up and illustrated in the personal experience of Sir Samuel Baker, as recorded in a work already quoted. Referring to the vast table-land stretching from the Atbara to the Nile, Sir Samuel states :—

"As usual, the land was dotted with mimosas, all of which were now bursting into leaf. The thorns of the different varieties of these trees are an extraordinary freak of Nature, as she appears to have exhausted all her art in producing an apparently useless arrangement of defence. The mimosas that are most common in the Soudan provinces are mere bushes, seldom exceeding six feet in height; these spread out towards the top like mushrooms, but the branches commence within two feet of the ground; they are armed with thorns in the shape of fish-hooks, which they resemble in sharpness and strength. A thick jungle composed of such bushes is perfectly impenetrable to any animals but elephants, rhinoceroses, and buffaloes; and should the clothes of a man become entangled in such thorns, either they must give way or he must remain a prisoner. The mimosa that is known among the Arabs as the kittar is one of the worst species, and is probably similar to that which caught Absalom by the hair; this differs from the well-known "Wait-a-bit" of South Africa, as no milder nickname could be applied than "Dead-stop." Were the clothes of strong material, it would be perfectly impossible to break through a kittar-bush.

"A magnificent specimen of a kittar, with a wide-spreading head in the young glory of green leaf, tempted my hungry camel during our march; it was determined to procure a mouthful, and I was equally determined that it should keep to the straight path, and avoid the attraction of the green food. After some strong remonstrances upon my part, the perverse beast shook its ugly head, gave a roar, and started off in full trot straight at the thorny bush. I had not the slightest control over the animal, and in a few seconds it charged the bush with the mad intention of rushing either through or beneath it. To my disgust I perceived that the wide-spreading branches were just sufficiently high to permit the back of the camel to pass underneath. There was no time for further consideration; we charged the bush; I held my head doubled up between my arms, and the next moment I was on my back, half stunned by the fall. The camel-saddle lay upon the ground; my rifle, that had been slung behind, my coffee-pot, the water-skin burst, and a host of other *impedimenta*, lay around me in all directions; worst of all, my beautiful gold repeater lay at some distance from me, rendered entirely useless. I was as nearly naked as I could be; a few rags held together, but my shirt was gone, with the exception of some shreds that adhered to my arms. I was, of course, streaming with blood, and looked much more as though I had been clawed by a leopard than as having simply charged a bush. The camel had fallen down with the shock after I had been swept off by the thorny branches. To this day I have the marks of the scratching."—*The Nile Tributaries of Abyssinia*, pp. 102-4.